THE EUROPEAN COMMUNITY AND THE DEVELOPING COUNTRIES

TRADE AND DEVELOPMENT

A series of books on international economic relations and economic issues in development

Edited from the National Centre for Development Studies, Australian National University, by Helen Hughes

Advisory editors
Juergen Donges, *Department of Economics, University of Cologne*
Peter Lloyd, *Department of Economics, University of Melbourne*
Gustav Ranis, *Department of Economics, Yale University*
David Wall, *Department of Economics, University of Sussex*

THE EUROPEAN COMMUNITY AND THE DEVELOPING COUNTRIES

ENZO R. GRILLI

World Bank *and*
Johns Hopkins University

Published by the Press Syndicate of the University of Cambridge
The Pitt Building, Trumpington Street, Cambridge CB2 1RP, UK
40 West 20th Street, New York, NY 10011-4211, USA
10 Stamford Road, Oakleigh, Melbourne 3166, Australia

First published 1993
Paperback edition published 1994

Printed in Hong Kong by Colorcraft

National Library of Australia cataloguing in publication data
Grilli, Enzo R.
The European Community and the Developing Countries.
Bibliography.
Includes index.
1. European Economic Community - Economic policy. 2. European Economic
Community - Developing countries. I. Title. (Series: Trade and development).
338.91401724

Library of Congress cataloguing in publication data
Grilli, Enzo R.
The European Community and the Developing Countries/Enzo Grilli.
(Trade and Development)
Includes bibliographical references and index.
1. European Economic Community—Economic assistance. 2. European
Economic Community—Developing countries. I. Title. II. Series: Trade and
development (Cambridge, England)
HC60.G72 1992
337.40172'4-dc20

A catalogue record for this book is available from the British Library.

ISBN 0 521 38511 3   Hardback
ISBN 0 521 47899 5   Paperback

To Vola Dominica and Mary Lina for whom, I hope, a United Europe will be a reality.

Contents

List of Tables

List of Figures

Preface

The European Community (EC) has long been the largest trading bloc in the world. It is also on the way to becoming the world's largest integrated economic zone. Its trade, aid and development cooperation policies are therefore of great importance to the developing countries. Yet, knowledge of these policies is neither widespread nor systematic. Over the years the European Community has developed its own development perspective, policies and practices, which somehow seem to have nearly escaped the attention of most professional observers as well as the general public. As a result, debate over these policies and practices has been rather mute at the general political level and partial, at best, at the academic level. Public scrutiny of them has also been minimal. Neither the EC Parliament nor the other participatory bodies of the Community have had much success in raising the overall level of attention given to economic cooperation with developing countries.

Debate over development policies has normally taken place within the EC Commission and between the Commission and the EC Council. It has therefore occurred in sheltered and often subdued environments, outside the view of most interested parties. This practice may have kept EC development cooperation policies "safely" in the hands of technocrats and responsible government representatives, and thus perhaps ensured a degree of continuity and stability which otherwise may not have been sustained. It may also, however, have stymied innovation or slowed down the path of adaptation of these policies to new needs and emerging realities. Available evidence does in fact point to considerable stickiness in the development cooperation policies pursued by the Community.

Limited participation in, and at times limited transparency

of, decision making in the domain of EC development cooperation are reflected in the paucity of documentation available and in the difficulty of access to the relevant sources. It is also reflected in the attention paid at the official level to certain aspects of EC policies, at the expense of others. The Commission, for example, has traditionally emphasized EC cooperation with African countries, at the expense of relations with other developing areas. It has, therefore, privileged the preparation and diffusion of documentation relating to Community cooperation with associated countries in Africa, the Caribbean and Pacific (the ACPs), countries which were former colonies of key member countries. As a consequence, whatever outside attention there has been, has been concentrated only on selected aspects of EC cooperation with developing countries. The so-called Lomé model, and previously the Yaoundé policies, have been "overstudied" in a relative sense, while cooperation between the Community and Latin America or Asia has been "understudied".

I discovered this rather strong bias towards Africa when I began teaching a course on the development cooperation policies of the Community at the Johns Hopkins University. There was relative abundance of analysis of EC-ACP cooperation, including several good books and many specialized articles, but considerable scarcity of everything else—as if the rest did not really matter. As I systematically evaluated the primary material coming from the Community, I realized that the bias was built into the information flows from Brussels and was then reflected in the choices made by the authors of the more academic works on these subjects. Outside observers used what they could from the available stream of information and were guided by it in their choice of study subjects.

Until now the determinants, overall logic and evolution of EC development cooperation at large have not been subject to much systematic analysis. This book was written in order to begin this process and to provide some interpretative hypotheses based on the examination of policies towards *all* of the most important developing areas since the early 1960s. Despite the efforts made to focus the analysis on the entire set of EC cooperation policies and practices, the book still reflects the weight of tradition, as it takes as a key organizing principle the associative model first pursued by the Community in its relations with the "countries and territories" belonging to the members at the time of the Rome Treaty. However, the book goes well beyond that, as it examines not only the adaptations of EC "associationism", first to the Mediterranean area and subsequently to Eastern Europe, but also the different forms that development cooperation has taken in Asia and Latin America—the areas lying at the periphery of EC interests and development reach.

After recomposing what constitutes the mosaic of EC-developing country ties established over the years, the book deals with questions of the determinants, logic and justification (or lack thereof), of Community policies. Of the possible explanations for the apparent lack of design shown by these policies, some are only sketched. The political economy of many of the choices made, or not made, by the Community has also received in the book less attention than it deserves. More systematic and monographic analysis of some of the key questions raised here will have to follow before more convincing and complete answers to them can be put forward. Yet, in posing these questions within a certain analytical framework and offering at least a perspective based on theory, history and careful examinations of facts, the book establishes a first layer for the factual and analytical construction that others will hopefully complete in the future.

The book is intended for students of European affairs, and in particular for those interested in the external development perspective of the European Community. I hope that professionals and practitioners of development economics will also find it of some interest, at least for the light that it attempts to throw on the internal characteristics and external effects of EC trade and aid policies. Finally, by improving the state of knowledge of EC practices and making the basic facts more widely available, it is hoped that the book will also contribute to raising the level of general consciousness of the role of the Community in development cooperation, to highlight the need for more effective action in some key fields and to underscore the minimum requirements for success in a difficult, but worthwhile, area of EC external policies.

Acknowledgements

There are many people whom I wish to thank for assisting me in various ways during the preparation of this book. Without their help this undertaking would have been much more difficult, if not impossible. None of them, of course, is in any way responsible for the views and judgements expressed in the book, which are solely mine.

Among those who helped me, I would like to recall the reference librarians in the World Bank–IMF Joint Library and in the Office of the European Communities in Washington D.C., Mr Francesco Abbate of UNCTAD in Geneva, Mr Jurgen Koppen of the EC Commission in Brussels (formerly with the EC Office in Washington D.C.), Prof. Carlo Secchi and Prof. Sergio Alessandrini of Bocconi University in Milan, Prof. André Sapir of the Free University in Brussels, Prof. Sandro Sideri of the Institute of Social Studies in The Hague, Dr Christopher Stevens and Dr Tony Killick of the Overseas Development Institute in London, Dr Rolf Langhammer of the Kiel Institute of World Economics, Dr Wolf Grabendorff of IRELA in Madrid, Mr Jan Thorpe of the Overseas Development Administration in London, Dr Alfonso Lasso de la Vaga of CIDEAL in Madrid, Miss Susana Pezzano of SELA in Caracas, Ms Patricia Lee of the World Bank in Washington, Mrs Debbie Fischer who typed the manuscript, Ms Tikka Wilson who edited it with care and competence, and my wife Marlie for her unfailing support.

Abbreviations

AAMS	Associated African and Malagasy States
ACP	African, Caribbean and Pacific signatories to the Lomé Conventions
AfDB	African Development Bank
ALA	Asian and Latin American countries
AsDB	Asian Development Bank
ASEAN	Association of East Asian Nations
CAP	Common Agricultural Policy of the EC
CCP	Common Commercial Policy of the EC
CET	Common External Tariff of the EC
CID	Center for Industrial Development
CIDEAL	Centro de Communicación, Investigación y Documentación Entre Europa, España y América Latina
CIS	Commonwealth of Independent States
CFF	Compensatory Financing Facility of the IMF
CMEA	Council for Mutual Economic Assistance (also known as COMECON)
DAC	Development Assistance Committee of OECD
DG	Directorate General
DOM	Overseas Department of France
EBRD	European Bank for Reconstruction and Development
EC	European Community(ies)
ECLA	Economic Commission for Latin America of the United Nations
ECSC	European Coal and Steel Community
ECU	European Currency Unit (as from 1 January 1981)

EDF	European Development Fund
EEC	European Economic Community
EFTA	European Free Trade Area
EIB	European Investment Bank
ESC	Economic and Social Committee of the EC
EUA	European Unit of Account (until 1980)
EURATOM	European Atomic Energy Community
FAO	Food and Agricultural Organization of the United Nations
GATT	General Agreement on Tariffs and Trade
GDP	Gross Domestic Product
GNP	Gross National Product
GRULA	Group of Latin American Ambassadors to the EC
GSP	Generalized System of Preferences
IBRD	International Bank for Reconstruction and Development
IDA	International Development Association
IDB	Interamerican Development Bank
IMF	International Monetary Fund
IRELA	Instituto de Relaciones Europeo–Latino-americanas
JUNAC	Junta of the Andean Pact
LAFTA	Latin American Free Trade Association
LDC	Less Developed Countries
LTA	Long Term Arrangement on Cotton Textiles
MFA	Multifiber Arrangement
MFN	Most Favored Nation
NATO	North Atlantic Treaty Organization
NGO	Non-Governmental Organization
NICs	Newly Industrializing Countries
NIEO	New International Economic Order
NMC	Non-member Mediterranean Countries
OAPEC	Organization of Arab Petroleum Exporting Countries
OAS	Organization of American States
OAU	Organization of African Unity
ODA	Official Development Assistance
OECD	Organization for Economic Cooperation and Development
OPEC	Organization of Petroleum Exporting Countries

PHARE	Poland-Hungary: Assistance for the Reconstruction of the Economy (subsequently extended to the whole of Eastern Europe)
SAARC	South Asian Association for Regional Cooperation
SELA	Sistema Económico Latinoamericano
SITC	Standard International Trade Classification
STABEX	System for the Stabilization of Export Earnings (in Lomé)
SYSMIN	System for the Promotion of Mineral Production and Exports (in Lomé) MINEX in French
TOM	Overseas Territory of France
UNCTAD	United Nations Conference on Trade and Development
UNDP	United Nations Development Program
VER	Voluntary Export Restraint

I

European Associationism: New Beginning or More of the Same?

It was the weight of colonial inheritance that forced the European nations, engaged in the late 1950s in the creation of the European Community (EC), to deal in a common fashion with the diverse "countries and territories" still under their national jurisdiction. The desire for continuity in relations led EC countries almost naturally to deal in familiar ways with their dependencies, by then on the way towards political and institutional emancipation, mixing only a few new elements with known and time-tested responses. Extending association linkages to the countries and territories of Africa still under European authority was one of them; EC associationism has clear, strong roots in European colonialism.

Also clear, from the historical point of view, is the direct influence on the forms of EC associationism exerted by those EC members that had maintained the widest and longest colonial presence in Africa—France in particular. France had responded to the challenge of decolonization with its own transitional philosophy and associative policies. The notion of association, based on the theory of complementarity between metropolitan areas and colonies—especially those in Africa—and the corollary of mutuality of benefits from economic and political cooperation between them, had acquired considerable credibility in France by the end of World War II.[1] It came to be fervently practiced when the continuation of old-style colonialism turned out to be manifestly impossible. Association, based on Euro-Africanism, was then extensively used to try to preserve the influence of the metropole, while allowing the colonies to acquire various degrees of autonomy.

Among the major European powers France was not alone in experimenting with associative relations with colonies and former colonies. In Great Britain the practical tendency towards forms of association with the colonies had merged over the years with the doctrine of indirect government of the colonial possessions—a politically discreet way of dealing with a far-flung and diverse colonial empire.[2] And Great Britain, like France, was trying hard in the period immediately after World War II to establish a commonwealth with its present and past colonies.

Associationism was built into the French Constitution in 1946, which explicitly foresaw a variety of links with colonial possessions: on one hand the Union of Associated States (*Etats associés*), which enjoyed a certain amount of autonomy; on the other the Overseas Departments (*Départments d'outre-mer*), which were declared integral parts of France. In between there were the Associated Territories (*Territoires associés*) and the Overseas Territories (*Territoires d'outre-mer*). The French Constitution referred to equality of rights and obligations between the metropole and the associated states and territories and to the pooling of resources and efforts to develop their respective civilizations. France vigorously pursued a policy of association in the period of decolonization, especially towards Africa.

The Constitution of 1958, drawn and approved after France had joined the EC, still attempted to adapt and extend the existing associative framework through the creation of a French Community, offering self-administration to the African colonies within a quasi-federal structure dominated by the metropole, which maintained authority in matters of defense, economy, justice, higher education and external relations. The French Community, more or less imposed by de Gaulle on the African colonies in 1958 (only Sekou Touré's Guinea refused it), did not last long in the political climate of the 1960s, when rapid decolonization and the quest for independence became unstoppable everywhere in Africa. Yet, the fundamentals of French colonial theory and many elements of its practices, which had been inserted into the Treaty of Rome, survived and took on a life of their own in this new framework. Part IV of the Treaty unilaterally established a form of association between present or former African colonies of France, Belgium and Italy and the European Community. This linkage was subsequently updated and even partially reshaped, but never altered in a fundamental way even when the countries and territories of Africa became independent states.

Associationism suited well the basic ideologies and morals of some of the political forces that dominated Europe in the post-war period. Socialists and social christians believed in humanism and solidarity. They also tended to feel a deep sense of moral, aside from political, responsibility for the former colonies and their populations. They inevitably felt uneasy about their countries' colonial past, often going as far as to condemn it for its negative effects on the colonial possessions, and always asserted the obligation of their countries to care for the former colonies and their people.[3] These sentiments are clearly reflected in the French Constitution of 1946, which recognized France's intention "to conduct the peoples of whom she had taken charge to the liberty of self-determination".[4] Such perceptions and political attitudes influenced to a considerable extent the behaviors of the various governments that presided over Italy, the Netherlands and the Federal Republic of Germany during the post-World War II period in matters pertaining to aid, trade and industrial relations with the former colonies.

European conservative parties, on the other hand, felt no obvious guilt about colonialism. They tended to consider the former colonies as components of the national domain and as ingredients of national power, usable to expand or sustain it in time and space. They saw the colonies as having some importance in certain cases, while being fully expendable in others. Many Gaullists in France and conservatives in Great Britain maintained an unemotional view of their colonial pasts and dealt with former colonies largely from the standpoint of national interest.[5] Seen in this perspective, the celebrated "volte face" of de Gaulle regarding Algeria was not only internally consistent, but also fully compatible with the subsequent strenuous defense of *Francophonie* by Gaullist France.

Communist parties, a force to be reckoned with in France and Italy after World War II, held a rather idiosyncratic position vis-a-vis the former colonies. At the abstract political level they resolutely condemned colonialism as an inevitable excess of capitalist regimes and genuinely supported the independence of the colonies even when it entailed national liberation wars. At a more concrete level, however, they remained wary of taking too antagonistic a position towards the bourgeois governments of their countries in regard to the specifics of the post-colonial challenge. Colonial wars always put communists in a very awkward position, as they made them vulnerable to accusations of lack of patriotism, if not treason. In Italy, where the UN mandate over Somalia did not raise any serious internal political issue, the Communist Party contented itself with firm political opposition to colonialism in its various forms. In France, however, the situation was much more difficult for the communists, as the war experiences of Indochina and Algeria penetrated deeply into the national psyche and created nationalistic responses from which even rank and file communists were not immune. Consequently, the positions taken by the French Communist Party had to be more ambiguous than those of the Italian communists.[6]

The political and economic content of the post-colonial problem that Europe at large had to face beginning in the 1950s was also greatly influenced by the colonial experience of the most important European states. There were not only the results of broadly different colonial constructions, often exemplified by the French and the British colonial empires, but also the effects of colonial rules that had varied in time and content from one colony to another even within the same "empire". Diversities in colonial experiences and the effects thereof posed almost as many problems for Europe in the post-World War II period as the common traces left by colonial rule did for many African, Asian and Pacific territories.

In Africa, for example, diversity in administrative, legal and cultural traditions exported by the various colonial powers constituted a formidable obstacle to intra-African political and economic relations.[7] Superimposed on colonial economic structures that were dominated by the production of similar tropical agricultural products, that were deficient in means of transport and communications except with the metropolitan centers and that offered minimal scope for alternative production choices,[8] the specifics of the colonial heritage would shape for years to come the path of economic development that the former colonies of Europe were able to follow. Dependency on the production and export of primary commodities severely limited their economic choices and kept them tied to the former metropoles where the markets lay. Lack of investment capital, and thus strong dependency on financial assistance from Europe, pushed them in the same direction. Extreme scarcity of trained personnel made them look to Europe as a prime source of technical assistance in key sectors such as education, health, agriculture and communications. For these and other reasons, Europe was a crossroads that the newly independent states of Africa could not avoid. But Europe also became in many ways a prisoner of the social and economic realities it had helped create in the former .colonies. These realities dictated in practice many of the forms that the economic cooperation of Europe with Africa actually took.

The Origins of EC Associationism

Decolonization and its Challenges

The momentum of decolonization in Africa caught all the European colonial powers by surprise. France and the United Kingdom had given up, early after the end of World War II, their mandates in the Middle East. The United Kingdom had concluded that it could not hold on to India against the will of 500 million Indians and had granted independence to this country as early as 1947 (if after a bloody partition between the Hindu and Moslem parts). After a rather half-hearted attempt to hold on to Indonesia, the Netherlands had faced reality and granted the island country independence in 1949. Only France seriously attempted a restoration of colonial power in the East—in Indochina where it faced strong nationalistic resistance. Yet, by and large, the pattern followed by most European colonial powers in the years following the end of World War II was one of rapid retreat from the eastern possessions and continuation of colonial rule in black Africa.

The African continent, divided and redivided among the European powers in the eighteenth and nineteenth centuries, had been transformed into an idiosyncratic patchwork of territories having few of the traits that make for viable nations. The colonial possessions of Europe often lacked tribal homogeneity; their economic foundation was weak, or non-existent in certain instances; and their political and institutional structures were in most cases underdeveloped to the extreme. These territories were, in other words, generally considered not ready to claim, let alone receive, political independence.

There were exceptions to this broad rule. Among the British colonies, Ghana, for example, had a solid economy, stable social conditions, good general levels of literacy and developed national political structures. Nigeria was another large and seemingly solid colony, with potential for successful statehood. Ivory Coast, among the French colonies, was a model of internal stability and economic viability, based on a local class of modern farmers-entrepreneurs, who maintained strong ties with Paris and seemed well integrated into the cultural and economic structure of France. Yet, these were the exceptions. Most African territories were not ready for political independence, and more importantly, most lacked economic viability as would be expected of territories and diverse people drawn together not by tradition or volition, but by often capricious decisions taken in far away colonial offices.

The common wisdom in Europe in the mid-1950s was that, while decolonization of Africa was probably inevitable, an adequate time span was essential to it. Unlike many of the former European colonies in Asia or the former League of Nations mandates in the Middle East, most of the African colonies needed time to prepare before they could survive on their own. The presence of indigenous movements agitating for immediate independence did not negate the basic conclusion that independence was for most African territories far in the future. There was much less clarity on what this preparation actually entailed and on the most appropriate ways to achieve it, but accelerated development of education, creation of a better infrastructure for transportation, communications and health, and increased investments in agriculture and mining seemed to be integral parts of the strategy.

This European "common wisdom", though correct in many of its factual premises (which were the consequence of many years of mindless, when not exploitative, colonialism), totally misjudged the attractiveness that the idea of independence had for the local populations, and especially for the European-educated elites who were leading them. It also underestimated the strength of the influence exerted by the successful attainment of political independence by other former European colonies in Asia and the Middle East in the aftermath of World War II and by the international movement that was advocating rapid decolonization, political non-alignment and autonomous economic development of the former colonies as a viable alternative to continued colonial rule and dependent development. In Africa, in addition, there was a strong movement that expounded the ideals of Pan-Africanism and took an uncompromisingly negative position towards the prospects of continued political and economic cooperation with the former colonial powers.

So much did the Europeans underestimate the timing of decolonization in Africa, that in the process that led to the formation of the European Economic Community no particular awareness was shown by most of the principals of the question of future relations with colonial possessions in Africa and elsewhere. It was not until 1957, at the end of this process, that the problem of the relationships that needed to be established with current colonial possessions even surfaced. And colonies, in one way or another, were a reality for at least three, if not four, of the five key member countries. France had possessions in Africa and Asia as well as in the Caribbean and the Pacific. Belgium had the Congo and the trusteeship of Ruanda-Urundi. The Netherlands had given up its last African colonial possession in 1872, but maintained dependencies in other parts of the world. Italy had a UN mandate over Somalia. Only Germany at that time had no colonial connections anywhere in the world.

Association Under the Rome Treaty

Association of the members' territories to the European Economic Community (under articles 131-36, Part IV, of the Treaty of Rome) was adroitly sponsored by France, aided by Belgium, mostly against the objections of Germany and the Netherlands.[9] France wanted to ensure free access to the Community for the exports coming from its former colonies and, eventually, to share with the EC partners the costs of providing economic assistance to France *d'outre mer* that it then shouldered.[10] Germany and the Netherlands were less than eager to do so and to be seen as backing, economically and politically, the main colonial power of continental Europe. To the extent that these two countries were interested in development cooperation, they preferred to pursue humanitarian or foreign policy objectives which were not necessarily confined to a specific set of developing countries.

Hard political realities, however, prevailed over intentions regarding development cooperation: confronted with a French ultimatum, Germany and the Netherlands opted to save the emerging European Community and accepted, with minor modifications, France's associationist designs. The Treaty of Rome in art. 131 established the association between the Community and the countries and territories of Africa (Table 1.1) as well as its official purposes: "To promote the economic and social development of the countries and territories and to establish close relations between them and the Community as a whole".[11] Of the two stated objectives, the first can be said to belong to the German vision of development cooperation. The second translated into acceptable language the French goal of transferring to the Community as a whole the type of commercial and financial relationship that France had with its colonies.

The association system embodied in Part IV of the Treaty contained two main elements, namely rules regarding trade between the EC and the associates and aid from the Community to the associates. The French, who had at one point proposed that the economic union to be established among the six European states be extended outright to the colonies, could well live with what they obtained: an association agreement that tied French colonial possessions in Africa in a free-trade area with the Community and at the same time lightened the economic burden that the colonies represented for the French treasury. The only cost paid by France was to let the European partners share its formerly exclusive colonial markets.

The specific elements of the association system were as follows: (a) duties on imports between the EC members and the associates, and between the associates themselves, were to be gradually abolished, even though the latter maintained the right to protect infant industries and to keep or establish tariffs for revenue purposes (but without discriminating between EC member countries); (b) the EC was to supply financial aid to the associates through the European Development Fund (EDF) set up for this specific purpose; (c) labor could in principle circulate freely from the associated territories to the EC countries and vice versa; and (d) nationals and corporations from the EC countries could freely establish

Table 1.1 Evolution & Geographical Reach of EC Association

1957—Treaty of Rome

EC	*Partners*
Belgium	French West Africa, comprising:
France	Dahomey,[a] Guinea,[b] Ivory Coast, Mauritania,
Federal Republic of	Niger, Senegal, Sudan, Upper Volta[c]
Germany	French Equatorial Africa, comprising:
Italy	Cameroon (Trust Territory), Chad, Middle
Luxemburg	Congo, Gabon, Ubangi-Chari
The Netherlands	Other French territories:
	Autonomous Republic of Togo, Madagascar,
	Comoros, French Polynesia, French
	Southern and Antarctic territories, Algeria,
	Reunion, Guyane, Martinique, Guadeloupe,
	St Pierre and Miquelon, French Somaliland,
	New Caledonia, and dependencies
	Congo, Ruanda-Urundi
	Somaliland
	New Guinea

1963—Yaoundé I Convention

EC	*AAMS (Associated African and Malagasy States)*
Belgium	Burundi (formerly part of Ruanda-Urundi),
France	United Republic of Cameroon,[d] Central African
Federal Republic of	Republic, Chad, Congo-Brazzaville (formerly
Germany	French Congo), Congo-Leopoldville (formerly
Italy	Belgian Congo), Dahomey, Gabon, Ivory Coast,
Luxemburg	Madagascar, Mali (formerly French Sudan),
The Netherlands	Mauritania (formerly French Sudan), Niger,
	Rwanda (formerly part of Ruanda-Urundi),
	Senegal, Somalia,[e] Togo, Upper Volta

1969—Yaoundé II Convention

EC	*AAMS*
Belgium	Burundi, United Republic of Cameroon,[f] Central
France	African Republic, Chad, Peoples Republic of
Federal Republic of	Congo (formerly Congo-Brazzaville), Dahomey,
Germany	Gabon, Ivory Coast, Madagascar, Mali,
Italy	Mauritania, Mauritius (joined in 1972), Niger,
Luxemburg	Rwanda, Senegal, Somalia, Togo, Upper Volta,
The Netherlands	Zaire (formerly Congo-Kinshasa and before
	that, Congo-Leopoldville)

1975—Lomé I Convention

EC	ACP (African, Caribbean and Pacific countries)
Belgium	as in Yaoundé II plus:
Denmark	Commonwealth countries:
France	Bahamas, Barbados, Botswana, Fiji, Gambia,
Federal Republic of	Ghana, Grenada, Guyana, Jamaica, Kenya,
Germany	Lesotho, Malawi, Nigeria, Sierra Leone,
Ireland	Swaziland, Tanzania, Tonga, Trinidad and
Italy	Tobago, Uganda, Western Samoa, Zambia
Luxemburg	Non-Commonwealth countries:
The Netherlands	Equatorial Guinea, Ethiopia, Guinea-Bissau,
United Kingdom	Liberia, Sudan

1980—Lomé II Convention

EC	ACP
as before plus:	as before, plus:
Greece, which joined	Cape Verde, Comoros, Djibouti, Dominica,
the EC in 1981	Kiribati, Papua New Guinea, St Lucia, Sao Tome
	and Principe, Seychelles, Solomon Islands,
	Suriname, Tuvalu, Zimbabwe (joined in 1980
	after the Convention had been signed by the
	ACPs)

1985—Lomé III Convention

EC	ACP
as before plus:	as before, plus:
Spain and Portugal,	Angola (joined in 1985 after the Convention had
which joined the EC	been signed), Antigua and Barbuda, Belize,
in 1986	Mozambique, St Christopher and Nevis,
	St Vincent and the Grenadines, Vanuatu

1990—Lomé IV Convention

EC	ACP
as before	as before, plus:
	Dominican Republic, Haiti, Namibia

[a] Dohomey is now Benin.
[b] Guinea left the Association in 1958, but returned for Lomé I.
[c] Upper Volta is now Burkina Faso.
[d] Formed in 1961, through the union of French and British Trust Territories of Cameroon.
[e] Comprising former British Somaliland (1960).
[f] Later the Federal Republic of Cameroon.

themselves in the associated territories and vice versa. In summary, the Treaty of Rome unilaterally created a free-trade area between the EC states and their dependencies (as well as among the dependencies themselves), ensured rights of establishment for citizens and firms from either side (if in practice only from the EC) and established at the same time the presumption of collective responsibility of EC member countries to provide financial assistance to the former colonies of France, Belgium and Italy.

The two main elements of development cooperation present in the association package—free trade in both directions and economic aid—reflected existing economic realities, as well as the dominant thinking in the area of development cooperation. One reality was the free access to a particular metropolitan market that had been enjoyed by the producers located in the various colonies. This access was now extended from single metropolitan countries to the entire EC. For the non-associated countries whose exports to the EC remained subject to tariffs and other restrictions, free entry of associated countries' exports created a strong trade preference. Conversely, the right of free entry into individual colonial markets possessed by the producers of those EC member nations that had colonies—and thus the trade privilege that they enjoyed—was extended to all EC producers. Another economic reality was the bilateral aid supplied by the various European states to their colonies and former colonies. This could remain operative, but would now be complemented by EDF aid contributed by all member countries and administered by the Community.

Trade preferences granted to a specific group of developing countries posed a question of legality under the General Agreement on Tariffs and Trade (GATT), the regulatory framework of world trade to which all EC member countries belonged. GATT's foremost principle was non-discrimination in trade relations among "contracting parties". Trade preferences were instead discriminatory *par excellence*. Their whole purpose was to grant an advantage to the recipients, against third parties. In the case of EC preferences, these third parties were also GATT members. The Community itself was a preferential trading area, soon to become a customs union. If other GATT members, and most importantly the United States, were not keen to challenge the legal configuration of the Community as a customs union, and thus its permissibility under Art. XXIV, in 1958–59 the prevailing opinion in GATT was that the association extended to the "countries and territories" of Africa under the Treaty of Rome did not constitute a free trade area, and thus was not covered by the general waiver of the rule of non-discrimination built in to Art. XXIV.

The Latin American countries, in particular, were afraid that the exports of tropical products from the preferred African associates would displace theirs, and generally depress world prices. The negative expectations about the effects of EC preferences that they entertained were generally shared by orthodox economists, who feared that the association extended by the Community to the African colonies of its members would simply be trade diverting, and thus inimical to the world trade order sanctioned by GATT. The EC took instead, the position that the free-trade area between itself and the associates was permissible under GATT. It would not, moreover, be detrimental to other developing countries, as demand for tropical products in the Community was growing and any extra-production from the associates would be easily absorbed (thereby negating the two fundamental characteristics of demand for these primary products: its income and price unresponsiveness). The Community also maintained that the United Nations' Charter mandated that it should promote the economic and social development of the associated countries and territories. Trade preferences would be helpful to the economic development of these countries by sustaining their exports. Negative effects on third parties, especially other developing countries, would be minimal. Moreover, if proven wrong, the Community promised to consider compensation actions.

The controversy over the trade preferences granted to associated countries by the Community was never resolved within GATT. It re-emerged in the 1960s when the Yaoundé Convention was signed, and again in the mid-1970s, when the Lomé agreement was reached. But with the United States satisfied that at least the trade preferences received by the Community from its associates had been eliminated in the Lomé Convention, this controversy was *de facto* put in abeyance.

The readiness of the Community to skirt GATT rules in dealing with its associates may appear surprising, given its interest in an open and orderly trading environment, and thus in the solidity of the GATT. It may also be surprising, given the guardianship of the GATT order assumed by the United States, the principal ally of the EC member states. France and Great Britain, however, had clearly shown during the GATT negotiations that their acceptance of non-discrimination was tempered by the perceived need for a pragmatic application of this principle. In their views, dealing with developing countries required such pragmatism, since starting conditions in most of them were significantly different from those prevailing in the more developed members of GATT. If trade preferences could help the economic development of developing countries, they should not be automatically ruled out. This position re-emerged in the 1960s when generalized trade preferences in favor of developing countries were strongly advocated in various United Nations' fora by their representatives. Most European countries, on both ideological and economic grounds, considered them less unfavorably than the United States. In the late 1950s, moreover, EC countries were facing "existing realities" represented by the existence of countries and territories still under their jurisdiction, whose bilateral trade ties with the metropoles needed to be preserved. Real questions deserved, in their opinion, realistic answers. Extending free access to the whole Community to these countries was one of them.

But the dominant thinking on how best to help economic development in the associated territories was also clearly reflected in the notion that the EC would supply its own aid. The first European Development Fund (EDF I) covering the years between 1958 and 1963 was endowed with EUA 580 million. It was a small but not insignificant amount of additional financial resources, which represented an increase of 15 percent over existing bilateral aid flows to associated countries. Financing for the Fund came directly from the budgets of the six member countries. Prevalent economic orthodoxy then maintained that lack of savings was the major constraint to growth in poor countries. Trade could help developing countries by increasing the efficiency of local production or by providing a "vent" for surplus production of minerals and tropical agricultural products. External aid, however, was not only a net addition to domestic savings but also could be directed to much-needed capital investment projects. Foreign aid was, therefore, the simplest and most direct way to help economic growth in developing countries. In the debate over trade and aid as instruments of accelerated development, aid believers and promoters had the upper hand in the late 1950s. Aid was clearly the preferred instrument.

The Treaty of Rome, however, established the possibility of yet another kind of association. Under art. 238 "the Community [could] conclude with a third country, a union of states or an international organization, agreements creating an association embodying reciprocal rights and obligations, joint actions and special procedures". Under this legal umbrella the Community could thus enter into a wide range of associative relationships: from those envisaging future membership (limited to European countries by art. 237) to those aimed at special objectives such as trade preferences and economic cooperation.[12]

The scope for associationism left open by art. 238 was quite wide. In time the Community used it extensively, both to deal with the Mediterranean countries, and to enter into other cooperative relationships with individual countries or groups of countries in and outside Europe. Over time, the Community established cooperation agreements with such diverse partners as the countries of the Maghreb and Mashreq, Israel, Yugoslavia, Mexico, Brazil, India, China, Pakistan, as well as regional groupings such as the Andean Pact, the Latin American Common Market and the Association of South East Asian Nations (ASEAN) and most recently with Eastern European countries.

The Development of the EC Association System

The Road to Yaoundé

Much to Europe's surprise, African decolonization, instead of taking decades, occurred in the span of a few years. As late as 1956 there were only three independent countries in what is now known as sub-Saharan Africa: Liberia, Sudan and Ethiopia. In 1957 the Gold Coast (Ghana) became independent from Great Britain. In the following five years twenty-three newly independent states emerged in Africa, followed by another ten between 1963 and 1968. Among them were many EC-associated territories. For example, Guinea opted for independence outside the French Community in 1958; Senegal became independent in 1959; the French Sudan, Ivory Coast, Niger, Dahomey and Upper Volta followed suit in 1960. The same year, Belgium granted independence to Congo and gave up Ruanda and Urundi and Italy gave up Somalia. By 1968 only Portugal was holding on to its colonial possessions: Portuguese Guinea, Angola and Mozambique. In Rhodesia, white settlers managed to seize control of the government and to gain *de facto* independence from Great Britain, while South West Africa (Namibia) remained under South Africa's colonial rule, despite a 1968 UN declaration of assumption of direct control over this territory.[13]

The newly independent states, formerly associated to the EC ex officio (*association octroyé*), were obviously no longer bound by the content of articles 131–36 of the Treaty of Rome. Many of them, however, wished to maintain preferential access to EC markets for their exports and to continue to receive economic aid from the Community. Political independence had not lessened the dependency of their economies on the metropolitan countries, either in terms of trade outlets or capital inflows. In 1959 almost 80 percent of the associated territories' exports went to EC countries, and nearly all of the aid they received came from EC countries (Table 1.2).

Table 1.2 Trade with and Aid Flows to African Associates, 1958 (percentage of total)

To/From	Exports	Imports	Aid
EC (6)	79.0	82.3	98.0
United States	14.7	7.4	1.0
United Kingdom	2.7	4.9	—
Japan	0.4	0.8	—
Others[a]	3.2	4.6	1.0
Total	100.0	100.0	100.0

Note: African Associates refers to the group of Associated African and Malagasy States (AAMS).

[a] Industrial countries only for exports and imports. Multilateral organizations for aid.

Sources: Commission des Communautés Européennes, *Les Echanges Commerciaux entre la CEE et les Etats Africains Associés*, Série Aide au Développement, No. 2, Brussels, 1969; United Nations, *International Economic Assistance to the Less Developed Countries*, Doc. E/3395/Rev. 1, New York, 1961.

There was yet another complication. By 1961–62 the United Kingdom was trying to negotiate its membership in the EC and to find, in the process, an accommodation of the interests of its own former colonies, now part of the Commonwealth. For the existing associates this possibility created the problem of having to share the financial assistance received from the Community and the specter of competition from Commonwealth countries in the export markets of the six original members of the Community—markets where they enjoyed exclusive preferences. After all, the production and export patterns of the former British and French colonies in Africa were quite similar (Table 1.3). Agriculture dominated

Table 1.3 Structure of Production and Exports of Sub-Saharan Africa, 1960

	Distribution of Gross Domestic Product (percentage)		
	Agriculture	**Industry**	**Services**
Total Africa	49	16	34
Low income countries	(56)	(12)	(31)
AAMS	(46)	(14)	(39)
Commonwealth countries	(52)	(18)	(30)

	Distribution of Merchandise Exports[a](percentage)				
	Fuels	**Minerals and Metals**	**Food and Beverages**	**Other Primary Products**	**Manufactures**
Total Africa	3	7	62	21	7
Low income countries	—	(10)	(55)	(27)	(8)
AAMS	(1)	(6)	(63)	(23)	(7)
Commonwealth countries	(5)	(13)	(61)	(14)	(7)

Note: AAMS = Associated African and Malagasy States.
[a] In 1962.
Sources: World Bank, *Accelerated Development in Sub-Saharan Africa*, Washington D.C., 1981; World Bank, *World Development Report*, Washington D.C., 1989 (data files).

national production, and tropical foods and beverages dominated exports.

Competition between former British and French colonies in Africa was strong. Ghana and Nigeria produced and exported cocoa just like Ivory Coast. Kenya and Cameroon produced and exported coffee like the Congo and Ruanda. The Gambia produced and exported groundnuts, and so did Senegal. Tanzania and Kenya produced and exported sisal as did Madagascar. At that time bilateral aid was still mostly coming from France and Belgium and was primarily directed towards the associated countries. France also provided substantial aid to North Africa (Table 1.4). It was reasonable to fear that competition for multilateral EC aid would increase when association with Europe was extended to other African countries. Aid from the Community was in fact likely to be finite, or to increase much more slowly above a certain plateau even after the possible entry of the United Kingdom in the Community,

Table 1.4 Bilateral and EC Aid to Associated Countries, 1960

	Value (million US$)	As share of total aid to Sub-Saharan Africa (%)
A. Bilateral aid		
France[a]	280.0	91.2
Belgium[b]	86.0	100.0
Italy[c]	10.7	64.0
Germany, Fed. Rep.	0.1	2.0
Netherlands	—	—
Total	376.8	90.8
B. EC aid	0.5	100.0
C. Total aid from EC countries (A + B)	377.3	90.8

[a] In 1960 France's aid to Africa North of the Sahara was $383.2 million.

[b] Of which aid to Congo was $71 million.

[c] Total aid to Africa and to all developing countries excludes loans for $58.1 million, an abnormally high figure for 1960.

Sources: Commission of the European Communities, *Memorandum on a Community Policy on Development Cooperation: Appendices* Appendix 2, Brussels, 1972; OECD, *Geographical Distribution of Financial Flows to Less Developed Countries, 1960-64*, Paris, 1966.

since it would continue to come from member country budgets and would be subject to a high degree of national scrutiny and to many competing claims.

There were also opposite tendencies at work, pulling Africa away from cooperation with Europe. Pan-Africanism, then strong in many parts of Africa, extolled the virtues of continent-wide political union and of Africa-based development. It sharply contrasted with the Eurafricanism practiced by the EC and benevolently accepted by numerous Francophone African leaders. Sekou Touré, after spearheading his country's refusal to join the French Community in 1958, broke rank with the rest of Francophone Africa again by refusing to take part in the negotiations for the new association convention with the EC. Intense manoeuvering by Pan-Africanists in the aftermath of independence put on the defensive many African leaders who were willing to continue their special trade and aid relationships with Europe.[14]

However, by May 1963, when the first Conference of Heads of States and Governments of the Organization of African Unity (OAU) was held in Addis Ababa, Ethiopia, the Pan-African dream had, in effect, already been rejected in favor of national paths to development. An alliance of moderate Francophone and Anglophone leaders, from Houphouet-Boigny and Senghor to Neyrere and Tubman, prevailed and asserted the principle of "multiple roads" to the political, social and economic development of African nations as central to the purpose of the OAU. The turbulent unity dreams of Nkrumah and Touré were brushed aside in favor of continuity in national and regional cooperation with Europe. An alternative model of African political collaboration, based on the interests of each nation, was adopted.[15]

Africa of the Fatherlands, the accepted alternative to Nkrumah's "union now" objective, was reaffirmed at the third Conference of Heads of States and Governments of the OAU held in Accra, Ghana in October 1965. Mutual respect of national choices and non-interference in each other's internal affairs were underlined as the common rules of behavior. Not only were Nkrumah's interventionist tendencies in the name of Pan-Africanism rejected at the political level, but the notion of inward, Africa-centered development was also refused at the economic level. In the words of Arnold Rivkin, "after Addis, Cairo and

Accra, Eurafricanism, especially the EC rendition of it, found new acceptance in Africa, . . . that reached far beyond its immediate clientele".[16]

The draft association agreement between eighteen of the African nations by then independent and the Community was initialed in December 1962, before the final result of Great Britain's first attempt to enter the Community was known. Coalesced into the Associated African and Malagasy States (AAMS), comprising Burundi, Cameroon, Central African Republic, Chad, Congo Brazzaville, Congo Leopoldville, Dahomey, Gabon, Ivory Coast, Madagascar, Mali, Mauritania, Niger, Rwanda, Senegal, Somalia, Togo and Upper Volta, these countries signed in July 1963, in the capital of Cameroon— Yaoundé—a Convention of Association with the six EC members that was to become effective in 1964 and last until 1969. Association with the Community had changed from being involuntary and unilaterally granted, to being voluntary and negotiated (*association négociée*).

The Yaoundé Convention—or Yaoundé I, as it came to be known—covered trade and aid relations between the Community and the AAMS. It maintained preferential trade between the Community and the eighteen associated states, but on a bilateral basis. Each of the AAMS and the EC formed in practice a free-trade area. Associated countries did not enter into similar trade obligations vis-a-vis each other. The trade arrangements between each AAMS and the EC, however, continued to entail reciprocal obligations. Associated countries kept the right of preferential access to the EC markets that they had gained under the Rome Treaty, and also continued to grant to EC goods, at least in principle, the same right of access to their domestic markets. Existing trade obstacles between each AAMS and the Community were to be reduced at the same pace as those between the six members of the Community and to be eventually eliminated. Associated countries kept their privilege to limit in some areas the access of EC goods, but each AAMS also undertook not to discriminate in trade against any member of the Community. All members of the EC were to be treated equally. This provided, associated countries remained free to organize trade relations among themselves as they saw fit.

Under Yaoundé I EC aid to associated states was to continue

to flow bilaterally as well as multilaterally. The Community undertook to renew and expand the European Development Fund, in part to compensate for the abolition of the French *sur-prix*.[17] The second European Development Fund (EDF II) was endowed with EUA 800 million. It was authorized to provide loans as well as grants, and to finance investments as well as technical assistance and training. Loans could be "special" (EUA 50 million) and "ordinary" (EUA 70 million). The latter were to be provided by the European Investment Bank (EIB), which was authorized to operate in both member and associated states of the Community.

Yaoundé I *de facto* multilateralized the existing trade regime between the EC and the former colonies, while maintaining intact the aid system that had been set up by the Treaty of Rome. The adaptation of the trade regime was made necessary by the independent status reached by the former associated territories and by their consequent right to choose their trade policies vis-a-vis one another. The first decision that they took in this area was not to establish a free-trade area among themselves, but to regulate trade on an *ad hoc* basis. The Yaoundé Convention sought, however, to preserve in substance the rights of establishment of EC nationals and EC companies in the associated states, if more in the sense of non-discriminatory treatment than of unencumbered freedom of establishment. The Convention also sought to equalize the rights of nationals and companies of the six EC countries in the AAMSs. In practice the objective was to eliminate the special provisions in favor of French and Belgian nationals and firms in the former colonies of these two countries. In all these areas, therefore, the goals of Yaoundé I were somewhat more limited than those of the Treaty of Rome.

Given the new nature of association—a freely negotiated agreement among independent states—its administration could no longer be left to Community institutions alone.[18] It had to be multilateralized to reflect greater equality between the Community and the associates. A formal institutional structure was created in Yaoundé, patterned on that of the European Community (and of the French Community before it), but totally independent from it. An Association Council was set up to supervise the functioning of the association. A Parliamentary Conference was established as a vehicle to facilitate political dialogue between the EC and the AAMSs, and a Court of Arbitration was formed to help settle disputes arising from the Convention and its workings. The Council, comprising one representative from each of the six EC members and the eighteen AAMSs, plus one from the EC Commission, could delegate its powers to the Association Committee and be assisted by a secretariat. The Parliamentary Conference, established on a parity basis, was formed by members of the European Parliament and the national assemblies of the various AAMSs. The Court of Arbitration was made up of a president, nominated by the Association Council, and four judges, two nominated by the EC Council of Ministers and two by the AAMSs.[19]

Oil Crisis, British Accession and the Second Expansion of Associationism

Characteristically, the next quantum jump in EC relations with developing countries did not occur until 1975, two years after the oil crisis and the entry of the United Kingdom (plus Ireland and Denmark) into the Community. The accession of Great Britain presented the Six with a challenge that had been avoided in 1963: how to deal with the former British colonies in Africa, Asia and the Caribbean. This problem, carefully avoided in the aftermath of the first French veto of the United Kingdom's entry into the Community, could no longer be skirted.

The Declaration of Intent sponsored by the governments of Germany, Italy and the Netherlands in 1963, and reluctantly consented to by France, had left open the possibility for countries "having production structures comparable to those of the Associates" to become a part of the association Convention under art. 58, or to establish special association agreements with the EC. A third possibility was foreseen: that of trade agreements to facilitate commercial exchanges between the Six and developing countries. Nigeria had negotiated the first such association agreement (formally under art. 238 of the Treaty of Rome) in 1966. The so-called Lagos Convention, however, never came into effect as a consequence of the war in Biafra. Along the same lines, the Arusha Convention was signed in 1968 (and modified in 1969) between the six EC members and Kenya, Tanzania and Uganda.[20] This Convention, in practice, exhausted the efforts made by the Community to enlarge its collaborative reach towards developing countries in Africa. As for the Commonwealth countries of sub-Saharan Africa, Asia and the Caribbean, nothing new was to emerge until 1975, notwithstanding the reaffirmation by the European Commission in its 1967 opinion (revised in 1969) of the principles governing association contained in the 1963 Declaration of Intent.[21]

In 1969 the Community signed a trade agreement with Morocco and Tunisia. In 1973 it concluded a non-preferential trade agreement with Uruguay—the first with a Latin American country. But, on the basis of their content and the time it took to bring them to conclusion, these agreements can hardly be considered exceptions to the rather passive phase in EC–developing country relations that began after Yaoundé I and lasted until 1975, when the Lomé Convention was concluded. Demand for associative ties with the EC was not strong in these years, and the EC was not making any particular effort to render the possibility of association more attractive to developing countries.

In this period, within the framework of the United Nations Conference on Trade and Development (UNCTAD), most developing countries were concentrating their efforts on international rather than regional economic cooperation. Their efforts were aimed in two directions: the attainment of a measure of price stabilization for their primary commodity exports through international agreements financed by consuming countries, and the attainment of trade preferences for their exports of manufactures to industrial countries. The general strategy followed by most developing countries was to try to reduce their dependency on primary commodities—whose prices were thought to be always unstable in the short term and falling in the long term relative to those of industrial products, and whose export demand was growing very slowly— and to diversify as quickly as possible into the production of manufactures.[22] To do so, developing countries were strongly advised to protect their infant industries from outside competition, to substitute imports of manufacturers with domestic output until the necessary scale economies and production efficiencies could be achieved, and then to start exporting. In order to be helped in this difficult transition process, developing countries "needed" preferential access to industrial countries' markets for their manufactures.

During the early 1970s industrial countries, including those of Europe, were debating the need for and the costs and benefits of international price stabilization, and were maintaining a skeptical position towards it. France was the exception inside, as well as outside, the Community in so far as the French maintained a generally favorable position towards the idea of regulating primary commodity markets. In practice this debate led nowhere. A case by case approach was followed; a few international agreements were set up, but the developing countries' quest for a generalized approach was successfully blocked by a coalition led by the United States and supported, in general, by the European industrial countries.[23]

When developing countries concentrated their efforts on obtaining trade preferences for their manufactures, EC countries, which had already granted such preferences to a small subset of them (the AAMSs), were put in an awkward position. They could not disagree in principle, as the United States did, with the use of trade preferences, because it was an instrument that featured prominently in their own arsenal. At the same time, they could not eliminate the trade benefits already granted to their associates by extending similar preferences to all developing countries. The solution to this dilemma was to graduate trade preferences according to stages of development (or in practice per capita income), and to grant the largest preferences to the relatively poor countries (generally in sub-Saharan Africa) and the smallest preferences to the relatively rich developing countries (generally in Latin America and South East Asia). Yet, when the EC finally enacted its Generalized System of Preferences (GSP) in 1971, the system was not general in either country or commodity coverage, nor was it strongly income-graduated. The AAMSs maintained higher preferences relative to non-associated countries. Among non-associated countries, however, the low-income countries of South Asia were not treated uniformly better than the middle-income countries of Latin America and South East Asia. Also some industrial products which were particularly important exports for the developing countries (including textiles and clothing goods) were exempted from the GSP.

Aside from being engaged in a protracted "holding action" vis-a-vis the demands posed by developing countries, the six EC members remained otherwise occupied, from the mid-1960s onwards, with the implementation of the Common Commercial Policy (CCP), the establishment of the Common Agricultural Policy (CAP) and the protection of their first ailing industrial sector: textiles and clothing.

The first agricultural product—olive oil—was covered by the CAP in 1966. In the next two years the reach of the common policy was extended to most agricultural products of importance to the Community: grain and grain products, rice and rice products, meats, milk and dairy products, sugar, oilseeds, and fruits and vegetables. Wine was subsequently added to the list. With this addition, the CAP virtually isolated the internal European market for temperate-zone food products from the rest of the world. This affected the export interests of Latin American countries more than those of associated African countries. The developing countries of Latin America were among the largest producers and exporters of competing temperate-zone food products (grains, sugar, meats and dairy); while those of Africa mostly exported non-competing tropical food (seeds and oleaginous fruits, tropical oils, coffee, cocoa) and non-food agricultural products (cotton, rubber, sisal) to the EC. Yet, the CAP did affect the export interests of the AAMSs, because 4 to 5 percent of their exports consisted of temperate-zone agricultural products (Table 1.5).

The first set of quantitative restraints on exports of cotton textiles and clothing was established in 1961 by Europe and the United States, and was followed in 1962 by longer lasting arrangements that were periodically renewed throughout the 1960s and early 1970s. But while the 1961 Short Term Arrangement on Trade in Cotton Textiles was almost exclusively directed against Japan, the Long Term Arrangements, which started in 1962 and lasted until 1973, became progressively directed against developing countries' exports (even though the associates were formally exempted from EC import restrictions).

The renewal and expansion of European associationism in the early to mid-1970s were the products of two external events: the United Kingdom's accession to the EC and the oil crisis. The Community reacted swiftly to these challenges. Its response contained elements of continuity as well as innovation. In dealing with the English-speaking countries in Africa, the Caribbean and the Pacific, the Community continued to follow

Table 1.5 Commodity Structure of Associated Countries' Exports to the EC
(percentage of total exports)

	1958	1962	1966
Food, beverages and tobacco			
of which:	36.9	30.3	26.8
Bananas	(4.9)	(4.7)	(4.2)
Coffee	(17.2)	(12.8)	(11.6)
Cocoa	(8.4)	(6.5)	(5.3)
Tobacco	(1.1)	(0.8)	(0.5)
Raw materials of which:	45.2	43.3	41.6
Wood	(8.1)	(12.3)	(13.3)
Cotton	(5.9)	(3.8)	(2.5)
Rubber	(1.2)	(1.3)	(1.0)
Mineral ores	(2.8)	(4.4)	(9.6)
Groundnuts	(11.3)	(8.6)	(5.5)
Groundnut oil	(5.0)	(5.0)	(3.9)
Palm oil	(3.5)	(2.8)	(2.1)
Energy products	1.1	1.6	1.2
Metals of which:	15.0	22.7	28.4
Copper	(13.2)	(17.1)	(23.7)
Manufactures	1.8	2.1	2.0
Total exports	100.0	100.0	100.0
(CAP-affected exports)	(4.6)	(4.1)	(4.0)

Source: Commission des Communautés Européennes, Les Echanges
Commerciaux entre la CEE et les Etats Africains et Malgache Associés, Série
Aide au Développement, No. 2, Brussels, 1969.

its standard association model, but adapted its contènt to the
requirements of the new situation.

The most important new factor of the early 1970s was
undoubtedly the success of the Organization of Petroleum
Exporting Countries (OPEC) in gaining control of the world
oil market and the strong demonstration effects that its actions
were having on all commodity producers. The perception of
the power of producer cartels such as OPEC was heightened
in Europe by the concomitant emergence of real shortages of
raw materials caused by strong inflationary growth in the
industrial West. On the coat-tails of the sharp increases in the

prices of oil and other primary commodities rode the fears of a newly-acquired "commodity power" that developing countries seemed more than willing to use to achieve their self-proclaimed goal of a new international division of labor, that is, a redistribution of wealth on a global scale. Europe felt particularly vulnerable in those years to commodity power, given its widespread dependency on imported oil and non-oil raw materials.[24]

The other new factor that the EC confronted was the problem of the Commonwealth countries, which the United Kingdom did not wish to cut loose after joining the Community and which the Community soon came to perceive, at least for a brief period, as possible additional allies in the quest to strengthen the security of its raw materials supplies on a regional basis. If not suddenly transformed into a "hot pursuer" of developing countries' good will, the Community did feel a new sense of urgency and purpose in dealing with African countries after the oil crisis of 1973. Africa came again to look like one of the few reliable outside reference points for Europe, especially since even the American hold over client states in the Middle East could no longer be relied upon to ensure an adequate supply of petroleum, and since Latin American countries seemed to have grown detached from Europe, if not become hostile to it. Europe in the early 1970s rediscovered itself as the industrial area most exposed to the threat of action by commodity producers, with only Africa to rely on as a source of vital raw materials. The presumed benefits of EurAfrica were assuming an added and concrete dimension: secure supplies of raw materials in very uncertain times.

The invitation extended, via Protocol No. 22 of the January 1973 Treaty of Accession, to the English-speaking countries in Africa and elsewhere (the associables), to negotiate association agreements with the EC, and the invitation to the Asian Commonwealth countries (the non-associables) to negotiate trade agreements, soon assumed a sense of strategic urgency that was not anticipated at the time of issuance. In November 1973 the first oil crisis developed, supplies of oil were embargoed by the Organization of Arab Petroleum Exporting Countries (OAPEC) and Europe physically sensed its high exposure to, and dependency on, a suddenly hostile developing world. Past association with Africa, colonial and post-colonial, came to be seen as a fixed point on which to anchor a strategy for lessening a serious structural weakness of Europe.

In addition, contrary to deep-rooted expectations, the AAMSs that had seemed in the past so reluctant to share their trade and aid privileges with the associable countries of Africa, the Caribbean and the Pacific, quickly forged an effective alliance with them in 1973-74, giving birth to a cohesive and aggressive negotiating group. Led by Senegal and Nigeria, the Francophone and Anglophone countries of Africa found considerable unity of interest in dealing with the EC and derived strength, not weakness, from jointly bargaining with it. Unity also helped these countries to focus their demands on some of the goals emphasized by the New International Economic Order (NIEO). One goal was stabilization of receipts from commodity exports; another was non-reciprocal trade concessions.

What the EC members had envisaged as a simple extension of Yaoundé terms became a more complex and a somewhat novel type of association. The transformation of Yaoundé into Lomé occurred not only in terms of geographical coverage, but also in content. The new Convention signed on 28 February, 1975 in Lomé, the capital of Togo, extended association to forty-six countries, including most of the former British colonies in Africa (Table 1.1). It also contained features that Yaoundé II did not have. Among them were: (a) the explicit recognition of the need for export revenue stability of the associated countries of Africa, the Caribbean and the Pacific (ACP); (b) the establishment of the System for the Stabilization of Export Earnings (STABEX), financed totally by the Community; (c) the abandonment of reciprocity in trade relations between the associated and the nine EC countries; (d) a Sugar Protocol; and (e) provisions covering industrial cooperation. Among the old elements, trade cooperation and continuation of financial (and technical) assistance to the associated countries certainly remained the most important. The institutional framework that had started with Yaoundé I was also maintained and strengthened in the new convention (Table 1.6).

Not unexpectedly, in the new political and economic circumstances of the 1970s, STABEX was the most important innovation of Lomé I. It met one of the long-standing demands of developing countries to have a measure of insurance against commodity revenue instability without having to pay too dearly

Table 1.6 Basic Characteristics and Contents of the Association Arrangements Made by the EC

Treaty or Convention	Rome Treaty (1958–63)	Yaoundé I (1964–69)	Yaoundé II (1969–75)	Lomé I (1975–80)	Lomé II (1980–85)	Lomé III (1985–90)	Lomé IV (1990–2000)
Nature of instrument	Treaty among 6 European countries	Convention between EC and developing countries	Same as Yaoundé I	Same as Yaoundé II	Same as Lomé I	Same as Lomé II	Same as Lomé III
Parties to Treaty Convention	EC Countries only (Treaty unilaterally extended to 22 countries and territories)	EC(6) and 18 African states (AAMS)	EC(6) and 18 AAMSs	EC(9) and 46 African, Caribbean and Pacific (ACP) countries	EC(9) and 58 ACPs	EC(9) and 65 ACPs	EC(12) and 68 ACPs
Stated purposes	"To promote the economic and social development of the countries and territories and economic relations between them and the community as a whole." (Preamble)	"Furthering the industrialization of the associated States, and the diversification of their economies." (Preamble)	Same as in Yaoundé I (Preamble)	"Intensify efforts for the economic and social progress of ACP States" and "establish a new model of relations between developed and developing countries". (Preamble)	Same as in Lomé I	"Promote and expedite the economic, cultural and social development of ACP states and consolidate and diversify relations in a spirit of solidarity and mutual interest." (Art. 1)	Same as in Lomé III
Basic principles	Reciprocity and non-discrimination in trade relations	Reciprocity and non-discrimination Equality of partnership	Same as in Yaoundé I	Non-discrimination in trade relations (reciprocity dropped) Partnership Equality of relations	Same as in Lomé I	Same as in Lomé II	Same as in Lomé III

Treaty or Convention	Rome Treaty (1958-63)	Yaoundé I (1964-69)	Yaoundé II (1969-75)	Lomé I (1975-80)	Lomé II (1980-85)	Lomé III (1985-90)	Lomé IV (1990-2000)
Main areas of cooperation	Trade	Trade Right of establishment of firms and individuals	Same as in Yaoundé I	Trade Commodities Industrial development Establishment, payments and capital movements	Trade Commodities Industrial development Establishment, payments and capital movements Agriculture	Trade Commodities Industrial development Establishment, etc. Agricultural and rural development and conservation Investments Fisheries Transport and communications Regional cooperation Cultural and social cooperation	Trade Commodities Industrial development Enterprise development Agriculture, food security, rural development Investments Fisheries Transport, communication and other services Regional cooperation Cultural and social Energy Environment
Main instruments of cooperation	Free-trade area between EC(6) and countries and territories EC aid	18 free-trade areas between EC(6) and each associate EC aid	Same as in Yaoundé I	EC unilateral trade preferences EC aid STABEX Center for Industrial Development (CID)	EC unilateral trade preference EC aid STABEX CID SYSMIN Technical Center for Agricultural and Rural Cooperation	Same as in Lomé II	Same as in Lomé III

for it. Unlike the existing Compensatory Financing Facility (CFF) of the International Monetary Fund (IMF), STABEX was to compensate for revenue instability deriving from single commodities, irrespective of what happened to other export revenue.[25] STABEX was thus more accessible to the beneficiaries than the IMF facility, which became operational only when total export receipts fell below a historical norm. In addition, while the CFF foresaw interest charges on the resources drawn from it and repayments by the users of the facility in all cases, Lomé contemplated at least a partial conversion of STABEX compensatory payments into grants. This would happen whenever export receipts from a primary commodity did not return to a pre-existing norm within a given time period. Least developed countries were exempted from repayments; and, even when repayable, STABEX credit did not carry an interest charge.

Revenue stabilization, it was hoped, would simplify the macroeconomic management of economies, such as those of the associates, which were highly dependent on primary commodity exports and on Community markets. For thirty-three of the associates one product accounted for more than 50 percent of total exports to the EC as late as 1977.[26] Compensation for permanent losses in export revenue, when it occurred, was to constitute in practice a new way to distribute EC aid. Through STABEX, some of the Community aid resources were in fact becoming allocated on the basis of the objective needs of associated countries, instead of the political and other considerations of importance to the donors. They were also being almost automatically, instead of discretionarily, allocated to beneficiaries.

Abandonment of reciprocity in trade relations with a group of developing countries was another significant concession made by the Community to the demands of the New International Economic Order. Like revenue stabilization, this was a demand by developing countries dating back to the 1950s, when the basic rules concerning international trade enshrined in GATT—non-discrimination and reciprocity—began to be criticized as unsuitable to the special needs of the underdeveloped countries. A waiver to the rule of non-discrimination had already been granted by GATT in 1971, just before the Generalized System of Preferences, extended to developing countries by the EC and Japan, entered into effect. Non-reciprocity in GATT trade negotiations had been recognized even earlier.[27] With Lomé the Community made a regional exception to this principle, which it had followed under both the Rome Treaty provisions and Yaoundé I and II. Lomé, therefore, signaled the abandonment by the Community of the old notion of free-trade areas between the member states and the associates, and the generalization of the principle of unilateral trade preferences.

The Sugar Protocol was another example of special treatment for Lomé associates. It allowed them to export to the Community for an indefinite period of time guaranteed amounts of cane sugar at predetermined prices. Since prices were to be fixed within the annual CAP price range, the sugar convention carried in itself an element of price indexation for one of the exports of the ACP countries.[28] With this action the Community came to extend to all the members of the Lomé convention the regime practiced by Great Britain in the Commonwealth Sugar Agreement. For the countries associated under the Yaoundé Conventions, which did not include any special regime for this product, the Sugar Protocol represented a net gain. Most significant was the fact that sugar, unlike bananas and rum, which were covered under separate protocols in Lomé, was a competing product. One of the agricultural products covered by the CAP was thus recognized as having enough importance for the ACPs to warrant the special treatment of duty-free imports as well as guaranteed prices.[29]

The export regimes for ACP countries built into Lomé I mirrored closely that of Yaoundé II. These countries, like the associates before them, could now export to the Community duty-free tropical products and manufactures, amounting by then to 90 to 95 percent of their exports. The remainder was competing agricultural products covered by the CAP, for which the Community nonetheless granted a somewhat preferential entry. Associates were given either a reduction on the levy payable, or a waiver, or a percentage reduction in the tariff applicable to imports of these products. And these were not insignificant concessions. According to some estimates, 70 percent of the exports of competing products originating from ACP countries had *de facto* duty-free entry into the Community.[30]

Industrial cooperation received increased attention in Lomé I, without assuming, however, the importance that many of the ACP countries would have liked. EC commitments in this field remained long on words and short on deeds. Being overlooked by both parties was the fact that industrial cooperation, going beyond the external financing of new industrial infrastructure, is very difficult by nature. Industrial partnership generally involves arrangements between established firms. Transfer of technology cannot be engineered easily by governments. Outside public assistance can be used to finance new industrial projects, but even in these cases not much more than the supply of industrial capital is possible for the foreign public donor. Much needed managerial skills, merchandising capacity and marketing channels can hardly be supplied as quickly and as easily by public donors as by private investors.

The EC chose the route of direct financial assistance for infrastructure in the transport and communications sectors through the EDF, accompanied by the undertaking to establish institutions that could promote joint ventures between EC and local firms. In fact, Lomé I foresaw the setting up of an Industrial Cooperation Board and a Center for Industrial Development (CID). These institutions were common to and jointly managed by ACP and EC countries. Another feature of EC industrial cooperation policies was the explicit pledge not to try to influence the industrial development models followed by the ACP countries. The Community undertook to assist the plans autonomously worked out by the ACP governments. At the insistence of the ACP members, a key element for any successful industrial development drive—security for foreign investors— did not become part of Lomé I. EC private investors did not, therefore, acquire any new form of insurance against political risk in ACP countries. There was no appreciable difference between investing in associated or non-associated developing countries, at least in terms of explicit coverage of political risks.

Direct financial assistance to associates, a key feature of past associations, remained pre-eminent in Lomé. In comparison with EDF III under Yaoundé II, which had been endowed with EUA 918 million, the total package of EC financial resources made available under Lomé I in 1975 was EUA 3,462 million, more than three and a half times larger in nominal terms (Table 1.7). The funding included EUA 2,100 million for straight grants; EUA 446 million for special loans (having 40-year maturity with a 10-year grace period and carrying a 1.0 percent yearly interest

Table 1.7 EC Association Arrangements: Resources and Reach

Convention (Funds)	Date of Entry into Force	Total Aid (nominal)[a] (millions EUA/ECU)	Total Aid (real)[b] (millions of 1958 EUA/ECU)	No. of Countries (at time of signature)	Associated Countries' Population (millions)
Treaty of Rome (1st EDF)	1-1-58	581	534	19[c]	55
Yaoundé I (2nd EDF)	1-7-64	730	530	18	69
Yaoundé II (3rd EDF)	1-1-71	918	464	19	80
Lomé I (4th EDF)	1-4-76	3,462	1,021	46	250
Lomé II (5th EDF)	1-1-81	5,049	913	57	348
Lomé III (6th EDF)	1-5-86	8,500	1,224	66	413
Lomé IV (7th EDF)	1-3-90	12,000	1,377	68	493

a Includes EDF and EIB own resources.

b Nominal aid deflated by EC GDP deflator index centered in the mid-year of each "convention period".

c Plus 12 other territories (see Table 1.1).

Sources: Commission of the European Communities, *Ten Years of Lomé*, Brussels, 1986; *The Courier*, No. 120, March–April 1990 (for total aid, number of countries and population); *European Economy*, November 1989, No. 42 (for EC GDP price deflators).

rate, reduced to 0.75 percent for the least developed ACPs); EUA 99 million for risk capital for industrial, mining and tourism projects; and EUA 377 million for the STABEX scheme. In addition, the financial assistance package envisaged EUA 390 million in European Investment Bank (EIB) loans, at subsidized interest rates (an automatic interest subsidy of 3 percentage points).

Despite this very large increase in financial assistance envisaged in the first Lomé Convention compared with Yaoundé II, when the increase in European inflation is taken into account the increment in real purchasing power of EC financial assistance was considerably smaller (from 370 to 220 percent). In addition, if one considers that ACP population stood in 1975 at 250 million, 3.1 times higher than AAMS population when Yaoundé II was signed, the per capita real value of EC financial assistance actually decreased under Lomé I.[31]

Lomé did not represent the only major expansion of EC relations with developing countries in the mid-1970s. The United Kingdom's entry into the Community and the OAPEC oil embargo of 1973–74 added urgency to Europe's need to establish relations with its developing neighbors to the south and to the development of the "Global Mediterranean Policy" that had been announced in 1972 at the Paris Summit of the Community's Heads of State.

On the one hand, the potential loss of the British market for horticultural exports had spurred some of the countries of the Maghreb to push for compensating tariff preferences. On the other, the Arab oil embargo had highlighted Europe's extreme vulnerability in the energy field and its need to strengthen ties with the countries of the Mediterranean basin, to ensure greater security of supply of oil. The Maghreb countries needed the EC markets for their exports, while the Community needed the Maghreb to show that it was capable of productive relations with its nearest Arab neighbors.

The rather dormant preferential trade arrangement signed by the Community in 1969 with Tunisia and Morocco became the anchor for the push towards enhanced cooperation with the Maghreb. In 1976, after three years of negotiations, the EC concluded "overall cooperation agreements" with Tunisia, Morocco and Algeria. Similar agreements were concluded in 1977 with Egypt, Jordan and Syria—the Mashreq countries. The *overall* referred to the content of these new agreements, differentiating them from the previous ones that had dealt simply with trade.

The Lomé Era: The Stagnation of the Model

The extension of the areas of cooperation envisaged in the Lomé Convention, the beginning of a *European* response to the core demands of developing countries (non-reciprocity in trade relations, stabilization of export revenues and some indexation of export prices), the extension of the institutional framework for cooperation based on equality between two sets of countries at extremely different stages of development—the nine EC members and ACPs—made Lomé look, at least for a while, like the most advanced system of North–South development cooperation and a model for things to come. One can discount heavily the hyperbole of EC Development Commissioner Claude Cheysson, and Minister Babacar Ba, Chairman of the ACP Council of Ministers, who at the signing of Lomé I respectively referred to the new Convention as "an agreement unique in history" and "a somewhat revolutionary agreement". Yet, when Percival Patterson, Jamaican Minister for Industry and Trade, characterized Lomé I as "an agreement whose value [was] greater than that of the sum of the elements it contained . . . and a new system of [North–South] relations", he was expressing a fairly widespread view, although few disinterested observers would share it fifteen years later.[32]

Great new experiment in development cooperation or old colonial wine in new bottles, new model of North–South relations or unique historical development, elephant or mouse, the first Lomé convention and its successors have nonetheless come to symbolize the European attitude towards, and policy of, development cooperation more than any other set of decisions taken before or after. The Lomé policy has, therefore, elicited strong interest and its changes, its effects on the EC and associated countries, its direct and indirect economic impacts on the rest of the developing countries, its role as model for developed country–less developed country relations, and

its influence on the development of the post-colonial relationships between Europe and Africa have all been studied.[33]
    Despite its obvious linkages with the past, Lomé I turned out to be a largely non-replicable product of its time. When Edgard Pisani, the EC commissioner for development cooperation, wrote in his 1982 Memorandum on the Community's development policy that "the Community has a fundamental interest in the existence of a stable, well regulated, and predicable system of international relations" and that "it is naturally concerned to promote a system which speaks the language of interdependence, rather than conflict", he was surely distilling the main lessons of the 1970s and articulating some of the key determinants of the external projection of the Community that began with Lomé I.[34] But at the same time he was reiterating strategic concepts that had already lost much of their political and economic value for the EC nations. In just a few months the South was to fall into a serious debt crisis, oil and non-oil commodity prices were to collapse, and the much heralded interdependence between North and South would begin to look, from the South's standpoint, more and more like the old dependence on the industrial North. The 1980s, with their brutal effects on the growth and welfare of many developing countries, re-established the balance of international economic and political power in favor of the North. With it, the external conditions surrounding EC–ACP development cooperation changed drastically and became almost antithetical to those that had prevailed during much of the 1970s and had, in some of the ACP leaders' eyes, produced the small "miracle" of Lomé I.
    Three conventions and fifteen years later, it has become quite evident that Lomé I did not become a new model of development cooperation between Europe and the developing countries in general. The Lomé paradigm did not extend to either regional or global North–South cooperation.[35] It is also highly doubtful that it served as a model even in the narrower context of EC–Africa relations. Far from constituting a generalizable approach to development cooperation, Lomé appears to have been an *ad hoc* device, useful to Europe during a transitional period.[36]
    The strongest support for the conclusion that the role and significance of Lomé became progressively discounted in the

1980s can be found in the fact that Lomé policy stagnated in content and innovative thrust. Lomé II and III were nearly exact copies of Lomé I (Table 1.6). The official rhetoric surrounding them was drastically toned down by both the Community and the ACPs. Philosophies of development cooperation and surrounding conditions changed so much during the 1980s, that simply conserving Lomé became a key objective of both the associates and the most cooperation-minded EC members. With the fading of the bargaining power that commodity producers appeared to have gained in the 1970s and even OPEC falling on hard times, the ACPs had little of value to bring to the bargaining table. But aside from bargaining strength, in the 1980s developing countries also lost part of the legitimacy that in the past had accrued to them as "victims" of the outside world. Instead of being seen as entitled to increased economic help, given the external shocks to which they were being subjected, in the 1980s the domestic policies of the developing countries came under scrutiny by the donors, and were now considered a key to their sub-standard economic performance. Assistance to them was made strongly conditional to policy performance and was closely monitored by international organizations. So much and so quickly did the environment around Lomé change, that in the opinion of some authoritative observers, even the simple renewal of Lomé II was to be considered a respectable deal for the ACP countries.[37]

The effective content of the Lomé Conventions hardly changed over time. The only significant innovation of Lomé II, which entered into effect in 1980, was the System for the Promotion of Mineral Production and Exports (SYSMIN). An insurance system against reductions of mine output in ACP countries—introduced as an alternative to the ACP's proposal to extend STABEX to mineral exports—SYSMIN was from the very beginning an instrument designed more to ensure mineral supplies to EC consumers than to stabilize or increase export revenue in ACP producers. In this light the establishment of SYSMIN can be seen more as an indication of the weakening of ACP bargaining power vis-a-vis EC countries than as a further concession by the Community to the wishes of the associates.[38]

Lomé III, which started to operate in 1985, contained some emphasis on the new so-called thematic actions, that is, on long-range efforts to counter major climatic, environmental and health problems at the regional level, with priority on the fight against drought and desertification in Africa. Lomé III also contained a new chapter on cultural and social cooperation, a new section on tourism and some additional attention to trade promotion. On the whole, however, these were verbal concessions to developing countries' goals and concerns, void of real substance. When a few EC members insisted on the inclusion in Lomé III of safeguards for EC private investments in ACP countries, the latter had to agree to a joint statement of willingness to negotiate investment protection agreements.

Such agreements were clearly needed to encourage EC private investors, and thus were also in the interests of the developing countries that signed the new convention. Yet, the fact that this was the first time the ACPs had to bow to EC pressures on this point, although the subject had been discussed for years within the Lomé framework, is indicative of the change that had been taking place in the relative strength of the two groups of countries since the early 1970s. The same trend can be seen in the shift of EC grant resources from traditional projects to the financing of adjustment lending foreseen in Lomé IV. Structural adjustment is clearly a priority for most ACPs, but the fact that the EC could obtain agreement to a highly conditional use of grant resources from the same countries that five years earlier had successfully resisted even Commissioner Edgard Pisani's efforts towards a more systematic policy dialogue with the Community, is again indicative of a drastic change in relative bargaining power. The Community, moreover, which in earlier years had prided itself on strictly respecting the development priorities of the associates and had left to them the decision on the final destination of the aid resources it provided, was now in effect trying to establish control over the policy environment governing the use of the aid resources as a condition of the disbursement of part of its economic assistance.

By the time Lomé III was negotiated most of the African countries south of the Sahara were in the midst of a profound economic crisis, of which debt was the most visible external manifestation, but by no means the most important. Their need for assistance, regular and special, was so high, and their bargaining strength so low, that the early 1970s could have been in a different century, not just the previous decade. Yet,

Europe did not launch any autonomous special action programs for Africa. It did extend additional financial assistance to sub-Saharan Africa, but through international channels (such as the World Bank and the IMF), that is, outside the framework of Lomé. Bent on not creating new precedent, the EC nations avoided using Community channels to deal with the African crisis.

EC Europe, moreover, did not take, either alone or with other industrial areas, any debt reduction initiative vis-a-vis Africa until 1988, despite the evident and urgent need for debt relief in most sub-Saharan African countries, despite the official nature of much of the debt contracted by these countries and despite the innumerable calls for help that it received. When EC Europe took the initiative, the first sign of it came from the heads of state of the four largest EC countries when they agreed with their US, Canadian and Japanese counterparts on actions to be taken on debt relief for African countries. It was the so-called G-7 (the seven largest industrialized nations) that officially took the decision. Again, the avoidance of the existing EC–ACP institutional framework could not have been clearer in political meaning. The concession over debt was once more unilateral, and not negotiated with the ACPs. It is significant that Germany, France, the United Kingdom and Italy also chose to advance their proposals for the reduction of official debt of low-income countries to the United States, Japan and Canada, instead of dealing first with their EC partners in Brussels. This choice was not solely aimed at achieving equitable burden sharing with the other major industrial creditors, an objective that could have been achieved in other ways, but was also to underline the non-regional nature of their efforts and the fact that the more favorable terms of debt renegotiation were to be unilaterally *granted*. In addition, the Paris Club, the informal union of official creditors, was kept as the negotiating forum, no doubt to signal that even in the exceptional circumstances of the mid-1980s, debt questions were to be kept within the established fora and dealt with using established procedures. The form and substance of the European debt initiative could not have been farther away from the model of Lomé.

The EC shyness on the question of debt relief for ACP countries, surprising as it may have appeared to those who understood both the origin and consequences of the debt problem faced by these countries, as well the opportunity for furthering the European strategy of cooperation with Africa that was at hand, did not constitute a sharp deviation from existing policy trends. EC Europe, in fact, far from trying to extend the Lomé model in functional scope or geographical reach, had been intent for many years on only managing the existing relationship, accepting some marginal adaptation to either its specific goals or to the resources devoted to it, but no real innovation. In freezing the Lomé model and in reducing EC efforts to simple management of the existing mechanisms, the coalition of conservative EC member states that prevailed in Brussels found a natural, if perhaps unwilling, ally in the bureaucratic apparatus of the Community. Like any bureaucracy, the EC Commission is normally more inclined to preserve the status quo, or to marginally improve upon it, than to attempt to innovate or radically change it. This tendency is more pronounced in a situation where the Commission's role in shaping development policies is neither constitutionally clear, nor well-accepted by the Council.[39]

Does Lomé still hold any value for the Community? This question is worth asking. The significance of Lomé for EC Europe cannot, however, be evaluated in isolation. Lomé is a phase in the evolution of a phenomenon—associationism—that has deep roots in the history of Europe and derives its impetus both from changes in the politics and the economics of the "Old Continent" and from changes in world political and economic circumstances.

It is the purposes of European associationism that are reflected in Lomé, and not vice versa. For EC Europe associationism was from the start a defensive policy. It served first to protect Europe from the possible negative effects of decolonization, one of which was the threat to the regular supply of industrial raw materials to European industry. From this perspective a minimum level of political stability and economic development in the newly independent states of Africa was in the interest of the Community as well. Associationism was also an attempt to keep for Europe a measure of political influence in a world dominated by the two superpowers—the United States and the Soviet Union.

Aid and trade concessions, believed to be helpful in attaining these results, were used. If the framework of the EC was originally set up to unite Europe economically, it also offered advantages in managing the relationship with the newly independent states of Africa in turbulent and difficult times. Because the EC's political image was less obtrusive than the former colonial images of its members, it could be used to further this objective too. And used it was.

EC Europe's goals of maintaining political continuity and the economic status quo of EC Europe in its relations with the former colonies largely overlapped those of the political elites of many African states. The new rulers had to deliver at least a modicum of the well being and national progress promised in pre-independence days, and to be able to do so, or at least to show some positive results, they needed increased economic assistance from the outside. European states were a natural source of this much needed external help. Europe understood better than anyone else the internal requirements faced by the African political elites now in power. What Robert Lemaignen recounted is perfectly credible: the candidacy of a Frenchman as the first EC Commissioner for Economic Development found strong support in official political circles in Africa. Present and future heads of government in Africa preferred to have an "interlocutor" in Brussels who knew them and their needs rather than one who did not.[40]

As time progressed and post-independence tensions lessened in Africa and elsewhere, the policy of associationism became more and more a testimonial to the Community's willingness to play an active role in helping Africa to realize its economic potential and to develop economically. It also began to acquire some of the dimensions of an original collaborative approach. Some who saw this trend evolving stressed the importance of the institutional arrangements between donors and aid recipients that were built into the various associations sponsored by the Community and the importance of the principle of parity which, at least formally, governed these relationships. Others, more pragmatically, stressed the certainty and multi-year dimension of EC aid allocations.

Full use of the potential of EC associationism as proof of a forward-looking and truly collaborative development posture, however, was not made by the EC until the early 1970s, when the threat of commodity power suddenly loomed over Europe and a new type of defense had to be mounted against it. This defense centered around the early acceptance of some of the "more reasonable" demands contained in the NIEO and the establishment of the Community's good faith as a credible partner in this process. Lomé was a symbolic innovation that could be brandished to accredit this new image of the Community.

Associationism, as a model, seemed to be easily extensible to the Mediterranean and usable to protect Europe from its main structural weakness: dependency on imported energy. In pursuit of this objective in the new political circumstances of the 1970s, the EC never ceased to stress the positive value of interdependence between North and South and the duties that rested on all parties in a closely intertwined world. Key among them was the duty of economic cooperation. The EC was fulfilling it by providing trade and financial help on the basis of the principles of parity and non-interference. In turn, its African partners were expected to behave reasonably and fulfill their part of the bargain: the delivery of raw materials and the maintenance of friendly political relations with the Community. Commissioner Pisani, in his characteristically direct and honest way, explicitly recognized the objective of a secure supply of raw materials built into EC development policy in his 1982 Memorandum.[41] This, according to Pisani, was what characterized it most clearly and set it apart from other policies.

In the 1980s associationism lost most of the defensive objectives that it had assumed in the 1950s and again, and more strongly, in the 1970s. With the waning of the defensive dimension attached to it, associationism ceased to develop and adapt to changing circumstances. Lomé consequently stagnated.

Associationism, however, did not fully recoil, even after the disappearance of developing countries' commodity power, the collapse of the oil market and the emergence of the debt crisis. It went, instead, on a sort of "automatic pilot" under the watchful eyes of the Commission and some of the EC members. Whether this standing still of associationism and development cooperation, in the midst of political and economic circumstances favorable to the Community, can be taken to represent a lag in adjustment or the sign of "true development grit" by the EC, remains a matter of interpretation and some dispute. Lomé IV, however, seems to signal to some the continuance of associationism, although perhaps following different principles than in the past. This continuity could signify that, freed from its defensive clothes, EC associationism can survive as part of a more truly developmental EC cooperation policy. To others, Lomé IV signifies instead the beginning of a substantial movement in EC-ACP relations away from any pretense of partnership and towards a more traditional (and thus inherently unequal) North-South relationship in both trade and aid—a relationship strictly conditioned by the priorities, ideology and economics of the North. While no one has yet officially proclaimed that *"Lomé est morte"*, cheers of *"Vive Lomé"* are hard to hear from any quarter.

Notes to Chapter I

1 H. Deschamps, *Les Methodes et les Doctrines Coloniales de la France*, Paris, Librairie Armand Colin, 1953, pp. 142-54, 167-76 and 198-207. The tradition of association goes back to 1875, to the exploration of Central Africa by Pierre Savorgnan de Brazza, who developed the idea of peaceful French penetration of Africa and of a commonwealth of interest between Africans and Europeans: P. Manning, *Francophone Sub-Saharan Africa 1880-1985*, Cambridge, Cambridge University Press, 1988, p. 15. The concept was refined and further developed by Harmand, who saw in association a policy designed to "establish a certain equivalence or compensation of reciprocal services" between the colonizers and the colonized, in drastic contrast to assimilation: J. Harmand, *Domination et Colonisation*, Paris, E. Flammarion, 1919, p. 160. The idea of association became respectable in French intellectual life and was influential until recently. See F.R. Betts, *Assimilation and Association in French Colonial Theory: 1890-1914*, New York, Columbia University Press, 1961, p. 170.

2 K. Robinson, *The Dilemma of Trusteeship: Aspects of British Colonial Policy Between the Wars*, London, Oxford University Press, 1965; and D. Austin, "The Transfer of Power: Why and How", in W.H. Morris-Jones and G. Fischer, eds., *Decolonization and After: The British and French Experience*, London, Frank Cass, 1980, pp. 3-5. On the influence of French, British and Belgian colonial policies on the process of decolonization, see C. Young, "Decolonization in Africa", in L.H. Gann and P. Duignan, eds., *Colonialism in Africa: The History and Politics of Colonialism*, Vol. 2, Cambridge, Cambridge University Press, 1970, pp. 450-502.

3 See, for example, A. De Gasperi, "Propositi e Direttive del Primo Governo della Repubblica", Speech to Parliament of 15 July 1946, and 'Sull'Amministrazione Fiduciaria della Somalia", Speech to Parliament of 4 February 1950, in De Gasperi, *Discorsi Parlamentari*, Vol. 1, Rome, Ufficio Pubblicazioni della Camera dei Deputati, 1985, pp. 83–94 and 725–30.

4 For a history of relations between France and Africa during and after World War II, see E. Mortimer, *France and the Africans: 1944–1960*, London, Faber and Faber, 1969.

5 See, for example, C. de Gaulle, *Memoirs of Hope: Renewal and Endeavor*, New York, Simon and Schuster, 1971, pp. 37–40, and A. Eden, *Facing the Dictators*, Boston, Houghton Mifflin Co., 1962, pp. 587–8.

6 F. Fejto, *The French Communist Party and the Crisis of International Communism*, Cambridge, The MIT Press, 1967, pp. 36–9 and 96–106.

7 R. Rathbone, "The Legacy of Empire", in M. Cornell, ed., *Europe and Africa: Issues in Post-Colonial Relations*, London, ODI, 1981, pp. 1–20.

8 B.P. Cousté, *L'Association des Pays d'Outre-mer à la Communauté Economique Européenne*, Paris, Librairies Techniques, 1959, pp. 53–94.

9 On the process that led to the association to the Community of the "countries and territories" of the member states, see M. Andreis, *L'Africa e la Comunità Economica Europea*, Turin, Einaudi, 1967, pp. 17–22; D. Vignes, *L'Association des Etats Africains et Malgache à la CEE*, Paris, Librairie Armand Colin, 1970, pp. 7–12; N. Delorme, *L'Association des Etats Africains et Malgache à la Communauté Economique Européenne*, Paris, Librairie Pichon et Durand-Auzias, 1972, pp. 17–19; C. Dodoo and R. Kuster, "The Road to Lomé", in A.M. Alting von Geusau, ed., *The Lomé Convention and a New International Economic Order*, Leyden, A.W. Sijthoff, 1977, pp. 16–19; C. Cosgrove Twitchett, *Europe and Africa: From Association to Partnership*, Westmead, Saxon House, 1978, pp. 1–16.

10 M. Lister, *The European Community and the Developing World*, Aldershot, Avebury, 1988, pp. 14–17.

11 Office for Official Publications of the European Communities, *Treaties Establishing the European Communities*, Luxemburg, 1987, p. 349.

12 Jacqueline Matthews calls the first type of association "full association" and this second type "special association": J.D. Matthews, *Association System of the European Community*, New York, Praeger, 1977, pp. 10–27.

[13] Young, "Decolonization in Africa", pp. 450-502; H. Magdoff, *Imperialism*, New York, Monthly Review Press, 1978, pp. 94-116.

[14] A. Rivkin, *Africa and the West*, New York, Praeger, 1962, pp. 36-7 and 118-21.

[15] As candidly explained by President Leopold Senghor of Senegal, in *Cahiers de L'Afrique Occidentale et de l'Afrique Equatoriale*, 15 June 1963, "at no time [during the Addis Ababa Conference] did we renounce collaboration with Europe or with Asia or with France. Also in Africa we did not envisage the disappearance of the Union of African and Malagasy States. I have the same idea of African unity as General de Gaulle has of European Unity. It is necessary to build an Africa of the Fatherlands" (translation mine).

[16] A. Rivkin, *Africa and the European Common Market: A Perspective*, Monograph Series in World Affairs, No. 4, Denver, University of Denver, 1966 (revised 2nd edition), p. 5. On the interaction between the ideologies of Pan-Africanism and EurAfricanism see G. Martin, "Africa and the Ideology of Eur-Africa: Neo-Colonialism or Pan-Africanism", *Journal of Modern African Studies*, Vol. 2, No. 2, June 1982, pp. 221-38.

[17] Cosgrove Twitchett, *Europe and Africa*, pp. 86-7. The *sur-prix* system guaranteed prices to colonial producers that exceeded those prevailing in world markets, thus providing them with a subsidy from the French treasury. The system encouraged overproduction of the products covered by price guarantees and thus created a considerable financial burden for France.

[18] Vignes, *L'Association des Etats Africains*, p. 29.

[19] The experience of Yaoundé has been thoroughly examined. Aside from Cosgrove Twitchett, *Europe and Africa*, the economic provisions and effects of Yaoundé are analyzed in: H.R. Wartman, *Essays on the European Common Market*, Information Bulletin No. 57, Bloomington, Ind., Indiana University Graduate School of Business, 1966, pp. 23-49; F.B. Jensen and I. Walter, *The Common Market: Economic Integration in Europe*, Philadelphia, J.B. Lippincott Co., 1965, pp. 112-31; T. Balogh, "Africa and the Common Market", *Journal of Common Market Studies*, Vol. 1, No. 1, 1962, pp. 79-112; C. Young, "Association with the EC: Economic Aspects of the Trade Relationship", *Journal of Common Market Studies*, Vol. 11, No. 2, 1972, pp. 120-35; A. Ouattara, "Trade Effects of the Association of African Countries with the European Economic Community", *IMF Staff Papers*, Vol. 20, No. 2, 1973, pp. 471-98. The historical, legal and political characteristics of the Convention are examined in: Andreis, *L'Africa e la Comunità*

Economica Europea; W. Gorell Barnes, *Europe and the Developing World*, London, Chatham House-PEP Paper, 1967; U.W. Kitzinger, *The Politics and Economics of European Integration*, New York, Praeger, 1963, pp. 97-119; G.M. Adams, "Community Foreign Policy and Political Integration: Lessons of the African Association", in S.J. Warnecke, ed., *The European Community in the 1970s*, New York, Praeger, 1972; Delorme, *L'Association des Etats Africains et Malgache*. On the history and politics of negotiations see I.W. Zartman, *The Politics of Trade Negotiations Between Africa and the European Economic Community*, Princeton, Princeton University Press, 1971, pp. 24-76. For a more political view of European associationism at this stage of its development see G. Curzon and V. Curzon, "Neo-Colonialism and the European Community", in *The Yearbook of World Affairs*, London, Stevens and Son (for the Institute of World Affairs), 1971; and G. Galtung, *The European Community: A Superpower in the Making*, London, Allen & Unwin, 1973.

20 P.N.C. Okigbo, *Africa and the Common Market*, London, Longmans, 1967; Zartman, *Politics of Trade Negotiations*, pp. 77-115; Matthews, *Association System*, pp. 26-7.

21 Commission of the European Communities, *Opinion on the Application for Membership Received from the United Kingdom, Ireland, Denmark and Norway for Submission to the Council Under Art. 237 of the EC Treaty*, Doc. COM(67) 758, Brussels, 29 September 1967, p. 92; Commission of the European Communities, *Economic Union and Enlargement: The European Commission's Revised Opinion on the Application for Membership from the United Kingdom, Ireland, Denmark and Norway*, Brussels, October 1969, p. 57.

22 The first characteristic—instability of prices—is due to the unresponsiveness of both demand and supply of primary products to price changes, at least in the short term. The second—slow demand growth—is due to the unresponsiveness of demand for many primary commodities to income changes.

23 J. Isaken, "Western European Reaction to Four NIEO Issues", in E. Lazlo and J. Kurtzman, eds., *Western Europe and the New International Economic Order*, New York, Pergamon Press, 1980, pp. 12-13.

24 See, for example, Commission of the European Communities, *Europe and the Third World: A Study in Interdependence*, Collection Dossiers, Development Series No. 2, Brussels, February 1978, pp. 13-49, where European dependency on oil and other primary commodities is depicted in the starkest terms and overdramatized by the inclusion of tropical beverages, bananas and vegetable oils among the products imported from developing countries on which the Community was

most severely dependent. The critical importance of raw materials supplies from developing countries to the Community was still greatly emphasized by the Commission as late as 1984: Commission of the European Communities, *Commodities and Stabex*, Europe Information No. DE 49, Brussels, September 1984, pp. 10-14, where the role of the Community as a natural mediator between the developing countries and other industrial countries, such as the United States, in the North-South dialogue on commodities was justified on the basis of the special interest of Europe in the security of supplies of primary products. See also the emphasis attributed to the commodity dependence of the EC in Commission of the European Communities, *Europe-South Dialogue*, Brussels, 1984.

[25] These were: cocoa (including paste and butter), coffee, tea, groundnuts (including oil and cakes), cotton, raw sisal, coconut products, palm products, leather and skins, wood products, bananas, coffee, and iron ore. These products accounted for 30 percent of all ACP exports in 1975.

[26] Statistical Office of the European Communities, *Analysis of Trade Between the European Community and the ACP States*, Brussels, 1979, p. 2.33.

[27] D. Tussie, *The Less Developed Countries and the World Trading System*, New York, St. Martin's Press, 1987; R.E. Hudec, *Developing Countries in the GATT Legal System*, Aldershot, Gower (for the Trade Policy Research Center), 1987; E. Grilli, "Contemporary Protectionism in an Unstable World Economy", in G. Sutija and G. Fels, eds., *Protectionism and International Banking*, London, Macmillan, 1991, pp. 144-72. On the relationship between Yaoundé-Lomé and the GATT, see Matthews, *Association System*, pp. 62-89; Delorme, *L'Association des Etats Africains et Malgache*, pp. 264-77. The political significance of the abandonment of reciprocity by the EC in Lomé I, depicted as an acceptance of a kind of voluntary disequilibrium in trade relations with the ACPs, is stressed in M.P. Roy, *La CEE et le Tiers Monde: Les Conventions de Lomé*, Paris, La Documentation Française, 1985, pp. 15-16.

[28] Indexation of prices of commodity exports was one of the key demands made by developing countries in the framework of the NIEO. On its economic rationale see J. Cuddy, *International Price Indexation*, Lexington, Mass., Lexington Books, 1976.

[29] An examination of the special regime concerning sugar in Lomé can be found in J. Ravenhill, *Collective Clientelism: The Lomé Conventions and North-South Relations*, New York, Columbia University Press, 1985, pp. 219-41.

30 Cosgrove Twitchett, *Europe and Africa*, p. 150.

31 See Table 3.4.

32 The remarks of Commissioner Cheysson, Minister Babacar Ba and Minister Patterson may be found in "Dossier Lomé", *The Courier*, No. 31, May 1975, Special Issue, pp. 7–8 and 12–13.

33 The most important books written on Lomé are: E. Frey-Wouters, *The European Community and the Third World*, New York, Praeger, 1980; P. Bouvier, *L'Europe et la Coopération au Développement: La Convention de Lomé*, Brussels, Editions de l'Université de Bruxelles, 1980; C. Cosgrove Twitchett, *A Framework for Development: The EC and the ACP*, London, George Allen and Unwin, 1981; J. Moss, *The Lomé Conventions and their Implications for the United States*, Boulder, Col., Westview Press, 1982; Ravenhill, *Collective Clientelism*; Lister, *European Community and the Developing World*; Roy, *Les Conventions de Lomé*; and most recently S. Sideri, *La Comunità Europea nell'Interdipendenza Mondiale*, Milan, Unicopli, 1990, which provides an in-depth analysis of EC cooperation policies with all developing areas. The essays written on Lomé are too numerous to be listed. Some of the most significant are: I.W. Zartman, "Europe and Africa: Decolonization or Dependency", *Foreign Affairs*, Vol. 54, No. 1, January 1976, pp. 325–43; I.V. Gruhn, "The Lomé Convention: Inching Towards Interdependence", *International Organization*, Vol. 30, No. 2, Spring 1976, pp. 241–62; R.H. Green, "The Child of Lomé: Messiah, Monster or Mouse?", in F. Long, ed., *The Political Economy of EEC Relations with African, Caribbean and Pacific States*, Oxford, Pergamon Press, 1980, pp. 3–31; A. Hewitt, "The Lomé Conventions: Myth and Substance of the Partnership of Equals", in M. Cornell, ed., *Europe and Africa: Issues in Post-Colonial Relations*, London, DDI, 1981 pp. 21–42; M. Kahler, "Europe and its Privileged Partners in Africa and the Middle East", *Journal of Common Market Studies*, Vol. 21, Nos. 1–2, September/December 1982, pp. 199–218; E. Olu Sanu, "The Lomé Convention and the New International Economic Order", Lecture Series, No. 18, Lagos, Nigerian Institute of International Affairs, 1982; C. Stevens, "The European Community and Africa, the Caribbean and the Pacific", in J. Lodge, ed., *Institutions and Policies of the European Community*, New York, St. Martin's Press, 1983, pp. 142–53; M. Dolan, "The Changing Face of EEC Policies Towards the Developing Countries: Reflection of Economic Crisis and the Changing International Division of Labour", *Journal of European Integration*, Vol. 7, Nos. 2–3, pp. 161–96; J. Ravenhill, "Europe and Africa: An Essential Continuity", in R. Boardman, T.M. Shaw and P. Soldatos, eds., *Europe, Africa and Lomé III*, Lanham, Md., University Press of America, 1985,

pp. 35–58. Other recent essays on Lomé are referred to in notes 35, 36 and 37.

34 Commission of the European Communities, "Memorandum on the Community's Development Policy", Supplement 5/82 to the *Bulletin of the European Communities*, 1982, p. 12. This is called the Pisani Memorandum after EC Commissioner Edgard Pisani who prepared it.

35 A. Hewitt, "The Lomé Conventions: Entering a Second Decade", *Journal of Common Market Studies*, Vol. 22, No. 2, 1984, pp. 95–8.

36 I.W. Zartman, "Lomé III: Relic of the 1970s or Model for the 1990s", in C. Cosgrove and J. Jamar, eds., *The European Community's Development Policy: The Strategies Ahead*, Bruges, De Tempel, 1986, pp. 59–64.

37 T. Killick, "Whither Lomé? A Review of the Lomé III Negotiations", *Third World Quarterly*, Vol. 7, No. 3, July 1985, p. 676.

38 STABEX only covered iron ore among the mineral exports of the ACPs.

39 On the relationships between Council, Parliament and Commission in the area of community aid, see C. Jackson and P. Price, "Who Controls Community Aid", in Cosgrove and Jamar, eds., *The European Community's Development Policy*, pp. 163–71.

40 R. Lemaignen, *L'Europe au Berceau: Souvenirs d'un Technocrate"*, Paris, Plon, 1964, p. 57.

41 "The Community is not a multilateral development institution: being the expression of a European identity, the Community's development policies embody geographical preferences. Although it is a manifestation of solidarity with certain developing countries, it also reflects the Community's economic interest in the organization of its relations with countries on which it depends for the security of its supplies and its markets." Commission, "Memorandum on the Community's Development Policy", 1982, p. 14.

2

The Aid Dimension: Europeanization of Development Assistance or Two-Track Policy?

Economic assistance constitutes the traditional component of European development policy. It is a part that has roots in the colonial past of most EC member countries and is closely interlinked with their bilateral policies of development cooperation. It is also by far the most important in terms of domestic resources devoted to helping developing countries.

In Part IV of the Treaty of Rome, the main goal of the relations between the EC and the colonial dependencies of its members— eventually to become independent national entities—was put in terms of promoting the dependencies' economic and social development. Art. 131 was clear in this respect: "The Association shall serve primarily to further the interests and prosperity of the inhabitants of these countries and territories and to lead them to the economic, social and cultural development to which they aspire." Oddly, economic aid was never mentioned in the Treaty as a means to achieve the desired goals. Only provisions concerning trade between the Community and the associated countries and territories were specified in it.[1]

Though relegated to the "Implementing Convention on the Association of the Overseas Countries and Territories to the Community", the first real innovation in the relationship with the associated countries established by the Rome Treaty was the setting up of the European Development Fund as the instrument for channeling multilateral aid from the Community directly to the associates. The direct Community aid was to co-exist with the aid bilaterally distributed by the member countries, and be additional and complementary to it.[2] The EDF was small, both in absolute terms and relative to the size of the bilateral aid programs of some of the member states. At the time, however, the value of the Fund was its existence not its dimensions. Despite coming from member countries' special contributions, and not from the budget of the Community, direct EC aid symbolized both the common will to foster the economic development of the associates and the new ways of doing it being initiated by the member countries.

Since the beginning the Community had emphasized the importance of its direct economic assistance to the associated developing countries. Provisions pertaining to financial and technical assistance made up Title II of the Yaoundé Conventions and were placed immediately after those related to trade. The first authoritative review of the ways in which the EC was helping the developing countries, made public by the Commission in 1971, was significantly entitled *European Development Aid*, despite its concomitant coverage of trade and other matters.[3] Similarly, the first extensive official document on development policies, issued by the Commission in July 1971, specifically singled out direct financial assistance from the Community as the type of action most pleasing to the recipient countries.[4]

Most of the countries and territories referred to in Part IV of the Treaty of Rome were in Africa. Given past colonial ties, the concentration of direct EC aid in Africa south of the Sahara was almost a natural development, and was acknowledged as such. Inevitably, therefore, the countries first touched by Community aid were the African colonial possessions of France and Belgium, the African trust territories of Italy and France, the autonomous Republic of Togoland and a few other colonial possessions of the members located in various other parts of the world. These were the same territories that received sizeable bilateral transfers and other forms of assistance from some of the member states, especially France.[5] They not only remained at the center of attention of the national assistance policies of their current or former metropoles, but also became the preferred recipients of bilateral aid from those members of the Community that no longer had colonial possessions at the time of the Treaty of Rome. From the beginning, the concentration of aid on the Francophone associates of Africa was so clear that some analysts have argued that EC direct financial assistance was a form of compensation for the loss of benefits they incurred as a consequence of the phasing out of the price subsidies for exports that France had previously granted them.[6]

The particular focus of its development cooperation on Africa was openly, and often proudly, acknowledged by the Community. In 1971, for example, in a comment on the significance of art. 131 of the Treaty, the Commission simply and plainly stated that it showed "the member countries' willingness to contribute to the development of the developing world *within the particular geographical framework bequeathed by history*" (emphasis added).[7] In the same year, presenting to the Council its first extensive memorandum on development cooperation, the Commission again indicated matter-of-factly that the Community had originally embarked on "a *regional policy of development cooperation*" which was now "part of the Community patrimony" and had to be "maintained, improved and reinforced" (emphasis added).[8] This identification with Africa was further reinforced in the 1970s by the entry of the United Kingdom into the Community, and the consequent extension of privileged aid (and trade) relations to practically all the former British colonies of Africa.

Helping the poor countries of Africa in their quest for accelerated social and economic development necessitated continued resource transfers from the former metropoles and supplements from Brussels. The "additionality" of direct EC aid, an aspect which the Commission never ceased to emphasize, was indeed a tangible and new dimension of the Community's development assistance policy in the late 1950s. Yet, the political economy of multilateral EC aid was also clear from the very start: it offered a way to diffuse assistance burdens among the members of the new Community, which had assumed with the Rome Treaty the new joint obligation to help the development of the associated countries and territories. France and Belgium were able to get some respite at the margin, as Germany and the Netherlands started contributing substantially to the European Development Fund.

Aid from the Community turned out to be an effective and politically adroit way of achieving a new burden sharing among the members of the Community.[9] Germany, without looking like it was being forced into it, assumed the financing of EDF I on the same basis as France (at 34 percent of the total). The Netherlands, which had no territorial possessions in Africa, also contributed handsomely (12 percent of the total); Italy would do the same in later years. On the whole, the EC members that no longer had direct colonial offshoots in Africa supplied nearly half of the financial resources of the Fund set up to help the "region bequeathed by history".

The Many Appeals of Direct EC Aid

Financial aid is no doubt a form of assistance highly preferred by the recipients. Its attractiveness to developing countries has hardly waned over time, despite the numerous criticisms leveled against it. The African countries associated with the Community were no exception to this rule, rhetoric to the contrary (e.g. in favor of trade) notwithstanding. As late as 1989, in their background document for the negotiation of Lomé IV, the ACP countries after stating that trade was "central to the economic relationship" between them and the EC, hastened to reiterate the importance of aid by observing that "in terms of factors required for production, possibly the greatest lack in ACP states is the financial resources".[10] As early as 1971 the Commission had publicly noted that the Associated States had "on several occasions expressed their satisfaction with the objectivity and effectiveness of [EC financial and technical] cooperation".[11]

The position of aid recipients can generally be well understood. While trade is an exchange of commodities for other commodities, and thus an exchange of domestic for foreign resources, aid is a net addition to the recipients' national resources. Moreover, foreign aid constitutes international purchasing power. The resource augmenting effects of economic aid are not simply quantitative. Aid also allows those who receive it to acquire goods, services and technologies from abroad that otherwise would not be available or would be much scarcer. In general, African countries remained short of investment resources and/or foreign exchange. They also had to rely heavily on foreign assistance to organize the supply of nutrition, education and health services seen as essential to human development and to the satisfaction of basic human needs of their growing populations. For many of the poorer African countries foreign aid filled major public revenue and expenditure gaps.

Aid also had strong general appeal for the donors. Aside from being generally considered, at least in the 1960s, as one of the most effective instruments for fostering development, it was a visible and tangible sign of continued European commitment to Africa, and it could be delivered at specific times and aimed at specific objectives. These characteristics of aid allowed the satisfaction of multiple objectives—external as well as internal— and the fulfillment of the goals of the numerous aid constituencies existing in each of the EC members. To those who supported assistance to Africa on humanitarian grounds— a strong component of the domestic aid lobby in many EC countries—governments could point to the recognizable contribution to the recipients' welfare that was being made. To the various industrial and commercial concerns interested in public procurement, governments could indicate that *tied* bilateral aid was an assured form of support to home businesses and that even EC multilateral aid, tied only at the European level, was not open to procurement by non-members. To the recipients aid did not have to be justified, but, many of its benefits could be suitably evidenced.

There were also important foreign policy concerns that could be pursued through the supply of economic aid, particularly when it was channeled in new and less colonial forms than in the past. The second goal stated in Part IV of the Treaty of Rome, under the rubric of association with overseas countries and territories, was "to establish close economic relations between them and the Community as a whole". Multilateral- ization of the existing colonial relationships was an important objective sought by the signatories of the Treaty. The new institutions set up at the European level had no colonial past. They were, therefore, well suited to project the image of a Community that wished to keep "cooperation free of any hegemonic intent of domination and any strictly mercantile considerations".[12] The Community institutions could creditably embody the development concerns of the new Europe, which in turn fit well with the post-colonial era that everybody saw as setting in. Aid administration, moreover, gave Community institutions a much coveted foreign policy function to perform.

As a first step, since a set of "close economic relations" already existed between each colony and its metropole, the Treaty sought to extend these relations to all the members of the Community. Trade regimes were critical to this goal, as trade had been, up to then, largely a bilateral affair between each metropole and its overseas territories. Trade relations with associates had, therefore, to be multilateralized, and the Treaty of Rome provided for the creation of a free-trade area between the associated countries and territories and the EC as a whole. But economic aid, and in particular direct Community aid, was essential in smoothing the transition from bilateral to multilateral relations between the African territories and the European Community. Reaching this goal required significant amounts of aid from the Community in appropriate forms. If size and objective value of EC aid resources were important for the recipients, the forms of European financial assistance were not simply incidental. Aid that could not be construed as neo-colonial was appreciably better than aid that could. It made it easier for many associates to remain tied politically and economically to Europe in the post-colonial era. From the Community's standpoint direct aid accredited the new institution as an actor with an international political role to play.

EC trade and aid concessions, moreover, were tied to one another in many ways. Through the additional economic assistance extended by the EC, the associates could also take more full and rapid advantage of the trade preferences they enjoyed inside the Community. More aid meant larger investment possibilities and increased production potential. Diversification of markets and products could be better achieved with economic assistance than without it, as taking advantage of EC trade preferences required the capacity to supply new products as well as existing ones.

In an effort, therefore, to adapt to a post-colonial environment, while at the same time maintaining privileged relations with Africa, if on a collective basis, EC nations transformed part of the domestic resources once directly devoted to colonial development into foreign aid and acted as if they were adding appreciably to it. The "addition", as previously noted, came in part from those members that no longer had colonial ties in Africa or elsewhere in the developing world—the Netherlands, Germany and subsequently Denmark. In performing this transformation of aid relations, EC member nations as such lost control over the management of part of their aid resources, but continued to derive from them significant benefits, political as well as economic. They did so by geographically concentrating financial assistance, by targeting a portion of it towards the attainment of concerns "shared" with their privileged partners in Africa and by maintaining an implicit, but nonetheless clear, relationship between economic assistance and foreign policy objectives.[13]

As time went by, and trade preferences lost most of their importance for the associates, aid from the Community became even more appealing to the governments of the associated countries. It was seen as the greatest, if not the only, tangible benefit of their association with Europe. It was also most of what they could show to their citizens as coming from Brussels and a sizeable portion of what they could reliably depend on. A good deal of what Marjorie Lister calls the "discrete entente" between the Community and the associated developing countries of Africa was realized by direct EC aid.

The Main Dimensions of Aid from EC Europe

The EC members—bilaterally and through the Community— have become the main source of aid to developing countries since the late 1960s when, taken together, they overtook the United States. Apart from the dip registered in the late 1970s and early 1980s, when balance of payments problems due in part to the oil price increases temporarily lowered their relative contribution to world aid, the overall share of the EC members moved steadily up, to reach 36 percent of all Official Development Assistance (ODA) to developing countries in 1986–88.[14] Total ODA from the Community, in current US dollars and exchange rates, amounted to $19,000 million in 1986–88, of which, about $13,000 million was financial aid (bilateral and multilateral) and $500 million was food aid (Table 2.1). In addition there was France's aid to overseas departments and territories— $1,800 million; and $3,300 million was contributed by EC members to international organizations such as the World Bank, the Asian, the African and Inter-American development banks and the specialized UN Agencies. Among the industrial countries, the EC members taken together also devote the largest share of their GNP to aid: around 0.45 percent compared with 0.2 percent by the United States and 0.31 percent by Japan.[15]

Table 2.1 Total Aid from the EC to Developing Countries (million US$)

	1964-66 (average)	%	1976-78 (average)	%	1986-88 (average)	%
Bilateral aid[a]	1,388	93.0	4,038	87.0	11,419	84.8
Direct community aid of which:	104	7.0	602	13.0	2,055	15.2
EDF	(104)	(100)	(355)	(59.0)	(1,066)	(51.9)
Financial aid to non-associated countries	—	—	(32)	(5.3)	(479)	(23.3)
Food aid	—	—	(215)	(35.7)	(510)	(24.8)
Total aid disbursed	1,492	100	4,640	100	13,474	100

[a] Bilateral aid from France, Italy, Germany, United Kingdom, Belgium, Netherlands and Denmark. The total does not include French aid to overseas departments and territories (1,800 million in 1966–88) and EC countries' contributions to international organizations other than the EDFs ($3,300 million in 1986–88).

Sources: OECD, *Development Cooperation: Annual Report,* Paris (various issues); Court of Auditors of the European Communities, *Annual Reports,* Brussels (various issues).

The rate of growth of total aid closely paralleled that of the Gross National Product (GNP) of the EC members. As a result, when measured as a share of GNP, a good proxy for their capacity to contribute domestic resources to developing countries' development, total aid supplied by the Community directly and by its members has remained remarkably stable over time. This was on the whole a better performance than that of the United States, whose aid in relation to GNP has declined steadily since the end of World War II.

Despite the emergence of direct aid after 1957, the overall external assistance of the Community remained strongly bilateral in origin and dominated by financial flows. The relative importance of EC direct aid grew, if slowly, from the mid-1960s to the late 1980s. However, much of this growth occurred in the first part of that period. Since the mid-1970s, 85 to 87 percent of total ODA from the Community has continued to come from the bilateral programs of the member countries. Food aid, despite its growing importance in direct Community assistance to developing countries, where it now accounts for about a quarter of this total, never became a big factor in the overall flows of assistance originating in the Community. As a percentage of total bilateral and direct Community ODA, food aid is less than 5 percent. Financial aid has remained dominant.

Since the start, direct Community aid has been largely aimed at the former colonial possessions of the member countries, reproducing in this way many of the patterns of the colonial expenditures and subsequently of the bilateral aid programs of France, Belgium and Italy. Partial multilateralization of external aid did not change, therefore, the regional focus of overall EC assistance to developing countries. Since the early 1970s it has become even more concentrated on sub-Saharan Africa, at the expense of North Africa and South Asia, whose shares of total Community ODA have declined progressively (Table 2.2).

Because of its size and continuous growth, overall assistance from the Community has become critical to many developing countries, particularly the poorest in sub-Saharan Africa, which still receive from it more than half of their total ODA. Aid from the Community, however, has also become very important to other developing areas, such as Central and South America, where it accounts for about half of total ODA actually received.

Table 2.2 Geographical Distribution of Total ODA Flows from the EC (percentage of actual disbursements)

Recipient countries	1966-68 (average)	1976-78 (average)	1986-88 (average)
North Africa	13.0	11.0	7.0
Central and South America	2.0	5.0	7.3
Middle East	5.3	3.0	3.0
Asia	19.0	24.0	16.7
Southern Europe	10.6	4.0	3.0
ACP countries	43.6	43.0	46.0
Unallocated	6.5	10.0	17.0

Note: Total ODA = EC(7) bilateral and direct Community ODA.
Source: OECD, *Geographical Distribution of Financial Flows to Developing Countries*, Paris (various issues).

Moreover, the relative importance of aid from the Community to areas such as South America and Oceania, areas traditionally at the periphery of EC development cooperation, has increased in recent years—in part because more direct EC aid was directed to non-associated countries as the result of the incipient internationalization of Community aid, and in part as a consequence of the growing weight of the bilateral aid programs of some members.[16] Correspondingly, flows to North African, Middle Eastern and (in part) Southern European countries have become relatively smaller within total Community aid and less important to the recipients—partly because economic conditions in many of these countries improved over time and their needs for external assistance correspondingly declined (Tables 2.2 and 2.3).

From the very start there were exceptions to the general configuration of EC countries' aid relations described above. Perhaps the most important was the bilateral aid program of the Federal Republic of Germany, which was clearly global in reach. After granting independence to West New Guinea in 1962, the bilateral aid program of the Netherlands also developed along global, rather than regional, lines. The geographical diffusion of the assistance from these two EC members—demonstrated by the higher share of their aid going to Asian, and subsequently Latin American, developing countries relative to those of sub-Saharan Africa—conformed more to a notion

Table 2.3 EC Aid as a Percentage of Total Aid Received by Developing Countries

Recipient country groups	1971	1981	1988
North Africa	55.8	30.4	41.4
Africa South of Sahara	64.0	57.5	55.6
Central America and Caribbean[a]	52.5	52.5	45.6
South America	24.4	57.1	52.7
Middle East	47.3	13.2	17.4
South Asia	25.2	32.2	23.9
East Asia	15.9	18.9	19.2
Southern Europe	45.4	73.5	67.9
Oceania	28.9	41.0	53.2

Notes: EC aid = EC(7) bilateral and direct Community ODA. Total aid = ODA from all countries on the Development Assistance Committee (DAC) of the OECD.
[a] Includes Mexico.
Source: OECD, *Geographical Distribution of Financial Flows to Developing Countries*, Paris (various issues).

of a global development responsibility and to the public's perception of recipient country needs, rather than to special area interests or domestic commercial concerns.

Yet, the bilateral aid programs of the Netherlands and Germany were small in the immediate post-war period, and their importance in shaping overall trends within the Community was quite limited. When the relative weight of their aid within the Community grew, solidarity with other EC partners contributed to making the allocations of their bilateral aid more in tune with those of the rest of the Community. The choice of privileged recipients of Community aid (the "chosen few" in David Jones' characterization) made within the framework of the Treaty of Rome, perpetuated through the Yaoundé Convention and enlarged with the Lomé Convention, had the apparent effect of pushing even the aid programs of the most globalist members of the Community towards a more regional allocation of bilaterally supplied assistance.

Beginning in the 1970s the share of most EC members' bilateral aid going to associated states increased steadily, and by 1987 had come to account for 30 percent of the total in Germany, 35 percent in the Netherlands, 46 percent in France and 60 percent in Italy. The exceptions were the United Kingdom, whose share of bilateral aid going to associated countries remained fairly stable over time, and Belgium, which actually reduced its (high) quota of financial aid to ACP countries (Table 2.4). Given the continued preponderance of bilateral aid in total aid coming from the Community and the growing importance of aid from France, Germany, and (more recently) Italy in the bilateral assistance from Community members,[17] more and more of the economic resources transferred to developing countries from EC Europe became concentrated on the subset of countries that remained tied to the Community by the special relationship which dated back to colonial times. The increasing concentration of EC bilateral aid on Africa, the Caribbean and the Pacific was critical in preserving the overall aid privilege of the associated countries, particularly when—as in the 1970s—the regional bias of direct Community aid came under increasing criticism and pressure to change its geographical distribution became impossible to resist.

The expansion of the quota of bilateral aid from EC countries received by sub-Saharan Africa, which came mostly at the expense of South Asia and North Africa, did in fact reflect increasing acceptance of an ACP priority in German, and (to a lesser extent) Dutch, bilateral aid. It also reflected the concomitant emergence of a strong pro-ACP bias in Italian bilateral aid during the 1980s. Only the United Kingdom maintained a strong Asian component in its aid distribution during both the 1970s and the 1980s, while the share of British bilateral aid going to ACP countries remained unchanged.

The fall in the share of total Community aid going to North Africa during the 1970s and 1980s seems to run against the increasing attention paid by the Community to that region after the first oil price shock of 1973, the joint emphasis put on a Mediterranean policy, and the pro-Arab tilt in the foreign policies of some of the Southern Mediterranean members of the Community (such as France and Italy) during the 1970s. Clearly, actual aid actions fell short of policy intentions, at least when the whole of the Community is considered. Some aid, moreover, may have been diverted to other more needy recipients when some of the countries of North Africa acquired new oil wealth. The fall in the relative importance of the aid received from EC Europe by North African countries may also be explained by the substitution of OPEC for Western aid, which occurred everywhere in Arab countries during the 1970s. OPEC aid

Table 2.4 Geographical Destination of Bilateral Aid from EC(7) Countries

	1960-62 (average) %	$	1970-72 (average) %	$	1980-82 (average) %	$	1985-87 (average) %	$
France								
ACP countries	39		35		50		46	
of which Yaoundé countries	(39)		(26)		(38)		(33)	
Other countries	61		65		50		54	
Total value in million US$[a]		730		619		1,913		2,646
Italy								
ACP countries	20		25		58		60	
of which Yaoundé countries	(15)		(11)		(11)		(22)	
Other countries	80		64		42		40	
Total value in million US$		79		84		160		1,354
Germany, Fed. Rep.								
ACP countries	7		14		29		30	
of which Yaoundé countries	(1)		(7)		(12)		(11)	
Other countries	93		86		71		70	
Total value in million US$		303		520		2,241		2,475
Belgium								
ACP countries	100		77		64		64	
of which Yaoundé countries	(100)		(77)		(59)		(56)	
Other countries	—		23		36		36	
Total value in million US$		72		110		370		342

Netherlands				
ACP countries	29	31	39	35
of which Yaoundé countries	—	(3)	(6)	(6)
Other countries	71	69	61	65
Total value in million US$	34	139	1,063	1,050
United Kingdom				
ACP countries	55	37	39	37
of which Yaoundé countries	(3)	(1)	(2)	(3)
Other countries	45	63	61	63
Total value in million US$	330	403	1,122	854
Denmark				
ACP countries	5	42	49	49
of which Yaoundé countries	(5)	(7)	(6)	(7)
Other countries	95	58	51	51
Total value in million US$	0.8	39	221	341

[a] Excluding aid to Overseas Departments (DOMs) and to Overseas Territories (TOMs).

Sources: OECD, *Geographical Distribution of Financial Flows to Less Developed Countries*, Paris (various issues); OECD, *Geographical Distribution of Financial Flows to Developing Countries*, Paris (various issues).

distribution did turn out to be quite strongly ethnocentric and biased in favor of Arab, and, in part, Muslim countries. Yet, at a time when preoccupations over security of supply of oil (and other raw materials) were very strong, when a Euro-Arab dialogue was being launched with much fanfare, and when a new determination to entertain closer relations with Mediterranean neighbors was emphasized at every occasion, the reduced use in North Africa of the bilateral aid instrument by some members of the Community is quite puzzling, and indicative of the possible existence of a free rider problem in their midst. It also shows how large the gap between stated goals and actual deeds can be in a situation where nations belonging to a regional group have not yet reached a degree of centralized decision making sufficient to ensure consistency between national policies and stated common objectives. The EC was in such a transitional phase in the 1970s.

From the standpoint of the receiving areas, it was previously noted that overall aid from the Community became overwhelmingly important for sub-Saharan Africa, a region that receives almost a quarter of total world ODA. Here aid from the Community accounted for almost 60 percent of the total for two decades. Yet, for South Asia and the Far East, which, because of their very large needs for foreign assistance, also absorb large portions of world bilateral aid (11 and 17 percent respectively), the share of Community aid in the total is much smaller (24 and 11 percent respectively). To get at least a rough idea of comparative aid needs, one may note here that sub-Saharan Africa accounts for only 11 percent of the total population of developing countries, while Asia as a whole accounts for 70 percent, and that 60 percent of the world's poor are in Asia. Total aid from the Community is also very important, in share terms, in Latin America where it is more than half of total overseas development assistance received. But this region, which in income terms is often characterized as the "middle class" of the developing world, receives only 3 percent of world ODA.[18]

The distribution of total EC aid has been quite uneven not only between associated and non-associated countries, but also among the associates. Geographically, aid going to associated countries is highly concentrated: twenty countries receive more than 75 percent of both bilateral and direct Community aid, although the countries receiving the largest share of EC direct assistance are not the same as those getting the major portion of member countries' bilateral aid.[19] The distributions of bilateral and direct EC aid only partially overlap at the country level, indicating that coordination between the two types of economic assistance is less than full, even in the case of the associated countries.[20]

The Regional Focus of EC Aid Policies

The regional focus of direct EC aid did not extend without difficulty from the members that had strong colonial traditions, lasting political influence and strong economic interests in Africa, to those that did not have or that did not make an interest in Africa an overriding objective of their foreign economic policies. Nor did the regional focus become so entrenched and accepted early in the life of the community that it avoided being the subject of further debate and periodic challenge.

Two distinct and partly conflicting "souls" of development cooperation have remained alive within the EC countries. Despite a series of adjustments and compromises reached in the name of group solidarity, noticeable differences of views still exist inside the Community on aid strategies. The globalist soul, which favors a developmental projection without continental frontiers, has deep and lasting roots in both Germany and the Netherlands, the two more open and outward looking countries within the Community.[21] The regional soul has long been personified by France, and supported at different times and in different degrees by Belgium and Italy. It favors a more limited and guarded development projection that is bounded by history, geography and time-tested relationships. Such a view is steeped in the tradition of "EurAfrica". The position of the United Kingdom has straddled across the two. While never limited to Africa, UK development cooperation concerns have never become truly global. This country has continued to balance Asian and African priorities, which broadly correspond to its sphere of former colonial interests.

Often obscured by other factors or events, these two almost viscerally different views of European development cooperation have uneasily coexisted inside the Community.[22] Globalist positions survived notwithstanding the successive victories of the regionalists until the mid-1970s, and the predominant influence maintained by regionalists within the Commission.[23] This influence has led, among other things, to a systematic downplaying—at the official level—of the significance of globalism inside the Community and often to the denial of its very existence.

The first victory of the regionalists was Yaoundé I, when the Rome Treaty policy of privileged association, instead of ceasing to exist, given the changes that had occurred in the political circumstances of the associates, was extended and reinforced through a convention negotiated between EC members and the newly independent states of Africa. Nor was a balance between the two views re-established by the "Declaration of Intent of the Member Countries" of 2 April 1963. Despite its apparent openness, this statement of policy regarding future associations with the Community did not represent any substantive concession of the victorious regionalists to the globalists. The six EC members did offer to the developing countries then outside the framework of Yaoundé the chance of joining it. But much like the choice of colors offered by Henry Ford to his T-model car buyers, non-members could become members only "as long as" their economic structures and production patterns were "comparable" to those of the Yaoundé associates. This meant in practice that only African countries could share in the privileges of association with the Community. The declaration of intent in all its practical effects was an extension and consolidation of the regional focus of the development cooperation policy of EC countries, not a change in it.

Yet, despite the conclusion in Yaoundé II and the apparent consolidation of the regional approach, the declaration by the Heads of State and Government of the Six issued in Paris in October 1972 seemed to lean significantly in the direction of globalism, as it mandated that alongside regional cooperation the Community pursue and develop links with the rest of the developing world.[24] The necessity of a global push in EC relations with developing countries, if only as a parallel track to regional cooperation with Africa, had already been recognized by the Commission in its 1971 Memorandum on development policy. This document contained, among other things, the explicit recognition that "as a result of the growing responsibilities which flowed from the Community's spreading international influence and from its power of attraction over developing countries, it was not possible to impose *strict* geographical limits on its activity in the field of financial and technical cooperation" (emphasis added). Yet the operative word was the adjective *strict* and its actual meaning was left undefined.[25]

That the struggle between the advocates of the two models of cooperation continued is shown by the 1973 Memorandum of the Commission on the future relations with the countries referred to in the Act of Accession of the United Kingdom to the Community—in practice the former British colonies—which came in the wake of the Summit Conference of 1972. Interpreting the EC Summit call for a policy of world-wide development, the Commission document stated that "the Heads of State and Government *did not wish to abandon the policy of association and replace it by a world-wide policy as yet to be formulated*" (emphasis added). In the same vein the Commission attempted to reassure the present and future associates that no substantial change in approach had occurred. Community policy of development cooperation, it said, "will be characterized by a combination of a *high* degree of cooperation at the regional level, with a necessarily *less intense* degree of cooperation on a world scale" (emphasis added). The regionalists in the Commission seemed determined to emphasize that the globalists had not prevailed at the Summit. Business was going to be regional nearly as usual.[26]

The economic, as opposed to the political, defense of the regional choice was set out in full in the so-called Fresco Document of 1974. Here the Commission sought to build its argument around the point that strong diversity existed in the development situations of third world countries. Because of this diversity, Community policy had to be selective in the use of its instruments of cooperation and in the choice of its country focus. Priority was placed on the smallest and poorest developing countries. The associates of Africa generally belonged to this category. They were poor, small and dependent on the export of primary commodities. Strong focus was to remain on them, mostly through the supply of Community aid. Large, poor countries, such as those of the Indian subcontinent at least had their sizeable internal markets to fall back on. Middle-income countries, half dependent on primary products and half industrializing, such as those of Latin America, could instead derive benefit from market access and efficient industrial cooperation. They already were the beneficiaries of the EC GSP scheme. As far as EC direct aid was concerned, the conclusion of this document could not be clearer: "The poorest countries— unfortunately the ACP group contains many—will benefit not only from the upgrading in money terms agreed by the Council, but, additionally, from some transfer of Community aid previously allotted to less deprived countries."[27]

Regionalism was finally enshrined in the Lomé construction. The extension promised in the Declaration of Intent of 1963 occurred twelve years later in almost exactly the terms envisaged earlier. EC financial assistance, in the form of both bilateral and multilateral aid, was concentrated on the ACP countries, of which sub-Saharan Africa constituted the preponderant part. The Mediterranean policy, developed shortly thereafter, could simply be construed as an extension to North Africa of the standard EC regional approach. It was presented as such by the regionalists in the Commission, who had in Development Commissioner Claude Cheysson (a future foreign minister of France) a convinced and dedicated leader.

Yet, the globalists survived with some help from the new members of the Community (such as Denmark), and their influence on EC policies, though still small, began to be more clearly felt in subsequent years. In 1976, for example, a system for extending financial aid on a regular, if limited, basis to some of the non-associated countries of Latin America and Asia was finally put in place. This was only a modest success for the globalists. EC direct financial assistance was very small in size and limited in practice to supporting food production in the poorest countries of the two regions. An outline regulation setting out the aims of this type of aid, and specific guidelines for its use, had to wait until 1981. The program remained small in size and scope. Asian countries—India, Bangladesh and more recently China— were the main beneficiaries of it, together with a handful of Central American countries.[28] Globalization of EC aid began with very modest steps and proceeded at a snail's pace. Financial and technical assistance to Asian and Latin American (ALA) countries never exceeded one-sixth of that extended to the ACPs (Table 2.5).

Table 2.5 Direct EC Aid to ACP and Non-Associated Developing Countries (million ECU)

	1976–78 (average)	%	1980–82 (average)	%	1986–88 (average)	%
ACP countries	298	91.7	598	72.1	960	67.5
Non-associated developing countries	27	8.3	231	27.9	463	32.5
of which:						
ALA countries	(8)	(29.6)	(64)	(27.7)	(163)	(35.2)
Others	(19)	(70.4)	(167)	(72.1)	(300)	(64.8)
Total aid disbursed	325	100.0	829	100.0	1,423	100.0

Notes: Financial aid only (food and emergency aid not included); ACP = African, Caribbean and Pacific; ALA = Asian and Latin American.
Sources: Court of Auditors of the European Communities, Annual Reports, Brussels (various issues); Commission of the European Communities, *Thirteenth Annual Report from the Commission to the Council and Parliament on the Implementation of Financial and Technical Cooperation to Developing Countries of Asia and Latin America*, Brussels, 1990.

The memorandum on EC development policies produced by Development Commissioner Edgard Pisani in 1982 only validated the modest enlargement of the sphere of action of Community financial assistance that had occurred in the previous years. The memorandum singled out the economic development of the Mediterranean countries as an objective worth supporting "by every means available", and stressed the willingness of the Community to "make available certain funds, to help carry out specific operations of mutual interest" with Asian and Latin American countries in the framework of cooperation agreements with them.[29] Both the limited initiative concerning financial assistance to the poorest Asian and Latin American countries and the more substantial aid initiative for the Maghreb and Mashreq countries, begun in 1978, were thus destined to survive. Globalists even got an open acknowledgement of their existence by Edgard Pisani himself, but not much more.[30]

Bilateral aid policies of EC member states continued to become more and more attuned to the original African focus of EC direct aid during the 1970s, when the Dutch and German aid programs assumed a much stronger ACP direction than they had previously. The United Kingdom's entry into the Community also helped to consolidate the African preference among its members. This trend in EC bilateral aid became even more pronounced in the 1980s, when Danish and Italian aid programs also focused on Africa, and assistance to this continent became a general priority for donors in Europe as well as outside it.

Thus, even if not totally attributable to the influence of the regional tradition established early on in the Community by France and Belgium, the African orientation of total European aid became nonetheless stronger with the passage of time, as the focus of the bilateral aid of EC members became progressively more aligned with that maintained by the Community. While the relative tendencies of these two forms of development assistance are difficult to interpret at the aggregate level, some relaxation in the regional preference of direct Community aid seems to have occurred only when bilateral aid was clearly becoming more oriented towards Africa, making it possible for the regionalists to accept the diversion of a part of Community aid to Asia and Latin America. The timing of these changes makes it possible to hypothesize that only the consolidation of the regional focus of the bilateral aid programs of key members created the premise for a slightly less regional posture in Community assistance to developing countries. This hypothesis implies growth in the complementarity between bilateral and EC aid, a point that is at least partially confirmed by available empirical evidence.[31]

The Determinants of Direct EC Aid

Foreign aid apparently has more widespread and deep-rooted public support in the EC countries than in any other area of the industrial world, with the exception of Scandinavia, and this support has seemingly grown over time. According to opinion polls, support for the general concept of development aid in the Federal Republic of Germany was 74 percent in 1984, as against 58 percent in 1958. In the early 1980s, 75 percent of those polled in the Netherlands favored aid at least at current levels (an exceptionally high 1 percent of GDP). In 1983, 59 percent of the people sampled in the United Kingdom favored economic aid to poor countries, as against 39 percent in 1977.[32] And in Italy aid has been supported by more than 70 percent of the sampled population. In a Europe-wide survey taken in 1987, 34 percent of those interviewed were "very much in favor" of aid, while 54 percent were "rather in favor". In 1983 the corresponding shares had been 27 and 55 percent.[33] Increasing acceptance of aid was common to eight of the ten member countries covered in both the 1983 and 1987 surveys. The exceptions were Belgium and France where support for aid to developing countries had eroded. The levels of public support for foreign aid existing in EC countries compare with a 40 percent acceptance of aid in Japan and 50 percent in the United States, where those who favor aid are also on the decline.

Some of the reasons for the widespread popular support for aid to developing countries that exists in Europe can be gauged from the same attitude surveys. Aid is favored by nearly 50 percent of the people polled because of the poverty and needs of the recipient countries. Only 20 percent see aid as an instrument necessary to ensure continuation of growth in Europe. A main reason for supporting aid to developing countries is therefore found in the moral convictions of European citizens, for whom the reduction of poverty and fulfillment of basic needs in the third world is a worthwhile goal. Indicative of the strong public support for humanitarian aid to developing countries is the fact that in the same 1987 survey only 24 percent of the respondents thought that less attention should be concentrated on the third world and more on fighting poverty in Europe. Characteristically, most Europeans indicated that the most useful aid to developing countries was provided by voluntary organizations (31 percent) and international organizations such as the United Nations (28 percent), while confidence in national governments as effective sources of assistance to the third world was low (12 percent).[34]

In EC Europe, as in most other parts of the industrial world, the amount of aid resources made available on a yearly basis depends on real income. The most powerful trend determinant of real aid flows is the growth of national product, a proxy for capacity to afford foreign assistance. The cycle of aid, however, has slightly different economic determinants. Given the predominance of official aid over private aid, the cycle in aid flows depends on the budgetary and/or the balance of payments situations in the donor countries. In times of budget stringency, usually when revenues are lower than expected because of lower than normal activity and resource utilization, European governments appear to be tighter with their aid expenditure. The same applies, to some extent, to situations of temporary balance of payments difficulties, when overall expenditure policies need to become restrictive.[35]

As for the domestic determinants of the allocation of public aid among developing countries, two competing hypotheses have long been found applicable in Europe as well as elsewhere in the industrial world: donor interests or recipient needs. The former can be political or economic in nature. Among the political goals of the donor countries one can consider the maintenance of the allegiance of the recipients to the Western bloc or the preservation of their neutrality, the degree of support sought in international fora such as the United Nations (and thus the voting behavior of the recipients) and the donors' regional political interests. US bilateral aid has often been tied to the positions taken by recipient countries in East–West conflicts. The Federal Republic of Germany for many years refused to extend aid to countries that recognized the German Democratic

Republic. Regional stability goals have also featured prominently, as shown by the bias of US aid towards Israel and Egypt, and more recently Central America. Regional–colonial interests have also been found to be important determinants of the bilateral aid of France and Italy. Among the economic interests of the donors, important ones are defending exports to the recipient country or sustaining national investments. The needs of the recipients are evidenced by their per capita incomes, their poverty alleviation goals and their capacity to supply basic services (such as health and education) to their populations.

Available empirical evidence has tended to show that bilateral aid from EC countries has been allocated among developing countries much more on the basis of donor interests than on that of recipient country needs.[36] Recent analysis, based on models that account simultaneously for the importance of different types of motivations, has shown a more composite picture and the emergence of significant recipient need motivation in the allocation of bilateral aid from the major EC countries. The fulfillment of human needs seems to be a major influence on the aid allocation of the Netherlands, while the defense of export interests is a significant determinant of the aid allocations of the United Kingdom, Germany and Italy. Aid distributions by France seem, instead, to be determined only by commercial interests and to have a strong bias in favor of Francophone countries.[37]

The political economy of Community aid to associated countries, the subject of recent studies, has also shown a composite set of motivations. Considered as a whole, aid directly distributed by EC member countries appears to have been driven, until recently, by both donor interests (exemplified by the support of EC exports to the associated countries), and recipient needs (exemplified by the fulfillment of basic health and education requirements). However, the consideration given to member country commercial interests in the aid allocation process seems to have considerably declined in the 1980s, while the fulfillment of basic human needs has remained an important factor.

The model underlying the country distribution of direct Community aid appears, therefore, to have lost part of its original balance and become tilted toward recipient country needs.

Europeanization of Development Aid: The Failures in Coordination

Despite the progress achieved, Europeanization of development aid is still nowhere in sight more than thirty years after the creation of the European Community and two major enlargements of its membership. Multilateralization of EC aid, the most direct route towards Europeanization of external assistance, spearheaded efforts towards this goal but failed to reach decisive results. Less direct forms of Europeanization of aid, from making assistance practices more homogeneous among EC members to the establishment of more common aid objectives among EC partners, have not advanced much either. After a promising start, this process seems to have slowed down to the point where progress is hardly discernible.

The first attempt to Europeanize aid was made by EC members with the Treaty of Rome, and resulted in the establishment of the European Development Fund, which was centrally administered at the Community level, if still bilaterally financed. Given that the resources expected to flow annually from EDF I amounted then to less than 10 percent of total aid originating from member countries, the Treaty of Rome achieved only a partial Europeanization of EC aid by source. In spite of the hope that the process would continue and the share of EC external aid going through newly created multilateral channels would increase over time, the obstacles to this happening were quite formidable. As the EDF was set up for an *ad hoc* purpose— the supply of some common aid to the associated countries— no general responsibility in the field of external aid assistance was assigned to Community authorities by the Treaty of Rome.

In distributional terms, moreover, direct EC aid ended up reinforcing directly as well as indirectly the concentration of European external assistance on Africa. Somewhat paradoxically, therefore, multilateralization of European aid narrowed its overall geographical spread, thus highlighting in some way the exceptional nature of collaboration among EC partners in aid giving. As long as the priorities represented by the associated countries were approximated by bilateral aid from member countries, the main objective of cooperation in this field could be seen as fulfilled, and neither additional multilateralization nor additional coordination would become strictly necessary. In a certain sense Europeanization of external assistance inside the Community became a prisoner of the *ad hoc*, exceptional, goals assigned, since the start, to EC aid policies.

An important push towards multilateralization of aid relations came, however, during the 1960s from the developing countries which demanded it as a key concession in the area of international development policies. Although the main target of developing countries' pressures was then the United States, at that time by far the single largest bilateral aid donor, this trend also affected the EC countries. Developing countries insisted on requesting that economic aid coming from the West be multilateralized in order to lessen their political dependence on single donors and to make the aid resources that they received more effective in helping their development.[38]

Apart from the quest for reduced political dependence, which many found desirable as a way to shield developing countries from the intense East–West competition that seemed to envelop the entire world, orthodox economists everywhere stressed the need to maximize the development effectiveness of aid, which in their view depended on both the claim over real resources that a unit of aid actually entailed and the final uses to which it was put. Development effectiveness, it was argued, would be greater the larger the portion of aid going to productive purposes, the greater the efficiency in the use of aid resources and the more targeted to the development potential of the recipient aid projects could be made. By releasing the recipients of external assistance from the obligation to spend it in the donor countries, at least the real purchasing power of a given amount of aid could also be increased. If able to convert aid resources into goods and services wherever they bought the most, recipients could stretch the value of their "aid dollar".

The other arguments also appeared to militate in favor of multilateral aid, administered by neutral technical bodies that could ensure, together with non-politicization of aid relations, the highest compatibility of aid allocation with national development plans and priorities in recipient countries, maximum efficiency of aid use within the priority sectors and maximum claim over outside resources for each unit of aid. These arguments also strongly supported utilizing explicit and objective criteria for country allocation of available international aid, transparent and effective methods for evaluating aid uses and general methods of maximizing aid reach. International aid agencies seemed to meet many of these requirements. They could ensure aid effectiveness through careful evaluation of country needs, objective assessment of economic priorities within countries and the implementation of appropriate investment analysis. They could also ensure that truly international competitive bidding would take place for the procurement of the implements of projects or programs financed with aid.[39]

Planning and welfare economics also seemed to be able to supply most of the technical tools necessary to ensure the achievement of maximum economic effectiveness of aid, provided that their use could be systematically enforced. If aid resources could be effectively allocated among competing uses (through intersectoral planning) and productively used in the chosen sectors (via cost-benefit analysis), aid could work better to help development in recipient countries. Aid administration for development purposes thus seemed to fall logically within the domain of international financial institutions.

The World Bank—the market-based development agency created at Bretton Woods in 1944—was complemented with an aid administering window in 1960, when the International Development Association (IDA) was established. EC nations contributed 21 percent of the resources of the first IDA endowment. The remainder of Europe supplied another 21 percent of the total. Aside from borrowing in capital markets and relending to member countries at the lowest possible market interest rates, the World Bank Group could now also make loans at highly concessional terms to the poorest of its member countries using the financial resources provided by the more prosperous ones. In making these loans, the World Bank would apply objective criteria, utilize its direct knowledge of development needs and country priorities, and above all, evaluate each investment project for which financing was considered using rigorous cost-benefit criteria.

The United Nations was also endowed with a development aid agency, the United Nations Development Program (UNDP), set up in 1965. Three regional development banks were also established in close succession: the Interamerican Development Bank (IDB) in 1959, the African Development Bank (AfDB) in

1964, and the Asian Development Bank (AsDB) in 1966. The last two were given concessional resources to administer, in addition to capital and capital guarantees that enabled them to borrow in financial markets, much like the World Bank. EC nations contributed to most of these initiatives, thus accepting that a higher share of the domestic resources devoted to external aid would be administered by international bodies. Overall contributions of EC countries to international aid went up from $189 million in 1960-61 to $433 million in 1970-71, equivalent to about 0.03 percent of their GNP.

As for direct Community aid, the trend towards modest enlargement continued with the carry over of the EDF from the Treaty of Rome to the Yaoundé Conventions (EDF II in 1963 and EDF III in 1969). At the end of the 1960s, multilateral EC aid still represented 10 percent of total Community aid (Figure 2.1) and also remained strongly focused on African countries, if on a subset of them: the largely Francophone associates. The transition from Yaoundé to Lomé in the mid-1970s, and the consequent extension of the EC network of association to practically the whole of Africa, gave the last push to multilateral EC aid—which reached around 15 percent of the total—and at the same time cemented the regional character of EC aid. After this, the share of multilateral in total EC aid ceased to grow, and the aid policies of the Community proceeded on a parallel track to those of the member countries.

The dichotomy between bilateral and multilateral EC aid has become one of the key structural characteristics of the Community policies of development cooperation. The expectation entertained by some that sustained efforts at the Community level could achieve over time a better balance between the two types of assistance to developing countries was in practice proved wrong. That the process of Europeanization of aid was not to be automatic has become quite evident during the last fifteen years. For the first conscious attempt to change the aid policy equilibria which had been consolidated since Lomé, one had to wait until 1990, when the Italian government proposed a major overhaul of these policies, starting with a major increase in the resources devoted to development aid and the strengthening of the multilateral approach.[40]

The analysis of the political economy of European aid has

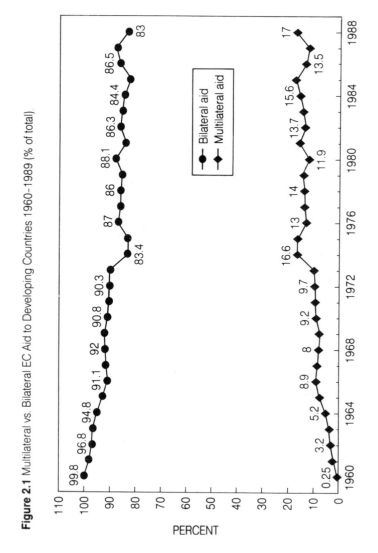

Figure 2.1 Multilateral vs. Bilateral EC Aid to Developing Countries 1960–1989 (% of total)

Source: OECD Geographical Distribution of Financial Flows to Developing Countries (various issues).

shed some light on the reasons for the lack of self-adjustment in the balance between bilateral and multilateral aid coming from the Community. Bilateral aid is generally seen by donor governments as an instrument capable of supporting the political and commercial needs of the donors. Thus control over domestic aid resources is not easily given up. Until the basic objectives (one could call them the systemic goals) of bilateral aid are changed, or subsumed into Community aid in the framework of a more complete political union among the EC members, one can argue that the existing preference for bilateral aid is destined to remain.[41] According to this view, the goal of Europeanization of aid would therefore be constrained by the pace at which political integration among members actually proceeds.

There is apparent merit in this explanation, even though failure to proceed along the road of political integration did not in itself prevent the pooling of substantial amounts of member country resources in other areas, such as agriculture. The critical difference, one can presume, must lie in the nature of development aid, which is still viewed by most member states as a direct instrument of national policy.

Yet, attempts by the EC Commission even to simply *coordinate* aid policies have met with so little success that the reasons for this failure can hardly be understood in terms of the mere national interests of member countries. Some coordination efforts at the European level would in fact be so cost effective and useful, and so clearly outside the political domain, that their absence can only be explained in terms of the national political economy of aid. The groups that most fear coordination of aid at the EC level, including the national bureaucracies that administer aid and state-owned (and often private) enterprises that often have *de facto* preferential access to procurement from national aid budgets, are probably so strong and effective in pressuring national authorities that they are capable of preventing even those modest steps towards Europeanization—through EC coordination—that would be useful also from the standpoint of national interest.

Outside the framework of the national political economy of aid it would be difficult to explain, for example, why simple exchanges of information over aid plans between national aid authorities and the Commission would have to be limited to aid to associated states,[42] or why the position of EC members in international organizations concerned with aid—such as the World Bank, the Food and Agriculture Organization of the United Nations (FAO) and other UN agencies—could not be coordinated at the Community level. The realization of the existence of powerful and influential interest groups, including national bureaucracies set against aid coordination, coupled with the more political fear of appearing to try to tip the balance of aid power in its favor or of simply upsetting the stability of burden sharing in multilateral EC aid financed outside the EC budget (i.e. EDF resources), may explain why the Commission typically has been so unassertive in the area of coordination vis-a-vis national authorities.

Coordination activities do not have to start with the harmonization of systemic goals, when it appears that existing differences among the members of a regional group are so large that they cannot be bridged by any amount of effort from its technical organs. There are areas of coordination that are by nature more neutral and thus less difficult to enter. In the case of the EC, the allocation of aid among recipients could, for example, be helped by systematic exchanges of (timely) information on past allocations and future intentions (multi-year country programs). Annual information and consultation meetings could be organized for the main recipient countries. This could avoid bunching bilateral aid in certain countries and regions at certain times and would also improve the efficiency of aid resource use in the recipient countries to the extent, at least, that bunching creates serious absorption difficulties. In time, these systematic exchanges of information could lead to the development of more uniform or mutually compatible allocation criteria for bilateral aid used by each EC member.

Despite the existing differences in the ways in which aid administration is organized at the national level—central vs. regional or country-based structures—there would be merit in field coordination, that is with country authorities in recipient countries, not only in order to better understand needs and schedules, but also to coordinate the distribution of certain types of aid (food or balance of payments aid) more efficiently. Member countries' diplomatic missions could play a key role, acting in harmony with each other and with the local offices of the Commission. This implies, however, that aid ministries, where they exist, cooperate with their foreign ministries, an assumption that does not appear as far-fetched in principle as it seems to be in practice.

Coordination could be relatively easy and quite fruitful in the area of aid instruments (food aid vs. grant/loans, grant components, terms of loans, aid tying) and sectoral priorities (agriculture, industrial development, transportation and communications, education, etc.) to improve effectiveness and efficiency of bilateral aid, without unduly interfering with national priorities and decision making. These are technical aspects of aid cooperation *par excellence.*

Finally, coordination could take place in the international sphere of aid giving, from participation in commodity agreements, to consultative groups or aid consortia for individual countries, to IDA contributions and priority setting in the area of nationally financed but internationally distributed aid, to the decision making in international organizations that are involved in economic and technical assistance to developing countries (the World Bank Group, the regional banks, UNDP, FAO and more recently the IMF).

The EC Commission presented in 1972 a first set of proposals in the area of coordination at the Community level of aid and technical assistance. Its analysis concluded that "lack of harmonization in the various aids applied to the same developing countries or regions results in a definite reduction in the effectiveness of aid . . . The result is overbidding, double usage and gaps which local resources do not manage to fill." These were inescapable and hardly controversial conclusions stemming from the experience gained until then. The Community sought first of all to increase coordination of direct Community aid with aid coming from member states destined for associated countries to ensure better programing of country aid and better reviews of aid effectiveness.[43] It also sought from member countries a relaxation of financial conditions attached to bilateral aid (e.g. grant/loan balances, duration, grace periods and interest charged on loans), supporting the efforts made by the Development Assistance Committee (DAC) of the OECD in this area.[44] It also proposed the untying of bilateral aid at the Community level, to make it parallel to Community-dispensed assistance.

These were appropriate specific first steps that could in no way be construed as disguised attempts by the Commission to extend its jurisdiction into areas not explicitly assigned to it by the Treaty of Rome. The reaction nonetheless must have been so negative that no further action in the field of aid harmonization and coordination was proposed in any of the subsequent documents of the Commission on development policies, be they official proposals,[45] communications to the Council,[46] or simple staff reviews.[47] In most of them the subject is not even broached.

Particularly striking is the virtual absence of treatment of these problems in the Pisani Memorandum of 1982, a document that was intended to break the mold of caution and tradition in many areas and to make path-breaking proposals; a document, moreover, that was the brainchild of a development commissioner who was used to speaking his mind. In the area of policy coordination and coherence the document only obliquely referred to aid when it stated that the Commission "intends to report periodically to the Council and Parliament on the progress made and difficulties encountered in coordinating bilateral and Community cooperation policies".[48] Mr Pisani seemed to be threatening to let the Council know what it already knew all too well!

Undoubtedly mindful of the lukewarm response it had elicited from the Council to its earlier proposals for better coordination of member states' cooperation policies,[49] the Commission waited until 1984 before revisiting the subject.[50] And it did so gingerly, and apparently in response to the rebukes of the Court of Auditors, which had noted that even in the field of information exchange, flows were largely one way, from the Commission to the member countries, and not vice-versa.[51]

The Commission stressed the need of operational coordination, taking pragmatic, *ad hoc* forms "adapted to the interests and particular sensitivities of each member state in respect of specific regions, countries or sectors". It explicitly shunned "institutionalized, formal coordination".[52] Its suggestions were thus low-key and conventional: improving the exchange of information, the strengthening of coordination in the field and more systematic use of co-financing. The Commission ended its communication to the Council stressing that "the purpose [it was pursuing] was not to achieve a common overview of all community aids in the context of development policy or, *a fortiori*, establish a common policy of development cooperation".[53]

Even at the end of the 1980s, after the Council itself had recognized both the need for more systematic coordination of the member countries' and the Commission's action in support of structural adjustment in sub-Saharan Africa,[54] the Commission was still quite conservative in suggesting aims for coordination and specific courses of action.[55] In endorsing some of the Commission's ideas and suggestions in the area of support for adjustment, the Council showed no evident taste for change. It limited itself to advocating the obvious, without mandating any action from the members or the Commission. In terms of objectives, it stressed the need to "increase consistency and convergence between the approach of the Commission and the Member States at all levels". In terms of action, it recognized the usefulness of informal meetings on country situations (organized by either the Commission or a member state) to "exchange views and information on each member state's experience, perceptions and intentions" and to "help draw up, country by country, a coherent Community approach to the process of adjustment".[56]

That a tacit understanding to leave things pretty much as they were in the contentious area of aid administration must have been reached among EC members, or between the Commission and the national bureaucracies, can be deduced also from their unwillingness to face the problem of budgetizing Community aid to associated countries.

The first EDF was set up at a time when there hardly was an EC budget. Its financing had to come from direct contributions of member states as much as a matter of necessity as of choice. The sharing of the burden of aid to associated countries and territories was also the inevitable result of political negotiations among members. Agreement on member country contributions, with France and Germany making equal (and preponderant) contributions to the Fund, was in fact an achievement that mirrored the degree of cooperation being established among the six original member states.

Six EDFs and more than thirty years later, with a Community budget equal to one percent of EC GNP, the continued funding of aid to associated countries through special contributions from member states can either be taken as representative of the will of key members to maintain a sharing of the burden of external aid that differs significantly from that of the EC budget, or of the unwillingness of the majority to reduce their fairly direct control over substantial flows of financial assistance going to developing countries.

Notes to Chapter 2

1 In arts. 132, 133 and 134.

2 Art. 1 of the Convention reads: "The member states . . . participate in measures which will promote the social and economic development . . . [of the associates] by supplementing the efforts made by the authorities responsible for those countries and territories. For this purpose a Development Fund for Overseas Countries and Territories is hereby established, into which the member states shall . . . pay contributions . . . The Fund shall be administered by the Commission". See Office for Official Publications, "Implementing Convention on Association", p. 577.

3 Commission of the European Communities, *European Development Aid: How the European Community is Helping the Developing Countries*, Brussels, 1971.

4 Commission of the European Communities, "Commission Memorandum on a Community Development Cooperation Policy", Supplement 5/71 to the *Bulletin of the European Communities*, 1971, p. 11. In the same section of the document the Commission noted, instead, the erosion of the trade preferences granted to the associated countries and their fear that the trade element would soon disappear from the economic content of the association.

5 France devoted more than 2 percent of its GDP to aid in 1960, mostly to its present and former colonies. Official aid alone accounted for almost 1.5 percent of GDP. Of the $750 million of official development assistance distributed by France, more than 90 percent went to Africa, with North Africa taking 50 percent and sub-Saharan Africa 40 percent. France alone accounted for 62 percent of all EC development assistance to developing countries and for 73 percent of all official aid flows to sub-Saharan Africa. Of the $380 million going to the associated states of Africa as bilateral aid from EC member countries, $307 million (or 74 percent) came from France. Another 22 percent of the total came from Belgium. Belgian aid, however, went almost

totally to Congo. See Commission of the European Communities, *Memorandum on a Community Policy on Development Cooperation: Appendices*, Brussels, 1972, pp. 170–204.

6 D. Wall, "The European Community's Lomé Convention: Stabex and the Third World's Aspirations", London, Trade Policy Research Center, 1976 (mimeo.), p. 2.

7 Commission, *European Development Aid*, 1971, p. 8.

8 Commission, "Community Development Cooperation Policy", 1971, p. 4.

9 All unrequited transfers of resources from the Community, its member countries and their citizens acting in a private capacity constitute aid. Technically, however, to qualify as development assistance the transfer must be given with the promotion of economic development and welfare of the developing countries as its main objective and contain a minimum grant component. Current conventions put it at 25 percent of the value of the flow. Standard practices, moreover, separate private from official aid flows to developing countries. Only the latter are included in the common definition of "Official Development Assistance" or ODA, the standard by which aid is measured and compared across countries. ODA includes net official grants, grant-like flows and official development lending. Official grants are gifts in money or kind for which no repayment is required. Grant-like flows are, for example, loans made in the donor's currency, but payable in the recipient's currency. Official development lending includes loans with maturities of more than one year extended by governments and official agencies for which payment is required in convertible currencies or kind. Interest charged is usually below market rates or grace periods are granted before repayments become due.

10 ACP Group, *Memorandum on ACP Guidelines for the Negotiations for a Fourth ACP/EC Convention*, Brussels, 1989, pp. 121 and 148.

11 Commission, "Community Development Cooperation Policy", 1971, p. 11.

12 *Ibidem*, p. 28.

13 That in many ways the privileged relationship between the Community and its African associates had a clear political dimension was clear to both parties. As for the associates, in addition to the already mentioned quotation from President Leopold Senghor of Senegal, one can recall the statement of Jacques Rabemananjara, Malagasy Minister of Foreign Affairs, who declared in 1963 that

"the Association is a political act. It would be false and dangerous to hide this profound truth behind a facade of economic technicalities". The statement is reported in Cosgrove Twitchett, *Europe and Africa*, p. 33. As for the Commission, its perception of the associates' views was equally clear and has been clearly expressed since 1971: "the most authoritative voices in the AAMS stress increasingly and emphatically the fact that the association is in the first place a political option". See Commission, "Community Development Cooperation Policy", 1971, p. 11.

[14] When aid is defined as ODA, at constant 1987 prices and exchange rates. According to this definition, the Community's share of world ODA was 27.3 percent in 1960-61, 31.7 percent in 1970-71, 28.9 percent in 1980-81 and 35.6 percent in 1987-88. The corresponding shares of the United States were 45 percent, 27 percent, 17 percent and 19 percent; those of Japan 4.3 percent, 9.0 percent, 10.9 percent and 15.6 percent and those of the Arab countries 4.9 percent in 1970-71, 23.9 percent in 1980-81 and 5.7 percent in 1987-88. See, OECD, *Twenty-five Years of Development Cooperation: A Review*, Paris, 1985, and OECD, *Development Cooperation in the 1990s*, Paris, 1989. The EC is here defined as EC(12), minus Luxembourg, Greece, Spain, Portugal and Ireland, or EC(7).

[15] Only the Arab countries do better than the Community as a whole, with 1.2 percent of their GNP going to aid. There are nonetheless large differences even within the EC(7). Bilateral aid as a share of GNP is highest in the Netherlands and Denmark (around 1 percent in 1987-88) and lowest in the United Kingdom (0.3 percent in the same years). OECD, *Twenty-five Years of Development Cooperation*.

[16] France, for example, has substantially increased aid to French Guyana in recent years (from $45 million in 1975 to $138 million in 1987).

[17] The combined share of aid from these three countries increased from 65 percent of total EC bilateral aid in 1973-75 to 71 percent in 1986-88.

[18] See Overseas Development Administration, *DAC, Arab and Multilateral Aid: Geographical Distribution: 1982-88*, London, 1990; World Bank, *Population Data Files*, BESD Data Bank, Washington D.C. The figure of EC aid is also inflated by the presence of overseas departments of France such as Guyana.

[19] E. Grilli and M. Riess, "ED Aid to Associated Developing Countries: Distribution and Determinants," in *Weltwirtschaftliches Archiv*, Vol. 128, No. 2, 1992, pp. 202-20.

[20] The Spearman rank correlation coefficient between the country allocations of bilateral and direct EC aid to ACP countries in 1985, for example, had a value of 0.437.

[21] Bouvier, *L'Europe et la Cooperation au Développement.*

[22] The first official reference to the existence of profoundly different views of development cooperation can be found in the Commission's Memorandum of 1971, which explicitly refers to them (if to dismiss their actual importance) in a soon to become characteristic, summary fashion: "it is important to stress [that the Community has sought a balance between the active and complete, but geographically circumscribed policy it had adopted in its relations with the AAMS and the solutions which it felt it should offer to other developing countries] because it disposes of a fruitless quarrel between regional and universal solutions to the problems of development", in Commission, "Community Development Cooperation Policy", 1971, p. 4.

[23] Symbolic of the prominence of the French tradition of development cooperation inside the Commission is the fact that all the commissioners in charge of cooperation policies were French nationals from 1958 (Robert Lemaignen) to 1985 (Edgard Pisani). After them came an Italian, Lorenzo Natali, and in 1989 a Spanish national, Manuel Marin.

[24] Council of the European Communities, "Final Declaration of the Conference of the Heads of States and Governments of the European Community", Paris, 19-21 October, 1972 (mimeo.)

[25] Commission, "Community Development Cooperation Policy", 1971, p. 22.

[26] Commission of the European Communities, "Memorandum to the Council on the Future Relations Between the Community, the Present AAMS States and the Countries in Africa, the Caribbean, the Indian and the Pacific Oceans Referred to in Protocol No. 22 to the Act of Accession", Supplement 1/73 to the *Bulletin of the European Communities*, 1973, p. 5. This document is sometimes referred to as the Deniau Memorandum, after the commissioner who prepared it.

[27] Commission of the European Communities, "Development Aid: Fresco of Community Action Tomorrow", Supplement 8/74 to the *Bulletin of the European Communities*, 1974, pp. 16-18.

[28] The EC Council annually established the guidelines for the regional distribution of this aid. Asia was assigned 80 percent of the total

in 1976–78 and 75 percent since then. The share of Latin America went from 18 percent in 1976–78 to 20 percent in 1980–82 and to 25 percent in 1986–88. The remainder went to Angola, Mozambique and Zimbabwe until they became members of Lomé: M.P. Roy, *La CEE et le tiers Monde: Hors Convention de Lomé*, Paris, La Documentation Française, 1984, pp. 83–90; and L.L. Ntumba, "L'Aide Financière et Technique de la CEE aux Pays En Voie de Développement d'Asie et d'Amérique Latine", *Revue du Marché Commun*, No. 328, June 1989, pp. 339–41.

29 Commission, "Memorandum on the Community's Development Policy", 1982, p. 6.

30 E. Pisani, *La Main et l'Outil*, Paris, Robert Laffont, 1984, pp. 15–16.

31 The Spearman rank correlation coefficients between the country distributions of bilateral and direct EC aid to developing countries have a positive sign and increase in value over time: from 0.395 in 1970 to 0.645 in 1975, to 0.782 in 1980.

32 Development Committee, *Aid for Development: The Key Issues*, Washington D.C., The World Bank, 1986, pp. 55–6.

33 European Cooperation and Solidarity, EC Commission and Council of Europe, *Europeans and Development Aid in 1987*, Brussels, 1988, p. 27.

34 *Ibidem*, p. 32.

35 M. Beenstock, "Political Econometry of Official Development Assistance", *World Development*, Vol. 8, No. 1, 1980, pp. 137–44.

36 See A. Maizels and M. Nissanke, "Motivations for Aid to Developing Countries", *World Development*, Vol. 12, No. 9, 1984, pp. 245–53, where this result applies to the country allocations of France, Germany and Great Britain, in addition to the United States and Japan.

37 A. D'Agostino, *Bisogni Essenziali ed Aiuti allo Sviluppo*, Doctoral Dissertation, Milan, Bocconi University, 1989, pp. 177–207; and F. Daveri and E. Grilli, "Modelli di Distribuzione Geografica degli Aiuti Pubblici allo Sviluppo", Istituto per gli Studi di Politica Internasionali (ISPI) Working Paper, Milan, 1991 (mimeo.).

38 See United Nations, *Proceedings of the United Nations Conference on Trade and Development*, Vol. 1, New York, 1964, pp. 42–8; and *Proceedings of the United Nations Conference on Trade and Development—Second Session*, Vol. 1, New York, 1968, pp. 38–44.

39 See, for example, the recommendations contained in the influential report, released in 1969 by the Commission on International

Development chaired by Mr L.B. Pearson: L.B. Pearson, *Partners in Development*, New York, Praeger, 1969, pp. 14-22.

[40] The proposal was presented by the Italian government to the EC Council in July 1990, at the initiative of Foreign Minister Gianni De Michelis during the period in which Italy held the presidency. It called for an increase in the amount of aid to 1 percent of the Community's GNP beginning in 1993, a quarter destined to Eastern Europe, another quarter to the Mediterranean areas and 50 percent to the remainder of the developing countries. The note called for the implementation of a common aid strategy, skewed towards multilateralism, so as to avoid the difficulties encountered in the past: Italian Ministry of Foreign Affairs, "Iniziativa dei Paesi CEE verso i paesi dell'Est Europeo, del Mediterraneo e dei Paesi in Via di Sviluppo", note presented to the EC Council of Ministers, 16 July 1990 (mimeo.).

[41] K. Billerbeck, *Europeanization of Development Aid: Integration Through Coordination of National Aid Policies of EC Member States*, Berlin, German Development Institute, 1972, pp. 4-6.

[42] The Internal Agreement concluded on 20 November 1979 between the member states within the framework of the second Lomé Convention stipulates that the member states "shall notify the Commission of any bilateral aid which has been granted or which is envisaged" and that "each member state and the Commission shall periodically bring such information up-to-date" and "shall provide each other with available data on other aid granted or proposed for the ACP states". Quoted in Court in Auditors of the European Communities, "Special Report on the Coordination of Community Aid to Third Countries", *Official Journal of the European Communities*, No. C224, Vol. 27, 25 August 1984, p. 6.

[43] Commission of the European Communities, "Memorandum from the Commission on a Community Policy on Development Cooperation: Program for Initial Actions", Supplement 2/72 to the *Bulletin of the European Communities*, 1972, pp. 20-21.

[44] *Ibidem*, p. 17.

[45] Commission, "Memorandum on the Community's Development Policy", 1982.

[46] Commission, "Development Aid: Fresco of Community Action Tomorrow", 1974.

[47] Commission of the European Communities, "The Development Cooperation Policies of the European Community from 1971 to 1976",

Brussels, April 1977 (mimeo.); Commission of the European Communities, *The European Community's Development Policy: 1981-1983*, Brussels, 1984.

[48] Commission, "Memorandum on the Community's Development Policy", 1982, p. 27.

[49] Council Resolution of 16 July 1974 entitled, "Harmonization and Coordination of Member States' Cooperation Policies", had only "recommended" that: (a) the exchange of information be increased; (b) mutual consultations on aid policies be encouraged; (c) mutual consultations on the positions to be adopted by Member States and the Community in international organizations be held. The main emphasis of the Council resolution was on political coordination. Technical coordination was scarcely emphasized and the Commission was given no special mandate in this area: Court of Auditors, "Coordination of Community Aid to Third Countries", 1984, p. 6.

[50] Commission of the European Communities, *Commission Communication to the Council on Better Coordination of Development Cooperation Policies and Operations within the Community*, Doc. COM(84) 174 final, Brussels, 26 March 1984.

[51] Court of Auditors, "Coordination of Community Aid to Thrid Countries", 1984, p. 7.

[52] Commission, *Better Coordination of Development Cooperation Policies*, 1984, p. 7.

[53] *Ibidem*, p. 13.

[54] "Council Resolution of 31 May 1988 on the Economic Situation and Adjustment Process in Sub-Saharan Africa", in Council of the European Communities, *Compilation of Texts Adopted by the Council, 1981-1988*, Brussels, 1989, pp. 101-3. Paragraph 7 of the Resolution, specifically concerned with coordination between member states and the Commission, is so garbled as to be almost incomprehensible beyond the advocacy of better coordination. Confused language was, no doubt, the result of disagreement among members over the forms of coordination.

[55] Commission, *Better Coordination of Development Cooperation Policies*, 1984.

[56] Council of the European Communities, "Resolution of 16 May 1989 on Coordination in Support of Structural Adjustment in ACP States", *Bulletin of the European Communities*, No. 5, 1989, pp. 117-18.

3

The Community's Aid Model: Continuation of Colonial Patterns or a New Form of Cooperation with Associated Developing Countries?

In no other area more than economic assistance to developing countries has the claim to have developed a "new model" been made more regularly and perhaps more credibly by the Community. In many respects direct EC aid was made the symbol of the Europe being constructed: new, unencumbered by global strategic burdens and focused on the maintenance of justice and peace in the world. The claim of a new aid model had to do not only with volume, although the Community appeared for some years to be the channel for more and more European development assistance, but also, and above all, with the forms of direct Community aid. EC aid was said to be stable (multi-year), non-political, negotiated (for the most part) with the recipients, administered in association with them, utilized to fit the recipients' priorities and free of narrow commercial ties. In addition, EC aid was mostly given in the form of grants. If pressed to show how the Community's development practices differed significantly from those of the member states, or if challenged, to show how EC development policies could really be considered a significant step in the direction of a New International Economic Order, the Commission could always refer to its aid and aid practices.

In the first comprehensive document on development policies sent by the Commission to the Council in 1971 the point is proudly made that "in the sector of financial and technical cooperation, the Community's contribution to the economic and social development of the AAMS is continuous and free from the disturbances which sometimes arise in the political relations between some of these countries and one or other of the Member States".[1] This point is plainly repeated in a report on the European Development Fund issued by Court of Auditors of the Community eleven years later.[2] The stability and predictability of EC aid were in one sense closely linked to the non-political nature of the relationship between the Community and its associates, a claim often made by Community officials.

That the recipients appreciated EC aid for these reasons may not have sounded like a credible claim when made at such a general level by the Community itself. In fact, stability and predictability of EC aid applied more to commitments than to actual disbursements. If the former almost represented multi-year entitlements, the latter were always subject to practical difficulties (and some discretion by the Commission) that caused considerable fluctuations in disbursement flows, particularly in the case of project aid. Numerous complaints by the recipients about the slowness and lumpiness of EDF disbursements were heard throughout the years. Yet, as late as 1989, right at the beginning of their document setting the approach to the negotiations for Lomé IV, the ACP countries were still stating the belief that "in the area of financial cooperation, EDF resources tended to facilitate economic planning and budgeting in ACP countries in view of their predictability and availability".[3]

Despite the practical difficulties encountered with EDF disbursements, the greater than average predictability of EC multilateral aid seems to have been genuinely appreciated by the associates. However, this was certainly not the case for the generosity of EC aid, either in its terms or its volume. The terms of EC financial assistance have been denounced as insufficiently liberal by the associates at least since Lomé I.[4] Volumes were considered to be below expectations almost from the beginning of the association, a judgement that the associates never changed. In the early years of the association the major complaint was about bilateral aid from some EC countries whose growth was sluggish. In some cases (e.g. Belgium) the share of aid going to associated countries was dropping. In later years, the complaints had two aspects. On the one hand, the AAMSs felt cheated. The promise to protect their previous real aid levels, given by the EC in the Deniau Memorandum, was not maintained and they were therefore made to pay (in terms of real aid given up) for the extension of the association to the former British colonies.[5] On the other hand, total real flows of aid to associated countries, considered in their entirety, fell with Lomé I and the drop was never corrected. The ACP countries went as far as appending a unilateral declaration on the subject to the text of Lomé II, in which they characterized the amount of aid foreseen in it as neither adequate nor fully reflecting previous understandings.[6] Capping years of complaints and criticism over the quantity of EC aid, the approach document of ACP countries to Lomé IV, immediately after the positive appraisal of the predictability and availability of Community financial assistance, reads: "However, the quantum of these resources has remained too low to have a visible impact on the ACP economies."[7]

The principle of *parity*, or *equality*, between the Community and the associates in financial and technical cooperation was also strongly emphasized by the Commission. The associates were described as having "contributed very directly towards the design and organization, and later the adaptation, of this cooperation" during the ten years of Yaoundé.[8] The adaptability of EC technical and financial assistance was credited to the parity principle built into the conventions of association and to the spirit of close cooperation with the associates on which they were based. In furthering associationism and adapting it to the new international political reality faced by the enlarged Community in the mid-1970s, the first Lomé Convention strongly emphasized the equality of the *partners* in the cooperation between Europe and the ACPs.[9]

In the field of financial and technical cooperation parity implied active participation of the ACP states in all aspects of the aid process: the programing of aid, project preparation, *ex-ante* project evaluation, financing decisions, project execution and *ex-post* project evaluation.[10] The participatory nature of aid administration—what Mr Pisani called *cogestion* (joint-management)[11]—was a unique trait that, in the view of the Community, put EC aid in a category by itself, with respect to both standard bilateral and standard multilateral aid practices. The aspect of joint responsibility in the management of financial assistance is greatly emphasized in the text of Lomé III.[12] The strong attachment of the Commission to the joint management of the aid it supplies to associated countries was still shown as late as 1988 in the guidelines issued by Development Commissioner Lorenzo Natali for the negotiations of Lomé IV, despite the radical change that had already been introduced into the Community's attitudes towards aid conditionality and policy dialogue with recipient countries.[13]

The Unique Characteristics of Direct EC Aid

Even though in going from principles to practice some of the innovation and originality avowedly built into the EC multilateral aid model becomes lost, the key characteristics of the EC model of direct aid deserve special attention. Additionally to bilateral aid supplied by EC member countries, its political–economic neutrality and joint-management are among the most important.

Additionality

In assessing the effective value of the claims made about EC aid, a preliminary but important question is whether the financial resources administered by the Commission, and particularly those contributed from member countries' budgets in the framework of the association policy, complement the bilateral aid directly supplied by the member states or substitute for it. If additionality were present, the many unique characteristics of EC multilateral aid policies and practices would more clearly denote a real change from the past. If Community aid were instead a simple substitute for bilateral aid, not only would the effective value of the innovations built into EC aid policies be much less, but these policies could also be seen as an attempt to diversify standard behaviors only at the margin, and possibly obtain maximum political advantage from the innovations that were introduced but at the minimum cost (i.e. the amount of bilaterally administered aid resources given up). The net result could be interpreted more as a token than as a meaningful innovation.

Additionality of EC aid has been maintained almost as an article of faith by the Commission since the very beginning of its direct responsibility for aid administration. The principle goes back to the Treaty of Rome and the establishment of the first European Development Fund. In the spirit of the Treaty, the EDF was the most tangible sign of the new collective responsibility assumed by the EC partners in aiding the associated countries and territories.[14] Moreover, the Treaty's implementing convention was rather explicit on this point: the joint participation of member countries in actions aimed at promoting the social and economic development of the associated countries—such as the Development Fund—was not to be in lieu of, but in addition to, the efforts of the countries that were directly responsible for them.[15] In its 1971 document on European development assistance, the Commission simply reiterated this basic principle, by stating that "the financial aid given [by the EC], besides being multilateral, is *additional to and never substituted for other contributions to the developing world from the Community*" (emphasis added).[16] This was a claim that seemed to ignore the difficulties of proving or disproving aid diversion but one that is nonetheless still widely accepted, especially by Francophone analysts.[17]

Passing judgements on additionality of aid is difficult and always somewhat subjective. Money is fungible and the final destination of capital flows always uncertain.[18] Yet, no massive diversion of bilateral aid flows to non-associated countries by either France, after 1958, or the United Kingdom, after 1974, seems to have occurred. In the late 1950s, France, which was by far the largest single supplier of aid among the prospective members of the EC, was the target of widespread suspicion that the association to the Community of overseas countries and territories it so strongly advocated could be a ploy to reduce the financial burden imposed by its colonies. Germany and the Netherlands were also worried that establishment of the first EDF would allow France to put more resources behind its efforts to hold on to Algeria. They did not wish in any way to become involved in or even identified with French colonial policy.[19]

Total French public sector contributions to developing countries and multilateral organizations (including contributions to the EDF), however, increased between 1958 and 1962 in both nominal and real dollar terms. France apparently did not seek an immediate reduction of its total aid burden, which did not fall appreciably, either in absolute terms or in relation to GNP, until the end of the Algerian war. As for diversion of aid from one group of recipients to another, the share of French public bilateral aid going to associated countries decreased by three percentage points between 1960 and 1962, but this decline turned out to be temporary. Similarly, the amount of total British ODA after 1974 remained roughly constant in real terms and as a share of GNP for at least five years,[20] while bilateral ODA going to Lomé countries also remained constant as a share of total ODA during the next several years (Table 3.1).

In more recent times, however, and in practice since the Deniau Memorandum,[21] the claim of additionality of Community aid has generally been made in a weaker form, by stressing: (a) the continuous growth of the resource envelope made available by the Community for the purpose of financial and technical cooperation, within Lomé[22] as well as outside it;[23] and (b) the efforts made by the Community to keep the value of aid to associates constant in real terms. This weaker claim notwithstanding, the Community has shown over time a consistent preference for dealing with nominal aid figures even at times of high inflation[24] and a strong reluctance to supply any satistical basis for the claims made about real aid.[25] It has also systematically avoided providing figures on per capita real aid received by the associates.[26]

Table 3.1 Country Distribution of French and British Aid after EC Membership

France		1960	1961	1962	1963	
Aid to:						
AAMS		42	35	39	44	
North Sahara		53	59	54	46	
Rest of LDCs		5	6	7	10	
United Kingdom	1974	1975	1976	1977	1978	1979
Aid to:						
ACP countries	32	33	29	30	34	33
Asia	48	39	47	45	46	43
Rest of LDCs	20	28	27	25	20	24

Source: OECD, *Geographical Distribution of Financial Flows to Developing Countries*, Paris (various issues).

This apparent unwillingness of the Community to show the per capita aid that it actually delivered, and above all to show it in real terms, can be seen as part of a conscious effort not to validate, even indirectly, associates' expectations about aid, at least after the mishap caused by the unfulfilled promises made in the Deniau Memorandum. The Commission's position is probably due also to the need to counter accusations of aid diversion coming from the associates, which deeply resented the extension of multilateral aid from the Community to non-associated developing countries. While wary of making public this criticism of Community aid policies for fear of being seen as breaking intra-developing country solidarity in dealing with industrial countries, ACPs never refrained from expressing it privately and in the strongest possible terms. Even in their 1989 paper on how to approach the Lomé IV negotiations, the ACPs flatly noted that "pressure on the EEC to globalize its Lomé policy has over the years led to a considerable reduction in the special treatment of Lomé vis-a-vis non-Lomé developing countries. This is evident in . . . [the fact that] in the context of declining per capita aid flows to the ACP since Lomé I, the Community since 1976 has been increasing its aid flows to the non-Lomé developing countries."[27]

Some of the most bitter criticism leveled against the Community by ACP countries came over the unwillingness of the EC members to live up to the commitments concerning financial assistance that they made at the time of the enlargement of the association. The general commitment made by the Community then was to increase aid substantially so as to maintain the level of assistance already granted to AAMSs, while at the same time not discriminating against the new associates.[28] The specific commitment that the Community made was to consider "in real terms" the advantages obtained by the AAMSs and to afford "similar treatment of comparable situations". It promised that "the total volume of aid must be fixed so that all the countries formerly and recently associated can be treated similarly on the basis of their needs resulting from their respective social–economic situations, their levels of development, specific obstacles which are retarding this development and the resources which each has at its disposal".[29]

These were pretty clear promises that could only be interpreted to mean that aid to AAMSs would be maintained at least at constant levels in real terms and that aid to the new associates would be set at comparable real levels. This did not happen. Real per capita aid declined drastically from Yaoundé II to Lomé I, and again from Lomé I to Lomé II despite the substantial increase in real resources made available for financial assistance to associated countries by the Community members (Table 3.2). This explains the sense of betrayal by the Community often expressed by the ACPs.

In time, the Commission made other extravagant claims about aid. The Pisani Memorandum, for example, states that "development cooperation is a cornerstone of the European integration", thus making aid, one of the key elements of integration policy, central to the very construction of the Community.[30] It is sufficient to compare the EC resources devoted to aid to those that go into the Common Agricultural Policy (CAP) to see the oddity of such a claim.

The Commission was not trying, on these and other occasions, to mislead the associates on aid. It was simply stating its views and goals, which were generally supportive of the associates' expectations and needs. It was at the same time fighting for control of aid sources and greater centralization of the aid function within the Community, a battle that nearly always saw the Commission at odds with the Council. In some respects the Commission and the associates were allies in the quest for more and more stable Community development aid. The success of the Commission in carving out for itself a wider role in the area of assistance to economic development depended in many ways on the success attained by the associated countries in extracting more aid resources from the Community. The realization that there was a commonality of interests between the Commission and the associates, probably contributed to the more conservative and circumscribed position taken by the Council on matters of development aid, including volumes, sources and budgetization.

The Commission showed at different times that it was less than fully satisfied with the amount of Community financial aid to developing countries and with its limited reach. Aside from institutional disputes over the control of aid to developing countries, such dissatisfaction was no doubt also tied to the continuous debate between the regionalists and the globalists inside the Commission. Yet, it would be difficult to discount,

Table 3.2 Value of EDF Financial Aid Allocations to Associated Countries

	Rome Treaty	Yaoundé I	Yaoundé II	Lomé I	Lomé II	Lomé III	Lomé IV
EDF current value (million EUA-ECU)	581	666	843	3,072	4,724	7,400	10,800
EDF constant 1958 value[a] (million EUA-ECU)	534	484	427	906	855	1,066	1,240
EDF/per caput current[b] (EUA-ECU)	10.5	9.7	10.5	12.3	13.5	17.9	21.9
EDF/per caput constant[c] (EUA-ECU)	9.7	7.0	5.3	3.6	2.5	2.6	2.5

[a] Current values deflated by the EC GDP deflator index centered in the mid-year of each "convention period".

[b] EDF current values divided by associated countries' population at beginning of each convention period; millions 55, 69, 80, 250, 348, 413 and 493 (estimated) respectively. Population of Lomé IV includes that of Haiti and Dominican Republic.

[c] EDF constant values divided by same population figures.

Sources: Commission of European Communities, *Ten Years of Lomé*, Brussels, 1986 (for current value figures and population up to Lomé III); Commission of European Communities, *Fourth Lomé Convention*, Brussels, 1989 (for current value figures of Lomé IV); EUROSTAT, *ACP Basic Statistics: 1988*, 1988 (for population figures in years to 1986); *European Economy*, November 1989, No. 42 (for EC GDP price deflator); ACP population in 1990 and EC GDP deflator in 1992 estimated by author on the basis of trends.

among the reasons for the Commission's dissatisfaction, the awareness, matured through time and experience, that without a sufficiently large and far-reaching aid network the development policies of the Community would not maintain much credibility among developing countries. The waning of the effects of EC trade preferences, publicly recognized by the Commission as early as 1971;[31] the enlargement of the reach of the trade restrictions applied to exports of textiles and clothing from developing countries via the Multifiber Arrangements (MFAs) in the early 1970s; the progressively larger negative effects of the CAP, especially on non-associated countries; and the stalemate reached on industrial cooperation early in the life of Lomé I, all conspired to make it more and more difficult for the Community to brandish "a new model" of North–South cooperation and to maintain credibility as a true "partner in development". The Commission, or at least parts of it, understood this all too well.

If aid was to be projected as a distinguishing feature of EC development policies, the Commission believed, it had to be strengthened in kind, enlarged in total size and, more moderately, also in geographical reach. Thus came the specific proposals, first made in 1971, for the gradual untying of aid at the Community level and for progressively greater coordination of aid and technical assistance from Brussels.[32] Thus came the subsequent proposal, contained in the Pisani Memorandum of 1982, to establish the figure of 0.1 percent of the Community's GNP as its autonomous development aid target for the 1980s.[33] Thus followed the attempt to globalize (within strict limits) EC aid, made in the 1975 Commission proposals to establish a separate program of financial and technical assistance for non-associated developing countries, covering both Asia and Latin America.

The adequacy of aid, as the key residual instrument of EC development policy, again became a heated issue in the late 1980s, particularly with respect to the financial assistance needs of Eastern Europe and the Mediterranean area. As the contours of the economic situation of Eastern Europe became clearer, and the external assistance requirements of this region were perceived as large and lasting into the medium term, the elaboration of the EC policy response became totally intertwined with the debate over the sufficiency of EC development aid to meet old and new objectives. A push in the same direction also came from the pressures of immigration, mostly from North Africa, being increasingly felt in Southern Europe. Here again, a key issue of policy was the influence that trade and aid could exert on the supply of migrant labor, especially from the Maghreb countries. While not fully articulated, fears of massive migrations from Eastern European countries also added urgency to the debate over a coordinated and focused policy response to these new challenges that the Community was facing from its eastern neighbors.

One important strand of the response envisaged as possible or desirable at the Community level by some of the members, emphasized the necessity for much greater aid flows from the member countries, which were better coordinated than in the past and focused on the attainment of a few key common goals. These goals included the rapid restructuring of the Eastern European economies, increasing their reliance on market forces, and a more rapid industrialization of North Africa, based on labor-intensive manufacturing.

Political and Economic Neutrality

According to the Commission, another important characteristic of EC aid was that it was largely untied, either politically or commercially. The beneficiaries of the Community's financial assistance would therefore be helped by the lack of either political or economic "strings" attached to it. This claim can be examined more easily in its weaker form: EC aid is less tied than most bilateral aid coming either from European or other industrial nations. Part of the credibility of such a claim stems from the fact that Community aid can be seen as originating from a quasi-multilateral source. And multilateralism should in theory reduce for the recipient the political costs associated with aid dependency, as well as the economic costs deriving from the limited procurement possibilities that are normally attached to bilateral aid.

The Community, however, is not a multilateral organization in the traditional sense. Nor is it a multilateral development organization. Its major objective is to attain economic cooperation within Europe. Aid given through the Community is part and parcel of a limited foreign economic policy function that the member countries elected to perform in common. The Commission has at times explicitly recognized these facts, denying that the Community is "a multilateral development institution", and instead characterizing it as "the expression of a European identity".[34] Yet, it has often underlined the non-traditional and non-political character of the Community's financial cooperation with developing countries.

The affectation of political neutrality by the Community in part reflected its desire for credibility among developing countries, which it also pursued by taking weak positions (in between those of the superpowers) on some NIEO and regional political issues. In part it also represented a continuation of the attempt to present to the third world a new image of Europe, in particular, one free of any vestige of colonialism. Many of the Development Commissioners steeped in the French national tradition of *"troisième force"* distinct from both the United States and the Soviet Union, stressed the political neutrality of the Community when dealing with developing countries. Commissioner Claude Cheysson, for example, justified it as follows: "The Community is weak, it has no weapon . . . it is completely inept to exercise domination . . . The European Community is young, it has no past."[35]

The non-political nature of EC aid has normally been associated with the non-political nature of the Community. "The Community . . . has neither the attributes nor the ambitions of a State", claimed the Commission in 1982. "Its development policy is increasingly becoming the *expression of fundamental objectives assigned to it by European public opinion*" (emphasis added).[36] Former Commissioner Pisani concluded the syllogism as follows: "Not being a State, the Community does not have a strategic vision, nor does it have an historical past. Not partaking in the political passions of the States, only the Community can elaborate a development aid policy that can be . . . politically neutral".[37] This position had well established roots inside the Commission. Ten years earlier its director general for external relations had declared: "The non-interference in the internal affairs of the partner countries imposes on the Community an attitude of strict self-discipline, preventing in practice any *a priori* specification of economic cooperation policies [to be followed by partners]. Such cooperation cannot thus but be the result of continuous consultations and permanent dialogue."[38]

How does the logic of Mr Pisani's conclusion stand up to close scrutiny? How does it stand up to political reality or history? The state is clearly not the only political entity that exists. Not being a state does not, therefore, by itself qualify the Community as a non-political entity. The EC is a transitional political construction built by established political entities: its member states. If it has not yet become an autonomous political body, it undoubtedly absorbs and reflects some of the basic political dimensions that emanate from its constituent elements. Its decision making, for example, in general is clearly political in nature. And decision making in the field of aid policies is no exception to this rule. The Council of Ministers shapes and controls development policies through the conventions and agreements that it concludes and the decisions it adopts.[39] The Community's policies are political, if derivative in nature.

In the 1972 Memorandum on Development Cooperation one finds the statement that "through the position of principal partner which it has achieved in international trade and through the growing influence which it enjoys in the world as a powerful economic entity approaching completion and tending towards *political* unification, . . . the Community exerts a genuine attraction" on developing countries (emphasis added).[40] Even the Pisani Memorandum, at least in some of its parts, admits to the political nature of the EC and to one of the foreign policy concerns that lie at the base of its development policy: *"as a political and mercantile power* [the Community] is naturally concerned to promote a system which speaks the language of interdependence and not of conflict" (emphasis added).[41] Whenever it found it expedient, for example in negotiating the size of financial assistance to be extended to the associates in the framework of the Lomé conventions, the Community never shied away from stating, often rather bluntly, that the decisions about the size of the aid package were political in nature, a position well understood by at least some of the key players on the associates' side.[42]

Political neutrality in aid giving would presumably mean that "whatever the internal developments in recipient countries, they would continue to benefit from [the] Community's assistance".[43] If its aid giving had been politically neutral, Europe would have shown that "it does not only help her friends and sanction those who are not like-minded", and that Community assistance "is applied in the exclusive consideration of the objective needs of her partners".[44] But is this the reality of the Community's behavior? Is it really true that "there does not exist [inside the Community] a political debate [over aid], despite the many attempts made at provoking it"?[45] Recent, and not so recent, emphasis on human rights as a factor in the allocation of multilateral Community aid would seem to counter, at least in part, the claims of strict political neutrality.

While political debates within the Council, or at summit meetings, can only be inferred from incomplete information, the aid behavior of the Community is much more open and certain. Special political interests of member countries, in particular of associates, have always had a bearing on EC aid allocations. At a most basic level, the country distribution of EC aid has always had a political flavor. Even during the first three EDFs, certain Francophone African countries were clearly more privileged than others: e.g. Madagascar, Gabon, Congo, Mauritania, Senegal, Togo and Central African Republic.[46] In general, Francophone West and Central African countries seem to have remained among the preferred recipients of EC aid under the first three Lomé conventions (Table 3.3), getting on a per

Table 3.3 Regional Allocation of EDF Aid Commitments (ECU/per capita)

	Lomé I	Lomé II	Lomé IIIᵃ
Sahel	12.7	14.0	16.2
West Africa			
Francophone	11.8	12.7	16.2
Anglophoneᵇ	1.5	2.1	3.8
Eastern Africa	6.8	6.5	8.2
Madagascar	58.1	58.2	81.7
Central Africa	6.7	7.0	9.0
Southern Africa	8.8	12.0	13.1
Caribbean	14.7	18.3	25.5
Pacific	11.0	16.0	21.5
Total aid commitments (million ECU)	1,934.0	2,516.0	3,827.0

Note: Programmed aid only.
ᵃ As of 31 December 1989.
ᵇ The unweighted averages for Anglophone West Africa are: 10.6 (Lomé I), 12.2 (Lomé II), 15.5 (Lomé III).
Source: Court of Auditors of the European Communities, *Annual Reports—Part II, The European Development Funds*, Brussels (various years).

capita basis several times the aid of their Anglophone neighbors. Caribbean and Pacific countries, small in size and high in per capita incomes, also received a disproportionate amount of EC economic assistance. Outside the Lomé conventions, the EC has never hidden the broad political purposes pursued through financial assistance—for example in the Central American countries.[47] Cooperation with the countries belonging to the Association of East Asian Nations (ASEAN) has also always had an international political dimension for the EC.[48] More recently aid to Eastern Europe has become overtly political in nature.[49]

Internal political developments in recipient countries have also affected both EC cooperation policies and aid management, if less than uniformly across recipient countries. The Lagos Convention of 1966, establishing the association of Nigeria to the Community, was never ratified by the Community after the start of the civil war over the secession of Biafra. The negotiations for an economic and financial cooperation agreement between the EC and the Andean Pact were suspended in July 1980 after a coup d'etat in Bolivia. In the late 1970s, aid to Uganda and Equatorial Guinea was practically suspended at the peaks of the political and human right abuses perpetrated by the Amin and Macias Nguema regimes. Economic assistance to China was frozen after the massacre of Tiennamen Square and to Haiti after the military suppressed the election results that followed the fall of Duvalier. Yet, the EC continued to assist the Central African Empire during the worst excesses of Bokassa and to send aid to Burundi and Ethiopia despite serious instances of genocidocal behavior attributable to the authorities of both countries. It also concluded an agreement for economic and commercial cooperation with Brazil, despite the military dictatorship in power there.

One can either accept these discrepancies of behavior as inevitable or condemn them as manifestations of political opportunism. One can either agree or disagree with the use of economic aid to pursue broad political objectives in the recipient countries or regions, such as in the case of Central America, where the Community openly acknowledged that "it firmly believed that political dialogue and economic cooperation [with the region] could help reinforce democratic principles and human rights [in it]".[50] Yet, one can hardly turn around and make the claim that EC financial aid, or development cooperation at large, is politically neutral, either in design or in management.

What may be true is that the Commission tried over time to minimize the domain of overtly political decisions concerning aid, made on the basis of stated principles and according to clear behavioral rules, preferring instead a more discreet and pragmatic type of decision making.

Technically speaking, however, the Community's aid to developing countries—associates and non-associates is not even untied commercially. Recipient countries still have to procure within the European Community. Given the size of the Community market, it can be argued that the economic costs of this type of aid tying are probably not very high as a rule. Prices of European goods and services may not be significantly higher than world (or alternative regional) prices. Yet it is difficult to see how, given physical distance and the differences in factor intensities and technology that are embodied in goods produced in different parts of the world, the requirement for EC procurement would not reduce the purchasing power of at least a part of Community aid.[51]

Over the years the Community has taken steps to relax somewhat the procurement ties attached to its aid. With respect to associated countries, the parity principle embodied in the Lomé Conventions naturally led to the explicit affirmation of the notion that "participation in invitations to tender and contracts be open on equal terms to all natural persons, companies or firms" from the Community member states and ACP countries.[52] To ensure the widest possible participation on equal terms of European and ACP firms, contracts are normally awarded on the basis of international invitations to tender.[53] Yet, in the same convention that enshrines the equality of treatment of EC and ACP firms, one finds it explicitly stated that third countries can participate in contracts financed by the Community only on an exceptional basis, at the request of the ACP state concerned, and that any such participation must be authorized by the Community.[54]

Competition between EC and ACP firms, while desirable in principle, can hardly substitute for third country competition in procurement. In fact, while exceptions to the rule of international tendering have assumed increasing importance, the ratio of contracts split between EC and ACP firms has not changed much over the years, and third country competition has remained insignificant. For example, over the life of EDF

IV and EDF V (Lomé I and II) firms from EC member states have been awarded a stable 70 percent of all contracts, while ACP firms won appreciably less than 30 percent of the total. During both of these EDFs third country firms were awarded only 1.7 percent of all contracts.[55]

Joint Management

The organization of EC technical and financial cooperation has contained since the beginning important innovations, with respect to the norms of both bilateral and multilateral aid. The management of financial cooperation has been inspired by some original principles, including commitment to the initiative and responsibility of the beneficiaries.[56]

Active participation of beneficiaries in the management of aid resources was not only an innovative, but also an extremely ambitious, objective. Reaching it necessitates, in the best of circumstances, the creation of an unusual amount of mutual confidence between the donor and the recipient of aid, although the aid relationship is by nature asymmetrical. Mr Lemaignen well captured the priority assigned to establishing a new dimension in the cooperation between the Community and the associates in the first "directive" to his colleagues of Directorate General VIII (DG VIII) after its constitution: "Every possible political or economic controversy in associated countries will be more profoundly affected by the confidence that you will be able to inspire in your counterparts than by the logic of your reasoning."[57] Even the slight hyperbole can be overlooked, so well does the directive illustrate the priorities assigned to the confidence factor by the first administrator of Community aid.

Aid practices under the Yaoundé Conventions were characterized as follows by the Commission in the early 1970s; "Aid is implemented on the basis of real and close cooperation between the relevant authorities of the Associated Countries and the Community Commissions and the European Investment Bank. The initiative for all the projects [financed by the Community] comes from the associated states concerned. The evaluation, with a view to finance, is conducted by the Community in dialogue with these states. The latter are totally responsible for implementing the projects concerned."[58] Until the implementation stage of the project, with or without an additional round of consultation, Community practices could hardly be characterized as revolutionary (Figure 3.1). Most multilateral banks followed roughly the same procedures. Giving control to the beneficiary country of the implementation of a project financed by Community resources was the only real innovation. Multilateral banks, let alone bilateral aid donors, did not then, and still do not relinquish control over the implementation of the projects that they finance to the authorities of the country concerned. Nonetheless, the conclusion of the Commission's evaluation appears a bit too strong: "It is therefore the associated countries which direct their own development on the basis of their own decisions, with the Community's financial aid and support."[59] But, in evaluating its own aid model, the Community was never constrained by excessive modesty!

A few years later, in reviewing aid practices under the Lomé Convention in the mid-1970s, DGVIII showed again that neither had it lost the flare for words instilled by its first Commissioner nor had modesty spread widely inside the Commission when evaluation of aid cooperation was at stake. Explaining the meaning of the procedures governing donor–recipient relations under Lomé, the Commission stated: "Put in a word, these procedures amount to the co-management of Community aid by the EC and the ACPs, . . . a practice which has no parallel."[60] What was the basis for such a claim, one can legitimately ask? Did Lomé innovate enough in this area to justify this claim of the uniqueness of the EC model of technical and financial cooperation with the associated countries?

In the "Fresco" document of 1974, where selectivity in the Community's development cooperation policy was strongly advocated, the collaborative relationship between the Community and its associates in the field of aid was described in near ideal terms: "Our Associates and ourselves sit around the same table; in this club, priorities and programs are set by our Associates and not by ourselves; mutual aid is 'de rigueur'."[61] Even in the Pisani Memorandum of 1982, which represented a frank, often critical review of EC development practices, not only did the Commission take pride in the reach and volume of EC aid, but it also restated some of the guiding principles of EC aid policy, including that "governments of

Figure 3.1 EDF Aid Procedures: Stages, Purposes and Participation

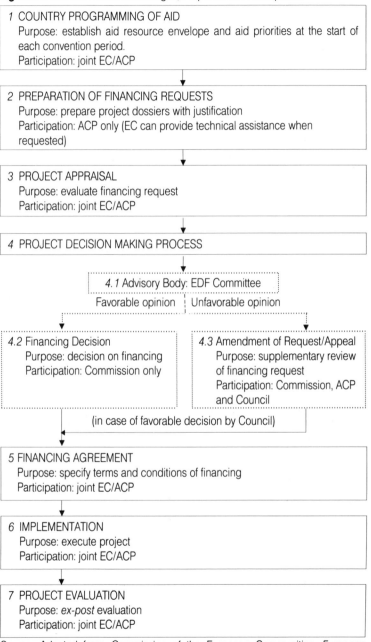

1 COUNTRY PROGRAMMING OF AID
Purpose: establish aid resource envelope and aid priorities at the start of each convention period.
Participation: joint EC/ACP

2 PREPARATION OF FINANCING REQUESTS
Purpose: prepare project dossiers with justification
Participation: ACP only (EC can provide technical assistance when requested)

3 PROJECT APPRAISAL
Purpose: evaluate financing request
Participation: joint EC/ACP

4 PROJECT DECISION MAKING PROCESS

4.1 Advisory Body: EDF Committee

Favorable opinion   Unfavorable opinion

4.2 Financing Decision
Purpose: decision on financing
Participation: Commission only

4.3 Amendment of Request/Appeal
Purpose: supplementary review of financing request
Participation: Commission, ACP and Council

(in case of favorable decision by Council)

5 FINANCING AGREEMENT
Purpose: specify terms and conditions of financing
Participation: joint EC/ACP

6 IMPLEMENTATION
Purpose: execute project
Participation: joint EC/ACP

7 PROJECT EVALUATION
Purpose: *ex-post* evaluation
Participation: joint EC/ACP

Source: Adapted from: Commission of the European Communities, *European Development Fund Procedures*, Development Series No. 4, Brussels, 1981.

countries receiving Community aid have the sovereign right to determine their priorities; they decide on how to use their own resources and those which the Community places contractually at their disposal". If true, these claims made by a commissioner who had nonetheless tried to strike a balance between the "rigid conditionality imposed by financing bodies and the irresponsibility of non-conditionality" by aid donors, could indeed be taken as indicators of a brand-new attitude in multilateral aid policies, which stressed stability, non-politicization of aid relations and neutrality of aid cooperation.[62]

The institutional dimension of joint management of aid between the Community and the associates was also emphasized by Commissioner Pisani after he left the Commission: "At both the Ambassadorial and at the Parliamentary–Ministerial level, there exist organs that associate the beneficiaries to the management of aid and to the improvement of the conditions of use of aid in the beneficiary countries."[63] He made this remark in spite of the palpable difference, in tone and substance, which he had attempted to introduce in the basic dimensions of the "aid dialogue" between the Community as the external provider of funds and the local decision makers in ACP countries. A dialogue that was to be over policies and thus go "beyond the process of mere haggling or simply discussing the technicalities of schemes requiring finance".[64]

For Commissioner Pisani the time had come in the early 1980s "to extend the political dialogue [between the Community and the associated states] beyond the mere negotiations on projects to be financed, . . . [to] the effectiveness of policies it is supporting".[65] This was an extension for which the ACPs did not show much appreciation, possibly in view of the strong rhetoric previously used by the Community to characterize the total respect of national development objectives present in EC aid practices. However, to understand Mr Pisani's, and the Commission's, change of heart, one must not look too far. In the same document, when the reasons why external aid had not achieved the full effect sought by both donors and recipients are examined, one finds the explicit judgement that "the countries of the Third World are also partly responsible for these disappointing results", because of poor administration, urban bias in their policies, preference for large projects, and often the inability to define a development policy and stick to it.[66]

The innovations of Lomé in the area of aid administration had not, in effect, been very drastic. The Lomé Conventions emphasized the general principle of equality in the negotiation of the "collective contract" between the Community and the associates, and the joint administration of it. Yet, in the specific field of aid, practices remained roughly unchanged as far as project selection and implementation were concerned, even though, in the interest of speed, Commission involvement in project selection and evaluation became more pronounced. The principle that the Community could "propose schemes and programs for technical cooperation", with the consent of the associate concerned, had actually already been recognized in Yaoundé II (art. 22). Lomé I simply generalized this principle (art. 50), when it mandated the "the active participation of the ACP country concerned in all stages of a project", thereby also legitimizing the Commission's involvement in all of them. It went further than Yaoundé II, however, in establishing that "upon request of an ACP country, the Community could extend technical assistance to the evaluation of projects or programs" (art. 52).

The most significant changes introduced by the Lomé Conventions have to do with the programing of country aid by the Community. This was a key innovation, whereby the Community undertook the specific obligation to program country aid at the beginning of each convention period, in order "to permit the beneficiary country to have a clearest possible idea of the aid that it could expect over this period, and specifically of the amount of aid, modalities and objectives to which it could be applied" (art. 51 of Lomé I). This programing, moreover, was envisaged as being established by the Community on the basis of proposals made by each ACP country, in which priority objectives would be identified. Again full and active interaction between the Community and the associated countries was envisaged in the programing of EC aid.

Programing of aid, therefore, was intended, on the one hand, to provide foreseeability (*prévisibilité*) and, on the other, to be the vehicle for clearly identifying country development priorities and making them compatible with EC priorities. Aid programing at the country level did in fact establish the basis for a more effective injection of Community development goals into the overall development strategies of the ACPs. The principle of neutrality of the Community with respect to ACP development strategies and priorities, while not reversed, was thus being narrowed in its practical sphere of application. Five years later, the Commission's emphasis on food security and rural development (a main practical result of Mr Pisani's review of the Community's development policies and priorities) was prominent in Lomé III; and even the links between EC aid and food security objectives were fairly clearly spelled out (art. 33).

The assertiveness of the Community in shaping some of the development policies of the associates clearly grew over time. In Lomé IV the continuation of this trend was most evident in the specification of the amount of aid destined for structural adjustment in ACP countries. What had begun with a modest proposal by Mr Pisani to extend the Community–ACP political dialogue beyond the mere technicalities of project financing, in order to find a third way between too rigid a conditionality and no conditionality,[67] had developed in less than a decade into the explicit adoption of policy conditionality by the Community for a consistent part of its aid to ACPs. The ACPs' opposition to Mr Pisani's ideas does not appear to have helped them stem the tide of their declining economic and political influence vis-a-vis the EC.[68] This trend clearly culminated in their rather resigned acceptance of adjustment lending aid in Lomé IV.

Adaptability of Direct EC Aid: Forms, Instruments and Conditions

Another important characteristic of EC aid was its adaptability to changing needs and circumstances in both donor and beneficiary countries. Naturally, the Community has tended to underline the flexibility of its approach to development cooperation and the adaptability of its forms to the changing requirements of the recipient developing countries, particularly its associates.[69] Specifically, the Community has claimed that financial instruments available, methods and forms of intervention, as well as sectors of application of financial aid, were adapted over time to the developmental requirements of the associates, often with their input and help. But the influence of conditions in Europe and in the rest of the world on the changing forms and instruments of Community aid is also quite clear.

Starting with the range of financial instruments made available, grants were the rule under the Treaty of Rome. The first EDF was totally made up of grant resources for the benefit of overseas countries and territories. Loans from the European Investment Bank and risk capital were added in Yaoundé I (Table 3.4). The EIB loans were to finance investment schemes in the associated countries that had the potential for direct profit and were to be made on "special terms".[70] Lomé I established the possibility of special loans from the EDF.[71]

Parallel to the widening of the range of financial instruments available in the area of cooperation with associates, the Community diversified the modes of its aid distribution. Under the Rome Treaty aid could go only to finance investment projects. The Yaoundé Conventions made it possible for Community aid to go towards the financing of technical assistance, including general development studies, project-related technical assistance and training programs. The same Convention foresaw the possibility of extending aid to trade promotion, and of granting special aid in the case of natural disasters affecting associates.[72] In addition, Lomé I introduced STABEX financing, to compensate the ACPs for shortfalls in export earnings from specific commodities, complemented by SYSMIN financing (in Lomé II) to sustain production of minerals.[73]

By and large, the expansion in the range of financial instruments available for aid cooperation reflected more the needs of the Community than those of the associated countries. To expand financial assistance to the associates, within the constraints imposed by the member country governments on grant resources, which parliaments had to approve, the Community resorted to the introduction of loans, first from the EIB and then from the EDF itself. The diversification of aid modes, on the other hand, reflected the recognition that associates had a variety of development needs that could be helped by aid (from project financing to technical assistance), and that these needs evolved over time. At times the addition of new modes of financing reflected the effect of a gradual acceptance by the Community of demands made by the

Table 3.4 EC Financial Aid to Associated Countries: Typology and Actual Commitments (million EUA/ECU)

	Rome Treaty	Yaoundé I	Yaoundé II	Lomé I	Lomé II	Lomé III	Lomé IV
EDF	581	666	828	3,072	4,724	7,400	10,880
Grants[a]	(581)	(620)	(748)	(2,150)	(2,999)	(4,860)	(7,995)
Special loans	—	—	—	(446)	(525)	(600)	—
STABEX	—	—	—	(377)	(634)	(925)	(1,500)
SYSMIN	—	—	—	—	(282)	(415)	(480)
Risk capital	—	(46)	(80)	(99)	(284)	(660)	(825)
EIB "own resources" loans	—	64	90	390	685	1,100	1,200
Total[b]	581	730	918	3,462	5,409	8,500	12,000

[a] Includes subsidies on EIB loans.
[b] Includes aid to overseas countries and territories.

Sources: Commission of the European Communities, *European Development Aid*, Brussels, 1971; Commission of the European Communities, *Ten Years of Lomé*, Brussels, 1986; *Fourth Lomé Convention*, Brussels, Europe Information, p. 76, 1989.

associates, whose political and economic importance increased with changing external circumstances. This is the case of STABEX, for example, which met a long-standing demand of associated developing countries for compensatory financing to counter the effects of commodity export shortfalls, but which was granted by the Community only in the mid-1970s, when Europe felt it had to make at least one highly symbolic concession to the pressures of NIEO demands.

The Community, however, not only adapted its instruments of financial cooperation to changing realities, but also expanded the scope of utilization of accepted instruments and introduced flexibility into some of the conditions attached to their use. These changes were clearly in the interest of the developing countries. The meaning of investment financing, for example, was liberally interpreted to also include projects in the social area and in the domain of general technical cooperation. Programs were added to projects in the Lomé Conventions. The conditions for access to STABEX financing were liberalized, in terms of the number of products covered, access ceilings and repayment conditions, making it over time more and more grant-like.[74]

Perhaps even more importantly, the fields of application of Community aid were widened in the course of time. When the first EDF was set up the main destination of EC aid was physical infrastructure. Transport and communication projects alone absorbed nearly 45 percent of EDF resources. Water and urban infrastructure received another 9 percent. By comparison, aid going to production activities—rural and industrial—reached only 17 percent of the total. In the course of Yaoundé I and II aid to productive sectors was increased considerably. First agriculture, then industry became the focus of greater attention. The share of agricultural investments increased to 37 percent of the total in EDF II and remained around 30 percent in EDF III. Industry came to account for 7 percent of all EDF III investments, up from practically zero in EDF I. The emphasis on industrialization continued to grow under Lomé I and II. Rural production became again central in Lomé III, absorbing 33 percent of total resources (Table 3.5).

These broad changes in the sectors of application of Community aid can be seen to reflect largely the effects of external circumstances, having to do with the evolution of

Table 3.5 Sector Destination of EDF Resources (percentage)

	1st EDF Rome Treaty	2nd EDF Yaoundé I	3rd EDF Yaoundé II	4th EDF Lomé I	5th EDF Lomé II	6th EDF[a] Lomé III
Transport and communications	43.5	32.3	37.5	23.8	18.3	14.2
Rural production	16.5	37.2	29.6	23.2	24.7	33.1
Education and training	19.5	9.8	10.4	8.0	6.0	3.0
Health	8.7	4.1	0.9	2.3	2.6	1.8
Water, urban infrastructure, housing	8.5	7.0	4.7	3.6	6.1	2.4
Industrialization[b]	0.7	5.6	7.2	13.7	20.2	11.8
Trade promotion and tourism	—	0.2	1.3	1.3	1.8	3.0
STABEX	—	—	—	12.4	13.6	20.0
Emergency and other aid	2.6	3.8	8.4	11.7	6.7	10.7
Total	100.0	100.0	100.0	100.0	100.0	100.0
Amount of resources (million EUA/ECU)	570.9	717.7	637.7	3,133.5	4,639.3	5,966.1

Note: Data were determined on the basis of financing decisions.
[a] As of 31 December 1989 for the 5th and 6th EDFs, and 31 December 1986 for the 4th EDF.
[b] Including energy and mining.

Sources: Court of Auditors of the European Communities, "Annual Report 1987", *Official Journal of the European Communities,* C336, 15 December 1987; Court of Auditors, "Annual Report 1990", Official Journal of the European Communities, C313, 12 December 1990; Commission of the European Communities, *European Development Fund,* Brussels, 1976.

mainstream economic development policies and with the priorities implicit in the demands of the associates. Emphasis on infrastructural investments clearly reflected the development orthodoxy of the 1950s. Greater attention to the specific needs of the productive sectors in developing countries mirrored the change in accepted development policies and priorities that occurred in the 1960s, especially concerning the role of industrialization in economic development. EC aid fully reflected these needs in the 1970s. Similarly, food security and rural development, mixed with a strong component of human needs, were favorite themes of development practices in the 1970s. They were strongly reflected in Commissioner Pisani's 1982 review of EC development policies and in Lomé III, only to be quickly superseded by the debt problem and structural adjustment needs.

During the 1960s the developing countries lobbied strongly, inside and outside UNCTAD, for greater emphasis on industrialization. The EC associates reflected some of this general thrust in their request for industrial cooperation in Lomé I. This convention not only began with an explicit recognition of the desirability of industrial development in ACPs, but also specified a set of collaborative measures designed to realize this objective.[75] The whole of Title III of the Convention was dedicated to this purpose. The ranking of the section concerning industrial cooperation, after those related to trade and raw materials, but ahead of aid, is quite indicative of the preferences given by the ACPs to this area of development cooperation with the Community. Rural development never became as popular, and as generally accepted an objective of economic development, as industrialization among developing countries. The ACPs were no exception to this tendency. The main thrust towards redirecting aid to both food security and human needs came, as already observed, from the Community. The same can be said for the emphasis on structural adjustment in Lomé IV.

Geographical Distribution of Direct EC Aid

If the sector distribution of direct Community aid reveals the broad development priorities attached to EC development policies and some of the key changes that occurred in them over time, geographical distribution shows some key dimensions of the political economy of EC aid.

A first important element of the distribution has to do with the priority assigned to associated developing countries, or the degree of regionalism in EC development cooperation. Changes in the balance between aid to associates and aid to non-associates are significant indicators of the changes in the overall balance between regionalism and globalism in Community development policies. Figure 3.2 shows the broad geographical distribution of EC aid as far back as it can be reconstructed from available data on country destination of aid.

If one considers the countries in Africa south of the Sahara as the nearly exclusive domain of EC associationism, irrespective of when associative links were actually established, one can see quite clearly that economic assistance to these countries (and the Caribbean and Pacific partners) declined from about 80 percent of the total in the early 1970s to about 70 percent in the mid-1970s, but it has remained in the 60 to 70 percent range ever since. Even after the adjustment in the distribution of aid in favor of non-associates that occurred in the late 1970s, the Community managed to maintain a steady regional preference in aid distribution. In fact, the share of EC aid going to sub-Saharan Africa has again been on the rise in the last few years, largely as a result of the Community response to the worsening economic and social conditions of most sub-Saharan African countries. Outside sub-Saharan Africa, a significant portion of EC aid went to Mediterranean countries (first Southern European and subsequently North African) and Asia. Latin America became slightly more important as a recipient of EC aid only in the 1980s, and largely at the expense of Asia.

The overall picture is not very different if one considers the distribution of EC aid in conjunction with the various stages of Community association policy, differentiating strictly between associated and non-associated countries. What this differentiation makes clear, however, is the fact that up to Lomé I, EC aid to sub-Saharan Africa was almost exclusively concentrated in the AAMSs which received 85 to 90 percent of the total aid going to that region. After 1975 the AAMSs and the rest of the associates came to split nearly evenly the direct EC aid going to sub-Saharan Africa. Moreover, the

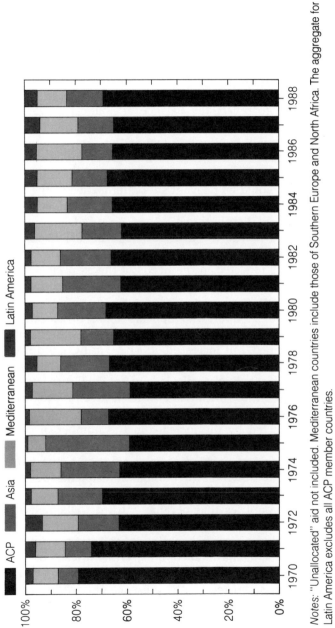

Notes: "Unallocated" aid not included. Mediterranean countries include those of Southern Europe and North Africa. The aggregate for Latin America excludes all ACP member countries.

Source: OECD, *Geographical Distribution of Financial Flows to Developing Countries*, Paris (various issues).

correspondence between sub-Saharan Africa and the associated countries increased so much that the two aggregates became virtually indistinguishable in terms of EC aid distribution. Aid to ACP countries shows almost exactly the same tendencies as total aid to sub-Saharan Africa.

Another important dimension of EC aid practices has to do with the distribution of financial assistance within the group of associated countries. Which sub-group is more privileged often seems to reflect the balance of political power among the members of the Community, on the assumption that former metropoles might continue to take better care of the interests of their former colonies than of the rest of the associates. In other words, within the general pattern of collective client-elism, there would be relevant subpatterns, tied to the colonial past of the main EC member countries, made evident, for example, by aid distribution practices. A related, if more general question, is whether the distribution of EC aid to associated countries is more influenced by economic development objectives, as reflected in the needs of the associates, than by the political and economic interests of the member states of the Community.

On the question of who appears more privileged in aid distribution, available data indicates that West Africa has not only maintained, but increased, its share of EC aid during the first three Lomé Conventions.[76] East Africa, on the contrary, has been allocated relatively less of total EC programed aid since 1975. Central Africa has also been given a progressively larger share of the Community's program aid, but the data is partially affected by the increase in the number of southern African countries that became associated to the EC after Lomé I. If one considers, instead of total aid, per capita aid, thus controlling for growth in the number of recipients, due to both increases in population in the associated countries and in the number of countries that became entitled to Lomé-type aid, the pattern of preference for Francophone African countries in EC financial assistance becomes even more evident. Aid allocated to Sahel and Francophone West Africa is on average four times higher than to Anglophone West Africa. Even when the figures are adjusted for the presence of Nigeria among the Anglophone West African countries—as Nigeria received on a per capita basis much less aid than any other African neighbor—

aid to Francophone West Africa is still 30 percent higher than that going to the Anglophone portion. Roughly the same disparity in per capita aid allocations under the Lomé III Convention still exists between the largely Francophone Central African countries and those that are Anglophone.

On the question of the determinants of EC aid distribution, the evidence is less clear cut. We saw in the previous chapter how the distribution of bilateral aid from the main EC member countries generally has tended to be influenced more by considerations of national interest than by the development needs of the recipients, even though the latter seem to have been gaining in importance in recent years. The first issue that arises, therefore, is whether EC aid is allocated on the basis of the same objectives as bilateral European aid. The answer to this question is negative. The model of allocation that explains members' aid does not work nearly as well in explaining Community aid, or more accurately, the variables that are most relevant in explaining bilateral aid distribution—trade and investment flows—lose some of their relevance in the case of EC aid to associates. The determinants of EC multilateral aid thus appear to be different from those of bilateral aid.

Analyses of the factors that best explain the intercountry allocation of aid from the Community to the ACPs show that the social and economic needs of the recipients have been important since the early 1970s and have since kept their importance. The claims of the Community (in the Lomé Conventions and elsewhere) that EC aid is aimed at the economic and social development of the developing countries appear to have some foundation, at least as far as associated countries are concerned. The crucial qualification is that such foundation is limited to about 15 percent of all aid resources going to these countries from the Community. Political–strategic considerations, however, are not totally absent in EC aid distribution. The franc zone seems to enjoy some preference on political grounds and the countries that are most important as suppliers of raw materials are also somewhat favored among the associates as recipients of EC financial assistance. The importance of political–strategic considerations, especially when strongly embraced by one of the key EC members, were underscored by the large increases in EC direct aid to countries such as Ivory Coast and Senegal granted in the late 1980s, when economic stagnation, and often decline, hit the previously prosperous countries of the monetary area linked to the French franc.[77]

The Effects of Community Aid on the Associates

The developmental impact of multilateral aid from the Community in the associated countries is uncertain at best. Aside from the serious problems of evaluating aid effectiveness that one normally encounters, the aid administered from the EC Commission has been generally too small in volume to make an identifiable difference in many recipient countries. EC multilateral aid, moreover, has never been publicly evaluated, either by the Commission itself, or by any outside technical body. In terms of scale, the closest the Community has come to a public and representative evaluation of the aid extended to the associated countries is the 1981 and 1982 Reports on the European Development Funds by its Court of Auditors.[78] Aid to non-associated countries has only recently and partially been reviewed, at least publicly.[79] Reviews by other public bodies, such as the House of Lords in Great Britain, have on the whole been unflattering.[80] But this is quite common in non-technical outside reviews of aid policies and achievements.

The size of EC multilateral aid needs to be taken into account at the very beginning of any attempt to look at its developmental effectiveness. In the period 1986–88, for instance, the Community directly disbursed an average of $1,500 million a year in total aid, of which nearly $1,100 million went to associated countries. In volume terms the Community aid program was slightly more than half that of the bilateral aid program of France or Germany, and not much bigger than the aid program of the Netherlands.[81] These ratios have not changed much since the mid-1970s, when the share of the multilateral aid program in total aid coming from the Community and its members ceased to increase. To give yet another perspective on the relative size of multilateral EC aid, one can consider that in the period 1985–87 concessional aid to developing countries from IDA (the aid arm of the World Bank Group) was $3,100 million a year, and that another $1,800 million came from other multilateral financial institutions. In addition, more than $3,000 million a year came from United Nations agencies. Direct Community aid has, therefore, always been quite small, relative to both the bilateral aid of member states and multilateral aid flows coming from other sources. The relative importance of aid coming directly from Brussels was naturally greater for some recipient countries than for others. In the early 1970s, for example, Cameroon, Zaire and Senegal received more than 8 percent of their total ODA from the Community; Madagascar and Ivory Coast, about 5 percent. In the early 1980s, India got 9.4 percent of its total ODA directly from the Community, while the EC share was 3 to 4 percent for Sudan, Egypt, Bangladesh and Senegal. In the period 1988–89 Ivory Coast received 6.6 percent of its total ODA from the Community; India, 5.1 percent; Ethiopia, 4 percent; and Cameroon, 3.6 percent. For some countries, during some periods of time, direct EC aid was non-marginal, but even in the more preferred Francophone countries of Africa, Community assistance was never consistently a major factor in the total external aid picture.

The relatively small size of multilateral aid from the EC and its country dispersion make it difficult to assess its overall development effectiveness even for the privileged recipients. There is no general evidence, for example, of the contribution made by EC direct aid to the investment performance of ACP countries, which always were the most privileged recipients of Community assistance. Even sectoral evaluations of the development effectiveness of EC aid are lacking. At a more aggregate level of economic relevance, there is evidence that in many sub-Saharan African countries external aid permitted the financing of imbalances in external payments on a nearly continual basis, thus postponing domestic adjustment and helping to maintain overvalued exchange rates.[82] But this important negative macroeconomic effect of aid cannot be attributed only to the portion coming from the Community. Food aid, moreover, a mainstay of the EC aid program in Africa, has been extensively criticized for creating consumption habits that recipient countries in Africa could hardly afford and even less keep; and for stifling local production of traditional food staples—a criticism that appears to be more emphatic than persuasive.[83]

The only meaningful evidence of the effects of EC aid has come from a few analyses of country experience conducted on a project-by-project basis. This type of evidence, however, does not allow for many easy generalizations. At the micro level, the performance of specific projects is by nature subject to wide variations not only across countries, but also within the same country, and caution is needed in drawing conclusions. Even in the sectors where most of the project financing from the EDFs has occurred—agriculture, infrastructure, education—the summation of project evidence is subject to wide sampling errors.

In Malawi, for instance, EDF-financed projects seem to have been relatively successful in a variety of sectors at least until the early 1980s, and government authorities appear to have been able to take advantage of the new source of aid by effectively using EC funds as aid of last resort.[84] In Sierra Leone, on the contrary, the developmental effectiveness of agricultural and road transport projects financed by EDF I seems to have been poor. Wrong and hurried choices were made and poor implementation further complicated matters.[85] Similarly, in Zaire, of four agro–industrial projects examined by the Court of Auditors of the Commission, not one was still viable after ten years. They all continued to operate only because the local government or external sources were supporting them.[86] In Cameroon the record seems to have been only slightly more mixed—most EC aid went to transport projects, which failed to generate strong benefits for the country, and failed to adapt to changed circumstances and priorities.[87]

The administration of EDF aid has been subject to many criticisms. Indeed no aid administration, national or international, has been spared this type of criticism over the course of time. The criteria for country allocation of EC aid, for example, were never clarified beyond vague generalities. This lack of transparency has often been noted. Project appraisal has often been criticized as too lax technically, and EC administrators as too prone to let social and political considerations override economic facts. Management of EDF funds has been found neither very efficient nor always very transparent by auditors. Recipients have criticized the slowness of disbursements. Rural development, agro-industrial, education and health projects have been found wanting more often than not. Water supply and sanitation projects, however, have generally been considered more successful, while transport projects have accumulated a mixed record.[88]

Yet, it appears that aside from the organizational and administrative problems affecting the EDFs, much of the lack of project success depended as much on conditions in the recipient countries as on the technical modes of project evaluation and execution that were actually followed by the Community. What Trevor Parfitt elegantly, if somewhat euphemistically, called the recipient country's "developmental ecology", is of critical importance in determining the success or failure of any project.[89] This ecology includes the quality of economic policies being pursued in the host country, the degree of competence and honesty of its administration, the efficiency of its aid planning and in some cases the level of popular mobilization and participation that it is possible to ensure. The cases of Malawi and Sierra Leone, previously referred to, offer some stark contrasts. In Malawi a more competent government was able to take full advantage of EC aid, to integrate it into its planning cycle and to use it effectively in project financing. In Sierra Leone, a less competent and less dedicated government administration was able to obtain funds from the Commission for doubtful projects, which did not yield many lasting benefits.

The debate over the developmental effectiveness of EC direct aid has not been the only one conducted with passion over the years. Equally, if not more, engaging has been the dispute over the broader political and economic effects of such aid on the associates.

The growing importance that economic and financial assistance has assumed in EC–ACP relations, a mirror image of the decline in the value of the trade preferences granted to associated countries by the Community, has been generally recognized.[90] The central role played by EC aid in maintaining the overall value of the ACP relationship with the Community over time has also been increasingly underlined.[91] Without the growth of financial assistance to ACP countries within the Lomé Conventions, the privileged relationship between EC Europe and Africa may have not have survived.

The realization of the critical importance of aid in holding together the EC–ACP partnership is unlikely to have escaped the Council, a political organ *par excellence*, sensitive to the necessity that the other side of the partnership be put in a situation where it could show tangible signs of benefits from cooperation with the EC. Up to a point the associated developing countries and the EC needed one another. The leaders of the ACPs needed the Community to enable them to harness more resources to achieve their economic and political goals at home, among which the preservation of their often personal regimes was important. The Community needed the associates to enhance its standing with developing countries, to preserve a modicum of influence over many of them in troubled times and to maintain a minimum of economic security in the supplies of energy and raw materials. With the passage of time, however, the dependency of the associates on the Community grew, while that of the Community on the associates waned. The economic and political fortunes of the ACPs, after the years of hope (some would say illusion) of the 1970s, darkened in the 1980s. The opposite occurred in the Community. An association asymmetric since birth, became even more so, as the interests and expectations of its components, diverged with the passage of time.

Nonetheless, whatever remained open to salvage in the shifting balance between the expectations of the associates and the interests of the EC members in the association was preserved largely because of the powerful bond represented by aid. The associates had at least this to show as a tangible and unmistakably positive reward of association. EC aid was an extra cushion of outside resources. It was also the most targetable to internal political priorities, given the influence of the recipients in deciding its destination, and thus the most valuable to the political elites that held power in many of the associated countries. The Council well understood this reality. Every "entente", overt or discreet, has its price. Aid was in many ways the price that the EC had to pay to keep EurAfrica going. The key goal, as usual, was how to minimize this cost. And knowing its relative strength, the Council made sure that this would happen. Every time the Lomé Conventions were renegotiated, the Council set in advance the amount of aid it was ready to offer. The offer would then be made to the associates as a "take or leave" proposition, and the associates could only complain— at times bitterly—and then accept the Council's proposal. In this bargaining the Council never gave any latitude to the Commission. It did not want to, and did not need to.

In this sense a fairly common criticism of EC aid, that it generated clientelism among developing countries, particularly African countries, seems to miss the point that clientelism was largely a consequence of economic asymmetry between industrial Europe and underdeveloped Africa, cemented by colonialism. It preceded, not followed, EC aid. At most, one can probably say that EC aid contributed to perpetuating clientelism. What should not be forgotten, however, is that in some circumstances collective clientelism is not an unreasonable alternative from the standpoint of the clients, and thus even its perpetuation may be as much a function of demand as it is of supply.

Notes to Chapter 3

1 Commission, "Community Development Cooperation Policy", 1971, p. 11.

2 "Community aid is also generally appreciated by the beneficiaries as being generous and non-political, i.e. given without ulterior motives or political strings attached." See Court of Auditors of the European Communities, "Annual Report Concerning the Financial Year 1981, Part II, The European Development Funds", *Official Journal of the European Communities*, No. C344, Vol. 25, 31 December 1982, p. 118.

3 ACP Group, *ACP Guidelines for Negotiations*, p. 6.

4 As shown in Table 3.4, up to Yaoundé II, financial assistance was provided by the Community at very favorable terms: 87 percent of the total in the form of grants, the rest in the form of loans at subsidized rates. Aid to associated countries, moreover, was untied within the EC. Beginning with Lomé I, i.e. EDF IV, grants (direct and through STABEX) dropped to 73 percent of total financial aid to associated countries. In Lomé III they declined further to about 68 percent.

5 Commission, "Future Relations Between the Community, the Present AAMS States and the Countries in Africa, the Caribbean, the Indian and the Pacific Oceans", 1973, pp. 32–3.

6 *Annex* XLIII to the Lomé II Convention, reprinted in *The Courier*, No. 58, Special Issue, November 1979, p. 106.

7 ACP Group, *ACP Guidelines for Negotiations*, p. 6.

8 Commission, "Future Relations Between the Community, the Present AAMS States and the Countries in Africa, the Caribbean, and the Indian and Pacific Oceans", 1973, p. 21.

9 See, for example, the Preamble of Lomé I, which declares the contracting parties as "anxious to establish, *on the basis of complete equality between the partners*, close and continuing cooperation" (emphasis added): reprinted in *The Courier*, No. 31, Special Issue, March 1975, p. 3.

10 Art. 50 of Lomé I, *Ibidem*, p. 15.

11 Pisani, *La Main et l'Outil*, p. 225.

12 Art. 186(g) and Art. 192.3 of Lomé III, reprinted in *The Courier*, No. 89, January–March, 1985, pp. 41–3.

13 In the Natali guidelines one finds, among the key characteristics to be preserved in Lomé IV, the "permanent dialogue both at the technical level (aid programming and policy dialogue) and at the political level (the joint institutions)". The section of the guidelines from which this quotation is taken is reported in A. Hewitt, "ACP and the Developing World", in J. Lodge, ed., *The European Community and the Challenge of the Future*, New York, St. Martin's Press, 1989, p. 294.

14 F. Baron and G. Vernier, *Le Fond Européen de Développement*, Paris, Presses Universitaires de France, 1981, p. 6.

15 See Art. 1 of the Implementing Convention of the Association, in Office for Official Publications, *Treaties*, p. 577.

16 Commission, *European Development Aid*, 1971, p. 9.

17 See, for example, M.P. Roy, "La Convention de Lomé: Amorce d'une Nouvel Ordre Economique International", *Notes et Etudes Documentaires*, Vol. 30, No. 4313-4315, 1976, pp. 31-32, and I. de Limbourg, "Aide au Développement de la CE en Chiffres", *Objectif Europe*, Vol. 4, No. 2, 1979, pp. 22-4.

18 These aspects are emphasized by many Anglophone analysts, generally more skeptical about the claim of additionality of EC aid resources: Wall, *European Community's Lomé Convention*, pp. 13-14, and C. Rajana, "The Lomé Convention: An Evaluation of EC Economic Assistance to the ACP States", *Canadian Journal of Development Economics*, Vol. 2, No. 2, 1981, pp. 306-8. The exception is Ravenhill, *Collective Clientelism*, pp. 275-80.

19 On this point see Delorme, *L'Association des Etats Africans et Malgache*, pp. 17-18; Dodoo and Kuster, "Road to Lomé", pp. 17-18, and Cosgrove Twitchett, *Europe and Africa*, p. 14.

20 The trends in total ODA of both the United Kingdom and France from 1950-55 to 1984 can be found in OECD, *Twenty-five Years of Development Cooperation*, pp. 334-6.

21 Commission, "Future Relations Between the Community, the Present AAMS States and the Countries in Africa, the Caribbean, the Indian and Pacific Oceans", 1973, p. 7.

22 See, for example, the recent review of the Lomé conventions published by the Commission: Commission of the European Communities, *Ten Years of Lomé*, Europe Information Doc. DE 55, Brussels, 1986, pp. 15 and 20.

23 Commission, *Development Policy: 1981-83*, 1984, p. 75, and Commission of the European Communities, *Official Development Assistance from the European Community and its Member States*, Europe Information Doc. DE 57, Brussels, 1988, p. 20.

24 Commission, *Development Policy: 1981-83*, 1984, pp. 64-74; Commission of the European Communities, *The Europe-South Dialogue*, Brussels, 1988, pp. 15-18; or the latest document of the Commission, *Official Development Assistance*, 1988, where not a single indication is given about real aid.

25 Commission, *Ten Years of Lomé*, 1984, p. 15.

26 In fact, to get from the Commission the first systematic indication of per caput nominal aid granted to ACP countries one has to wait until 1986, Commission, *Ten Years of Lomé*, 1986, p. 15.

27 ACP Group, *ACP Guidelines for Negotiations*, p. 9.

28 The Deniau Memorandum reads: "As regards financial and technical cooperation, the enlargement of the Association will necessarily mean that the Community will have to increase its financial aid substantially. Anything else would have the result of penalizing the countries at present associated or giving differential treatment to future partners; neither is a tenable hypothesis", Commission, "Future Relations Between the Community, the Present AAMS States and the Countries of Africa, the Caribbean, the Indian and Pacific Oceans", 1973, p. 7. A similar, if more vague, promise was contained in a protocol annexed to the Treaty of Accession to the Community of Great Britain, Ireland and Denmark: "The accession of the new Member States to the Community and the possible

extension of the policy of association should not be the source of any weakening of the Community's relations with the Associated African and Malagasy States which are parties of the Convention of Association signed on July, 29, 1969", Office for Official Publications of the European Communities, *Documents Concerning the Accessions to the European Communities*, Vol. II, Luxemburg, 1988, pp. 80–81.

29 Commission, "Future Relations Between the Community, the Present AAMS States and the Countries in Africa, the Caribbean, the Indian and Pacific Oceans", 1973, p. 32.

30 Commission, "Memorandum on the Community's Development Policy", 1982, p. 8.

31 Commission, *European Development Aid*, 1971, p. 21.

32 Commission, *Community Policy on Development Cooperation: Program for Initial Actions*, 1972, pp. 18–21.

33 Commission, "Community Development Cooperation Policy", 1971, p. 24.

34 *Ibidem*, p. 14.

35 C. Cheysson, "Security and Development: A View from Europe", Lecture Delivered to a World Bank Managers' Retreat, Annapolis, Md., April 1981 (mimeo.).

36 Commission, "Memorandum on the Community's Development Policy", 1982, p. 14.

37 Pisani, *La Main et l'Outil*, p. 20.

38 J. Loeff, "La Communauté Elargie et l'Espace Méditerranéen", in H. Brugmans et al., eds., *La Politique Economique Extérieure de la Communauté Européenne Elargie*, Bruges, De Tempel, 1973, p. 111.

39 Jackson and Price, "Who Controls Community Aid", p. 164.

40 Commission, "Memorandum on the Community's Development Policy", 1982, p. 17.

41 *Ibidem*, p. 12.

42 A recent example of this position taken by the Community can be found in the negotiations for Lomé II. When ACP countries proposed at their 1979 ministerial meeting in Freeport, Bahamas, that some objective criteria for the determination of the aid package be part of the new agreement, the Community responded by noting that fixing the size of EC multilateral aid to the associates "was a global problem of political nature". See Ravenhill, *Collective Clientelism*, pp. 302–3.

43 Pisani, *La Main et l'Outil*, p. 225 (translation mine).

44 *Ibidem*, p. 226. See also Commission of European Communities, *The Lomé Convention and the Evolution of EEC-ACP Cooperation*, Information Note No. P-74, Brussels, July 1978, p. 3, where one finds the following statements: "Our approach leaves up to the partners to take the essential decisions concerning the priorities to be adopted in the use of the various [cooperation] instruments. The Community shows clearly that it is for the developing countries to decide freely for themselves what their development models should be."

45 Pisani, *La Main et l'Outil*, p. 225.

46 Ravenhill, *Collective Clientelism*, p. 67.

47 Commission, *The Europe-South Dialogue*, 1984, p. 91: "The European Community has backed the efforts of the Contadora Group to find a peaceful solution to the regional conflicts in Central America from the beginning—Declarations of the European Council at Stuttgart in June 1983 and in Dublin in December 1984. Since 1987 it has also supported the Arias peace plan. It is also helping to consolidate the efforts of the Central American countries to promote the economic and political factors which unite them."

48 S. Harris and B. Bridges, *European Interests in ASEAN*, London, Routledge and Kegan Paul (for the Royal Institute of International Affairs), 1983, p. 46.

49 See Chapter 8.

50 Commission, *Europe-South Dialogue*, 1984, p. 91.

51 Some EC aid, of which STABEX-related transfers are the most important example, is not subject by its nature to procurement.

52 Lomé II, art. 125.

53 Exceptions are possible under both "restricted invitation procedures" and "accelerated procedures" in the case, for example, of emergency aid. Commission of the European Communities, *European Development Fund Procedures*, Development Series, No. 4, Brussels, 1981, p. 17.

54 Art. 125.3.

55 Commission, *Ten Years of Lomé*, 1986, p. 58.

56 J. Bourrinet, *La Cooperation Economique Euroafricaine*, Paris, Presses Universitaires de France, 1976, pp. 121-2.

57 Lemaignen, *L'Europe au Berceau*, pp. 117-18 (translation mine).

58 Commission, "Future Relations Between the Community, the Present AAMS States and the Countries of Africa, the Caribbean, the Indian and Pacific Oceans", 1973.

59 Commission, "Future Relations Between the Community, the Present AAMS States and the Countries of Africa, the Caribbean, the Indian and Pacific Oceans", 1973, p. 21.

60 Commission of the European Communities, "The Community Development Policy to Date", The Courier, November–December 1982, No. 76, p. 74.

61 Commission, "Development Aid: Fresco of Community Action Tomorrow", 1979, p. 9.

62 Commission, "Memorandum on the Community's Development Policy", 1982, p. 16.

63 Pisani, La Main et l'Outil, p. 225 (translation mine). The Commission had made the same claim in 1981 when explaining EDF procedures: "The recipient countries are afforded a degree of responsibility in the administration and management of aid which is of crucial significance and has increased over the years", Commission, European Development Fund Procedures, 1981, p. 22.

64 Commission, "Memorandum on the Community's Development Policy", 1982, p. 16.

65 Ibidem, p. 16.

66 Ibidem, p. 16.

67 Ibidem, p. 16.

68 J. Morrice, The EC's Development Policy: From Lomé to the North–South Dialogue, Brussels, Agence Europeénne d'Information, 1984, pp. 7–8.

69 Commission, "Future Relations Between the Community, the Present AAMS States and the Countries in Africa, the Caribbean, the Indian and the Pacific Oceans", 1973, pp. 21–2, which reads: "Community financial assistance has thus been directed towards even closer participation in the efforts made by AAMS. Joint research on improved measures for adapting financial and technical cooperation to the developmental requirements of the associated countries has gone hand in hand with the increase in Community financing. The adaptation's effects are visible in several essential areas, such as the application of Community financing by sectors of activity, the methods and forms of intervention, the range of financial instruments available, or work programs."

70 The special terms meant a 40-year maturity, a 10-year grace period and favorable terms of interest, including the possibility of a subsidy up to 3 percentage points over 25 years (Art. 19 of Yaoundé I and art. 12 of Protocol 5 attached to it).

71 The loans carried standard conditions of repayment: 40 years, with a 10-year grace and an interest of 1 percent per annum (art. 3 of Protocol No. 2 attached to Lomé I), reduced to 0.5 percent per annum for the least developed countries.

72 Arts. 19 and 20 of Yaoundé I.

73 SYSMIN was intended to finance maintenance, rehabilitation and expansion of mining production in ACPs (arts. 49 and 55 of Lomé II).

74 For a more complete review of STABEX and SYSMIN see Ravenhill, *Collective Clientelism*, pp. 99–1150. The functioning of STABEX is also examined by H. Kibola, "Stabex and Lomé III", *The Journal of World Trade Law*, Vol. 18, No. 1, January–February 1984, pp. 32–51; G. Faber, "The Economics of Stabex", *The Journal of World Trade Law*, Vol. 18, No. 1, January–February 1984, pp. 52–62; and more recently A. Hewitt, "Stabex and Commodity Export Compensation Schemes: Prospects for Globalization", *World Development*, Vol. 15, No. 5, 1987, pp. 617–31.

75 See the Preamble to the Convention, reprinted in *The Courier*, p. 3.

76 Grilli and Riess, "EC Aid to Associated Countries", pp. 22–6.

77 Between 1985 and 1988 direct EC aid to Ivory Coast went from $9 million to $206 million. Over the same period financial aid to Senegal increased from $6 million to $65 million.

78 Court of Auditors of the European Communities, "Annual Report Concerning the Financial Year 1980, Part II, The European Development Funds", *Official Journal of the European Communities*, No. C344, Vol. 24, 31 December 1981, pp. 147–62, and "Annual Report Concerning the Financial Year 1981", pp. 117–215. The 1981 evaluation by the Court of Auditors was based on the examination of seventy investment projects in six associated countries (Netherlands Antilles, French Guyana, Surinam, Kenya, Somalia and Zaire). From these projects, and others examined in the previous two years (over 200 in number amounting to an overall expenditure of ECU 1,300 million), the Court drew several general conclusions. The first was that EDF financial aid allocations had been unevenly distributed and utilized by recipient countries. Small Caribbean

countries, for example, were allocated too much aid relative to their needs, while poor countries encountered the most serious difficulties in using what was allocated to them. The second conclusion was that the building projects financed by the EDF showed a tendency to deteriorate rapidly. They had, according to the Court, to be better adapted to the maintenance capacities of the recipient countries. The third conclusion was that the initial estimates of the costs of projects had often proved to be inadequate. The fourth conclusion was that investment projects were badly synchronized with one another. Finally, the Court found serious defects in agro-industrial projects, which often failed to achieve their purposes because of their excessive size and lack of integration in the economies of the host countries. The 1982 evaluation was based on the review of seventy-two investment projects (plus emergency aid and micro-projects) in seven associated countries: Senegal, Ivory Coast, Lesotho, Malawi, Mauritania, Togo and Benin. The Court noted that while it found the overall situation "satisfactory", there were several general failings in Community practices. One was the limited feedback from past experience arriving to the Commission in the areas of preparation and implementation of projects. Another had to do with the "too isolated approach of the projects supported by the EDF". Projects, even when technically good, failed to improve regional or national welfare. Finally, recipient countries tended to be incapable of both managing the projects and financing the costs of management and upkeep. This created a large risk of rapid "project collapse" after conclusion. The Court's findings drew a detailed and defensive response from the Commission (*Ibidem*, pp. 207–15). The Commission, however, never published any of its own evaluation of EDF-financed projects, although some internal evaluations were apparently made. John Ravenhill, for example, cites extensively an internal paper covering the results of projects financed during Lomé I: Ravenhill, *Collective Clientelism*, pp. 305–7. Moreover, Mr Dieter Frisch, Director General for Development in the Commission, in a speech delivered in Berlin on 30 November 1984 drew some lessons from what he called "comparative assessment of hundreds of projects of all kinds from over 20 ACP states", concluding that "in the vast majority of cases the *technical* objectives were attained, usually at reasonable costs. But the situation was different with respect to the *development* aims: only about a third of the projects had been completely successful, another third had run into problems which, however, could probably be solved; but the remaining third were in serious difficulties" (original emphasis). See D. Frisch, *The Lomé Convention: Practical Aspects, Past Experience and Future Prospects*, Europe Information, Doc. X/57/1985, Brussels, European

Communities, March 1985, p. 21. In drawing what is in fact a rather strong negative conclusion about the development effectiveness of EDF-sponsored investment projects, the Director General of DGVIII did not specify whether it was based on direct project assessment by the Commission or on the findings of the Court of Auditors. The Court provided, in subsequent years, reviews of the Community's aid disbursed through STABEX and SYSMIN (in *Official Journal*, C321, 15 December 1986), of training and trade promotion aid (in *Official Journal*, C336, 15 December 1987) and of emergency aid (in *Official Journal*, C316, 12 December 1988), but never again revisited in depth EDF-financed projects.

79 Commission of the European Communities, *Thirteen Years of Development Cooperation with the Developing Countries of Latin America and Asia: Data and Results*, Doc. SEC(89) 713 final, Brussels, 10 May 1989.

80 House of Lords' Select Committee on the European Communities, *Development Aid Policy*, London, HMSO, 1981, pp. xxiii-xxvii and xxx-xxxiv.

81 Even excluding aid to DOMs and TOMs.

82 S. van Wijnbergen, "Aid, Export Promotion and the Real Exchange Rate: An African Dilemma", Economics and Research Staff Discussion Paper No. 199, Washington D.C., The World Bank, 1986 (mimeo.). On the more general aspects of aid to Africa, see T. Killick, "The Development Effectiveness of Aid to Africa", PRE Working Paper No. 646, Washington D.C., The World Bank, 1991 (mimeo.). On aid to agriculture in Africa, see U. Lele and J. Rahul, Synthesis: Aid to African Agriculture, in U. Lele, ed., "Aid to African Agriculture: Lessons from Two Decades of Donor Experiences", Washington D.C., The World Bank, 1989 (discussion draft).

83 On the various effects of food aid in recipient countries in Africa, including its impact on agricultural production, see C. Stevens, *Food Aid and the Developing World: Four African Case Studies*, London, Croom Helm, 1979, pp. 135-209; and his testimony, in House of Lords, *Development Aid Policies*, pp. 143-4; and Killick, "Development Effectiveness", pp. 55-7. The emerging consensus is that the negative effects of food aid on agricultural production in recipient countries are relatively small and can be avoided through appropriate design of aid projects and programs. On the general question of the usefulness of food aid see T.N. Srinivasan, "Food Aid: A Cause of Development Failure or an Instrument for Success?", *The World Bank Economic Review*, Vol. 3, No. 1, January 1989, pp. 39-66.

84 A. Hewitt, "Malawi and the EEC: The First Seven Years", in C. Stevens, ed., *EEC and the Third World: A Survey 4—Renegotiating Lomé*, New York, Holmes & Meier Publishers, 1984, pp. 100–42.

85 T.W. Parfitt, "EEC Aid in Practice: Sierra Leone", in C. Stevens, ed., *EEC and the Third World*, pp. 143–67.

86 Court of Auditors, "Annual Report Concerning the Financial Year 1980", p. 153.

87 A. Hewitt, "The European Development Fund as a Development Agent: Some Results of EDF Aid to Cameroon", *ODI Review*, No. 2, 1979, pp. 41–56.

88 Court of Auditors, "Annual Report Concerning the Financial Year 1980", pp. 153–62.

89 Hewitt, "Malawi and the EEC", p. 164.

90 Baron and Vernier, *Le Fond Européen de Développement*, pp. 10–11; Roy, *Les Conventions de Lomé*, Ravenhill, *Collective Clientelism*, pp. 309–40.

91 Lister, *European Community and the Developing World*, pp. 131–2.

4

Trade Policies Towards the Associates: The Privileges that Did Not Matter

EC trade policies towards developing countries were constrained from the start by the international goals of the Community; first, the creation of a customs union by the six member states, which eliminated internal barriers to trade and established a Common External Tariff (CET); then, the gradual transformation of the customs union into an economic union in which key sectoral policies would become common to all members; and more recently, a determined push towards total integration of domestic markets.

The decisions taken in 1957 by the "Six" to proceed towards the constitution of a trading group that would deal in a common fashion with third countries in matters of commerce had important consequences for all EC trading partners, developed and developing alike, and would shape the overall trade stance of much of Europe for years to come. The establishment of a customs union and the beginning of a common market among the main continental European countries put pressure on the United Kingdom and on the smaller countries of Western Europe (Switzerland, Austria, Denmark, Norway, Sweden, Portugal and Finland), which coalesced into the European Free Trade Area (EFTA) in 1960. Trade liberalization and economic integration in Europe thus became an irreversible tendency, and the leadership of this process fell inevitably to the stronger group of countries—those belonging to the EC. North America, on one side, and the developing countries, on the other, also had to face these new European realities.

In its early stages the orientation of the European Community was necessarily inward. Serious reservations were expressed about it by some developing countries, especially those of Latin America, but they did not exert much countervailing pull.[1] Their relative trade position did not permit it. Politically independent developing countries accounted for just a sixth of EC trade. In fact only the United States acted to ensure that trade liberalization within Europe would not occur at the expense of the rest of the world, by pushing in the context of GATT negotiations for a reduction of EC barriers to trade with the rest of the industrial countries. Japan at the time was not a major factor in world trade.

Economically weak and politically fragmented, developing countries were then rather passive subjects of policies, including trade policies; the primary actors were the industrialized countries of Europe and North America. Even subsequently, when decolonization increased the number of independent actors in the world economy and their potential influence on trade policy matters, developing countries failed to coalesce into a strong bargaining group. Those among them that could have provided the necessary leadership—in Latin America and Asia— were either skeptical of the benefits of free trade, or wary of international financial integration. India, for example, decided early on to pursue a near closed-economy model of development, largely based on the domestic market and central planning of investments. The experiences of the 1930s, when their relatively small and open economies suddenly had to confront a hostile trade and financial environment, were still too fresh in the minds of many Latin American policy makers to be overcome by the new trade and finance orthodoxy of the post-World War II period. Trade and financial linkages with the rest of the world were considered by many of them more as a necessity than an unmitigated blessing. Trade with the industrial North, in particular, was often seen as perpetuating inequality in economic relations between the two groups and as an obstacle to rapid industrialization of Latin America, the only real avenue to sustained development on the continent.

The GATT, with its free trade philosophy and general rules (non-discrimination and reciprocity), was not popular among developing countries.[2] The neo-classical trade model that was the basis of the GATT order was thought to be scarcely relevant to the situation of Latin America. It preached free trade among economies capable of shifting resources from one sector to another, of specializing in the production of the goods for which there existed a comparative advantage and of maintaining full employment of all available factors of production. These were conditions applicable at best to developed, not to developing countries, whose internal deficiencies and basic economic weakness prevented transformation and development.

The dominant view in many Latin American countries was that structural economic weaknesses and starting inequalities compelled them to seek both protection from industrial countries' competition in internal markets and privileged access to industrial countries' export markets. Without both domestic protection and external trade preferences, Latin America would not have been able to industrialize, that is to develop. Much of the theoretical and empirical underpinning for this view came originally from the UN Economic Commission for Latin America (ECLA), energetically led by Raul Prebish.[3] Some of these attitudes and policy preferences were sympathetically echoed by the leaders of the large developing countries of Asia, who were also prone to seeking economic development through industrialization behind the shield of domestic protection. The Asian countries had, however, the advantage of huge domestic markets, which insulated them to some extent from the world economy. In contrast, most Latin American countries were left with the "only" option of pursuing regional integration to create the market for the development of their infant industries.

Yet, the majority of the newly independent countries of Asia, the Middle East and North Africa seemed more interested in fighting for access to industrial country markets for their specific exports (such as tropical agricultural commodities and textiles) than for general principles. The leaders of these countries generally ignored GATT *tout court*, but remained at the same time strongly suspicious of the grand strategies of generalized market access for developing countries' exports advocated by their Latin American colleagues. But if the Latin American positions concerning global trade strategies did not seem to make much headway in the 1950s, neither did the practical, and ideologically more agnostic, quest of the newly established countries of Asia, the Middle East and North Africa for unencumbered access to industrial country markets for the products of major interest to them. The main industrial countries "ganged up" in the early 1960s to control imports of cotton textiles and clothing. The EC set up its common agricultural policy shortly thereafter, insulating its agricultural sector from outside competition and nearly preventing market penetration by non-EC produced temperate food products, including fresh fruits and vegetables. All this was in exception to GATT rules. International commodity agreements that developing countries advocated to get a better deal on export prices, on the other hand, were few and far between.

Finally, the European colonies of Africa were then fully integrated into the economies of their metropoles. Trade occurred mainly with their European colonial powers and capital inflows came exclusively from them. The only basic need felt by the African colonies in the trade area, had they been in a position to express it independently, was that the creation of a European Community should not reduce their free access to metropolitan markets. French colonies, for example, needed, at a minimum, to maintain free trade with France or, at a maximum, to gain free access to the common European market. However, lacking political autonomy, the colonies were unable to articulate their own positions, and could do nothing but hope that their colonial "masters" would make wise decisions about them and protect their economic interests, present and future. Dependence on Europe for export markets and capital inflows was not likely to change with political independence.

EC Trade Relations with Developing Countries

In the late 1950s trade with developing countries was critical neither to the macroeconomic well-being of the Community, nor to its security. As recipients of EC exports developing countries (excluding much of Africa, still under the direct control of the member countries and Great Britain) accounted for about 15 percent of the total. They also supplied no more than 20 percent of total EC imports. In 1958 a little less than 7 percent of exports from the Community went to Latin America, 3 percent to South and South East Asia and 6 percent to West Asia (including the Middle East). Independent North Africa accounted for another 2 to 3 percent. EC import shares from these country groups were little different (Table 4.1).

From the standpoint of product composition trade between

Table 4.1 Network of EC Trade, 1958, 1971 and 1985 (percentage share)

	EC[a]	Non-EC Western Europe	Other Industrial Countries	USSR and Eastern Europe	China[b]	Latin America	Africa	South and South East Asia	West Asia	Residual Trade
Imports from:										
1958										
EC(6)	32.1	25.8	10.8	2.6	1.3	7.4	11.5	4.6	3.0	0.9
1971										
EC(6)	49.3	21.9	11.2	3.4	0.4	3.6	4.7	2.1	2.1	1.3
EC(9)	50.6	16.1	13.9	3.3	0.3	3.9	4.9	2.8	2.4	1.3
1985										
EC(9)	54.2	13.3	12.8	2.6	0.4	3.0	5.4	3.4	3.2	1.7
Exports to:										
1958										
EC(6)	33.9	19.5	17.9	3.1	0.4	6.7	9.6	2.9	5.6	0.4
1971										
EC(6)	52.3	15.0	12.6	3.3	0.3	3.3	6.0	1.6	5.1	0.5
EC(9)	53.2	11.0	15.0	3.4	0.3	3.3	6.0	2.0	5.4	0.4
1985										
EC(9)	52.3	13.9	14.2	2.8	0.8	2.1	4.7	3.4	4.8	1.0

a Intra-trade.   b Includes other socialist economies in Asia.

Source: UNCTAD, *Handbook of International Trade and Development Statistics*, New York, 1976 and 1988.

the Community and developing countries (including the colonies) still exhibited prototypical colonial patterns in the mid-1950s: the Community mostly exported manufactures to developing countries and imported primary commodities, largely foods and agricultural raw materials. There were no significant exceptions to this pattern of trade relations across partner areas. About 70 percent of all EC exports to Latin America and South Asia were manufactured products. Roughly the same was true for exports to Africa. Most of the remainder was temperate-zone food products and processed metals. Food items and agricultural raw materials made up the bulk of EC imports. More than 50 percent of all imports from Latin America and Africa were (tropical) food and beverage products, while about 20 percent were agricultural raw materials. In the case of imports from South Asia the relative shares of food and raw materials were almost exactly the opposite of those of Africa and Latin America—56 percent agricultural raw materials and 27 percent food products—but the total did not change: three-quarters, or more, of EC imports were in these two product categories. Most of the remainder was minerals and metals. Fuel was an important import item from the Middle East and considerably less so from Latin America, where it constituted little over 12 percent of the total (Table 4.2).

Aside from being relatively small and patterned around the exchange of finished industrial products for primary commodities, EC trade with developing countries was also relatively unimportant from the standpoint of overall security of supply. If one looks at the share of total EC imports of primary industrial inputs coming from developing countries, one can see that overall Community dependence was not high, being 22 percent in the case of ores and metals. It was higher for agricultural raw materials and fuels, respectively 38 and 49 percent. Yet, most raw materials imported from developing countries had synthetic substitutes—synthetic rubbers and fibers—while production and distribution of fuels was solidly in the hands of multinational corporations controlled by US and European capital. Thus the idea of a Community held hostage since its inception by dependency on raw material imports from developing countries, often put forward at the official level in later years, was far from accurate even in the late 1950s. Vulnerability was obviously greater in specific

Table 4.2 Product Structure of EC Trade with Developing Areas (percentage of total)

Exports to:	Latin America				Africa				South and South East Asia			
Commodities	1955	1973	1980	1985	1955	1973	1980	1985	1955	1973	1980	1985
All food items[a]	6.8	6.6	9.4	8.4	14.3	14.7	13.0	15.7	10.3	9.1	6.1	5.1
Agricultural raw materials[b]	1.5	0.9	0.7	0.1	1.4	1.1	0.7	0.1	1.0	0.9	0.8	0.1
Ores, minerals and metals[c]	16.4	8.2	7.1	5.4	8.3	8.2	6.4	8.3	12.2	5.9	5.3	6.0
Fuels[d]	1.9	0.9	2.7	1.8	6.6	1.8	5.2	3.0	2.0	0.2	1.3	0.1
Manufactured goods[e]	72.3	81.8	77.5	83.4	64.6	73.6	72.9	72.0	72.6	82.7	84.5	87.7

Imports from:	Latin America				Africa				South and South East Asia			
Commodities	1955	1973	1980	1985	1955	1973	1980	1985	1955	1973	1980	1985
All food items[a]	50.7	60.9	41.1	42.0	58.9	22.6	13.7	12.8	26.9	22.2	16.6	14.3
Agricultural raw materials[b]	21.5	6.1	5.5	3.7	18.2	7.5	4.2	3.2	55.9	21.0	9.3	6.5
Ores, minerals and metals[c]	15.1	17.3	19.4	15.8	19.5	17.5	6.8	3.1	8.1	8.2	6.9	5.0
Fuels[d]	12.7	6.2	22.0	24.0	0.3	46.5	68.4	72.6	3.8	0.3	1.0	1.4
Manufactured goods[e]	1.7	8.0	11.4	14.3	3.8	6.0	5.7	6.0	4.4	45.6	63.8	71.8

Notes: EC(6) in 1955 and 1973; EC(9) in 1980 and 1985. Sub-totals may not sum up to 100 because of errors and discrepancies in trade statistics.

a SITC 0+1+22+4   b SITC 2−22−27−28   c SITC 27+28+67+68   d SITC 3   e SITC 5+6+7+8−67−68

Source: UNCTAD, *Handbook of International Trade and Development Statistics*, New York, 1976, 1983 and 1989.

products, particularly metals, but a few exotic materials for which EC nations were absolutely dependent on imports could hardly change the overall picture.

Strong EC private commercial interests still remained in developing countries—in plantations, mines, transport facilities—as the result of past and ongoing direct investments, the defense of which was articulated by some in terms of common strategic-security goals, but the overall dependency of the EC economies on such production operations was marginal.

Apart from the national interests of some of the EC members in specific areas, and their desire to protect them using, at least in part, the Community's shield, the overall economic importance of the developing world to the EC, in terms of either trade or payments, was quite small at the time of the formation of the Community. For this very reason EC member states could be relaxed, to the point of non-chalance, about their relations with developing countries. Once extensive influence over present and former colonies was safeguarded, the rest seemed to matter very little.

Neither the importance of trade with developing countries nor the commodity patterns of trade changed very much over time. Increasing focus on intra-EC trade (a consequence of both market integration and boundary enlargement) and the growing importance of transatlantic trade, conjoined to reduce even further the relative weight of developing countries' trade with the EC in the years to follow. In 1985 EC imports from all developing countries represented less than 15 percent of the total. Exports were just a little more than that. Similarly, manufactures continued to dominate EC exports to developing countries, while EC imports of primary commodities remained, until the 1980s, the rule from all areas except South East Asia (Table 4.2) and the Maghreb.

Dependency on imports of industrial inputs from developing countries declined over time, except for oil. In 1980 imports of agricultural raw materials from developing countries accounted for 18 percent of total imports, while the share was even lower for minerals and metals: 14 percent of the total. As for fuels, overall reliance on imports from developing countries increased over the years—from 49 percent in 1955 to 59 percent in 1980, with Africa becoming an important supplier (Table 4.3). Within Africa, however, two countries, Algeria and

Table 4.3 EC Dependency on Developing Countries for Raw Materials (import share by region and sector)

Source	Agricultural Raw Materials[a]			Ores and Metals[b]			Fuels[c]		
	1955	1973	1980	1955	1973	1980	1955	1973	1980
Latin America	9.4	3.4	3.9	7.1	4.8	6.1	8.6	1.8	2.8
Africa	10.7	7.0	5.9	12.3	8.3	4.2	0.3	22.8	16.7
West Asia	2.6	1.7	0.9	0.8	0.3	0.8	38.6	40.8	39.7
South and South East Asia	15.2	7.4	7.3	2.4	1.5	2.4	1.6	0.1	0.1
Total developing countries	38.1	19.8	18.1	22.7	15.5	14.1	49.5	65.3	59.4

Note: Totals include EC imports from other developing countries.
[a] SITC 2–22–27–28
[b] SITC 27+28+67+68
[c] SITC 3

Source: UNCTAD, *Handbook of International Trade and Development Statistics*, New York, 1976, 1983 and 1989.

Nigeria, account for most of the total. In the early 1990s the Middle East is still the major source of fuels for EC Europe, supplying about 40 percent of total import requirements.

Apart from oil, therefore, the overall sphere of EC trade and security interests affected by developing countries has tended to shrink over the past three decades. Wherever the trade interests of the Community collided with those of developing countries (as in the case of temperate-zone agriculture, textiles-clothing, footwear, steel and electronic equipment) the EC took defensive measures which restricted the ambit of competition by resorting mainly to non-tariff barriers. In the area of manufactures, restrictive trade policies have mostly affected the exports of the newly industrializing developing countries of East Asia and Latin America.[4] The other developing countries either did not pose any threat, or were contained by a mixture of compensatory trade concessions and informal pressure. In the area of agricultural trade, the EC took strong defensive measures against all imports in the 1960s and has continued to shield the domestic market ever since, affecting mostly, among the developing countries, the Latin American producers of temperate-zone agricultural commodities.[5]

The Making of EC Trade Policies Towards the Associates

The method chosen by EC Europe to deal with the countries and territories of Africa, associationism, went more in the direction of protecting the immediate trade interests of the associates in the Community than the Community's interests in the present and former colonies of the members. In this sense EC trade policies towards associated developing countries assumed early on, and maintained through time, a pre-eminent character of development policies.

The Rome Treaty, as previously noted, created a free-trade area between all the colonial territories and the Community. In time each colony was to gain free access to the markets of all EC countries for nearly all its exports. Quantitative restrictions on imports from the associated countries and territories in effect at the national level were to be removed by all EC members and import duties eliminated in three stages. Correspondingly, however, EC members were to gain progressive free access to the markets of all associate countries and territories. The associates were to lower their duties on imports from the EC members, and gradually eliminate import quotas affecting EC goods. The colonies, moreover, were to trade freely among themselves, mirroring the EC members. In practice, however, their right was recognised to maintain various types of duties on imports from EC countries for revenue purposes, as well as for infant industry protection.[6]

By foreseeing the creation of one single free-trade area between the European Community and all the associated countries and territories, the colonial powers of continental Europe were not only pushing for expanded market access for each of their colonies, but also for trade integration among them. This was a potentially "revolutionary" development, in so far as it also created the premise for the expansion of horizontal trade among the future African states and for effective multilateralization of their trade relations. While the potential for intra-trade among associated countries and territories might not have been very high at the time, given the consolidation of vertical trade links with the metropoles that had occurred during colonial times and the basic competitiveness of their economies,[7] the possibility of increasing such trade with the help of outside capital investments and in a wider and more competitive market framework could not be dismissed *a priori*. Moreover, it was the first time that the colonial powers had acted voluntarily to open up trade possibilities between their colonies, which they had hitherto maintained isolated from one another.

The Yaoundé Conventions did not change the export regime of the AAMSs vis-a-vis the Community, ensuring that they would continue to enjoy progressively freer access to EC markets.[8] The associates also maintained their individual obligations to cut tariffs on imports from EC countries (and to abolish quantitative restrictions). But, at the request of the newly independent African associates, the proviso of free trade among them was dropped in the first Yaoundé Convention. The single free-trade area envisaged by the Treaty of Rome was in practice replaced with eighteen free-trade areas between each of the associated countries and the Community.

This exercise of autonomous choice in the trade policy area by the newly independent states had several negative consequences. It sanctioned parcelization of trade among them, and eventually led to the acceptance by individual African countries of more protection of domestic markets than would have happened if a single free-trade area with the EC had been maintained. Both turned out to be serious obstacles to their economic development. Much time and effort were subsequently spent on regional integration efforts, which, in a context of heavy discrimination towards third countries, insufficient market scale and inconsistent national economic policies, failed to produce significantly positive consequences for the economies of the participating countries.[9]

As far as trade with the Community, however, the AAMSs continued to enjoy preferential treatment vis-a-vis non-associated countries, industrial and developing alike, whose exports to the EC were, at least until 1971, charged the normal most favored nation (MFN) tariff rates foreseen by the CET. After the establishment of the Generalized System of Preferences by the Community, non-associated developing countries were instead granted tariff rates on industrial products below the MFN ones, but above those applicable to imports from AAMSs. The preference margin enjoyed by the associated countries on exports of manufactures to the Community, was thus reduced, but not eliminated.

Preferential trade treatment for the former colonies was from the very beginning the hallmark of EC external trade policies towards developing countries. The regional focus of such policies was nearly a matter of course for the Commission, which wrote in 1971: "The policy of preferential access that the Community pursues in relation to some developing countries corresponds to special obligations and interests created not only by history and geography, but by the clearly complementary nature of their economies and by a host of traditional links which are not exclusively commercial."[10] Later on, official arguments in favor of the regional trade policy pursued by the Community de-emphasized the historical links and EurAfrica's economic complementarities. The stated objective became that of fostering the economic and social development of the associates through the growth of their trade, even though the regional character of the policy was not put in doubt.[11] The European Community was never to deviate seriously from regionalism in trade relations in the years to come. When it extended trade privileges to other developing countries, the Community always attempted to graduate them so as not to erode totally the preferences granted to the former colonies of Africa, which remained the most privileged among all developing countries in matters of trade.

The extension of the policy of association to the former British colonies that followed the 1973 enlargement of the Community (after the more limited Lagos Convention of 1966 and the Arusha Convention with East African countries of 1968) did not change the basic character of the trade treatment of associates. It just increased its sphere of application from twenty to forty-six countries, as well as the extent of the privilege connected to it. Under Lomé I associated developing countries gained duty-free access to the EC market for practically all their exports. The exceptions were those agricultural exports that were affected by the CAP. The new Convention, in addition, reduced the obligation of reciprocity of trade preferences, which the associates had honored since the Rome Treaty, to one of simple non-discrimination among EC members in their bilateral trade relations. With Lomé I, EC trade preferences towards ACP countries became in fact unilateral. No other set of countries, developed or developing, was ever granted such a privilege of generalized free entry into EC markets without any obligation of reciprocity.[12]

However, some adjustments in the trade relations between the EC and other developing countries had by then already become necessary. International political pressure had led the Community to extend to the rest of the developing countries at least some of the trade privileges previously granted only to associated states in Africa, the Caribbean and the Pacific. Pressure had come mostly from those developing countries that were beginning to industrialize or to significantly expand their existing industrial base. UNCTAD had been the main forum for such demands on the Community and the rest of the industrial world. The EC introduced a GSP scheme in 1971 that was applicable to the exports of manufactures from non-associated developing countries. Yet, since ACP countries did not export a large quantity of manufactures to the Community, the loss of some preference in the Community markets for these exports was far from being too onerous for them.

The Community, however, continued to treat its associates with special attention even in the area of manufactures exports. Only AAMS countries under Yaoundé, and the ACP countries under Lomé, were formally excluded from the special provisions regulating trade in textiles and clothing enforced within the frameworks of the Long Term Arrangements (LTAs) on Cotton Textiles until 1973, and the Multifiber Arrangements after 1974. Moreover, only ACP countries were given (under Lomé I) special privileges for even their exports to the Community of agricultural products included in the CAP, in addition to a special regime for sugar. For all other non-associated developing countries, exports of textiles and apparel to the Community became and remained subject to quantitative restrictions, while exports of competing agricultural products continued to be covered by variable levies and other CAP-related measures.[13]

In time, the trade policies of the European Community came to create a hierarchy of privileges which affected different groups of developing countries differently. The associated countries *latu sensu* were the most privileged from the very start and remained at the top of what has been called the "pyramid of privilege" created by the EC,[14] with free entry to EC markets for nearly all their exports. The other developing countries to which the EC extended special trade and cooperation arrangements, such as those of the Maghreb and Mashreq (respectively Tunisia, Morocco, Algeria and Egypt, Jordan, Syria, Lebanon) ranked second. These countries have enjoyed, since the late 1970s, extensive trade preference for their agricultural exports and (at least nominally) for their industrial exports as well. Finally come the rest of the developing countries, which were granted trade preferences only in the area of industrial products (again with the previously noted exception of textiles and clothing products).

In time the pyramid of EC trade privileges reached more countries and acquired new layers. The EC developed Preferential Trade and Cooperation Agreements with other Mediterranean countries—Israel in 1975 and Yugoslavia in 1980—which together with the special Association Agreements reached with Malta in 1970 and with Cyprus in 1972, either added beneficiaries to existing layers of trade privileges or created new layers. The EC, moreover, entered into (non-preferential) Commercial and Economic Cooperation

Agreements with single countries in Latin America (Brazil and Uruguay in 1974, Mexico in 1975) and Asia (India in 1973, Sri Lanka in 1975, Pakistan and Bangladesh in 1976, China in 1985). In terms of trade privileges these arrangements put the developing countries concerned well below the associates. However, some of these countries gained the possibility of obtaining special cooperation from the EC in selected areas of commerce. This put them slightly above those only receiving GSPs.

Some countries also changed position within the hierarchy, moving up or down the ladder of trade privileges. The most notable changes were those that occurred in 1975 for the East African countries, which moved from a position of limited association under the Arusha Convention to become full associates under Lomé. Guinea had refused to join the Yaoundé Convention in 1963, thus dropping from the top to the bottom layer of privileged countries, but moved up to the top again in 1975 when it became a signatory of Lomé I. Some countries exited the pyramid altogether. This occurred to the semi-developed countries of Southern Europe with which the EC had negotiated association agreements in the 1960s and 1970s, and which subsequently became full members of the Community—namely Greece, Portugal and Spain.

The trade treatment reserved by the EC for developing countries remained, therefore, highly differentiated over time, with different trade preferences going to different groups. Such trade treatment has often been characterized in negative terms, not only because of the type of dependent relationship that it tended to perpetuate for some countries, but also for the hierarchy that it imposed on the beneficiaries and the distinctions that it created among them. Associated countries, for example, became wary of trade concessions made by the Community to other developing countries under GATT and demanded compensation for any reduction in the trade preferences granted to them. They opposed the GSP in the early 1970s. Even in the 1980s they expressed great concern about the trade concessions made by the EC to the East European countries, thus acting at times as a conservative group that opposed trade liberalization in general and the extension of unilateral trade benefits to other developing countries in specific cases.

A specific design of the "divide and rule" type has been imputed by some to the European Community.[15] The historical evolution of the EC trade regime lends credence instead to the notion that the trade policy construction that emerged was shaped first by the colonial inheritance and subsequently by a series of *ad hoc* reactions to emerging circumstances. The actual content of the trade regime set up for developing countries by the EC, moreover, supports the conclusion that the primary objective of the trade policies followed through the years was a traditional one: the defense of European economic interests, sectoral or general, and the maintenance of the post-colonial economic order that allowed Europe to develop and prosper after the end of World War II.

The General Effects of Trade Preferences

In a very basic sense a trade preference yields a price advantage to the suppliers of the country (or area) that receives it vis-a-vis those of the countries (or areas) that do not (the rest of the world). In the case of tariffs, for example, the preference receiving country is normally charged a lower import duty than the others. Exporters operating from it are afforded a price advantage vis-a-vis those of the rest of the world equivalent to the difference in import duties. From the standpoint of the grantor, trade preferences effectively discriminate among imports according to their country or area of origin.

The trade enhancing effect of a tariff preference on the receiving country will thus depend in the first instance on the extent of the preference actually granted: the larger the reduction in the tariff rate, the wider the price wedge that it creates and, therefore, the greater the trade enhancing effect. This effect will also depend, however, on the height of the base tariff against which the preference is granted: the higher the base tariff, the larger the price advantage afforded by any given cut in rates.

Producers in preferred countries can therefore compete more effectively than before with those located in non-preference receiving countries whose export prices to the preference granting area must continue to reflect the full height of the tariff being levied on them. Exports from the non-preference receiving countries will thus be displaced from the markets of the preference giving country to the extent that preferred suppliers can export at or below the "world plus third country tariff price". Trade in these circumstances will be diverted from non-preferred to preferred outside suppliers. When the export capacity of the preferred suppliers at (or near) the prevailing prices is large enough, non-preferred suppliers may find themselves completely shut out of the markets of the preference giving area. In this case trade diversion is complete.

Whenever preferred suppliers can do better than simply meet the import requirements of the preference granting area at "world plus third country tariff prices", domestic prices in the preference granting area will decline. As a consequence, domestic producers will supply less and domestic consumers will consume more than before of the goods in question (where the "before" is the situation that prevailed prior to the granting of the preference). This means that total imports by the preference giving area will go up, and that exports from the preference receiving to the preference giving area will increase because of the displacement of domestic producers. New net trade is created when tariff preferences lower the domestic prices of the goods to which they apply and as a result domestic producers see their tariff protection reduced. The benefits of this new demand for imports spill over to the preferred exporters, and are additional to those coming from the displacement of former exporters from the non-preference receiving areas.

The increase in export volumes for preferred suppliers can thus come from two sources: *trade creation* and *trade diversion*. Trade creation derives from the capacity of preferred producers to compete more effectively than before with home producers in the preference giving area, as well as from the increase in total demand for the product that follows the internal price decline caused by the reduction in tariff. Trade creation, therefore, involves the replacement of higher cost domestic producers by lower cost foreign producers. Trade diversion derives, instead, from the price advantage that producers in the preferred area have vis-a-vis those of the rest of the world (that still face the full height of the tariff). As a result of trade preferences higher cost preferred producers can displace lower cost producers in the non-preferred areas and export in their stead.

As for their effects on the export volumes of the beneficiary countries, trade creation and trade diversion work in the same direction. They both tend to increase such exports. If larger volumes of exports also mean larger export earnings in preference receiving countries, and higher economic rents for domestic producers, these producers will be in a position to invest more, even when new investments require new imports. To the extent that an increase in investment takes place with respect to what would have been possible in the absence of the preference-induced increase in exports, economic growth may also accelerate in the beneficiary country.

This obviously constitutes the best economic rationale for tariff preference in favor of developing countries. It rests, however, on two key assumptions. The first is that preference receiving countries succeed in taking advantage of the opportunity granted to them and increase their exports. The second is that increasing exports can generate faster growth. Both are theoretical presumptions that need to be validated in actuality. Neither effect can be simply assumed to take place automatically, without reference to enabling conditions. Both are clearly influenced by the economic policies followed in preference receiving countries—in particular those that affect the supply of exportable goods and the expectations of domestic and foreign investors. The shape of the export supply function is of critical importance (and so is that of demand in the preference giving area).

All the direct trade benefits mentioned above are static and allocative in nature. They are destined to disappear as the effects of the tariff preferences work themselves out. There may be, however, additional benefits for the preference receiving countries. If, for example, after being able to expand export supply as a result of first round trade diversion, preferred producers also become more efficient as the scale of their production increases or as technical innovation is stimulated by increased export and competition, they can continue to gain from the tariff preferences and further displace existing suppliers (domestic and foreign) in the preference granting area. These would be dynamic gains from trade generated by secondary reactions to the receipt of tariff preferences.

Efficiency gains are also realized in the preference giving area, where both tariff protection of domestic producers and inefficient production are reduced. Yet, there are also drawbacks connected with the granting of tariff preferences. Tariff revenue, for example, is reduced by the amount of trade diversion that takes place. In the extreme case of complete trade diversion, the tariff revenue of the preference granting area is completely lost. It is in fact transferred to the preference receiving area and becomes part of the economic value that accrues to it as a result of the preference. If trade creation takes place, some domestic producers in the preference giving area are displaced by imports. The costs of their dislocation may have to be shouldered, at least in part, by the community. This is another (temporary) cost that may arise from the granting of a trade preference. Transfers of benefits occur inside the preference giving area as well—from domestic producers to domestic consumers. The former lose and the latter gain from the reduction in protection.

What is clear, however, is that producers in the preference receiving areas should unequivocally gain from the receipt of a tariff preference. If an increase in exports takes place at the expense of domestic production in the preference granting area, welfare is transferred from producers and government in this area to producers/exporters in the preference receiving one. If an increase in exports from the preference receiving area takes place only at the expense of third party producers, the gains of the former group are the losses of the latter. The international political economy of preference giving (and receiving) rotates around this set of economic effects. They explain why prospective recipients of tariff preferences seek them actively, while third country and domestic producers in prospective preference granting areas are opposed to them.

Reciprocal Trade Preferences Under Yaoundé: Extent and Specific Effects

The concession of trade preferences made by the Community to the associated countries and territories of Africa at the time of the Treaty of Rome was meant to be a significant one. The import tariff levied by France on the products of importance to her colonies were higher than those of most of her EC partners when the Community was set up. The preferences extended by the Treaty of Rome to associated countries and territories in the form of free entry for their exports, though lower than those that the French colonies enjoyed in the market of their metropole, applied to the entire EC.[16] Of the associated countries and territories, at least the French colonies traded the higher preferences enjoyed in a smaller market for lower preferences applicable to a much larger one. This trade-off, however, did not occur immediately, as the EC common external tariff was initially set at existing French levels. It was only with the passage of time, and the reduction of the CET, that tariff preferences enjoyed by the associated countries that were former colonies of France diminished appreciably with respect to those enjoyed before being associated to the EC.[17] In the beginning the other territories maintained whatever special trade arrangements they had with their current or former metropoles (e.g. the special regime for bananas enjoyed by Somalia in Italy, and by Guadaloupe and Martinique in France), but gained tariff preferences from all EC members.

The reciprocity of tariff concessions that the Treaty of Rome unilaterally established as an obligation for the associated countries and territories, and that the Yaoundé Conventions carried over by agreement of the two parties, meant much more to the EC countries than to the associates, not only because of the escape clauses left open to them, but also because many associates were exempted from granting tariff preferences. The Central African Republic, Chad, Congo Brazzaville, Gabon and Zaire could not apply tariffs discriminatorily because of the provisions of the Congo Basin Treaty of 1883; nor could Burundi, Rwanda, Somalia and Togo, being under the trusteeship of the United Nations. Reciprocity, however, was important to the EC partners of France, largely because it forced those associated countries and territories that granted tariff preference only to imports from France to extend similar treatment to all EC members, thus reducing the exclusive trade advantage enjoyed by France in its colonies.

In general terms, the expected effects of reciprocal trade preferences, such as those envisaged first by the Treaty of Rome and subsequently by the two Yaoundé Conventions, can be summarized as follows:
1 Exports of associated countries to the EC should have

increased, other things being equal, faster than those of other countries receiving lower tariff preferences. In practice, the share of the AAMSs in total exports to the EC (EC imports) should have gone up in time, or at least the share of AAMS exports in total exports from developing countries to the EC (EC imports from LDCs) should have increased. This weaker expectation is motivated by the fact that, at least in the short term, the main advantage of tariff preferences for the AAMSs should have come from trade diversion, as the EC preferential treatment for their existing exports should have put them at a comparative advantage only (or largely) vis-a-vis other developing countries exporting similar products to the EC (mainly tropical agricultural products). In the longer run, however, one would also expect some trade creation to have occurred, and AAMS exports to have substituted for some domestic EC production and the share of the associated countries in the total imports of the EC to have increased.

2 Exports of associated countries to the EC should have increased, other things being equal, faster than those going to other industrial areas where they did not enjoy the same degree of tariff preferences. In practice, the share accounted for by the EC in total AAMS exports should have grown in size.

3 Imports of associated countries from the EC should have increased, other things being equal, more rapidly than imports from the rest of the world, as the AAMSs granted the EC preferential access to their domestic markets. Thus the share of the EC in total AAMS imports should also have gone up in time.

The available evidence of the effects of the preferences on the AAMSs that can be derived from the analysis of actual trade flows in the period covered by the Rome Treaty and by the two Yaoundé Conventions is largely divergent from *a priori* expectations. In particular, AAMS exports to the EC, relative to both world and other LDCs exports, declined rather than increased between 1958 and 1973, and so did AAMS exports to the EC relative to total exports of the same countries. Only the share of AAMS imports from the EC increased as expected, but only marginally during the period under consideration. The analysis of *ex-post* trade flows would thus seem to lead to the conclusion that reciprocal trade preferences had little, if any, positive effect on the exports of the associated countries to the

EC, and only a very small export augmenting impact on those of the EC countries to the AAMSs.

Prior to 1958 the AAMS countries exported nearly 72 percent of their goods to the EC. This share remained virtually unchanged during the years of association under the Treaty of Rome and declined to 68 percent under Yaoundé I and to 60 percent during Yaoundé II (Table 4.4). The AAMSs, however, diversified the destination of their exports to a considerable extent within the Community, substantially reducing their dependency on the French market.[18] Exports to France fell from 38 percent of the total in 1953–58 to 31.5 percent in 1965–68.

The share of associated countries in total world exports to the EC, or equivalently the share of total EC imports coming from AAMSs, declined steadily throughout the period. In 1973 it was nearly two percentage points lower than in 1963. What is even more striking is the decline in the share of AAMS exports in total developing country exports to the EC. Even within developing country exports to the Community, whose product composition can be assumed to be more uniform and thus more significant for comparison purposes than that of world exports to the EC (which is dominated by manufactures exported by other industrial countries), the AAMSs lost market share throughout the period. Their share of developing country exports to the Community, which was 13.5 percent in 1956–58, declined to 11.5 percent in 1961–63, to 11 percent in 1968–70 and to 9.3 percent in 1971–73 (Table 4.4). In the Community markets preferred AAMS exports did less well than similar, but non-preferred, exports coming from other LDCs. This seems to indicate that the fears of trade diversion harbored by many developing countries, particularly those of Latin America and South Asia, which were kept out of EC associationism, may not have had as much foundation as they thought.[19]

The share of AAMS imports from the EC, on the other hand, did increase, as one would have expected, from 66.6 percent in the late 1950s to 68 percent in the late 1960s. France, within the Community, saw its quota of exports to the associated countries go up, particularly during the period of association under the Treaty of Rome. This increase was helped by the devaluation of its currency vis-a-vis those of the EC partners that took place in 1958 (which was reflected *pari passu* in the devaluation in the currency of the associates).

Table 4.4 AAMS–EC Trade Under the Treaty of Rome and Yaoundé Trade Regimes (percentage share)

	1953–55 (average)	1956–58 (average)	1961–63 (average)	1968–70 (average)	1971–73 (average)
AAMS exports to:					
EC(6)	71.9	71.7	72.8	67.5	59.5
Rest of the world	28.1	28.3	27.4	33.5	40.5
EC(6) imports from developing countries of which:					
AAMS	14.5	13.5	11.5	11.0	9.3
Other S.S. Africa[a]	12.7	11.7	9.5	8.5	8.5
Latin America	24.0	24.5	25.0	22.0	18.5
Others	48.8	50.3	54.0	58.5	63.7
AAMS imports from:					
EC(6)	65.2	66.6	66.7	68.0	67.0
Rest of the world	34.8	33.4	33.3	32.0	33.0

Note: Under these trade regimes trade preferences were reciprocal.
[a] Sub-Saharan Africa.

Sources: A. Ouattara, "Trade Effects of the Association of African Countries to the European Economic Community", in *IMF Staff Papers*, Vol. XX, No. 2, 1973; IMF, *Direction of Trade Yearbooks*, Washington D.C. (various years); EC *Monthly Statistics—External Trade*, Special Number 1958–74, Luxemburg, 1975; United Nations, *Yearbook of Trade Statistics*, New York (various issues).

There are several reasons that can be found to explain these trade outcomes that seem so sharply at variance with *a priori* expectations based on the theory of customs unions. The first is that simple *ex-post* analysis of trade trends may be misleading since it cannot disentangle the effects of trade preferences from those of other factors, affecting, for example, the demand for or the supply of AAMS exports (changes in tastes, substitution by synthetics, raw material saving technology, differential rates of technological innovation in production). The theoretical trade effects examined above are in fact predicated on the assumption that other things remain equal, aside from trade preferences, which can rarely be assumed to be the case in practice.

A study designed to account, albeit in an indirect way, for the factors that may have affected the export performance of the AAMSs in the EC market and the EC countries' performance in the AAMS markets—such as overall growth in the demand for imports in the importing area, price competitiveness of the exporting country and trade privileges—found that over the 1959–69 period direct trade preferences neither created nor diverted trade, while reverse preferences appear to have had some trade diversion effects.[20] These results are broadly consistent with the conclusions that can be derived from a simple review of trade shares.

Moreover, a fairly detailed analysis of the factors determining the direction of welfare gains and losses resulting from the AAMS–EC association in its early years, shows neither a clear pattern of gains for the associated countries nor one of clear losses for countries excluded from it.[21] What may have happened, instead, this analysis shows, are welfare shifts among EC countries: a reduction of the welfare burden of France that came from being the only provider of preferential access to many of the associates and a corresponding increase in the burden of other EC members.

Similarly, a detailed analysis of commodity trade flows over the 1958 to 1968 period indicates that the expansion of AAMS exports that occurred was largely due to products such as copper and timber that received non-preferential tariff treatment in the EC.[22] Income growth in the EC seems to have been transmitted to the associated countries, as growth in demand for their exports, through the known channel of elasticities, and to have swamped the price effect of the trade preferences. EC imports of relatively income elastic goods such as copper and wood grew, despite the absence of trade preferences on them, more rapidly than those of preferred products such as cocoa, coffee and vegetable oils, whose demand was relatively inelastic with respect to income in the preference giving area.

Non-Reciprocal Trade Preferences Under Lomé: Extent and Specific Effects

Under the trade regime established in the Lomé Conventions, the first two effects of trade preferences—relative expansion of associated countries' exports to the EC and of EC imports from the associated countries—should have remained at work. Since preferences became non-reciprocal, and the ACP states were no longer obliged to favor imports from the EC, the price advantage enjoyed by EC exports to associated countries' markets during the previous conventions should have ceased to exist.

Available trade data indicate that the share of total ACP exports to the EC remained constant between 1975 and 1988 (with a slight dip in 1980), while the share of EC imports from the ACP continued to decline during the entire Lomé period. EC imports from the ACPs fell relative to both the imports from developing countries and total imports, indicating, *prima facie*, the continued absence of substantive trade-diverting effects exerted by EC tariff preferences, as well as the lack of sizeable trade-creating effects even in the long run (Table 4.5).

The associated countries of Africa, the Caribbean and the Pacific did substantially less well in the EC market than the developing countries of South Asia, North Africa and Latin America (not to mention the newly industrializing countries (NICs) of East Asia) despite the trade preferences that they enjoyed. There also seems to be no major difference in outcomes within the ACP group, depending on the length of association with the EC. A decline in EC import shares is common to both the first and subsequent generations of associates. The overall results of the import share analysis do not change if petroleum is excluded from the totals.

EC imports from ACP countries also grew less rapidly than

Table 4.5 ACP–EC Trade Under the Lomé Trade Regime (percentage share)

	1974–76 (average)	1979–81 (average)	1987–89 (average)
ACP exports to:			
EC(12)	50.4	47.8	51.0
Rest of the world	49.6	52.2	49.0
EC(12) total imports of which:			
ACP	7.5	6.7	4.6
Mediterranean area	8.2	8.4	8.2
Latin America	5.7	6.0	5.8
ASEAN	1.9	2.4	3.2
Asian NICs[a]	2.3	3.5	6.3
Other LDCs[b]	20.9	17.8	2.9
EC(12) imports from developing countries of which:			
ACP	16.0	15.1	14.8
Mediterranean area	17.5	18.6	26.6
Latin America	12.1	13.4	18.9
ASEAN	4.0	5.4	10.3
Asian NICs[a]	5.1	7.6	21.1
Other LDCs[b]	45.3	39.9	8.3

Note: Under the Lomé trade regime preferences were non-reciprocal (they were granted unilaterally by the EC).

[a] Hong Kong, Singapore, South Korea and Taiwan.

[b] Including Middle Eastern oil exporting countries.

Sources: United Nations, COMTRADE database; EUROSTAT, *External Trade Statistical Yearbook: Recapitulation 1958–1989*, Brussels, 1990.

those of other industrial countries. The share of ACP countries in total EC imports in fact declined under the three Lomé Conventions, from 8.5 percent in 1974 to 4 percent in 1989. As suggested by Figure 4.1, this decline in the ACPs' share in the overall imports of the Community appears to be a long-term phenomenon, unaffected, or not sufficiently compensated for, by EC trade preferences. Non-ACP developing countries, on the contrary, expanded their share of the EC import market from 9.5 percent in 1974 to 17.1 percent in 1989. What is even more remarkable is that the declining trend in the market share

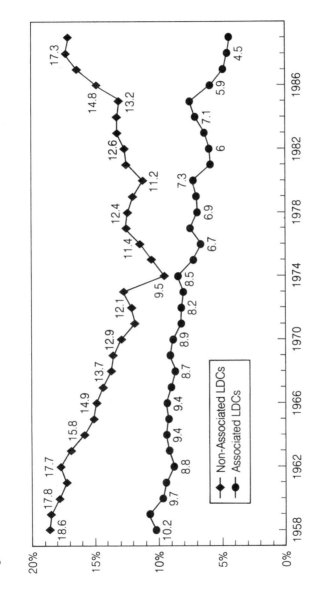

Figure 4.1 Share of Associated and Non-Associated Developing Countries in Total EC(12) Imports

Source: United Nations, COMTRADE data base.

of non-associated developing countries that had become apparent during the previous ten years was reversed during Lomé. The same tendencies are confirmed when petroleum is excluded from total EC imports.[23]

All these trade trends, which appear to indicate a *prima facie* lack of potency in EC tariff preferences, have attracted considerable attention in recent years. Numerous studies have examined the patterns of trade between the EC and the ACPs. They have uniformly come to the conclusion that the Lomé Conventions failed to have any marked impact on ACP aggregate exports. The representative interpretation of the data is that the trade preferences for ACPs contained in the Lomé Conventions may have been a necessary condition for promoting their exports to the EC, but by no means a sufficient one.[24]

Those analysts who focused on overall market shares have also concluded that the trade preferences for ACPs included in the Lomé Conventions appear to have had, by themselves, a minimal ability to sustain exports to the EC, and that the process of marginalization of ACP exports in EC markets seemingly continued through the 1970s and 1980s despite the existence of trade preferences.[25] In particular, these studies have shown that the changes in both EC shares of ACP exports and ACP shares of EC imports that occurred during the first two Lomé Conventions were statistically significant.[26]

While systematic studies of the various factors affecting the competitive position of ACP exports in EC markets are still wanting,[27] it is hardly surprising that ACP countries failed to maintain their shares of the Community's imports, not only in absolute terms, but also vis-a-vis other developing countries whose exports to the EC were not preferred to the same extent. On the one hand, the overall value of the preferences granted to the ACPs by the EC declined over time, as EC MFN tariffs on imports of primary products—and thus preference levels— were reduced as a result of trade liberalization completed under the auspices of GATT. By the mid-1970s tariff margins in favor of associated countries had already been drastically cut in products such as coffee, cocoa, vegetable oils and wood (Table 4.6). The erosion of preference margins for some of the principal exports of the associated countries was recognized early on by the EC Commission, which utilized it to argue for increments in EC aid.[28]

Table 4.6 EC MFN Tariffs on Imports and Implicit Preferences for Yaoundé Associated States (% ad valorem)

Products	EC Common External Tariff				
	1958[a]	1964	1973	1980	1986
1. Copper	—	—	—	—	—
2. Wood (not sawn)	5	—	—	—	—
3. Coffee	16	9.6	7	5	5
4. Cocoa	9	5.4	4	3	3
5. Seeds and oleaginous fruits	—	—	—	—	—
6. Bananas	20	20	20	20	20
7. Groundnut oil	18	10	10	10	10
8. Mineral ores	—	—	—	—	—
9. Cotton	—	—	—	—	—
10. Other metals	—	—	—	—	—
11. Palm oil	9	6	6	6	6
12. Wood (sawn)	—	—	—	—	—
13. Aluminum	10	10	7	6	—
14. Tin	—	—	—	—	—
15. Phosphates	—	—	—	—	—
Weighted average (1958=100)	100.0	63.4	52.2	45.7	44.5

Notes:— = zero tariff. Products are listed in order of importance, as export earners, to the associated states in 1962.

[a] In addition, zero tariff was set on imports of tea, rubber, sisal, hides and skins, gum arabic, tin, cobalt and petroleum.

Sources: B. Cousté, L'Association des Pays d'Outre-Mer, Paris, Libraries Techniques, 1959; Commission of the European Communities, Memorandum on Community Development Cooperation, Brussels, 1972, p. 276; Bulletin of the European Communities, Supplements (various issues); UNCTAD-UNDP, Market Access Conditions for Agricultural Raw Materials, Tropical and Natural Resource-Based Products of Sub-Saharan Africa, Geneva, 1987 (mimeo.).

In addition, no preferences ever applied to important exports such as copper, phosphates, cotton and particularly crude oil, whose relative importance in associated countries' exports increased substantially after 1973 as a consequence of the large increase that occurred in its relative price. An average of 50 to 60 percent of ACP exports to the Community were not given any preference because the products concerned were non-dutiable irrespective of source.[29] Another 5 to 10 percent of ACP exports to the Community were not covered by tariff preferences, being subject instead to special import regulations under the CAP.[30] For these exports, associated countries received better treatment than non-associated countries,[31] but it was still much less favorable than that afforded the EC domestic producers with which ACP producers competed in Community markets. On average, therefore, preferences for ACPs applied to only 35 to 45 percent of their exports,[32] and were heavily concentrated in tropical beverages, whose demand in the EC became increasingly saturated over time and was never very price sensitive.[33]

Exports of manufactures from the ACPs, which seemingly came to enjoy duty-free entry into the Community under Lomé, aside from constituting a tiny part of ACP exports,[34] in practice were not heavily preferred by the EC. A very large proportion of manufactures—more than 90 percent according to some estimates—had duty-free entry into the EC under MFN or GSP terms, if they satisfied the EC's rules of origin. Successive rounds of GATT-sponsored trade liberalization and the Community's GSPs granted in 1971 to almost all other developing countries, had by the mid-1970s already substantially cut the value of duty-free entry of ACP manufactures into EC markets. This is also one of the reasons why EC countries began to resort with increasing frequency to non-tariffs to protect their own markets from import competition from both industrial and developing countries. The biggest exceptions to the GSPs, and thus the area of greatest potential preference for ACP exports, were textiles and clothing exports. But here too appearances were better than reality.

The EC had first regulated imports of cotton textiles, and subsequently imports of textiles and clothing products made of both cotton and synthetic fibers, through special trade arrangements that were specifically aimed at slowing down the growth of supply from developing countries.[35] Their main regulatory instruments were import quotas that were applied by country of origin and product. ACP countries were excluded from the MFA import regimes, and thus apparently enjoyed strong preferences in the area of textiles and clothing exports, given the high MFN tariffs that the EC still levied on imports of these products,[36] and the even higher tariff equivalents of the quotas applied to imports from non-associated developing countries.

Yet, even in this area, preferences for ACP exports were largely fictitious. On the one hand, imports of textiles and clothing from ACPs were kept under permanent surveillance by the EC, to prevent trade deflection by other LDC exporters and to control the growth of export supply in ACP countries. Facultative ceilings on imports from ACPs (the "ACP line") were foreseen and acted as a powerful warning to actual or potential investors in export-oriented production of textiles and clothing in ACP countries. Later the EC acted to establish a network of intra-EC member country ceilings on overall ACP exports of "hyper-sensitive products" on a quota basis, as done for each MFA signatory.[37] The EC, therefore, never had to resort to the safeguard clause included in the Lomé Conventions. Individual members were less subtle at times. National safeguard actions were undertaken in the late 1970s against imports from ACPs (as in the case of knitwear products coming from Mauritius, against which the UK invoked the safeguard clause).

On the other hand, restrictive rules of origin imposed by the EC on all imports of manufactures coming from ACP countries contributed to the further reduction of the value of the nominal preferences that they enjoyed vis-a-vis suppliers of textiles and clothing products in other developing countries. The local content of ACP manufactured exports had to be between 50 and 60 percent of the total. Given the nature of most manufactures, which are produced from inputs supplied by specialized producers and are thus heavily dependent on intra-industry trade, and the economic size and level of industrial development of most ACP countries, these rules of origin, though cumulatively applied, constituted in themselves a powerful obstacle to EC market penetration.[38]

Aside from the stringency of the local content requirements imposed by the EC on ACP exports,[39] the ways they were applied could scarcely hide their protective content. Complementary to the tariff-jump rule, which became the basis for the definition of "sufficient working or processing" in the EC rules of origin,[40] the Community imposed lists of exceptions containing unilateral specification of the cases where a change in tariff heading did not constitute sufficient evidence of substantial transformation,[41] and of the specific transformation processes that were always considered insufficient to confer a product originating status.[42] Derogations from origin rules, moreover, could normally be granted for only two years. This made clear that they were considered to be provisional deviations from a rule that was to be applied in time. Even in the case of textiles and clothing exports, the cumulative effect of surveillance and other trade regimes applied to ACP exports and of restrictive rules of origin, discouraged non-EC investments—the only ones that could have helped ACPs to develop a local industry on the basis of market access to the Community.

But, even discounting the uncertainties regarding market access of ACP industrial products and the likely effects of uncertainty on investments in the export-oriented manufacturing of those associated countries that were subject both to special treatment by the Community and to restrictive rules of origin, the plain facts are that EC trade preferences under Lomé applied to little more than a third of ACP exports (most of which faced income inelastic import demand in the EC) and that the extent of the preferences declined over time. These basic facts go a long way in explaining why preferential treatment by the EC did not greatly encourage ACP exports to the Community.

Those analysts who, in addition to analyzing overall-market shares, examined the behavior of ACP commodity exports in detail, have concluded that trade preferences had favorable effects on only a handful of traditional exports. Commodity diversification did not occur on a significant scale even in the long term. Only at the margin, and quite recently, did ACP exports appear to have diversified a little, with certain categories of manufactures growing rapidly.

Changes in the overall commodity composition of ACP exports have occurred very slowly. In 1975–79 there was no significant change in the share of ACP exports to the EC accounted for by the top twenty-five commodities.[43] Between 1979 and 1983 the value share of ACP exports to the Community made up by the twenty-five most important export commodities actually increased slightly, indicating a *prima facie* failure by the associated countries to diversify their basic commodity export structure despite the tariff preferences that they received.[44]

ACP export trade with the EC is highly concentrated at both the country and the commodity level. The eight most important

ACPs account for about 70 percent of the group's total exports to the Community. The ten most important commodities account for nearly 80 percent of total ACP exports to the EC.[45] What happens to the export performance of a few countries and a few commodities can thus have a very large effect on overall trade trends. Nigeria, Gabon and Cameroon, which have accounted for a sizeable share of total ACP exports to the EC since the mid-1970s, for example, depend heavily on oil exports. Other key exporters such as Ivory Coast and Ghana depend to a considerable extent on coffee and cocoa exports. Zaire is largely dependent on copper. As primary commodity prices also fluctuate widely in international markets, the value shares of ACP exports, by commodity or country, may in fact largely reflect the cyclical movements of a few commodity prices or the export fortunes of a few ACPs.[46]

In the longer run trade preferences were expected to speed the development of an indigenous manufacturing capacity, oriented towards EC markets. This expectation is enshrined in the preamble of the first Lomé Convention. Yet, given the apparent lack of success that ACP countries had in developing an export-oriented industrial capacity, the question is whether too little time has passed or the incentives to develop it have been insufficient.

One body of opinion holds that expecting a substantive development of manufactured exports in ACP countries in the period since Lomé I would be unrealistic, given that many of these countries are either least developed or have small economies or both.[47] The positive development that recent studies emphasize is the growth, at the margin, of "new" export commodities, if from a low base.[48] This growth, moreover, seems to have endured over time and expanded to more commodities and countries, even though the increases in the absolute values of the new exports have not been enough to compensate for the decline in the traditional ones.

The most recent of the studies that have examined the marginal export performance of the ACP countries in manufactures indicates that in all groups of products on which analysis was focused there was evidence of rapid growth of exports to the EC by a small, but growing, number of ACP countries, some of which—like Kenya, Zimbabwe, Ivory Coast, Mauritius and Cameroon—are relatively developed, while others—like Ethiopia, Sudan and Ghana—are relatively undeveloped in terms of both per capita income and industrial structures.[49] But even for these new exports, success does not seem to have been strongly correlated with the existence of the highest preferences from the EC.

Those analysts who have examined the reasons, in addition to EC trade policies, which may explain the lackluster export performance of the ACPs in EC markets, have identified a series of supply factors affecting the competitiveness of ACP products. Incentives to produce traditional agricultural commodities and minerals—metals, for example—seem to have been insufficient in many countries, particularly during the 1970s, when changes in nominal exchange rates failed to compensate for the differential in inflation rates between the African exporters and their main competitors.[50] The share of African countries in world production and export of tropical beverages, vegetable oils and most minerals has declined rapidly since the early 1970s (Figure 4.2).

Aside from overvalued exchange rates and their disincentive effects, exports of traditional products were taxed, sometimes heavily, for revenue purposes. This constituted another powerful disincentive to production. Cocoa production in Ghana, for example, declined rapidly and smuggling became endemic. At times the oil bonanza exacerbated this trend, by contributing to overvalued exchange rates and to the decay of traditional agriculture. Nigeria is a case in point. Its entire agricultural sector has suffered heavily since the mid-1970s from the lack of incentives, and exports have nearly disappeared.

Government-controlled producer prices, export taxation and overvalued exchange rates have been credited, together with the structure of domestic protection, for the general anti-export bias that characterized the policies of many African countries during this period and thus for the lack of adequate incentives for both traditional and new exports.[51] High domestic protection of manufacturing, often in the presence of overvalued exchange rates, discriminated heavily against agriculture and led to the absorption of scarce investment resources in activities where factor productivities were relatively low. Competitiveness in manufacturing was never achieved because of limited market size, high unit costs and lack of competition. Instead of fostering domestic manufacturing, high tariff and quota protection put

Figure 4.2 Africa's Shares of World Production and Exports of Key Commodities: 1965–1988

Tea, Coffee, Cocoa

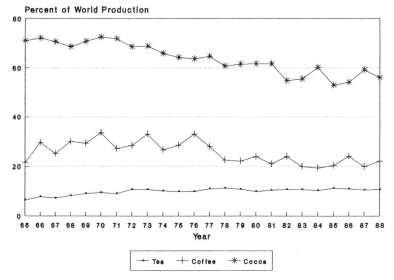

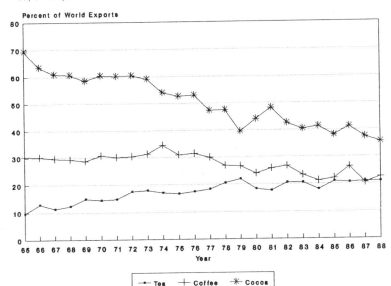
Tea, Coffee, Cocoa

Figure 4.2 *(continued)*

Iron Ore, Bauxite, Copper Ore

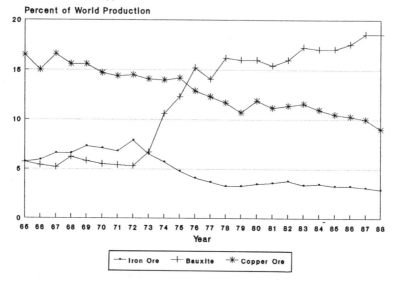

Iron Ore, Bauxite, Copper Ore

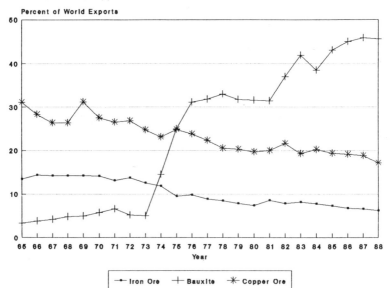

Figure 4.2 *(continued)*

Palm Oil, Groundnuts, Groundnut Oil

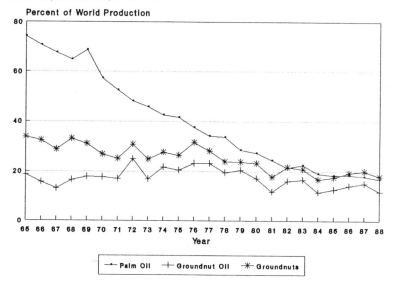

Palm Oil, Groundnut Oil, Groundnuts

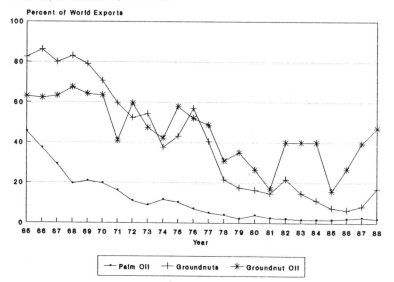

a premium on rent-seeking activities connected with both production and imports.

In these circumstances, inward-looking policies, especially in the realm of trade, would have had negative effects large enough to more than compensate for whatever preference in market access the EC was willing to grant. The "new orthodoxy" concerning the determinants of Africa's export failure in the 1970s and 1980s, stresses the importance of these factors, and thus the need for "structural" reforms, affecting the structure of the production incentives. Despite the doubts originally expressed by Development Commissioner Manuel Marin, structural adjustments has crept into Lomé IV.[52] The substantial amount of financial resources earmarked for it in the new Convention,[53] witnesses the acceptance by the EC of at least part of the orthodox diagnosis of the African failures and of the policy prescriptions that follow from it.[54]

Notes to Chapter 4

[1] The Latin American countries went as far as to consider the EC as constituting "near war on Latin American export perspectives": A.G. Mower, Jr., *The European Community and Latin America: A Case Study in Global Role Expansion*, Westport, Conn., Greenwood Press, 1982, p. 38.

[2] D. Tussie, *Less Developed Countries*, p. 2037; Hudec, *Developing Countries in the GATT Legal System*, 1987, pp. 23–55.

[3] R. Prebish, *The Economic Development of Latin America and its Principal Problems*, New York, United Nations, 1950.

[4] C. Secchi, "Protection, Internal Market Completion, and Foreign Trade Policy in the European Community", in E. Grilli and E. Sassoon, eds., *The New Protectionist Wave*, London, Macmillan, 1990, pp. 51–61; and E. Grilli, "Contemporary Protectionism in an Unstable World Economy", pp. 144–72.

[5] On the progression of the CAP, see P. van Den Noort, "The Political Realities of European Agricultural Protection", in P. Coffey and M.S. Wionczek, eds., *The European Community and Mexico*, Dordrecht, Martinus Nijhoff Publishers, 1987, p. 118.

[6] Art. 133 of the Treaty of Rome.

7 The colonies were producing many of the same tropical goods and minerals, and exporting them to their respective metropoles. The scope for complementary intra-trade was, therefore, not very large.

8 In fact the EC adopted ahead of time (in June 1964) a common external tariff on imports of a group of tropical products—fresh pineapples, desiccated coconut, unroasted coffee, tea, uncrushed pepper, vanilla, cloves, nutmeg, cocoa beans—from third countries, granting duty-free entry to the associates. This was a significant trade concession to the associates made ahead of schedule.

9 P. Robson, *Integration, Development and Equity: Economic Integration in West Africa*, London, Allen & Unwin, 1983, pp. 1-3; E. Berg, "Intra African Trade and Economic Integration", Vol. 1, Alexandria, Va., E. Berg Associates, 1985 (mimeo.), pp. 291-309; and more recently R. Langhammer and U. Hiemenz, *Regional Integration Among Developing Countries: Opportunities, Obstacles and Options*, Tubingen, J.C.B. Mohr, 1990, pp. 34-51 and 59-72.

10 Commission, "Community Development Cooperation Policy", 1971, pp. 26-27.

11 See article I of the Trade and Cooperation Title of Lomé I, repeated virtually unchanged in all the subsequent conventions.

12 Only the trade concessions to the Maghreb and Mashreq countries, granted in the context of the Cooperation Agreements signed in 1976-77, can be considered as somewhat comparable to them. See Chapter 5 for details.

13 Mediterranean countries were granted similar privileges as far as exports of industrial goods to the Community. In the case of textiles, however, the Community subsequently imposed quantitative limitations on imports from Mediterranean countries in evident violation of the letter of the cooperation agreements with these countries.

14 P. Mishalani, A. Robert, C. Stevens and A. Weston, "The Pyramid of Privilege", in C. Stevens, *EEC and the Third World: A Survey 1*, New York, Holmes & Meier Publishers, 1981, pp. 60-82.

15 See, for example, Galtung, *European Community: A Superpower*, p. 77.

16 In 1958 French tariffs on imports of foodstuffs, beverages and tobacco ranged between 20 and 25 percent *ad valorem*. Corresponding tariffs were around 10 percent in the Benelux countries and 15 percent in Germany. Tariffs on the imports of raw materials were 5-7 percent in France, 6 percent in the Benelux countries, 3-4 percent in Germany and zero in Italy.

17 The weighted average of French tariffs applicable to exports of French West Africa and French Equatorial Africa in 1957 was 8.1 percent. The corresponding EC tariff average in mid-1964, i.e. at the entry into force of the first Yaoundé Convention, was 4.8 percent. By then, moreover, large differentials between the original French tariffs on imports from outside the French area and the CET applicable to non-associates had materialised on specific items. The tariff preference enjoyed on coffee by former French colonies in the EC was about 10 percent, against an original preference in France's market of 20 percent. In the case of cocoa beans and processed wood, EC tariff preference was 5 percent and 10 percent respectively, as against 25 percent and 15 percent in the French market in 1957. Preference on unprocessed wood, which was at 10 percent in France in 1957 had disappeared in the EC market by 1964. See R. Lawrence, "Primary Products, Preferences and Economic Welfare: The EC and Africa", in P. Kennen and R. Lawrence, eds., *The Open Economy*, New York, Columbia University Press, 1968, p. 366; and Commission des Communautés Européennes, *Evolution du Regimé Douanier, Fiscal et Contingentaire des Principaux Produits Tropicaux Importés dans les Etats Membres de la Communauté Economique Européenne de 1958 à 1968*, Brussels, 1968.

18 Ouattara, "Trade Effects", pp. 508–10.

19 Several developing countries, including Brazil, Chile, the Dominican Republic, India, Pakistan voiced complaints inside GATT in 1958 about the possible trade diverting effects of the association of African colonies to the EC foreseen under the Treaty of Rome: Jensen and Walter, *Common Market: Economic Integration in Europe*, p. 120. The same concern about trade diversion was strongly voiced by a Panel of Experts assembled by GATT in 1958 to study the evolution of international trade and emerging trade policies. See General Agreement on Tariffs and Trade (GATT), *Trends in International Trade, A Report by a Panel of Experts*, Geneva, 1958, pp. 119–23.

20 Young, "Association with the EC", pp. 120–35.

21 Lawrence, "Primary Products, Preferences and Economic Welfare", pp. 240–60.

22 Ouattara, "Trade Effects", pp. 521–9.

23 J. Moss and J. Ravenhill, "The Evolution of Trade under the Lomé Conventions: The First Ten Years", in C. Stevens and J.V. van Themaat, eds., *Europe and the International Division of Labour*, London, Hodder and Stoughton, 1987, p. 113.

24 C. Cosgrove Twitchett, "Patterns of ACP/EC Trade", in F. Long,

ed., *The Political Economy of EC Relations with Africa, Caribbean and Pacific States*, Oxford, Pergamon Press, 1980, p. 171.

25 J. Moss and J. Ravenhill, "Trade Developments During the First Lomé Convention", *World Development*, Vol. 10, No. 10, October 1982, pp. 841–56; Moss and Ravenhill, "The Evolution of Trade", pp. 109–32.

26 This conclusion is based on non-parametric statistical tests used to evaluate the significance of the changes in the market shares across sample periods, before and after the entry into effect of Lomé. The conclusion applies to most ACP subgroups (newly preferred, previously associated, oil exporting and non-oil exporting).

27 One notable exception is the constant-market-share analysis of ACP exports performed by Jepma, which shows that both the small share of crude oil and manufactures in the exports of associated countries (the commodity effect) and the large share of the former metropoles in the geographical destination of associates' exports (the market effect) had a negative impact on their growth. Moreover, analysis of the competitive residual showed that by the beginning of the 1970s the positive effects of EC tariff advantages on associates' export growth had disappeared, and that competitiveness was falling behind that of comparator countries (the rest of the developing countries). See C. Jepma, "An Application of the Constant Market Share Technique on Trade Between the African and Malagasy States and the European Community: 1958–1978", *Journal of Common Market Studies*, Vol. 20, No. 2, 1981, pp. 175–82.

28 Commission, "Community Development Cooperation Policy", 1971, pp. 11 and 28.

29 J.P. Agarwal, M. Dippl and R.J. Langhammer, *EC Trade Policies Towards Associated Developing Countries: Barriers to Success*, Tubingen, Mohr, 1985, pp. 16–17. This report, also known as the Kiel Study, from the name of the institute with which the authors were affiliated—the Institut fur Weltwirtschaft an der Universitat Kiel—was commissioned by the EC.

30 It should be noted that the share of ACP exports to the EC covered by variable levies and other restrictions as a result of the CAP is constrained by the very existence of these access barriers (the share is small, in other words, because the restrictions applied to imports of these products into the Community are very strong) and thus does not constitute an indicative measure of the area of impact of the CAP and ACP exports.

31 Import duties were generally reduced or eliminated, even though other trade restrictions remained in effect.

[32] From the mid-1970s to the early 1980s, given the high prices of crude oil and the consequent increase in the share of ACP exports in this non-dutiable export, EC preferences covered only about 35 percent of ACP exports.

[33] One could argue here that the relevant price elasticity was that faced by the ACP countries, and not the overall one. But many ACP suppliers of tropical products, for example, were large enough to face less than infinitely elastic import demands with respect to prices (Ghana for cocoa, Ivory Coast for coffee, etc.). In addition some products such as coffee are not totally homogeneous (e.g. arabica vs. robusta coffees) and their demand can be somewhat differentiated by source.

[34] In practice, they amounted to exports of textiles and some clothing from Ivory Coast, Mauritius and Madagascar.

[35] For a review of the main features and effects on developing countries of the MFAs, see D. Keesing and M. Wolf, *Textile Quotas Against Developing Countries*, London, Trade Policy Research Center, 1980; and V.K. Aggarwal, *Liberal Protectionism*, Berkeley, University of California Press, 1985. Recent analyses of the MFAs can be found in W.R. Cline, *The Future of World Trade in Textiles and Apparel*, Washington D.C., Institute for International Economics, 1987; E. Grilli and E. Sassoon, eds., *The New Protectionist Wave*, London, Macmillan, 1990; C. Hamilton, ed., *Developing Countries and the Multifiber Arrangements*, Washington D.C., World Bank, 1990.

[36] The average tariff rate charged by the main industrial countries on imports of textiles and clothing after the Tokyo Round is still three times higher than that on manufactured goods as a whole: 17.9 percent, against 6.3 percent. See General Agreement on Tariffs and Trade (GATT), *The Tokyo Round of Multilateral Trade Negotiations*, Geneva, 1980, p. 38; J. Goto, "The Multifiber Arrangement and its Effects on Developing Countries", *The World Bank Research Observer*, Vol. 4, No. 2, July 1990, pp. 207-8.

[37] Agarwal et al., *EC Trade Policies*, p. 21.

[38] The cumulation rule, introduced in the first Lomé Convention, meant that inputs from any of the ACP states were considered as coming from the specific ACP country that was supplying the finished product for the purpose of weighing its local content. Another rule applied in this general area was the so-called cumulation of donor country content: inputs originating from the Community could also be counted as local content by the producing ACP. See, for example, art. 1 of Protocol No. 1 attached to the first Lomé Convention.

39 See, for example, the analysis of M. McQueen, "Lomé and the Protective Effect of Rules of Origin", *Journal of World Trade Law*, Vol. 16, No. 2, March–April 1982, pp. 124-7.

40 See art. 3 of Protocol No. 1 of the first Lomé Convention.

41 List A, in text of Lomé Convention.

42 List B, in text of Lomé Convention.

43 C. Stevens and A. Weston, "Trade Diversification: Has Lomé Helped?", in C. Stevens, ed., *EC and the Third World: A Survey 4— Renegotiating Lomé*, New York, Holmes and Meier, 1984, p. 29.

44 C. Stevens, "The Impact of EC Preferential Trade Policies", Background Paper, Washington D.C., The World Bank, 1986 (mimeo.), p. 12.

45 C. Stevens, "Obstructions to the Development of Trade Between the ACP and the EC", Paper Presented to the NIEO-Lomé Symposium, Amsterdam, 1988 (mimeo.), p. 3.

46 Stevens, "Obstructions to Development of Trade", p. 3.

47 Stevens, "Impact of EC Preferential Trade Policies", p. 13.

48 Stevens and Weston, "Trade Diversification", pp. 30-6; M. McQueen and R. Read, "Prospects for ACP Exports to the Enlarged Community", in C. Stevens and J.V. van Themaat, eds., *Europe and the International Division of Labour*, London, Hodder and Stoughton, 1986, pp. 89-91.

49 M. McQueen and C. Stevens, "Trade Preferences and Lomé IV: Non-Traditional ACP Exports to the EC", *Development Policy Review*, Vol. 7, 1989, p. 255.

50 Real exchange rates in most African countries appreciated, thus diminishing the incentive to produce tradeable primary commodities.

51 World Bank, *Accelerated Development in Sub-Saharan Africa: An Agenda for Action*, Washington D.C., 1981, pp. 24-30; B. Balassa, *Incentive Policies and Agricultural Performance in Sub-Saharan Africa*, PPR Working Paper No. 77, Washington D.C., The World Bank, 1988; and Agarwal et al., *EC Trade Policies*, pp. 60-96.

5

The Southern Policies of the EC: Keeping the Mediterranean Safe for Europe

Extending associationism to the Mediterranean region appeared to be a natural move for the European Community in the late 1950s and 1960s. The countries of this region were heavily dependent on trade with the EC, and thus interested in maintaining access to European markets. Europe had always had strong historical and cultural links with North Africa. Important political relationships between individual EC members and countries in the region, many of them colonial or quasi-colonial in origin and nature, were still in place. France had special links with the Maghreb countries—Algeria, Tunisia and Morocco, plus Syria and Lebanon. Italy had maintained a close relationship with its former colony, Libya, in addition to having traditionally strong ties with Malta and Tunisia. Germany was developing a solid rapport with Turkey.

The Mediterranean area, moreover, still represented an important outlet for EC exports. Nearly 8 percent of EC exports went to the Maghreb and Mashreq, another 2.5 percent to Greece and Turkey, and 4 percent to Spain and Portugal. Altogether, the region accounted for nearly 15 percent of all extra-EC(9) exports in 1960. The region was, in addition, strategically important for Europe. Much of the petroleum consumed in Europe came either from North Africa or the Middle East. The Suez Canal had been perceived to be important enough for at least two major European countries to react militarily to its takeover by Egypt in 1956. Defending the Mediterranean Sea from Soviet military threats, felt in those years to be all encompassing, required the amity, and possibly the active support, of the coastal states of North Africa.

Yet, associations between the Community and the Mediterranean countries outside it did not flourish. The EC long remained unable to even follow a coherent policy vis-a-vis this important neighboring area. This was not for want of trying. The Community attempted several approaches towards the Mediterranean, and is still trying to find a balance between outright integration and "special" ties with the non-European countries of the region.

The first phase of the "Mediterranean policy" of the EC was characterized by a case-by-case approach towards the countries of the region that led to the establishment of a variety of bilateral arrangements (Table 5.1). They ranged from unlimited association under art. 238 of the Treaty of Rome with Greece (1961) and Turkey (1963) foreshadowing membership in the Community; to limited associations such as those with Tunisia (1969), Morocco (1969), Malta (1970) and Cyprus (1972); to non-preferential trade agreements with countries such as Israel (1964), Lebanon (1965) and Yugoslavia (1970); to arrangements involving unilateral trade concessions such as those with Spain (1970) and Egypt (1972); or reciprocal concessions like the second agreement with Israel (1970).[1] Most of these agreements, however, looked like temporary, if not extemporaneous, responses to local trade problems.

But all had not been smooth sailing even to get to that point. In order to arrive at the 1970 agreements with Israel and Spain, for instance, the "orange policy" question had to be settled in a way that would satisfy the Italian citrus producers and protect their economic interests. The compromise reached involved the imposition of minimum import prices and the concession of graduated preferences to Mediterranean suppliers, with Greece at the top of this pyramid, Morocco and Tunisia in the middle, and Spain and Israel at the bottom, but still enjoying a substantial tariff privilege with respect to non-preferred countries.[2] Official rhetoric notwithstanding, nobody seemed very happy with this proliferation of agreements. To some it appeared that the Commission and the Council had proceeded in an outright "disorderly fashion".[3] To others, the mosaic of arrangements reached seemed to be at the border between pragmatism and arbitrariness.[4] Rather widespread was the perception that EC policy towards the Mediterranean was "accidental" at best.[5]

Table 5.1 Agreements between the EC and Mediterranean Countries

	Special Association Agreements Under Art. 238, with:	Trade Agreements Under Art. 113 and Art. 114, with:	
1st Phase of Mediterranean policy	Greece** (1961) Turkey** (1963)[a] Tunisia* (1969) Morocco* (1969) Malta* (1970) Cyprus* (1972)	*Preferential* Spain* (1970) Israel II* (1970) Lebanon II* (1972)[b] Egypt I* (1972) Portugal* (1972)	*Non-Preferential* Israel I* (1964) Lebanon I* (1965) Yugoslavia I* (1970)[c]
	Cooperation Agreements Under Art. 238, with:		
2nd Phase of Mediterranean policy	Israel III** (1975) Algeria** (1976) Morocco** (1976) Tunisia** (1976) Egypt II** (1977) Lebanon III** (1977) Jordan** (1977) Syria** (1977) Yugoslavia III** (1980)		

Notes: Dates of signature in parentheses. * means agreement of limited duration.
** means agreement of unlimited duration.
[a] An additional protocol defining the rules for achieving a customs union and developing economic cooperation was signed in 1980.
[b] This agreement never entered into effect.   [c] Renewed in 1973.
Sources: J. Loeffe, "La Communanté Elargie et l'Espace Mediterranéen", in H. Brugmans et al., eds., *La Politique Economic Extérieure de la Communauté Européenne Elargie*, Bruges De Tempel, 1973; K. Featherstone, "The Mediterranean Challenge: Cohesion and External Preferences", in J. Lodge, ed., *The European Community and the Challenge of the Future*, New York, St. Martin's Press, 1989; European Communities, *General Reports of the Activities of the EC* (annual), Brussels (various issues).

Particularly difficult to explain was how eleven years could have passed before special relations with Maghreb countries began to take concrete shape. At the time of the establishment of the Treaty of Rome, in a Joint Declaration of Intent, the EC member states had solemnly promised that in order to "maintain and intensify [their] traditional trade flows and to contribute to the social and economic development" of Tunisia and Morocco (then members of the "franc area"), conventions of economic association would be quickly negotiated with them.[6] But the association agreements concluded in 1969 only began to specify the content of the special relationship with these two countries of the Southern Mediterranean that were closest to Europe from the standpoint of history, geography and trade.

As a reason for this delay, one could consider with some benevolence the difficulties faced by the EC partners in liberalizing trade among themselves in the initial phase of the common market. Yet, the delay also clearly reflected the difficulty in reconciling the interests of the agricultural producers of the Community with those of the Southern Mediterranean.[7] In the field of agriculture, for example, none of the complementarities that existed between the Community and the Yaoundé countries applied to the Maghreb. Quite to the contrary, the basic relationship between the producers of the Maghreb and those of France and Italy (and subsequently Spain) was one of competition. In producing olive oil, wine, oranges and the like—crops originally developed by European settlers—the farmers of the Maghreb had often appreciable comparative advantages over their counterparts in Southern Europe. Protection of the interests of the latter was therefore incompatible, in principle, with the concession of preferences to the exports of the former.

Seen in the light of the Community's agricultural interests, the economic content of the association agreements of 1969 with Morocco and Tunisia (Algeria did not show much interest in following suit under the same conditions) becomes more understandable. The agreements ensured that almost all of the industrial exports from the two countries could freely enter EC markets, but extended only some tariff privileges to a limited number of their agricultural exports.[8] This was in some ways the Yaoundé trade model (without reciprocity), but adapted to a situation where the overlap of agricultural exports from the associated developing countries and domestic EC producers was extensive, instead of marginal.

At the same time, the initial posture that the Community took vis-a-vis the possible association of the Northern Mediterranean countries cannot be easily ascribed to economic or commercial considerations. The special association agreements reached early on with Greece and Turkey, aside from being of unlimited duration, were much more generous in content and forward looking in perspective. In the case of Greece, the agreement foresaw the establishment of a customs union with the Community, over a 22-year period, during which respective trade policies could be harmonized, as well as a host of joint institutions to administer the relationship that was being built. The agreement with Turkey, which followed suit, provided for a longer transition period and fewer joint institutions, but was set with the same ultimate goal of membership in mind. Greece and Turkey were not only European countries, but also political allies in the North Atlantic Treaty Organization (NATO), and yet at odds with one another over Cyprus and other matters. They had to be kept in the Western alliance and at peace with each other. In dealing generously with both Greece and Turkey from the economic point of view, the Community countries were shouldering part of their collective political responsibilities as members of the Western alliance.

Confirmation of the strength of the political dimension in the relations between the Community and the nations of the Northern Mediterranean can easily be found in the response to the 1967 military coup in Greece. Unwilling to accept as a close partner a military government set to stay in power for an indefinite period, the EC member countries "froze" the implementation of the association agreement with Greece beyond "current administration". The importance of political objectives can be seen again in the generous response of the Community to the requests of the democratic governments of Greece after the fall of the military from power in 1974.[9] It can also be found in the way the Community responded to the request for association by Spain in the early 1960s. Establishment of relations with Spain, beyond what was strictly needed at the commercial level, was postponed until the end of the Franco regime.[10] A manifestation of the same tendency occurred again in December 1980. When Turkey's civilian government was overthrown, the association agreement that had just been revitalized by the EC Council was put on hold. As in the case of Greece, financial assistance to Turkey was suspended and only the trade provisions of the agreements were maintained.[11]

The "Global" Approach Towards the Mediterranean

The second phase of the Mediterranean policy of the EC began in the early 1970s. The Heads of States and Governments of the member states formally signaled the change in strategy at the end of their October 1972 summit in Paris. They underscored in their final communique that the Community "attached essential importance to the fulfillment of its obligations towards the countries of the Mediterranean basin with which agreements had been or will be concluded, agreements which should be the subject of a global and balanced approach". The Foreign Ministers of the Community reiterated this objective in Copenhagen in December 1973, after the membership agreements with Great Britain, Ireland and Denmark had been signed, by declaring that "the EC will implement its undertakings towards the Mediterranean . . . in order to reinforce its long-standing links with these countries", and added that "the nine intend to preserve their historical links with the countries of the Middle East and cooperate over the establishment and maintenance of peace, stability and progress in the region".[12]

If "global" was not an entirely precise characterization, this new approach, as observed by Maurice Roy, could at least be differentiated from the previous one on two accounts. First, it was aimed at establishing a new coherence in the relations between the Community and all the Mediterranean countries, loosely defined so as to include among them those such as Jordan and Portugal which did not have shores on the Mediterranean Sea. This search represented, if not a total repudiation of the case-by-case approach followed until then, at least an appreciation of the need to treat the countries in the area in a more systematic and appropriate fashion than in the past. Second, the new agreements to be established were to include more than trade. They were to be extended to the social and financial spheres as well, enlarging the scope of development cooperation between the Community and its southern neighbors.[13]

Surely there was more to the declarations of intent of the EC Heads of States than met the eye. Dissatisfaction with the patchwork of agreements reached in the 1960s was widespread, as indicated by the Rossi Report to the European Parliament,[14] by the 1971 Commission memorandum on development policy,[15] and by numerous public pronouncements of high Commission officials.[16] Several bilateral agreements were due to be renegotiated soon. The first (northern) enlargement of the Community remained on the agenda, and was becoming progressively more likely. New international trade negotiations within the GATT framework (the Tokyo Round) were looming on the horizon.[17] Producers of strategic commodities, such as petroleum, were becoming more assertive in their claims over the "control" of natural resources, and traditional sea routes appeared to be much less secure than before, as Soviet naval presence in the Mediterranean was progressively increasing. Economic conditions in Europe continued to be good. Output was expanding rapidly and near full employment conditions prevailed in the Community.[18] It was, therefore, a favorable time for the Community to pay greater and more systematic attention to the Mediterranean basin.

The idea of a new approach had just not spontaneously emerged at the 1972 Summit. The Commission had clearly identified the critical importance of the Mediterranean area to the Community and called its development "a natural extension of European integration".[19] The Commission, moreover, had been given the task of preparing a plan for a "global policy", which it completed in September 1972. This followed a proposal by the French government to consider the establishment of a free-trade area with all the Mediterranean countries.[20]

The articulation of a "global approach" towards the area was being based for the first time on clear and explicit premises. Proximity, similarity of climatic and ecological conditions—and thus of agricultural productions—with Southern Europe, reciprocal interests in the areas of energy and labor supply, and the role of bridge between the Community and Africa played by the Maghreb and Mashreq countries, were among the reasons cited for priority interest in the Mediterranean area.[21]

In recognition of the economic status of the countries of the region, of the need not to increase their "dependence" on the Community, and in order to make the new arrangements compatible with GATT rules, trade relations were to be based on reciprocity, though reverse preferences from the Mediterranean countries to the Community could be graduated in time and extent to reflect the differences in levels of development of the various countries. The Community would phase out its import duties on industrial products by 1977 and liberalize its import regime on agricultural products as well. The objective was to extend concessions covering at least 80 percent of the agricultural products exported by each Mediterranean country to the Community,[22] and thus establish the basis for the creation of a free-trade area with these countries. Financial and technical cooperation between the Community and Mediterranean countries was also foreseen. In practice, this meant the extension of EC aid to them.

In addition to being based for the first time on clear premises, the Commission's proposals established an explicit ranking of the countries of the region, thus clarifying the ambit of application of articles 237 and 238 of the Treaty of Rome. There were non-European countries that could never aspire to membership in the Community—the majority in the region. There were European countries that could join at the expiration of existing agreements—such as Greece and Turkey. There were, finally, European countries that could conceivably join at a future date and under certain conditions, but whose membership path was not yet clear—such as Spain and Portugal. The global approach was meant to cover the first and third group of countries. Excluded were, naturally, those Southern European countries that were already tied to the Community by association agreements.

Misgivings inside the Council of Ministers concerning the extent of tariff concessions on agricultural imports and Community aid to the countries of the region, doubts about the wisdom of requiring trade reciprocity from all Mediterranean countries expressed by the British government,[23] and pressures from the United States government, which feared that trade preferences between Mediterranean countries and the EC would be directed against US interests, led to a substantial modification of the Community's plans, and, in substance, to the adoption of a graduated approach, beginning with the Maghreb countries, Spain, Israel and Malta.[24] Instead of being "global", at least in a geographical sense, the approach followed became simply an "overall" one.

As not even this modified global approach proved to be feasible, negotiations between the Community and the most important countries of the Southern Mediterranean became bilateral. Individual, if virtually identical, cooperation agreements were signed with three Maghreb countries in 1976—Morocco, Algeria and Tunisia—and with four Mashreq countries—Egypt, Jordan, Syria and Lebanon—in 1977.[25] When EC Development Commissioner Cheysson, in trying to put the best possible face on the rather meager results of efforts started with some fanfare by the Commission several years earlier, declared that "the policy that we are developing in the Mediterranean is the policy of Lomé", such a claim could not but sound hollow.[26]

The Mediterranean policy of the EC as it was being shaped in the mid-1970s was neither the twin of Lomé, and thus part of the "new model in North–South Cooperation" that the Community was claiming to have started, nor the "unplanned accident" that some of its sharpest critics called it. It was part of an evolving response to a long standing challenge that the Community was trying to face a little more coherently than in the past, without being quite able to systematize it.

The cooperation agreements reached with the Maghreb and the Mashreq countries after protracted and at time bitter negotiations were not only strictly bilateral (at the express request of the Mediterranean signatories intent on refusing even the symbolism of the Yaoundé and Lomé associations), but also failed to create the free-trade area earlier envisaged by the Commission as the pillar of the "global" approach of the Community. From the standpoint of the unilateral trade and aid privileges that they granted to the partners, the agreements fell short of matching those extended by the Community to the Lomé countries of Africa, the Caribbean and the Pacific. The level of cooperation established by the new set of agreements thus failed in many ways to meet the expectations of both the Southern Mediterranean countries and the Commission. The agreements placed the countries of the region at a level clearly lower than the ACP countries in the "pyramid of privileges" being constructed by the Community and they advanced by only a modest amount the goal of creating a free-trade area between the Community and its Southern Mediterranean neighbors.

Several factors had contributed to this outcome. The countries of the Southern Mediterranean, emboldened by the vision of "commodity power" in the roaring years of OPEC, and embittered by the results of the Yom Kippur war, wanted both formal respect and new tangible concessions from the Community. The Community, having changed its mind since the earlier phases of the "global" approach about the goals it wished to pursue, was weakly placed in the mid-1970s to offer both respect and substantive concessions to its southern neighbors. Powerful new realities seemed to have emerged and, as the negotiations with the countries of the Mediterranean region dragged on, they counseled a cautious attitude. A Euro-Arab dialogue, much more political in nature and potentially divisive in content, had begun with the purpose of establishing better relations with the major petroleum producers. Apart from Algeria, the other Southern Mediterranean countries were only marginal interlocutors in this new dialogue. The Community felt threatened by developing countries that suddenly demanded, as commodity suppliers, a redress of past economic torts that it was in no position to offer. By the time the new agreements were taking concrete shape the Community found itself again reacting to changes in external circumstances more than following carefully laid plans. Opting for temporary solutions, and waiting for the time when "the priorities of the dominant partner"[27] could be brought to bear, became in a way almost a natural response.

Even the inclusion in the new agreement of provisions concerning the supply of technical and financial aid by the Community, with the consequent extension of the earlier arrangements to new areas of economic cooperation, and the establishment of an *ad hoc* institutional setup for each agreement, somewhat following the Yaoundé and Lomé models, hardly constituted the breaking of new ground. The development cooperation agreements reached with the Mediterranean countries in the second part of the 1970s looked in the end like a faded copy of existing models. They seemed to reflect more the minimum price that the Community was willing to pay to offer something acceptable to its southern counterparts at that stage, than the innovation that it originally wanted to bring about in its relations with Mediterranean nations.[28]

Apart from the Yom Kippur war, the OAPEC embargo, the demonstration effect of OPEC and the related rhetoric of commodity power, there were other factors, such as the first enlargement of the Community in 1975 (and the consequent extension of the Yaoundé framework to the former British colonies of Africa, the Caribbean and the Pacific) and the membership application of Greece in 1975, that presented the Community with pressing challenges. The death of Franco in 1975 and the Portuguese revolution of the previous year had suddenly brought forward the prospect of a second (southern) enlargement of the Community.[29] What had begun for most EC members as a decade of consolidation and progress turned into a period of rapid change and formidable internal and external problems.

In addition, the prosperity of the 1960s and early 1970s had given way first to economic recession and subsequently to a difficult and uncertain phase of internal structural adjustment to higher oil prices. Economic difficulties and pessimism over the economic future of the Community became widespread. Reshaping the Mediterranean policy of the Community could hardly remain a strong priority in most EC capitals. The Commission was left to fend for itself, instructed, no doubt, to accept the lightest possible economic burden in order to bring the matter to a satisfactory conclusion.

The result was another set of differentiated responses, depending on Community interests and objectives, and to some extent on differences in partner country situations. For countries such as Greece and Turkey, the EC continued its policies of association, with membership in view, and extended this approach to Malta and Cyprus. For Maghreb and Mashreq countries, existing trade agreements were upgraded to cooperation agreements involving technical and financial aid. This approach was eventually extended to Yugoslavia. In the case of Spain and Portugal, as soon as political obstacles to membership subsided, integration into the Community was vigorously pursued. Alfred Tovias was broadly correct when he characterized the Community's approach to the

Mediterranean region not as global but simply as "common" to various groups of Mediterranean countries.[30]

Cooperation Agreements with the Maghreb and the Mashreq

If it was relatively easy for the Commission to argue, in principle, for closer relations with the Maghreb and Mashreq countries on the basis of their growing political, economic and strategic importance to Europe in the 1970s, defining the actual content of even a "common" approach to them was neither simple nor straightforward. The main obstacle was the so-called "organization of the Mediterranean agricultural space", a euphemism for the reconciliation of the agricultural interests of the Southern Mediterranean developing countries with those of the more developed countries to the north. Among the latter were the prospective members of the Community—Spain, Turkey, Greece and Portugal—as well as established members such as France and Italy. If such a reconciliation had proven to be difficult in the previous decade when membership in the Community was fixed, achieving it at a time when membership was becoming variable, in the face of both northern and southern enlargements, was an even more daunting task.

The Mediterranean area, moreover, despite the obvious similarities in agricultural production and exports, exhibited strong internal differences. The EC plan to treat the countries in the region as a whole was never strictly defined. Breaking the group down into relatively more homogeneous subgroups represented, at least conceptually, a more sensible approach. In the countries of the Northern Mediterranean, for example, industrialization was more extensive than in those of the southern part. In many of the northern countries it was also progressing more rapidly, under outward-oriented policies, than in most of the Maghreb. The exceptions inside the two subgroups were Turkey and Tunisia respectively (Table 5.2). Consequently the northern countries were relatively more interested in extending trade concessions to manufactures, while the southern countries tended to be more attentive to their agricultural interests when dealing with the Community.[31]

Table 5.2 Structure of Production and Exports of Mediterranean Countries

| | Production (% shares in GDP) | | | | | | Exports (% shares in total exports) | | | | | | | | |
| | Agriculture | | | Industry | | | Fuels, Minerals, Metals | | | Agricultural Products | | | Manufactures | | |
	1965	1973	1986	1965	1973	1986	1965	1973	1986	1965	1973	1986	1965	1973	1986
Southern Mediterranean															
Morocco	30	24	21	25	27	30	40	28	21	55	57	29	5	15	50
Algeria	15	8	12	34	43	44	58	84	96	38	13	1	4	3	3
Tunisia	22	20	16	24	27	33	31	43	19	51	35	17	18	20	64
Egypt	29	31	20	27	28	29	8	10	64	72	64	10	20	26	26
Jordan	23	14	8	17	21	28	27	24	43	54	34	10	19	42	47
Lebanon	12	10	n.a.	21	23	n.a.	14	4	n.a.	52	36	n.a.	34	60	n.a.
Syria	29	17	22	20	23	21	7	24	50	83	60	25	10	16	25
Israel	8	6	10	36	38	42	6	2	2	28	19	13	66	79	85
Northern Mediterranean															
Cyprus	20	14	8	27	29	29	40	17	8	59	62	32	1	21	60
Malta	8	7	5	30	35	39	7	2	1	30	18	5	63	80	94
Greece	24	20	17	26	31	29	8	24	15	78	39	30	17	37	55
Turkey	34	27	18	25	31	36	9	8	6	89	75	30	2	17	64
Yugoslavia	23	18	12	42	45	42	11	12	9	33	24	13	57	64	78
Spain	18	13	6	36	36	37	9	7	7	51	31	20	40	62	73
Portugal	21	15	10	41	45	42	4	3	4	34	28	16	62	69	80

Note: n.a. means not available.
Sources: World Bank, *World Tables*, Washington D.C., 1983 and 1987; World Bank, *World Development Report*, Washington D.C., 1990.

Among the more undeveloped and agriculturally oriented countries of the Southern Mediterranean, an important subdivision from the standpoint of resource endowments was between those that had petroleum—Algeria, Libya and Tunisia—and those that did not—Morocco, Egypt, Lebanon (and to some extent Syria).[32] The former faced less of a foreign exchange constraint than the latter in pursuing industrialization and modernization objectives. Development of oil exports also affected, both directly and indirectly, the political leanings of many of the countries of the region, with oil exporting countries taking more radical political postures at the international level than non-oil exporters. For the latter, interdependence with Europe was more of an unchangeable economic reality and collaboration with the EC more of a necessity.

In addition, development policies also varied a good deal among the Southern Mediterranean countries, particularly with respect to the restructuring of agriculture and the fostering of industrialization.[33] Algeria and Tunisia, for example, experimented extensively with cooperative forms of agricultural ownership, while Morocco maintained private ownership in agriculture. Industrialization was pursued more decisively, and through more massive state intervention, in Algeria and Egypt than in Morocco. Egypt remained strongly state-oriented in its development policies, particularly those concerning industry and trade. In all these countries industrialization strategies long remained resource-based and import-substituting. Only Tunisia, which had followed the Algerian model in the initial stages, shifted relatively early to a more export-oriented, private capital-based industrial strategy. The external trade policies actually followed were also quite different across the countries of this region. When the dynamics of the various country situations were taken into account, even following a "common" approach vis-a-vis country groups seemed difficult for the Community during the 1970s. And difficult it turned out to be.

When cooperation agreements were finally reached with the Maghreb countries in 1976 and the Mashreq countries in 1977, they appeared to be aimed at the same broad objectives of furthering the development of production capacity and developing the infrastructure of the partner countries and they were very similar to one another in structure and specific content. More specifically, all the agreements sought to promote the participation of the Community in the industrialization of the partner countries, the modernization of their agricultural sectors and the assistance of the Community in the marketing and promotion of their exports.[34]

The agreements all included a part dealing with trade preferences granted by the EC to the agricultural and industrial exports of the various Southern Mediterranean countries (with minor differences from country to country depending on individual export structures) and a part dealing with "economic, technical and financial cooperation" between the partner and the Community. This part specified, *inter alia*, the typology and volume of aid to be extended by the Community and financed through its budget. The various agreements had identical institutional structures: a Cooperation Council and a Cooperation Committee composed of representatives of the two parties and charged with the administration of the agreements. Cooperation Committees were explicitly mandated by the agreements between the EC and the Maghreb countries and left optional in those with the Mashreq countries.[35]

In the area of trade, the agreements formally recognized the goal of reciprocity of relations between the Maghreb and Mashreq countries and the Community, but left the actual implementation of the principle open in time and conditional to the "essential development requirements" of the partner countries. The partners only undertook a formal obligation to extend MFN treatment to EC member country exports.[36] In practice, the EC was again making unilateral trade concessions to these countries. More specifically, nearly all exports of industrial products originating in the Southern Mediterranean partners were granted free access to the Community.[37]

Agricultural exports from partner countries not covered by the CAP were also given unrestricted entry into the EC. Those covered by the CAP and of importance to Maghreb and Mashreq countries (e.g. meats, fish, vegetables, fresh fruits, fruit juices, prepared fish, vegetables and fruits, wine, olive oil) were instead granted tariff preferences ranging from 20 to 100 percent.[38] The tariff preferences were, in a rough way, inversely proportional to the self-sufficiency ratios prevailing in the Community as a result of the CAP.[39]

Imports of agricultural products judged to be "sensitive" by the Community were, in addition, subject to other protective measures. First, the reference prices set by the CAP were to be respected by Southern Mediterranean exporters for products such as fruits and legumes. Second, tariff preferences on some products—such as wine and rice—were limited to specified amounts. Third, tariff preferences on products such as fresh fruit and legumes were limited to off-season imports. Fourth, in case of serious disturbances in its internal market (i.e. excess supply), the Community could resort to the safeguard clause.[40] Fifth, the Community explicitly reserved the right to pursue anti-dumping and anti-subsidy actions under article VI of GATT, including the right to take unilateral precautionary measures in exceptional circumstances.[41]

In the area of technical and financial cooperation, the EC undertook the general obligation to participate in the financing of initiatives that would contribute to the economic and social development of the Southern Mediterranean partners. More specifically, the Community agreed to finance capital projects in the fields of production and infrastructure, technical cooperation—as a preliminary or a complement to capital projects drawn by the partners—and training projects. Financial assistance volumes were specified on a country-by-country basis for the periods of validity of the related protocols and broken down into two main components: budgetary contributions and European Investment Bank loans. EC budgetary contributions were in turn subdivided into grants and special loans. Grants were to go towards the financing of projects without direct financial returns (such as public health and education), to training and technical assistance and to subsidize EIB loans. Special loans, highly concessional in nature, were for risk capital participation, rural development or social infrastructure. The EIB's own resource loans were to be directed, as a matter of priority, towards the financing of agricultural projects, the support of small- and medium-size industrial enterprises (through local financial intermediaries) and the financing of productive infrastructure.

EC financial assistance destined to Maghreb countries grew from ECU 339 million in the first financial protocols to ECU 787 million in the third. Over the same period financial commitments to the Mashreq countries increased from ECU 320 million to ECU 768 million (Table 5.3). Although fairly equally divided between the two groups of countries in absolute

Table 5.3 EC Financial Assistance to Southern Mediterranean Countries (commitments, million ECU)

Recipients	1st Financial Protocols: 1978-81			2nd Financial Protocols: 1982-86			3rd Financial Protocols: 1987-91		
	Budget Funds[a]	EIB Loans[b]	Total	Budget Funds	EIB Loans	Total	Budget Funds	EIB Loans	Total
(A) Maghreb countries									
Algeria	44	70	114	44	107	151	56	183	239
Morocco	74	56	130	109	90	199	173	151	324
Tunisia	54	41	95	61	78	139	93	131	224
Total	172	167	339	214	275	489	322	465	787
(B) Mashreq countries									
Egypt	77	93	170	126	150	276	200	249	449
Jordan	22	18	40	26	37	63	38	62	100
Lebanon[c]	10	40	50	16	84	100	20	53	73
Syria[d]	26	34	60	33	64	97	36	110	146
Total	135	185	320	201	335	536	294	474	768
(A + B)	(307)	(352)	(659)	(415)	(610)	(1,025)	(616)	(939)	(1,555)
(C) Israel	—	—	—	—	40	40	—	63	63
Total (A+B+C)	307	352	659	415	650	1,065	616	1,002	1,618

[a] Includes grants and special loans at 1% a year over 40 years (with 10 years of grace).
[b] Loans at subsidized rate (2 or 3 percentage points below EIB lending rates).
[c] Including special reconstruction loans of ECU 20 million and 50 million under the 1st and 2nd protocols respectively.
[d] Aid to Syria under the 3rd protocol imputed from the residual balance in Table 17 of the Commission's XXIst General Report of the Activities of the European Communities—1987.

Sources: M.P. Roy, La CEE et le Tiers Monde: Les Conventions de Lomé, Paris, La Documentation Française, 1984, Table 4; and Commission of the European Communities, XXIst General Report on the Activities of the European Communities—1987, Brussels, 1988.

amount, EC financial assistance appears to have been strongly skewed in favor of the Maghreb, when differences in populations are taken into account. On a per capita basis EC commitments to the former group are 25 percent greater than to the latter. Moreover, until the third financial protocols, financial assistance for the Maghreb countries contained a larger element of concessionality than that for the Mashreq countries, as indicated by the higher share of budgetary aid in the total financial resources made available. Over time, however, the share of concessional aid decreased for both sets of countries to about 40 percent. In the case of the Mashreq, this decline was common to all countries, if relatively less pronounced for Egypt than for the rest. In the case of the Maghreb, Algeria—the main oil exporter in the group—saw its aid from the EC budget shrink the most in relation to total financial resources committed by the Community.

Actual aid disbursements from the Community show country and time profiles that are quite different from those exhibited by commitments. Mashreq countries received more than double the aid actually disbursed to Maghreb groups. Their aid, moreover, increased over time, from $60 million a year in 1980–82 to over $70 million a year in 1986–88, while EC aid going to the Maghreb countries never rose, on average, above $30 million a year. Egypt was by far the most preferred among the Southern Mediterranean aid recipients.

Finally, part of the cooperation agreements with the Maghreb countries dealt with the reciprocal treatment of workers. In each agreement the two parties extended each other's laborers a pledge of non-discrimination in working conditions and remuneration. They also extended each other's workers the same social security benefits to which their nationals were entitled.

The Enlargements of the EC and the Mediterranean Countries

If the northern enlargement of the Community in the mid-1970s extended the potential for trade diversion at the expense of the Mediterranean countries (as shown, for example, by Morocco's loss of free entry into the UK market for its fruits and vegetables and its consequent loss of market shares to the Northern Mediterranean suppliers inside the Community), the southern enlargement of the Community in the 1980s created much greater problems for the Mediterranean policy of the EC, and correspondingly stronger needs to adjust it to the new reality. The second enlargement occurred in two phases: Greece became a member of the Community in January 1981, Spain and Portugal joined five years later. The time it took for the second enlargement to be completed did not make its effects on the countries of the Southern Mediterranean any lighter. The entry of Greece merely foreshadowed the problems that were to come when both Spain and Portugal became full members of the Community.

In discussing the future of the Community's Mediterranean policy, the Commission itself put the issue squarely in focus in 1982 when it stated that "a double question mark hangs over the agreements [with the Mediterranean countries]: firstly, the conditions under which these agreements have been applied have already revealed that their technical and financial clauses are of little value if their commercial clauses are not rigorously observed; secondly, enlargement to include Spain and Portugal could further exacerbate the difficulties that have led to the present situation".[42]

The "less than rigorous" observance by EC countries of the commercial clauses of the cooperation agreements with the Maghreb and Mashreq had to do mostly with the quantitative restrictions to which imports of textiles and clothing from countries such as Morocco, Tunisia and Egypt had been subjected, despite the free access to the Community markets for all manufactures guaranteed by the cooperation agreements.[43] These limitations, introduced just a few years after the Southern Mediterranean countries had been promised free entry into the Community for their manufactures, were thwarting, or at least making it more difficult to achieve, a key objective of the cooperation agreements: the modernization of the economies of the partner countries and the support of ongoing industrialization processes. The limitations were also a destabilizing factor, specifically disturbing investments and slowing down the growth of a sector in which many of the Maghreb and Mashreq countries had sizeable comparative advantages over EC members.

The "present situation" had to do with the entry of Greece into the Community and the competition that the Southern Mediterranean countries were expecting in Community markets from increased exports of agricultural commodities such as olive oil, wine, fresh vegetables, and citrus and other fresh fruits from this new member of the Community. Aside from immediate trade deflection, the Southern Mediterranean countries were fearing the effects of the expansion in output of competing agricultural commodities that would follow the extension of CAP-induced producer prices to Greek farmers. Given the inverse correlation that existed between trade preferences offered by the Community to Maghreb countries and self-sufficiency ratios in Mediterranean foods, the increase in self-sufficiency expected immediately from the addition of Greek agricultural production to the Community's total and in time from the extension of the benefits of the CAP to Greek farmers, could not but reduce the scope and value of the trade preferences enjoyed until then by the Southern Mediterranean partners in Community markets.[44] The trade position of the Maghreb and Mashreq countries inside the Community was destined to worsen even further with the entry of Spain and Portugal. Spain would compete strongly with Morocco, and in part with Tunisia, as an exporter of Mediterranean agricultural products,[45] while Portugal would be a strong competitor in textile–clothing exports with both Egypt and Tunisia.[46]

At the same time and on the same occasion, however, the Community strongly reiterated the special political value it attributed to cooperation with its Southern Mediterranean neighbors, by stating first that "the Community did not underestimate either the difficulty or the time needed to carry out [a successful policy], but it refused to accept as inevitable the confrontation that has turned the Mediterranean into a crisis area for the past 40 years", adding that "the Community's approach in this area should go beyond development aid and commercial policy to try to create the conditions for a peace without which there can be no prosperity or security for anyone", and concluding that "the Community and its members should give the Mediterranean question a priority commensurate with what is at stake politically, backed up by the necessary financial and trade provisions".[47]

The Community had just shown that it could be

magnanimous. In an effort to keep Greece tied to Europe and to the Western camp, in addition to membership, it granted this country special economic development assistance. The new socialist government of Greece, originally opposed to entry, had requested and obtained a "special arrangement" in the form of increased agricultural and regional aid, and temporary derogations from import liberalization clauses and from EC competition policy, to support small business.[48] When an important political interest was at stake the Community had shown itself capable of acting in a forward-looking fashion.

In the case of the Mediterranean countries, however, this was easier said by the Commission than done by the Council. The southern enlargement itself stood in the way. As clearly and succinctly noted in a study conducted for the Community in 1984 by four important European research institutes, the second enlargement of the EC involved two basic tensions. The first derived "from the fact that the entry into the Community of Greece . . . and now the prospective entry of Spain and Portugal must give them some preference in the rest of the Community over all third parties formerly with equal access". To the extent that this damaged the development prospects of the non-candidate members, "it ran directly counter to the Community's member states' interest . . . to stabilize the Mediterranean for both security and economic reasons". The second tension was arising within the Community itself, as "all the areas and sectors in the Community threatened by the enlargement as such, or by the concessions third countries might demand in compensation, [would] tend to seek increasing protection regardless of the effects for third parties". Moreover, any response to the quandary faced by the Community's member states tended to be along a north–south divide[49] because the economic interests of the Southern European members—for which competition from Spain, Portugal and the Mediterranean area was strongest—were most threatened by the enlargements, while the economic interests of the Northern European members were most threatened by the prospective loss of export markets in the Mediterranean area and elsewhere.

Stripped to the essentials, the Community had three options. First, it could have essentially forced the Southern Mediterranean countries to absorb the loss of trade preferences entailed in the accession to the Community of Greece, Spain and Portugal and leave up to them the choice of maintaining a "scaled down" form of cooperation with the Community or seeking other ways. Second, it could have tried to compensate the loss of trade preferences suffered by the Mediterranean partners by increasing financial assistance to them and granting them additional preferences (at the expense of third parties) for those agricultural exports that did not compete with domestic production in the ten member countries plus the two new entrants, thereby trying to keep intact the cooperative framework so laboriously put in place in the late 1970s. Third, it could have attempted to change the terms and basis of its Mediterranean policy, accepting that integration of the Southern Mediterranean economies into the EC was an infeasible objective under the new circumstances and that a better goal of policy was to help to reduce their dependence on the Community. This would have entailed the supply of substantial diversification assistance, if for a limited time.

The Commission immediately showed its preference for the second alternative. Managing the southern relationship and preventing any abrupt reversal of policies was its natural response. In reporting to the Council on the exploratory talks with the Mediterranean countries and the applicant countries (then Spain and Portugal) held between 1983 and 1984, the Commission emphasized the need to increase Community aid so as to contribute to the social and economic development of the Southern Mediterranean countries and develop further the strategy of complementarity by extending cooperation to other functional areas—such as regional integration, scientific and technological cooperation, and development of small- to medium-sized enterprises. At the same time, since it was not feasible to rely totally on compensating tariff concessions on imports of non-competing agricultural products, the Commission proposed preserving during the transition period whatever trade was possible for Mediterranean countries in competing agricultural products. In practice, access privileges enjoyed by Southern Mediterranean countries were to be adjusted to ensure that they would not be negated by the upcoming dismantling of EC barriers against imports from Spain and Portugal. In the case of competing manufactures and textile–clothing products, the Commission's plan aimed to re-establish the principle of free-entry into the Community as originally envisaged in the agreements, thus foreshadowing the eventual abolition of the restrictive measures on imports that the Community had adopted in the early 1980s.[50]

The Commission, however, was acutely aware that such an option would be feasible in practice only if "keeping the Mediterranean safe for Europe" and in a "state of peace" remained a main policy goal for the Community. In fact it ended its report to the Council with a peroration that reflected rather clearly the uncertainties felt at the time. The next enlargement, the Commission wrote, "should prompt greater awareness [of the Community's responsibilities towards the region] and stimulate the political will to deal not only with the immediate consequences, important and difficult as they are, but also with the longer-term problem of the fundamental interests of the Mediterranean countries as a whole, set against which the cost and sacrifices to be borne in the short term can be rightly seen as very modest".[51] The strong certainties expressed in Commissioner Pisani's Memorandum concerning the political interests of the Community in the Mediterranean had, in the span of a few years, become hopes to be kept alive. With the accession of Greece and Spain to the Community, EC Europe was feeling more secure along its southern flank. With the apparent collapse of the oil cartel, the Community was also much less anxious than in the past about the security of the supply of this critical material. The Commission seems to have registered quite accurately that in the new circumstances the perceived political–strategic value of the Southern Mediterranean neighbors to some of the Community's member states was rapidly decreasing.[52]

The EC Council also seemed to endorse the second alternative, if in a more guarded way than the Commission, and with greater emphasis on aid than on trade. At face value the Statement it issued in March 1985, on the eve of the entry into the Community of Portugal and Spain, seems tilted towards the third alternative, at least in the medium term: supply financial assistance to the Southern Mediterranean countries and let them pursue their own ultimate development goals. As a guiding principle of the Community's Mediterranean policy, the Council proclaimed that it "be of an ongoing nature, and . . . in terms of economic development, make for significant and stable results in the medium-term". From an overall and long-term point of view, it pledged the Community to "direct its efforts to pursuing financial and technical cooperation with the Mediterranean partners in order to make an appropriate contribution to their economic and social development". In reality, however, the Council was more concerned with bringing the second enlargement to full fruition, to ensure that the EC construction could be widened, than with implementing a truly new Mediterranean policy. It was up to the southern neighbors to adjust and up to the Community to make the necessary marginal concessions to maintain the status quo in trade: the Community was simply to strive "to ensure the maintenance of the traditional export flows" of the Mediterranean countries.[53]

The Commission's guidelines for the economic cooperation between the Community and the Mediterranean countries issued in late 1985 stressed both familiar and partially new themes: reduction of food dependence, support for regional cooperation and attraction of risk capital. All of these, however, were rather general, if not outright vague. The principles that would be followed to re-adjust trade relations were never mentioned, let alone clarified with respect to the previous communication to the Council. Nor were the reform of the CAP or the return to free trade in textiles ever again cited. In the area of financial resources the guidelines stressed the need for "adequacy". Concretely, they indicated that the total amount of EC aid would be based on that of the previous financial protocols, with account taken of inflation, the enlargement of the Community, and the need to "give practical effect to the new priorities and qualitative improvements in cooperation".[54]

Particularly difficult to understand was the emphasis given to supporting the objective of food self-sufficiency in Mediterranean countries, whose "importance" was stressed by the Commission's document in a series of tables appended to it, which were meant to illustrate the dramatic deterioration that had occurred in the capacity of these countries to meet domestic consumption needs in cereals, meat and milk powder. These were the very products in which EC protection was creating continuous surpluses, and which could only be disposed of by generous food aid and export subsidies. The Community was now pledging resources to encourage more production of the same products in its Southern Mediterranean neighbors, while the more competitive agricultural exports of these countries were being deflected from the EC market by those of Spain and Portugal.

The trade provisions of the existing agreements with Maghreb and Mashreq countries were eventually modified on a country-by-country and product-by-product basis to account for some of the effects of the second enlargement of the Community. For the directly competing products, subject to import ceilings by country of origin, transitory arrangements involving reference prices and import calendars were made in order to smooth out the impact of Spanish and Portuguese products gaining free entry into the Community. The objective was the maintenance of existing export flows for products such as citrus fruits from Tunisia, Morocco, Cyprus and Israel, fresh tomatoes from Morocco, fresh potatoes from Cyprus, Egypt, Israel and Morocco, olive oil from Tunisia and wine from all Maghreb countries. The Community also extended some compensation to the Southern Mediterranean countries in the area of trade by gradually abolishing residual import duties on agricultural imports not directly competing with those of Spain and Portugal.[55] In the area of aid the Community raised the nominal amount of financial resources made available to the Maghreb and Mashreq countries by more than 45 percent in the fourth financial protocol.[56] By and large, however, a considerable amount of adjustment was left to the Maghreb and Mashreq countries to implement on their own.

Internal Community tensions were "solved" by awarding special assistance, under the Integrated Mediterranean Programs, to Greece and regional aid to Portugal. Southern European states were more generally compensated through the doubling of the EC's structural funds by 1992.[57]

Effects of the Mediterranean Policy

The trade effects of the preferences accorded by the EC to the Mediterranean countries are those on which most attention has been focused as one of the key dimensions of the Mediterranean policy. It is a question, as in the case of Lomé preferences, of the "value" that they held for the beneficiary countries. In making this evaluation it should not be forgotten that, while the ultimate test of the value of preferences lies in their effects on the well-being of the countries that receive them, their intermediate impact, which is more directly measurable, is the increase that they generate to the export trade of the beneficiaries. Additionally, the trade diversification impact of the preferences must be taken into account, particularly in view of the importance that this objective assumed in the development strategies of the beneficiary countries.

The Mediterranean countries, as earlier noted, are quite different from one another, in size, economic structure and resource endowments. They have also followed different growth and development strategies over the past thirty years. Some of them have changed policies quite drastically, particularly in the fields of trade and industrialization, during the period in question. Greece, for example, became much more export oriented in the 1960s. Tunisia switched from protection of domestic manufacturing output to positive encouragement of exports and foreign investments in the export sector in the early 1970s. Morocco did the same in the early 1980s. Turkey's industrialization policy also remained biased towards import substitution through the 1960s and 1970s, and significant change did not occur until the 1980s. Differences in starting points, as well as in the policies pursued, make it difficult to disentangle the effects of preferences on actual trade outcomes in *ex-post* studies. *Ex-ante* studies of the impact of EC preferences on beneficiaries are virtually non-existent.

Analysis of the geographical distribution of exports from Mediterranean countries indicates that the importance of the EC as an end market has increased for the Maghreb, but not for the Mashreq countries, whose export trade over time has become more tied to the Middle East. Israel increased its dependence on the United States, while reducing dependence on the EC as an export outlet (Table 5.4). Despite the presence of tariff preferences in the EC, several Mediterranean countries have substantially diversified the geographical destination of their exports. This notwithstanding, the EC remains a critical market for the Maghreb countries, as it still absorbs nearly half of their exports, and a very substantial market for all the other Mediterranean countries.

The trends in the shares of EC imports held by Southern Mediterranean countries in various types of products—competing food, raw materials and manufactures—are shown

Table 5.4 Geographical Distribution of Southern Mediterranean Countries' Exports (percentage share)

| Exports to: | 1976–77 (average) | | | | |
	EC(9)	US	Middle East	Developing Countries	Japan
Maghreb	44.2	36.3	0.2	8.2	0.5
Mashreq	26.3	2.6	6.8	28.7	1.9
Israel	35.7	18.3	—	22.0	3.1
Exports to:	1986–87 (average)				
	EC(9)	US	Middle East	Developing Countries	Japan
Maghreb	58.0	12.1	1.9	10.6	1.8
Mashreq	27.7	2.2	20.5	19.8	1.9
Israel	28.1	31.5	—	11.3	5.1

Source: International Monetary Fund, *Direction of Trade Statistics: Yearbook,* Washington D.C. (various issues).

in Table 5.5. The shares of the rest of the developing countries in the same product categories are also reported for comparison purposes. The figures indicate that the developing economies of the Southern Mediterranean basin experienced, despite preferential tariff treatment in EC markets, considerable difficulty in holding their own in competing food products, while they did better in traditional manufactures. The picture is more complex for raw materials. Maghreb and Mashreq countries lost market share in fertilizers, while both did better in petroleum and gas between 1977 and 1988.

Prima facie EC preferences seem to have helped the export diversification of Southern Mediterranean countries more than it helped their penetration of EC markets. Success in diversifying the structure of exports to the EC seems to have been greater for Maghreb than for Mashreq countries as shown by the gains that they made between 1977 and 1988 in the markets for manufactured fertilizers, clothing and, to a lesser extent, travel goods and footwear. Other Mediterranean countries, however, appear to have had much greater success in capturing a higher share of EC imports of both competing agricultural products and manufactures than their southern neighbors. Closer association and EC membership seem to have had their advantages.

More empirical evidence on the trade effects of the EC tariff preferences is available on a country-by-country basis from several sources.[58] Regarding Greece, the results of several studies indicate that EC trade preferences had a positive impact on the growth of its exports to Europe.[59] The evidence on Turkey is much less conclusive and no strong positive impact is found during the early period of association with the Community.[60] Available evidence points to favorable results for both Spain and Israel. Exports of both of these countries seem to have reacted positively to EC tariff preferences.[61] With respect to both the Maghreb and Mashreq countries, the evidence on the effects of the EC preferences is not as extensive as for the previous

Table 5.5 Shares of Mediterranean Countries in EC(6) Imports of Selected Products (percentage)

Origin of Imports:	1976–78 (average)			
	Maghreb	Mashreq	Other med[a]	Other LDCs
Competing food products				
Fish, fresh (031)	1.4	0.4	5.3	13.0
Fruit, fresh (051)	4.6	0.1	24.3	12.2
Fruit, preserved (053)	2.6	—	13.5	22.9
Vegetables, fresh (054)	5.4	0.6	10.8	16.4
Vegetables, preserved (055)	4.0	0.6	14.4	12.0
Alcoholic beverages (112)	1.7	—	11.4	—
Raw materials				
Fertilizers, crude (271)	44.5	10.6	0.01	22.7
Petroleum, crude (331)	5.3	2.7	2.7	35.2
Petroleum, products (332)	0.6	0.8	0.1	9.5
Gas, natural (341)	4.0	—	0.1	0.4
Cotton (263)	—	9.9	10.3	43.7
Manufactures				
Inorganic elements (513)	3.6	—	4.0	7.4
Fertilizers, manufactures (561)	3.7	1.8	4.5	4.3
Textile yarn (651)	0.2	0.6	12.3	5.0
Cotton fabrics, woven (652)	1.1	0.5	3.1	15.9
Textiles woven, non-cotton (653)	0.2	0.01	2.3	5.4
Other textiles (656)	1.0	0.3	7.5	25.6
Clothing (841)	2.3	0.01	11.1	25.1
Travel goods (831)	1.0	0.7	4.2	27.3
Footwear (851)	0.5	0.02	10.3	3.9

Table 5.5 *(continued)*

Origin of Imports:	1987-89 (average)			
	Maghreb	**Mashreq**	**Other Med**	**Other LDCs**
Competing food products				
Fish, fresh (031)	2.7	0.2	5.0	17.5
Fruit, fresh (051)	2.4	0.03	28.0	10.3
Fruit, preserved (053)	2.6	—	13.5	22.9
Vegetables, fresh (054)	1.7	—	15.0	32.5
Vegetables, preserved (055)	2.5	0.3	16.4	6.6
Alcoholic beverages (112)	0.4	—	13.1	—
Raw materials				
Fertilizers, crude (271)	32.6	3.6	0.6	34.1
Petroleum, crude (331)	6.8	4.4	4.0	28.9
Petroleum, products (332)	3.5	1.4	0.4	6.9
Gas, natural (341)	19.1	—	0.4	0.1
Cotton (263)	—	6.3	11.1	37.0
Manufactures				
Inorganic elements (513)	3.1	—	4.5	14.1
Fertilizers, manufactures (561)	8.0	1.5	6.5	6.7
Textile yarn (651)	0.5	1.4	11.7	6.2
Cotton fabrics, woven (652)	1.3	0.8	7.4	15.4
Textiles woven,				
non-cotton (653)	0.3	0.02	4.7	9.1
Other textiles (656)	0.3	0.3	19.8	28.7
Clothing (841)	5.2	1.7	19.3	29.3
Travel goods (831)	1.2	0.2	3.4	52.2
Footwear (851)	0.7	0.02	17.2	14.7

Notes: — means zero or negligible. SITC codes in parenthesis.
[a] Including Cyprus, Greece, Malta, Portugal, Spain, Turkey and Yugoslavia.
Source: United Nations, COMTRADE Data Base.

ones, particularly for the earlier period. Some studies point to positive effects on Tunisia and Morocco when considered individually.[62] Most studies of regional effects, however, indicate that they have been generally positive, even for the recent period,[63] if slightly more positive for the northern than for the southern countries.[64] Available evidence, moreover, indicates positive results for export diversification of associated countries in the Mediterranean. While the CAP appears to have severely hindered agricultural export growth, EC preferences on industrial products apparently provided positive incentives for the diversification of the export base of the beneficiaries in the Mediterranean basin, which occurred in both textiles-clothing and processed foods.[65]

Looking at the Mediterranean policy of the EC, one is struck by the apparent inconsistency between the moderately favorable economic results of the policy, even accounting for the variety of its economic consequences at the country level, and the general dissatisfaction with the results of the policy both in Europe and in its southern neighbors. Practically all recent documents of the Commission and even some of the declarations of the Council are apologetic in tone and specifically refer to the fact that the policy has not yielded the "expected" results. Similarly, dissatisfaction has been strong in both the Maghreb and Mashreq countries.[66]

Part of the explanation for this apparent paradox between results and the perceptions about them of both parties may lie in the differences in objectives being pursued. As Richard Pomfret accurately and succinctly put it, "the Community sought to create a sphere of political influence [in the Mediterranean region] while, the Mediterranean countries sought and obtained economic benefits".[67] Yet, because of an excess of caution, the Community may not have tried as hard as it would have liked to achieve strong political influence in the area. It opted instead for the transfer of some economic benefits to its southern neighbors, possibly at the expense of third parties. According to some observers, "all that the European Community had developed under the name of its global Mediterranean policy has been a trading system",[68] while the institutionalization of its undoubted security interests in the area, and their transformation into a formal political sphere of influence, was not pursued with sufficient determination. Instead of skillfully using an economic instrument—trade preferences—in the pursuit of a political objective, the Community wasted a political occasion and built instead yet another trading system of questionable value in the eyes of its partners.

The vastly different perceptions of the two parties reflect both the complexity of the preferential model actually applied by the Community, and the fragmented political and economic reality of the area upon which the model was superimposed. It also reflects the slowness and prudence—sometimes bordering on reticence—with which the Community dealt with the countries of the Southern Mediterranean. While not disguising its political intentions, the Community never fully articulated them and never coherently followed through with actions. At the same time, while openly brandishing the instrument of trade preferences, the Community never used it fully to create maximum advantages for its Mediterranean partners. The Mediterranean policy of the Community often resembled, in both choreography and motions, a slow baroque ballet, directed too conservatively, performed by technically competent, if unimaginative, dancers on a very slippery stage. Everybody was naturally dissatisfied at the end of the performance—the dancers about the boring director, the audience about the apparently soul-less dancers, and the director about the slippery stage upon which the ballet had to be performed and the unappreciative public to which the performance was directed. Yet, for lack of an alternative, the production went on.

Actually, the Commission did perform its technical duties quite well. It provided the Council with accurate analyses of the problems faced by the Community in the Mediterranean area and with reasonable proposals for action. It also supplied task continuity to the EC policy posture towards this important part of the developing world. The Council, however, consistently showed a lack of decisiveness and clarity of purpose in its decisions. It continued to react to changes in political and economic circumstances, and to act in a piecemeal, risk and initiative minimizing, manner. A main reason for this ineffectiveness is to be found in the north–south divide that has for many years characterized the appreciation of the Mediterranean problem within the Community. Until quite recently, the northern members generally tended to consider the southern Mediterranean as a border area and the problems originating from it as border problems, affecting only, and only marginally, the southern regions of the Community.

Agricultural trade problems between the Southern European members of the Community and the Maghreb–Mashreq countries were more often than not regarded with a degree of fastidiousness by the Northern European members, and seen either as the result of misplaced economic sensitivities or as a ploy used by the southerners to obtain greater internal transfers for their undeveloped regions. The same skeptical attitude was maintained by the northern members of the EC vis-a-vis the social and economic problems generated in countries such as France and Italy by immigration from North Africa (legal and illegal). The Community as a whole never addressed them, except for tacitly "blessing" individual member's attempts to regulate the immigration flows at the national level.

Redirecting (Again?) Mediterranean Policies?

The Mediterranean area has recently become the object of considerable attention inside the Community. After dealing with some of the consequences of the second enlargement through the negotiation of additional protocols to the existing cooperation agreements with Mediterranean countries in 1986–87, the Community focused again on its longer-term objectives in this area and on the related policy requirements. Between 1989 and 1990 the Economic and Social Committee of the Communities (ESC) first re-examined the Mediterranean policy of the EC and then expressed two "opinions" about it.[69] The Parliament also kept a close watch on the Mediterranean area and the problems emanating from it—particularly immigration and its consequences.[70] The Commission in turn sent two successive communications to the Council on "redirecting" Mediterranean policy.[71]

The concerns lying at the base of this flurry of activity by the various organs of the Community are quite clear. The most important has to do with the deterioration in the socio-economic circumstances of most Mediterranean countries and with the interest of the Community in alleviating it. Contractions in incomes and continued population growth generated substantial reductions in per capita consumption levels during the 1980s, especially in Algeria, Egypt and Morocco. Unemployment rates soared—particularly for young people— and immigration came to represent the only vent left for surplus labor in many of the countries of the region. While not generated by EC policies, the deterioration of socio-economic conditions in Southern Mediterranean countries was not effectively countered by them either. If anything, the ESC thought, the objective limitations of the existing cooperation agreements and the contradictions in their application, that is EC protectionism in agriculture and textiles, rendered Community policy less effective than it could have been. Similarly, the "social cooperation" provided for in some of the agreements had virtually been "a dead letter, because of [the] community's concern about employment and political pressure from member states". In conclusion, according to the Committee, the Community's Mediterranean policies "were not tailored to achieve their [new] main objective: the socio-economic development of the Mediterranean countries".[72]

The most interesting aspect of the 1989 ESC report was its explicit redefinition of the Community's policy goals in the Mediterranean area, changing them from security of supply of raw materials to socio-economic development of the area. In a period of diminishing global tensions the strategic importance of the Mediterranean could no longer be invoked as the sole justification for the Community's involvement. Yet, maintaining social and political stability in this area, the Committee thought, was still very much in the interest of Europe in order to safeguard peace in an unstable neighboring region[73] and to avoid immigration surges that would strain its absorption capacity.[74] Thus the ESC's concern with the socio-economic development of the area as a new, and key, objective of EC policies becomes quite understandable, and so does the attention to those measures that the Community could take to generate more employment in the Southern Mediterranean countries: liberalization of imports in agriculture and development of labor intensive manufactures—activities in which these countries have strong comparative advantages.[75]

These were needs that the Commission had openly stressed in the recent past,[76] and they stemmed from an analysis of the situation in the Mediterranean countries that was very similar to that of the ESC. According to the Commission, EC policy towards this area also needed to be changed, in order to address the needs of the countries of North Africa as well as the requirements of the Community. Increasing demographic pressures, worsening social imbalances and continued serious political instability in the whole Mediterranean area justified renewed interest in the economic development of the non-member Mediterranean countries (NMCs), at a time when "the expectations of the NMCs were quite obviously influenced by the Community's new developments". The new developments consisted of the completion of the EC internal market, with the trade and social implications that it carried, including "the anticipated impact of a common policy governing the granting of visas".[77]

While explicitly referring to the expectation in Mediterranean non-member countries of the completion of the EC internal market, the Commission was also implicitly making the point that the area's problems could no longer be treated by some of the Community members as border problems. Project 1992 had made them, perhaps for the first time, Community problems. Immigration was only one of them, if the most immediately worrisome. With the abolition of intra-EC checks on travel, immigration flows from North Africa could no longer be relegated to the southern countries of the EC.

In outlining five main areas of action for the Community— support of economic reforms in Mediterranean countries, encouragement of private investments, increases in aid flows to private investments, improved access to Community markets for their exports and strengthening economic and political dialogue with the southern neighbors—the Commission was not only signaling the urgent need for a comprehensive policy (which was only partially new), but also the general interest in such an approach (which was a key novel element in the EC–Southern Mediterranean political–economic equation). EC policy had to become truly "global" not only in scope and destination, but also in origin. It had to become a policy for the whole Community, in addition to being a policy for the whole Mediterranean region.

That the Commission's views and proposal must have fallen on sympathetic ears is confirmed in the 1990 Communication to the Council on the redirection of the Community's policy, which contained the specific proposals for the period 1992-96. This document states at the outset that "discussions in the Council and the Conclusions of the Strasbourg Council . . . have shown that views converge on the Commission's analysis and on the need to change the Community's Mediterranean policy".[78]

Two important aspects of the Commission's proposals were quickly acted upon by the Council, which approved in late 1990 the resource envelope for the financial protocols of the cooperation agreements with the Maghreb and Mashreq countries during the 1992–96 period, including a component designed specifically to support structural adjustment in these countries. In addition the Council backed the Commission's proposal for "horizontal" financial cooperation with the countries of the region, allowing the Community to support regional programs, particularly in the environmental area.[79] The request made by the Rome European Council that discussions on redirecting the Mediterranean policy be completed as rapidly as possible was thus honored, at least in part.[80]

The Council also agreed that trade arrangements with the countries concerned be improved in two ways: first by speeding up the dismantling of the Community's tariffs on imports of agricultural products foreseen in the Additional Protocols of 1986–87, and second by relaxing the tariff quotas and reference quantities on imports laid down in the same protocols.[81]

Lack of progress on the creation of a new institutional framework for cooperation, including the Development Bank for the Mediterranean (supported by Italy, France and Spain), and on the trade regime for textile exports, as well as the lack of an explicit endorsement of the Commission's guidelines for a new policy, make it difficult to judge if recent Council decisions represent the beginning of a true redirection of the Mediterranean policy of the Community or another minimum adjustment to the new circumstances. In order to affect the socio-economic conditions of the Southern Mediterranean countries in a tangible way, the Community will have to ensure that at least the conditions for the maintenance of employment in agriculture and for its expansion in manufacturing are put in place. This requires nothing short of the re-establishment of free trade in textiles (and thus the roll-back of protectionist measures erected after the signing of the Cooperation Agreements) and a substantial reform of the CAP regime for Mediterranean agricultural products. Measures providing direct encouragement to the flows of investment to the region will also be necessary. If these premises are not realized, no effective redirection of policy will be possible. Cooperation will remain piecemeal and become progressively less effective, while the propensity to adopt defensive postures in all areas, from trade to immigration, will most likely grow.

Notes to Chapter 5

1 All dates refer to the years of signature of the agreements. Dates of entry into effect vary considerably from one agreement to another. Some agreements, such as the second one with Lebanon, never entered into force. Some were subsequently amended. An additional protocol between Turkey and the EC defining the rules for achieving a customs union and expanding economic cooperation was signed in 1970. The agreements with Malta and Cyprus were augmented by financial protocols in 1976 and 1977 respectively.

2 S. Henig, "Mediterranean Policy in the Context of the External Relations of the European Community", in A. Shlaim and G.N. Yannopoulos, eds., *The EC and the Mediterranean Countries*, Cambridge, Cambridge University Press, 1976, pp. 316-20.

3 See, for example, the proceedings of the debate at the European Parliament over the commercial policy of the European Community in the Mediterranean Basin: Débates du Parlement Européen, *Politique Commerciale de la Communauté dans le Bassin Méditerranéen*, No. 133, Brussels, 9 February 1971, pp. 28-50.

4 This was the view expressed by an insider—the Director General for External Relations of the Commission Mr Joseph Loeff—at a symposium held in Bruges in March 1972: Loeff, "La Communauté Élargie et l'Espace Méditerranéen", p. 109.

5 See, for instance, W. Hager, "The Mediterranean: A European Mare Nostrum?", *Orbis*, Spring 1974, p. 231, who wrote that "nowhere on the periphery [of the EC] has the process [of establishing a mode of relations with neighbors] been so accidental as it has been towards the South". Similarly, G. Curzon, in introducing Tovias's book two years later, characterized the Mediterranean policy of the EC as "ill started, . . . an unplanned accident", in A. Tovias, *Tariff Preferences in Mediterranean Diplomacy*, New York, St. Martin's Press (for the Trade Policy Research Center), 1977, p. xvii.

6 Algeria at the time was still part of France. Morocco and Tunisia had by then just reached political independence. A similar declaration of intent was issued towards Libya: Office for Official Publications, *Treaties*, pp. 603-4.

7 Roy, *Hors Convention de Lomé*, p. 12.

8 Commission of the European Communities, *Cooperation Agreements Between the EEC and the Maghreb Countries*, Europe Information Doc. DE 36, Brussels, 1982, pp. 1-2.

9 L. Tsoulakis, *The European Community and its Mediterranean Enlargement*, London, Allen and Unwin, 1981, pp. 140-2; S. Verney, "Greece and the European Community", in K. Featherstone and D.K. Katsoudas, eds., *Political Change in Greece Before and After the Colonels*, London, Croom Helm, 1987, pp. 258-64; K. Featherstone, "The Mediterranean Challenge: Cohesion and External Preferences", in J. Lodge, ed., *The European Community and the Challenge of the Future*, New York, St. Martin's Press, 1989, pp. 188-190.

10 P. Holmes, "Spain and the EEC", in D. Bell, ed., *Democratic Politics in Spain*, London, Francis Pinter, 1983, pp. 165-79; M.M. Medina Ortega, "Les Relations entre l'Espagne et la Communauté Depuis 1945", in Institut d'Etudes Européennes, ed., *L'Espagne et les Communautés Européenes*, Brussels, Editions de l'Université de Bruxelles, 1979, pp. 8-10.

11 Commission, *The Europe-South Dialogue*, 1988, p. 62.

12 Council of the European Communities, *Copenhagen Declaration*, reprinted in *Bulletin of the European Communities*, 12/73, Annex 1, 1973.

13 Roy, *Hors Convention de Lomé*, p. 12.

14 Parlement Européen, *Rapport sur la Politique Commerciale de la Communauté dans le Bassin Méditerrannéen*, Document de Séance No. 246, February 1971.

15 The memorandum reads "the Commission considers that, taken as a whole, the agreements concluded with the Mediterranean countries are no more than *an inadequate expression of Europe's interest in this region* (emphasis added). Through these agreements the Community has so far made only a limited contribution to the economic development of this part of the world". Commission, "Community Development Cooperation Policy", 1971, p. 12.

16 As noted earlier, J. Loeff, Director General for External Relations of the Commission, had declared in March 1972 that "the moment seemed opportune for the Community to abandon the road of pragmatism and arbitrariness, and to appreciate fully the Mediterranean phenomenon and start a true Mediterranean policy based on a coherent overall doctrine aimed at promoting the development of the region". See Loeff, *La Communauté Elargie*, p. 109 (translation mine). Though more prudent, the Director General for Aid to Developing Countries of the Commission, Mr Hans Broder Krohn, during the same Conference also made critical assessment of the status and usefulness of the agreements reached with the Mediterranean countries. Such agreements, he stated, "had come to light over time in too diluted a fashion and in very different phases of the European construction". As far as their content, "one

must say that, in a period during which import duties are progressively losing their protective value and generalized trade preferences for industrial products are being put in place, actions limited to the domain of tariffs and quotas are but a small step towards the solution of the broad economic development problems of the Mediterranean basin": H. Broder Krohn, "La Communauté Elargie et les Pays en Voi de Développement", in H. Brugmans et al., eds., *La Politique Economique Extérieure de la Communauté Européenne Elargie*, Bruges, De Tempel, 1973 (translation mine), p. 161.

17 R. Pomfret, *Mediterranean Policy of the European Community*, London, Macmillan (for the Trade Policy Research Center), 1986, p. 21.

18 EC(10) gross domestic product had grown at 4.6 percent per year in real terms between 1961 and 1970. The unemployment rate in 1970 had fallen to 2 percent, from an already low 2.5 percent in 1960.

19 Commission, "Community Development Cooperation Policy", 1971, p. 12.

20 Tovias, *Tariff Preferences*, pp. 70-2.

21 See, for example, the Commission's Memorandum on development policy of July 1971, which states: "These countries' will to cooperate results from certain identities of interests and from a multiplicity of links due to proximity and tradition. This proximity and these affinities imply a considerable degree of interdependence, going beyond trade and extending to labor, tourism and all manner of invisible trade. The close interconnection of the political and economic interests involved, and the influence that Europe can exert in this region, contribute to making the development of the Mediterranean basin a natural extension of European integration." Commission, "Community Development Cooperation Policy", 1971, p. 12.

22 Agence Europe, *La Politique Globale de la CEE dans le Bassin Méditerranéen d'Après les Suggestions de la Commission Européenne*, Document No. 708, 30 November 1972, pp. 2-4.

23 The opinion of the United Kingdom was sought in view of its likely membership in the Community.

24 Tovias, *Tariff Preferences*, pp. 72-4.

25 Libya held out. All these agreements were to become effective in 1978.

26 In *The Courier*, No. 36, March-April 1976 (Actualités), p. I. Rather curiously, this claim was repeated in the Pisani Memorandum of

1982, where one reads that "in the implementation of its Mediterranean policy the Community took the Lomé model as its basis", only to recognize that "it was not able to give [the agreements with the Mediterranean countries] the solidity and political value of a collective contract". Commission, "Memorandum on the Community's Development Policy", 1982, p. 13.

27 This expression is borrowed from Pomfret, *Mediterranean Policy*, p. 100.

28 It was important and innovative that the aid to the Maghreb and Mashreq countries was to come from the Community's own budget, instead of being financed by specific budgetary contributions of the member countries as were the Development Funds in the Yaoundé and Lomé conventions.

29 Membership applications were submitted by both Portugal and Spain in 1977.

30 Tovias, *Tariff Preferences*, p. 12.

31 Israel partook of many of the structural traits of the northern countries and thus tended to behave like them in dealing with the Community, watching specific agricultural interests, but being mostly focused on market access for its manufactured products.

32 Syria and Egypt began to export oil in significant amounts in the early and late 1970s respectively.

33 Pomfret, *Mediterranean Policy*, pp. 16 and 52–5.

34 The wording of various agreements on the goals being pursued is identical. See, for example, article 4 of the Cooperation Agreement between the EC and Syria, *Official Journal of the European Communities*, No. L269/1, 27 September 1978, p. 4, and article 4 of the Cooperation Agreement between the EC and Tunisia, *Official Journal of the European Communities*, No. L265/4, 27 September 1978, pp. 4–5.

35 Aside from being exactly symmetrical in their structure, the agreements with the Maghreb countries are virtually identical in the number and general content of the provisions that they contain. The same is true for the agreements with the Mashreq countries. They are virtually identical to one another, if shorter than those that the EC concluded with the Maghreb countries.

36 See, for example, articles 9, 27 and 30 of the Cooperation Agreement between the EC and Morocco, *Official Journal of the European Communities*, No. L264/1, 27 September 1978, pp. 5 and 18, and articles 9, 24 and 27 of the Cooperation Agreement between the EC and

Egypt, *Official Journal of the European Communities*, No. L266/1, 27 September, 1978, pp. 5 and 12-13.

[37] All EC import duties and quantitative restrictions on imports from Maghreb countries were abolished, except for a handful of oil and cork products subject to annual ceilings. Imports in excess of what was specified in the ceilings could be made subject to import duties. The reintroduction of the duty, however, was not mandatory. A few additional exceptions to duty-free entry were retained in the case of industrial imports from Mashreq countries.

[38] See, for example, the Cooperation Agreement between the EC and Algeria, *Official Journal of the European Communities*, No. L263/1, 27 September 1978, and Cooperation Agreement between the EC and Jordan, *Official Journal of the European Communities*, No. L268/1, 27 September 1978.

[39] In the case of fresh citrus fruit, for example, where EC self-sufficiency was between 40 percent and 50 percent, import tariffs were cut by 80 percent. For potatoes, in which the Community was 98 percent self-sufficient, the tariff reduction was only 40 percent. In wine, where the EC was more than self-sufficient, tariff reductions were carefully circumscribed to ordinary wines (provided, always, that EC reference import prices were respected), while quality wines were subject to both very stringent tariff quotas and other restrictions (e.g. they could only be imported if they came from designated areas and bottled in containers of no more than two liters).

[40] See, for example, articles 15(1), 15(3), 21, and 36 of the Cooperation Agreement between the EC and Tunisia, *Official Journal of the European Communities*, pp. 8-14, 16-17 and 19.

[41] See, for example, articles 35 and 37 of the Cooperation Agreement between the EC and Tunisia, *Ibidem*, p. 19.

[42] Commission, "Memorandum on the Community's Development Policy", 1982, p. 13. Similarly, in its communication to the Council on the consequences of the second enlargement of the Community for the Mediterranean countries, the Commission had plainly stated that "the [Mediterranean] policy is not operating to the satisfaction of our partners, and it is necessary to take into account the reasons for the present difficulties". Commission of the European Communities, *Commission Communication to the Council on a Mediterranean Policy for the Enlarged Community*, Doc. COM(82) 353 final, Brussels, 24 June 1982, p. 1. Among the reasons, the Commission listed: (a) the fact that "far-reaching" concessions on the industrial side had not yielded the desired results, as recession in the EC had rendered its import policies more restrictive; (b) the

Community's internal Mediterranean problem, exacerbated by "a common agricultural policy skewed against Mediterranean crops"; and (c) the reduction in employment possibilities inside the Community for migrant labor for the Southern Mediterranean due to the economic recession, *Ibidem*, pp. 2–3.

[43] As noted earlier, all the cooperation agreements signed by the EC with the Maghreb and Mashreq countries contained a specific undertaking by the Community to ensure free entry of imports of industrial products. Access to the EC market was to be free of duties and similar charges, as well as of quantitative restrictions. The fact that informal restraints on imports of textiles and clothing products were agreed on in 1978 after the second MFA (and subsequently renewed in 1980 and 1982) with Morocco and Tunisia outside the specific framework of the Cooperation Agreements did not make them less contradictory of both the letter and the spirit of the EC Mediterranean policy. In the case of Egypt the contradiction was even stronger, as this country had been party to the MFA since the very beginning. The Cooperation Agreement with Egypt should have, therefore, superseded all existing restrictions. On the early MFAs and the informal agreements with Mediterranean countries in textiles see C. Cova, *La Politique Arabe de la Communauté*, Brussels, Bureau d'Informations Européennes, 1983, pp. 91–101.

[44] The entry of Greece into the Community increased prevailing self-sufficiency ratios in key agricultural products as follows: olive oil from 0.88 to 1.0; wine from 0.99 to 1.04; fresh vegetables from 0.94 to 0.95; fresh fruit (excluding citrus) from 0.77 to 0.81; citrus fruits from 0.41 to 0.49: Commission of the European Communities, *The European Community and the Mediterranean Basin*, Brussels, 1984, p. 106. Although the authors of this report do not specify the year to which the self-sufficiency ratios of the EC(9) apply, they presumably are those prevailing around 1980, just before the accession of Greece in the Community.

[45] According to the Commission, as a result of the accession of Spain and Portugal, the Community's self-sufficiency ratios would have reached 1.09–1.22 for wine, 0.89 for citrus fruits, 1.0 for most other fresh fruits and vegetables: Commission of the European Communities, "Problems of Enlargement: Taking Stock and Proposals", Supplement 8/82 to the *Bulletin of the European Communities*, 1982, pp. 12–15.

[46] S.A. Musto, "Southward Enlargement and Developing Countries: A Shift in the Community's Policy of Preferences?", in C. Stevens and J.V. van Themaat, eds., *Europe and the International Division of Labour*, London, Hodder and Stoughton, 1977, pp. 73–7.

47 Commission, "Memorandum on the Community's Development Policy", 1982, p. 22.

48 K. Featherstone, *Socialist Parties and European Integration: A Comparative History*, MUP, Manchester, 1988, pp. 179–80.

49 Commission, *European Community and the Mediterranean Basin*, 1984, p. 102.

50 Commission of the European Communities, *Commission Report to the Council on the Exploratory Talks with the Mediterranean and the Applicant Countries and the Commission Proposals Concerning the Implementation of a Mediterranean Policy for the Enlarged Community*, Doc. COM(84) 107 final, Brussels, 11 May 1984, pp. 15–25.

51 *Ibidem*, p. 26.

52 Economic recession in Europe and elsewhere had cut down the market strength of OPEC. Prices of oil were collapsing in international markets.

53 Reported in: Commission of the European Communities, *The Community and the Mediterranean Countries: Guidelines for Economic Cooperation*, Doc. COM(85) 517 final, Brussels, 26 September 1985, p. 1.

54 Commission of the European Communities, *Community and the Mediterranean Countries: Guidelines*, p. 13.

55 Additional protocols to the Cooperation Agreements were signed in 1987 with Algeria, Tunisia, Egypt, Jordan and Lebanon, and with Morocco and Syria in 1988. See Council of the European Communities, *Compilation of Texts, Vol. IV—Cooperation*, Brussels, 1988; *Compilation of Texts, Vol. V—Cooperation*, Brussels, 1989.

56 Council of the European Communities, *Press Release on the 1464th Council Meeting*, No. 10871/90, Brussels, 18–19 December 1990. The fourth financial protocol applies to the 1992–96 period. Of the ECU 2,375 million approved by the Council, ECU 775 million were regular budget funds, ECU 300 million were budget funds in support of economic reform and ECU 1,300 were EIB loans. The Maghreb/Mashreq split was not indicated.

57 Featherstone, "Mediterranean Challenge", p. 199.

58 The most recent survey of such evidence is that of Pomfret, who also offers his original results in several areas. See Pomfret, *Mediterranean Policy*, pp. 46–62.

59 See for example, T. Hitiris, *Trade Effects of Economic Association with the Common Market: The Case of Greece*, New York, Praeger, 1972,

pp. 138-41. G.J. Kalalmotousakis, "Greece's Association with The European Community: An Evaluation of the First Ten Years", in Shlaim and Yannopoulos, eds., *EEC and the Mediterranean Countries*, pp. 141-60; M. McQueen, "Some Measures of the Economic Effects of Common Market Trade Preferences for the Mediterranean Countries", in Shlaim and Yannopoulos, eds. *EEC and the Mediterranean Countries*, pp. 13-32.

60 M. McQueen, "Some Measures of the Economic Effects", p. 21; J.N. Bridge, "The EEC and Turkey: An Analysis of the Association Agreement and its Impact on Turkish Economic Development", in Shlaim and Yannopoulos, eds. *EEC and the Mediterranean Countries*, pp. 161-77.

61 J. Donges, "The Economic Integration of Spain with the EEC: Problems and Prospects", in Shlaim and Yannopoulos, *EEC and the Mediterranean Countries*, pp. 217-41; R. Pomfret and B. Toren, *Israel and the European Common Market: An Appraisal of the 1975 Free Trade Agreement*, Kieler Studien No. 161 Tubingen, J.C.B. Mohr, 1980.

62 M. McQueen, "Some Measures of the Economic Effects", p. 21.

63 R. Pomfret, "Trade Effects of the European Community Preferences to Mediterranean Countries", *World Development*, Vol. 10, No. 10, 1982, pp. 857-62.

64 G.N. Yannopoulos, "Patterns of Response to the EC Tariff Preferences: An Empirical Investigation of Selected Non-ACP Associates", *Journal of Common Market Studies*, Vol. 25, No. 1, 1986, pp. 15-30.

65 *Ibidem*, pp. 25-7.

66 See, for example, the report of the Commission to the Council on the exploratory talks with the Mediterranean countries before the second enlargement of the Community for a condensed summary of the grievances heard during that round of talks: Commission, *Exploratory Talks with the Mediterranean Countries*, 1984, pp. 3-5.

67 Pomfret, *Mediterranean Policy*, p. 102.

68 G. Minet, "Spanish and European Diplomacy at a Crossroads", in G. Minet, J. Siotis and P. Tsakaloyannis, eds., *Spain, Greece and Community Politics*, Sussex European Papers No. 11, University of Sussex, 1981, p. 29.

69 Economic and Social Committee of the European Committees, *Report on the Mediterranean Policy of the European Community*, Doc. CES(89) 386 final, Brussels, 26 June 1989 (this is the Amato report, from the name of the rapporteur); Economic and Social Committee of the European Communities, *Opinion of the Economic and Social Committee*

on the Mediterranean Policy of the European Community, Doc. CES(89) 835, Brussels, 12 July 1989; *Additional Opinion of the Economic and Social Committee on the Mediterranean Policy of the European Community,* Doc. CES(90) 512, Brussels, 26 April 1990.

70 The European Parliament went as far as to promote in 1989 a Conference for Global Cooperation in the Mediterranean Region at which the setting up of a Mediterranean Cooperation Council was discussed.

71 Commission of the European Community, *Redirecting the Community's Mediterranean Policy—Communication to the Council,* Doc. SEC(89) 1961, Brussels, 23 November 1989; *Redirecting the Community's Mediterranean Policy: Proposals for the Period 1992-96—Communication to the Council,* Doc. SEC(90) 812 final, Brussels, 1 June 1990.

72 Economic and Social Committee, *Report on the Mediterranean Policy,* 1989, pp. 6, 16 and 17.

73 The report reads: "Economic and social stability in the Mediterranean area is of immediate interest to the Community for a number of other reasons. The entire area is beset with social unrest which spawns not only domestic conflicts (e.g. the "bread war" in Algeria) . . . but also degenerative phenomena, such as terrorism and Islamic fundamentalism, which now pose a real threat within the Community as well". *Ibidem,* p. 22; and again: "The Community has an interest in greater political stability in the Mediterranean and a peaceful solution to the many local disputes . . . At the roots of these conflicts, in addition to political, racial and religious strife, are economic problems which can only be solved by adopting a joint approach to development throughout the Mediterranean." *Ibidem,* p. 23.

74 "Socio-economic development in Mediterranean countries is also vital for the Community in view of their rapid demographic growth. The population of the Mediterranean countries stands today at about 200 million, as against the Community's 321 million. By 2020, the figure will be 500 million in Mediterranean countries and 310 million in the Community . . . Demographic growth on this scale will pose enormous social problems for the Community." *Ibidem,* p. 21.

75 *Ibidem,* pp. 13-14 and p. 15.

76 Commission, *Mediterranean Policy for the Enlarged Community,* 1982, *op. cit.,* pp. 2-3; and Commission, *Exploratory Talks with the Mediterranean Countries,* 1984, pp. 15-19.

77 Commission, *Redirecting the Community's Mediterranean Policy,* 1990. The Commission concluded that "current trends in the Community and the Mediterranean non-Community countries would quickly make

a worsening of the economic and social imbalance between the two regions virtually unmanageable. Owing to its proximity and the volume of trade generated, the stability and prosperity of the Mediterranean region are essential to the stability and prosperity of the Community. In a wider sense, the security of the Community is at stake (local or regional conflicts, political instability, terrorism, drugs, environment)." These were nearly the same words used by the ESC in 1989.

78 Commission, *Redirecting the Community's Mediterranean Policy*, 1990, p. 2.

79 Council of the European Communities, *Press Release*, No. 10871/90, p. 1.

80 See Final Communique in *Bulletin of the European Communities*, No. 12, 1990, p. 14.

81 Tariff dismantling is to be completed by the beginning of 1993, instead of 1996. Tariff quotas and indicative ceilings fixed by the additional protocols are to be increased by 12-20 percent in four years according to products.

6

The Periphery of EC Reach: Trade and Cooperation Policies with Latin America

Latin America lies at the outer limits of the Community's development reach. Relative to that of sub-Saharan Africa and the Mediterranean, the position occupied by Latin America in the scale of development cooperation priorities pursued by the Community has not changed much since the 1950s. The region has remained a marginal concern for the Community, notwithstanding the attempts made at different times to expand the geographical reach of EC development cooperation.

Latin America's marginal priority for the EC is not the result of lack of links between the two continents. Europe had maintained strong cultural, religious and commercial ties with Latin America well past the time the continent had reached political independence from Spain and Portugal. Until World War I, Latin America had been Europe's most important trade partner. European capital, especially British, had played a key role in the development of the region.[1] The two continents are quite close in traditions and basic civilization.

Outside the direct political sphere, ties with Latin America in the late 1950s were at least as strong, if not stronger, than those that Europe had with Africa. From the standpoint of trade Latin America was almost as important to Europe as Africa, both as an export outlet and as a supplier of goods. In 1960, for example, total European exports to Africa (including North Africa) accounted for 7 percent of the total, against the 6.3 percent exported to Latin America. This region, unscathed by World War II, had been able to supply Europe with much needed food and raw materials in the immediate aftermath of the war. As for EC countries, exports to Africa amounted in 1958 to 9.6

percent of the total, while those to Latin America were a little over 6.7 percent. As a supplier, Africa (again including North Africa) accounted for 11.5 percent of total EC imports and Latin America for 7.4 percent (Table 4.1). Latin America, moreover, despite the relatively inward-looking trade policies started after the Great Depression and the drift towards autarky that ensued, retained a strong economic potential and appeared poised for continued growth. It was a continent rich in natural resources and endowed with relatively skilled labor and good infrastructure. Actual wealth and potential economic growth offered Europe enormous opportunities. Relative commercial importance was not, therefore, the key factor tilting the Community towards Africa in the late 1950s.

Latin America offered Europe in general, and the Community in particular, much of the same complementarity of economic interests that was sought in sub-Saharan Africa. It produced efficiently and cheaply many of the temperate zone foodstuffs that Europe needed—grains, sugar, meat and dairy products— and some of the agricultural raw materials and tropical foodstuffs that Europe imported from Africa. For a while, Latin America had been the main source of natural rubber in the world, and it still was a major producer of textile fibers such as cotton and sisal. It was the largest world supplier of coffee and bananas. It was also rich in wood and minerals—copper, zinc, tin, lead, bauxite, iron ore, and fossil fuels—and capable of meeting European needs in these areas, while requiring the advanced manufactures that Europe was capable of producing competitively and in abundance. In addition, it had a purchasing power that was twice as large in absolute terms as that of Africa, thus offering Europe a far superior potential for growth in trade and specialization in production.

Finally, trade with Latin America, though subject to higher transport costs than trade with much of Africa, afforded Europe many comparative advantages from the standpoint of security of supplies. The Atlantic Ocean was not subject to any significant Soviet threat, and trade with Latin America did not depend on the availability of the Suez Canal. For Northern Europe in particular, trade with Latin America could be at least as good, if not preferable, to trade with much of eastern and southern Africa when transport security was explicitly considered.

If Europe had wanted to pick a geographical area of

concentration for its cooperation policies on the basis of relative development needs, Asia would have been the natural choice. If Europe had instead been looking for an area offering strong economic complementarities, security of supplies and commercial advantages, Asia could not have competed successfully with Latin America or Africa. Either one of these two areas would have been preferable to Asia, on grounds of both distance and security. Also Latin America should have been preferred for the market potential that it seemed capable of offering to Europe. As it turned out, the Community chose in favor of sub-Saharan Africa, more as a result of the political and economic residues of colonialism, and French influence over EC members in that period, than as a result of a rational process of search and choice collectively undertaken by its members. It was a decision made more in the domain of members' national traditions and direct interests, than for the maximization of Community economic interests or of development effectiveness. For these reasons, those in the EC that remained in favor of a purer developmental posture continued to advocate a global reach for the Community's development policies and to reserve much of their sympathy for Asia. And those who valued economic rationality, aside from traditions, continued to be in favor of closer ties between the EC and Latin America.

The Community and Latin America: A Stillborn Relationship?

The overriding characteristic of EC-Latin American relations in the area of development cooperation is their near absence, after more than two decades of attempts made on both sides. Quite apart from existing cultural, ethnic and religious ties, when seen against the potential for mutual benefits that enhanced economic relations between these two areas always appeared to have, the lack of significant progress in EC-Latin American cooperation is on the surface almost mystifying.

Europe and Latin America are highly complementary in economic terms. Relative factor endowments have always pointed to a high potential for specialization based on comparative advantages: Latin America in land and other natural resource-intensive products such as foods, agricultural raw materials and minerals–metals, and Europe in capital-intensive, high technology industrial products, especially capital goods. In a range of labor intensive manufactures—such as clothing, footwear, leather goods—one could have envisaged, on the basis of either the product cycle theory or the more traditional comparative costs theory, that Latin America would have had strong advantages and a solid basis for progressive specialization and exports to the Community (and other industrial areas). In addition, intra-industry trade with Europe (and North America) could have been envisaged as a strong possibility in a range of consumer semi-durables, from transport equipment to electronics. In the post-World War II period Latin America had all the prerequisites for agricultural and natural resource-led development, compatible with a strategy of progressive industrialization and fitting the dictates of international specialization.

Latin America, in addition to size and purchasing power, had the natural resources, the human resources and the capacity to attract the capital and technology necessary for successful development. In the 1950s and 1960s Europe could have been a natural market for its agricultural products, its minerals and metals and some of its labor-intensive manufactures. Unlike the United States, Europe did not have a competitive agriculture, and did not pose any threat of continental domination to Latin America. European capital and technology could have flown to Latin America, either embodied in European direct investments or by itself. Latin America could have satisfied European needs for security of supply of raw materials, while offering attractive, and possibly fast growing, markets for some of Europe's consumer and capital good exports. Cultural affinities, similarity of tastes and superior understanding of each other's needs should have meant unparalleled ease of cooperation between these two areas in the economic, social and political spheres.

These were potentially important factors, and not the figments of imagination of a few European and Latin American nostalgics.[2] The fact that external factors and policy choices made by both sides prevented the development of a strong cooperative relationship between the countries of these two continents does not disprove either the existence of a wide potential for it or the relevance of this potential. The reasons for the non-cooperative outcome need to be understood.

The Elusive Beginning of EC–Latin American Development Cooperation

On Europe's side, Community development cooperation, born under the sign of regionalism, did not venture out of the chosen African path until the early 1970s. No systematic, or even significant, attention was paid to Latin America in the initial period of Community building. Only in setting tariff preferences in favor of the associated countries for products such as coffee and cocoa, did the Community attempt to strike a balance between Africa's economic interests and those of Latin America, whose access to the EC market was being impaired by trade preferences in favor of Africa.[3]

Latin America did not lack friends within the Community. Italy was keen on cultivating its historical and ethnic ties with several Latin American countries—Argentina, Chile, Uruguay, Peru and Venezuela among them—and kept a benign eye on their interests whenever they were affected by common EC policies. Yet, despite the role played in the establishment of the Community, Italy's influence on its affairs was not too great, and certainly not comparable to that of France or Germany. Still it was largely at the initiative of Italy that a declaration of intent was addressed to Latin America after the signature of the Rome Treaty. And when the Community began to look at Latin America in the late 1960s, it was again at the urging of Italy. But an EC approach to Latin America as a continent still took more than two decades to start. By the time the EC made its first serious attempt to establish intercontinental cooperative ties, the two areas had grown almost irreparably apart.

Latin America had suspected since the beginning that the very formation of the EC was likely to be detrimental to its trade interests. This fear had to do with both the common tariff policy envisaged by the Treaty of Rome and with the free-trade area that it set up with African colonies, whose primary exports competed to a considerable extent with those of Latin America (coffee, cocoa, bananas, tropical oils and fats). The EC Memorandum of Intention notwithstanding,[4] Latin America was acutely aware of the fact that its commercial interests in Europe were larger than those of Europe in Latin America. Its trade relationship with Europe was strongly asymmetrical. Latin America, therefore, felt threatened economically by the establishment of the EC,[5] and this perception was justified.

The trade dependence of Latin America on the EC was still very strong in the late 1950s. The Community was its second largest export market: about 17 percent of all Latin American exports went to the Community (Table 6.1). Dependence on the EC was even higher in key primary commodities. Over 35 percent of cotton, wool and copper, about 25 percent of meat, wheat, bananas and tobacco, and 20 percent of coffee and cocoa exports went to the EC. Some Latin American countries— Uruguay, Argentina and Chile—depended on the EC market for a third or more of their total exports. Others, like Peru and Paraguay, depended on the EC for one-fifth of their exports. Reduced access to Community markets, as a consequence of EC trade discrimination, would have made the "close relations and cooperation" with Latin America that the EC was apparently seeking very difficult, if not outright impossible, to achieve.[6] Latin Americans felt abandoned by Europe and at the same time bewildered by the lack of concern that Europeans were showing over the possible negative external effects of their common market.[7]

This turn of events highlighted for many Latin Americans the need for bargaining power to confront the emerging European economic bloc successfully, in addition to coping with the United States, the ever present, overbearing northern neighbor. This was a need that the newly created Economic Commission for Latin America (ECLA) saw as fitting well in the economic development strategy that it envisaged for the region, and therefore worth espousing immediately.[8] Coordination of trade and industrial policies at the regional level was then advocated by many as a precondition for both successful development and for safeguarding regional interests in international economic negotiations. And the defensive responses of Latin America were quick to come: in February 1960, with the Treaty of Montevideo, the establishment of the Latin American Free Trade Association (LAFTA) was agreed upon. The General Treaty on Central American Economic Integration, laying the foundations for the Central American

Table 6.1 Geographical Distribution of Latin America's Exports (percentage of total exports)

Exports to:	1958–61	1963	1973	1980	1985	1987
North America	45	38	37	36	40	42
EC[a]	17	31 (19)	26 (19)	22	21	20
EFTA[b]	12	3 (12)	3 (9)	2	1	2
Japan	3	4	5	4	4	5
Latin America[c]	9	15	17	21	17	14
Other developing countries	10	2	4	6	8	6

[a] EC(6) in 1958–61 and EC(12) from 1963. Figures in parenthesis for 1963 and 1973 are shares for EC(6).

[b] EFTA(7) in 1958–61 and EFTA(6) from 1963. Figures in parenthesis for 1963 and 1973 are shares for EFTA(7).

[c] Intra-trade.

Sources: General Agreement on Tariffs and Trade (GATT), *International Trade*, Geneva (various issues); Organization of American States (OAS), "The Effects of the European Community on the Latin American Economies", Washington D.C., 1963 (mimeo.).

Common Market, came later in the same year. While these decisions had other important determinants,[9] the desire of Latin American countries to respond in a coordinated fashion to the new challenge coming from the EC was present at the very creation of these mechanisms of regional cooperation.[10]

A type of dialogue of the deaf went on between the Community and Latin America during the 1960s. Low-level talks between their respective representatives were held. Questions were posed and answers provided by one party or the other, but no tangible results were reached.[11] The Community was then consolidating its preferential trade policies towards the former colonies and setting up its common agricultural policy, while Latin America was pushing for its own regional integration.

The development of the EC Common Agricultural Policy in the late 1960s appeared to many in Latin America to seal the issue of "special cooperation" with Europe. The danger posed by the CAP to Latin American interests had been spotted very early and clearly by local observers.[12] A narrowly protective policy concerning temperate-zone foods was by then prevailing within the Community, and Latin American exports of grains and meat were in the process of being shunted out of the EC market. Latin America felt its economic interests vitally threatened. Politically, it felt betrayed. Outright economic hostility from the Community had been feared, but possibly never expected in actuality. In trade and economic relations a sense of hostility between the two regions lasted until the late 1970s. The gusto with which Latin America led in the Group of 77, championed the quest for a "new international economic order" and castigated GATT for its effectiveness, when not for its duplicity, can only be understood against this background. At the political level, restoration of reciprocal understanding has yet to be fully achieved.

Not all the misunderstandings and lack of concrete results could be blamed on Europe. Much of Latin America had persisted since the end of World War II with inward-looking development strategies, first at the national, then at the regional level. The policies followed had considerably complicated trade and investment relations between Latin America and the rest of the industrial world, including Europe. In the post-war period, under the influence of the economics of ECLA, most Latin American countries had chosen to emphasize industrialization based on import substitution and reliance on domestic markets. The goal was to change the agrarian structure of most of the economies of the continent into an industrial one, based on modern technology.[13] Growth was as a matter of course believed to be dependent on technological progress, and industry was considered to be the natural conveyor of such progress. This phase, which is sometimes called "structuralism I",[14] lasted until the early 1960s.

When the limits to industrialization posed by the limited size of domestic markets and the distortions caused by strict protection of home manufacturing became evident, Latin America, again under the intellectual leadership of ECLA, attempted to continue the same strategy, but on a regional basis.[15] Through regional integration, it was thought, market size would be enlarged, more competition would be created, efficiency in production would be increased and the economic costs of import substitution would correspondingly be reduced. Structuralism II, as this phase is sometimes called,[16] lasted until the early 1970s. It provided another strong rationale for regional integration and economic cooperation among Latin American countries. Above all it continued to focus their attention inwards and led many Latin American policy makers to find in the notion of a hostile external environment the justification for pursuing, far beyond that prudence and good sense would have dictated, policies that were producing neither growth nor structural transformation, let alone greater internal equality. In these circumstances dialogue with the EC could not but be considered somewhat superfluous from the political standpoint and only very loosely justified economically. At best, Latin America could learn from the EC experience how to discriminate more efficiently, but not much more. During the 1960s both continents were looking inward and distance between the two grew inexorably.

Latin American countries, moreover, had by a vast majority refused to take part in GATT, leading the third world into an openly skeptical, if not hostile, position towards multilateralism in trade relations.[17] Because of such a position, another opportunity for dialogue with Europe was lost. On ideological grounds Latin America was also growing progressively more skeptical towards foreign investments. Reality and myths concerning multinational corporations were blending into an accepted philosophy of nearly *a priori* rejection of their usefulness to Latin American development. Foreign, including European, direct investments did not actually cease. But the environment in which they took place worsened. Several countries introduced restrictive codes on the basis of non-economic considerations. Finally, because of Cuba, and the ensuing preoccupations with the spread of Communism in the hemisphere, many Latin American countries leaned politically towards Washington. The US sphere of influence seemed to be regaining importance, notwithstanding the diplomatic forays of General de Gaulle into Latin America, and the bridges with Spain and Italy that remained intact during this period.

There were exceptions in the economic sphere. European, especially German and British, direct investments, for example, developed strongly in both Brazil and Argentina.[18] By and large, however, overall trade linkages were becoming progressively weaker, mostly as the result of the barriers to Latin America's exports erected by the EC via the CAP. And in the opposite direction they were weakening because of the constraints to

European exports created by the strict import-substitution and high-protection policies pursued by most Latin American countries. By the early 1970s, the share of EC exports going to Latin America had fallen to 3.3 percent of the total, and the share of EC imports from Latin America to 3.6 percent (Table 4.1). Europe was still occupying an important position among the export markets of Latin America, but its relative absorption of Latin America's exports was already falling significantly. Relative linkages through goods markets, traditionally the most important, were weakening between Europe and Latin America. The two continents were moving apart economically. Regional import substitution was increasing intra-trade in Latin America relative to external trade (Table 6.1). The southern hemisphere was in this sense following the footsteps of the Community: it was looking more and more inward when it came to trade. The key difference lay in the fact that while trade as a share of output was growing in Europe, it was declining throughout Latin America.

When called to justify this progressive estrangement from Latin America, EC officials resorted more and more to notions such as the political and economic fragmentation of the region, the lack of reliable interlocutors for the Latin American continent, and the want of realism in the expectations entertained by Latin American leaders about the CAP or financial assistance from the Community. After all Latin America represented the "middle class" of the developing world, and yet it still seemed to pretend that Europe should treat it in the same fashion as the "proletariat". Or so EC officials often said or seemed to imply.[19]

Dialogues Started but Not Developed

The first breakthrough in EC–Latin American relations occurred in 1970, with the beginning of the "Brussels dialogue", following the EC Council's Declaration of December of the same year and the establishment of an EC/LA Joint Committee. What looked like the creation of the first institutional link between the two regions and the start of a genuine interregional dialogue had antecedents in the Italian Memorandum to the Council of 1968, which had emphasized the need for Community relations with Latin America, and in the Commission's first report to the Council on relations with Latin America of 1969.

It also has antecedents in the Declaration of Buenos Aires of July 1970, in which the foreign ministers of the countries belonging to the Special Committee for Latin American Coordination[20] had proposed immediate ministerial-level consultations between the two regional blocs to establish an effective system of cooperation. Finally, there was the first serious setback suffered by LAFTA a year earlier, in the form of disagreement among its member countries over the implementation of trade liberalization, with the consequent postponement to 1980 of the establishment of a free-trade zone among them. Against this background, the beginning of regular meetings between the Group of Latin American Ambassadors in Brussels (GRULA) and EC representatives in what became known as the "Brussels dialogue", plus the enactment of the Community's GSPs in 1971, seemed to have ushered in a definite improvement in EC–LA relations. The preferences now being granted by the EC on the imports of industrial products looked like a definite and welcome change in its trade policies towards Latin America and Asia, which had been governed until then by reciprocity and the most favored nation principle. The GSPs also marked the beginning of a rebalancing of the positions of Latin America and Asia in the hierarchy of trade privileges granted by the Community to developing countries.

The EC, moreover, soon opened a second track in its relations with Latin America, by concluding bilateral trade agreements with certain countries of the continent: with Argentina in 1971, Uruguay in 1973 and Brazil in 1974.[21] While not amounting to much in effective content, as they did not foresee either the concession of trade preferences or the supply of financial assistance by the Community, these bilateral agreements seemed nonetheless to indicate at least a new EC interest in the region and augur better relations for the future. Not until much later did the agreements come to be considered much less favorably, as the manifestation of a "selective" approach towards Latin America simply aimed at solidifying existing bilateral links or even at establishing a base for competing better in traditional US markets.[22] In the same years the EC also decided to extend financial aid to Latin America, though only to some of the poorest countries in the region,[23] in line with the philosophy of aid allocation espoused in the "Fresco" Document.[24] From the beginning, therefore, EC aid privileged

Central American countries, a characteristic that never changed (Table 6.2). They continued to be the target of a preponderant share of EC economic assistance, given first as direct country aid, then as regional aid. The extension of EC financial assistance to Latin America, a potentially significant development, coincided, however, with LAFTA's indefinite suspension of the

Table 6.2 Direct Community Aid to Latin America (commitments, million ECU)

	1976-80 (average)	(%)	1981-85 (average)	(%)	1986-89 (average)	(%)
Central America						
Costa Rica	—		31.6		0.6	
Honduras	14.9		30.2		5.5	
Nicaragua	5.5		25.6		3.5	
El Salvador	—		3.3		9.5	
Guatemala	—		—		14.0	
Total	20.4	(26.8)	90.7	(34.4)	33.1	(15.0)
Caribbean[a]						
Haiti	13.9		7.1		—	
Dominican Republic	4.8		12.0		—	
Total	18.7	(24.5)	19.1	(7.3)	—	(0.0)
South America						
Bolivia	8.7		54.9		25.6	
Colombia	—		7.9		—	
Ecuador	2.9		5.9		9.0	
Peru	3.5		11.6		21.4	
Total	15.1	(19.8)	80.3	(30.5)	56.0	(25.0)
Regional organizations	22.1	(29.0)	73.1	(27.8)	131.1[b]	(60.0)
Latin America	76.3	(100.0)	263.2	(100.0)	220.2	(100.0)

Note: Includes financial aid for standard and disaster relief project (aid to agricultural research centers is not included).

[a] Non-associated countries only. Haiti and the Dominican Republic became "associates" under Lomé IV.

[b] Of which ECU 102.3 million to Central America, ECU 20.8 million to Andean Pact countries and ECU 8 million to other regional organizations.

Source: Commission of the European Communities, *Eleventh Annual Report to the Council and the European Parliament on the Implementation of Financial and Technical Assistance to Latin American and Asian Developing Countries*, Doc. COM(88) 715 final, Brussels, 1989.

goal of establishing a free-trade area. The ideal of regional integration was losing strength in Latin America.

While this was going on, however, the Community was still solidifying the regional focus on its development cooperation policies by extending preferential trade and aid regimes to the Anglophone countries of Africa. The signing of the Lomé Convention in 1975 did in fact put a practical end to the "new" phase in EC-LA relations, notwithstanding the establishment of SELA (Sistema Económica Latinoamericano) as a replacement for LAFTA as the locus for the design of regional development cooperation policies and coordination of external economic relations.[25] The Brussels dialogue, never too lively, became comatose soon thereafter. EC Europe, shocked by OPEC and economic recession was now seeking a Euro-Arab dialogue and focusing on the Mediterranean area as a matter of high priority. Official interest in Latin America, aside from oil producing countries such as Mexico and large mineral exporters such as Brazil, became again totally peripheral.[26] Latin America, on the other hand, could not but notice that the main thrust of EC development cooperation interests remained outside the South American continent.

Some efforts at reopening at least a channel for communication with the Community were made by GRULA in 1979, but they fizzled out, first over the ill-conceived admission of Cuba to this group,[27] and subsequently because of the Malvinas-Falklands conflict and the economic sanctions against Argentina adopted by the EC Council in 1982. The serious effort made by the Latin America Council, the governing organ of SELA, with its "Decision 44", to establish the elements of a common policy towards the EC in trade, aid, investments and technology transfers, including the definition of mechanisms of action to respond collectively to EC protectionism,[28] was in vain. Another "new" beginning had to wait until 1983-84, spearheaded by the sudden expression of political interest by the EC countries in Central America.

The Politicization of EC-Latin American Relations: The Current Phase

If it was SELA that again pressed for a resumption of dialogue in late 1983,[29] while the Community was completing its negotiations for a Cooperation Agreement with the Andean

Pact,[30] some significant movement had already occurred inside the EC Commission around 1980. In an internal paper prepared by the Directorate of External Affairs, the opportunity to make new efforts towards "one of the world's most important continents" had been underlined by Commissioner Haferkamp.[31] It was not, however, until the Conference between the Ministers of Foreign Affairs of the Community and those of Central American General Treaty and of the Contadora Group,[32] held in 1984 in San Jose, Costa Rica, that EC-LA relations were put on a new footing. It took EC Europe's solemn and open backing of the Contadora Group and its political objectives to generate the new "breakthrough". This expression of political will by EC Europe may not have signified the "end of the Monroe Doctrine", but it was certainly a turning point in relations with Latin America.[33] It marked the beginning of a phase in the political relations between the two continents that certainly had no precedent (and quite possibly no secure future).

The premise of the Commission's Communication to the Council in April 1984 on relations with Latin America and the ways to strengthen them was clearly political.[34] It referred to SELA's initiative, to the October 1983 resolution of the European Parliament, to the movement towards democracy in Latin America, and to the reinstatement of a civilian government in Argentina. Naturally, the document also referred to the economic crisis of Latin America and examined the options open in the field of economic cooperation, but it openly recognized that "the strengthening of relations between the Community and Latin America [went] beyond the economic sphere". It emphasized the importance of respect for human rights in the southern hemisphere, of the contacts with Latin American political circles being established by the European Parliament, and above all of the need "for massive Community support to the reawakening of democracy in Latin America".[35]

The accession of Spain and Portugal to the Community in 1985 gave rise to another serious problem in EC-LA relations, since as a consequence, the Latin American countries were going to lose access to the hitherto relatively more open markets of these two countries (particularly for their agricultural and food exports). They would also face increased competition in EC(9) markets from the new member countries' exports of labor-intensive manufactures.[36] The magnitude of these commercial problems, at least in the short term, seemed to outweigh the possible positive consequence in the political sphere deriving from the insertion of two "friends of Latin America" among the EC members.[37] At the urging of Spain and Portugal, the Community attempted to handle this issue by offering "to examine any problems in the field of trade with the view of finding appropriate solutions",[38] and by speeding up action on a broad front. The EC Council at its June 1986 meeting in the Hague invited the Commission to focus on specific ways to strengthen relations with Latin America. The Commission responded speedily with its Communication of December 1986,[39] which led to the first "conclusion" ever adopted by the Council on relations with Latin America the next year.

In endorsing most of the proposals of the Commission, the Council again emphasized the political importance of EC–Latin American cooperation.[40] The "promising developments which could bring the two regions closer together" mentioned by the EC ministers, were the return to democratic government and the setting up of regional integration areas in Latin America. The twelve ministers agreed that "increased cooperation and consultation on economic and commercial matters should be accompanied by stepping up of political relations", and that "by their actions, they will continue to support the establishment of democracy in all Latin American countries and endeavour to strengthen democratic governments in the regions". The decision taken by the EC member countries at the Hamburg Conference of 1988 to support the plan for the reconstruction and development of Central America presented by the isthmus countries, seemed typical of the open link established between economic and political cooperation initiatives. It was also a concrete example of the cooperation pledged by the Community when the first agreement with Central America was signed in 1985.

When closely examined, the guidelines adopted by the Council did not amount to much in the economic sphere: (a) continuation (and unspecified improvement) of official development assistance, as always, concentrated on the least developed countries of Latin America; (b) support of regional integration; (c) possible broadening of access to the Community's market through more effective use of GSPs; (d) support of trade promotion and a promise to take account of the export interests of Latin America in the Uruguay Round of GATT trade negotiations; (e) special emphasis on industrial cooperation "in the broad sense"; (f) support for training administrators or technicians; and (g) possible expansion of export credits. The Community did not promise more aid in support of South American democracies, nor did it appreciably improve Latin America's access to EC markets. Neither the MFA nor the CAP barriers to Latin American exports to the Community were mentioned by the Council, let alone reduced. The Commission's innovative proposal to extend EIB financing to Latin America was not endorsed. The debt problem of Latin America was only barely acknowledged. Nothing was offered in the way of assistance, either region-specific or general, in the area of debt.[41]

The politicization of relations between EC Europe and Latin America did not, therefore, prevent the EC from absconding when confronted with a problem critical to the survival of Latin economies: debt. The recognition of a debt–democracy link did not translate into any autonomous action by the Community to alleviate the burden carried by any of the Latin American countries. Here again, the "bourgeoisie of the developing world" did not seem to deserve the same treatment as the "proletariat" of Africa. The Community refrained from any autonomous initiative, general or country-specific, seemingly content to follow the US lead in the debt strategy, notwithstanding doubts entertained at the highest echelons of the Commission and at times openly expressed.[42] Lack of competence in the area of debt was at times mentioned.[43] At other times the need not to interfere with the actions of the commercial banks, or more generally the market, was stressed,[44] as if interventionist impulses had not emerged inside the Community every time a specific sector of its economy came under pressure and as if room had not been found for Community action in the interstices of the Treaty of Rome. Nor had any debt initiative come from EC members acting autonomously, outside the EC framework.

Difficult to understand in a climate of improving relations, the absence of EC action on Latin American debt is even more difficult to comprehend, let alone rationalize, when relations between the two regions were taking on, at the initiative of the twelve EC members, an increasingly political connotation.

Moreover, not only was much of Latin America responding to the debt crisis in a largely orthodox and responsible way,[45] but its overall economic policy thrust was also changing rapidly in the 1980s and moving towards outward-looking strategies, reduction of the role of the state in the economy, liberalization of goods and products markets and financial sector reform. In fact, after the first attempts to achieve more openness in the domestic economies and greater reliance on exports as an engine of growth made in the mid-1970s by several Latin American countries (particularly in the Southern Cone), economic policies throughout the continent took quite a drastic turn towards greater market orientation in the 1980s. Import-substitution policies were scrapped in favor of neutral or export-biased policies; liberalization became widespread and economic reforms were aimed at making the various economies more efficient and competitive through greater internal and external competition. These policy changes were in tune with the new economic orthodoxy prevailing in the decade of the 1980s; orthodoxy which was actively embraced and sponsored by many EC members and by the international organizations in which they wielded considerable influence. Neither orthodox short-term responses to the debt problem, aimed at reducing domestic absorption and generating export surpluses in order to service the external debt, nor widespread structural adjustment in the direction advocated by industrial countries and the multilateral institutions, seemed sufficient for Latin America to obtain special attention from the Community in the area of debt.[46]

The Policies that Mattered: Trade and Agriculture

Whenever asked what constituted the major obstacles to the development of cooperative economic relations with Europe, Latin Americans have nearly unanimously and consistently identified the Community's common agricultural policy and the trade preferences it granted to the associated countries of Africa. This view has remained dominant until today among Latin American economists,[47] and has found widespread acceptance in political circles as well. According to this view, the Community has been guilty from the beginning of trade discrimination against Latin America in the areas of tropical and temperate-zone agriculture, to the advantage of African countries in the first area and of domestic producers in the second. Despite being the main force behind the request for a generalized system of preferences from industrial countries, Latin America has traditionally discounted the practical significance of these preferences which were designed to help its exports of industrial goods to the Community.

The reasons for this concentration of attention on the agricultural interests damaged by the CAP and by the EC trade preferences in favor of associated African countries are not difficult to understand. Despite the industrialization efforts made by the Latin American countries in the post-World War II period, their success at exporting manufactures was quite small until recently, and limited to a few countries. For the most part, Latin American countries remained highly dependent on export of agricultural commodities (Argentina, Uruguay), ores and metals (Peru, Chile), and fuels (Mexico, Venezuela and Ecuador). Even in 1987 almost half of Latin America's exports to the EC were still food items, followed by industrial raw materials, fuels and manufactures in almost equal proportions (Table 6.3). Over time, raw material exports lost some of their importance for Latin America in EC markets, while the share of manufactures correspondingly rose. Similar trends have become evident in Latin America's trade with the United States, but the decline in the relative importance of exports of food has been more marked in the United States than in Europe, as has the increase in the share of manufactures in total exports. More than 40 percent of all Latin American exports to the United States were manufactures in 1987, against only 10 percent in 1980. Over the same period the share of manufactures in exports to the EC increased from 12 to 18 percent. Exports to Japan, much less important than those going to the Community or to the United States, remained dominated by raw materials and fuels, with manufactures accounting for a smaller share than in either of the other major industrial markets.

Latin America's overall export specialization has not changed much over time. Relative product emphasis has continued to be on food and minerals–metals to all three major industrial

Table 6.3 Product Structure of Latin American Exports to Major Industrial Areas (percentage of total)

	Food[a]	Raw Materials[b]	Fuels[c]	Manufactures[d]
Exports to EC				
1970	51.7	33.7	8.2	6.2
1975	50.7	23.5	14.1	11.1
1980	39.9	22.9	24.2	12.3
1987	46.0	19.4	15.8	18.1
Exports to US				
1970	38.4	18.6	32.4	10.2
1975	21.8	8.9	60.8	8.2
1980	21.4	6.9	61.3	10.0
1987	21.5	6.6	30.4	40.7
Exports to Japan				
1970	35.5	56.9	3.9	2.7
1975	40.5	50.5	2.1	6.7
1980	19.2	44.4	25.3	10.7
1987	23.4	39.6	21.5	14.9

Note: Rows may not add up to 100 due to statistical discrepancies.
a SITC 0+1+22+4
b SITC 2-22+67+68
b SITC 3
d SITC 5+6+7+8-67-68
Source: UNCTAD, *Handbook of Trade and Development Statistics*, 1986 and 1989.

markets, and on fuels to the US market. In all these cases the value of the specialization index shown in Table 6.4 is greater than unity, and often as high as 4 percent. The converse is a generalised "underspecialization" of Latin America in the export of manufactures. Between 1970 and 1987 the value of the index remains below unity in all three major industrial markets. Of the few changes in the sector intensity of Latin America's exports that seem to have occurred in this period, the most noteworthy are those in its trade with the EC, where the region's specialization increased in both food and mineral-metal products. Within the food group, the highest degree of specialization is still in exports of coffee and oil cake, where Latin America's share of EC markets is several times higher than its world market share. Within the mineral-metal group, Latin America specializes in the exports of copper and

Table 6.4 Latin America's Export Specialization by Product and Destination (specialization index)

	Food[a]	Agricultural Raw Materials[b]	Minerals, and Ores[c]	Fuels[d]	Manufactures[e]
Exports to EC					
1970	2.43	0.73	1.60	0.53	0.14
1975	3.25	0.82	1.90	0.43	0.35
1985	3.94	0.77	2.14	0.88	0.24
1987	4.73	0.78	2.68	0.90	0.31
Exports to US					
1970	2.48	0.42	1.29	3.80	0.18
1975	2.05	0.31	0.83	2.09	0.05
1985	2.91	0.54	1.13	3.00	0.82
1987	3.68	0.81	1.53	3.51	0.75
Exports to Japan					
1970	2.03	1.24	1.95	0.18	0.11
1975	2.33	1.74	3.97	0.05	0.30
1985	1.63	0.61	3.44	0.82	0.20
1987	2.01	0.67	4.39	0.75	0.16

Note: The specialization index is the ratio of the market share of Latin America in a given area for a given product to the overall export market share of Latin America in that area or $I = (X^i_{LAj}/X^i_{Wj}) / (X_{LAj}/X_{Wj})$, where j = area of destination; i = export product; LA = Latin America; W = world and X = exports.

When:

$I > 1$ Latin America tends to specialize in the export of product i to area j;

$I < 1$ Latin America tends to underspecialize in the export of product i to area j;

$I = 1$ Latin America is as strong an exporter of product i to area j as an exporter of all products to the same area (no specialization in product i to area j is present).

[a] SITC 0+1+22+4   [b] SITC 2-22-27-28   [c] SITC 27+28+67+68
[d] SITC 3   [e] SITC 6+7+8-67-68

Source. UNCTAD, *Handbook of International Trade and Development Statistics,* 1988 (for trade data).

iron ore. All these are products in which Latin America does not directly compete with the EC.

General reliance on traditional exports of primary commodities, whose demand grows slowly relative to income, and EC market barriers for temperate-zone food products, where Latin America could easily displace local production, account for a good deal of the "marginalization" of the region's exports to the Community. The region's share of total EC imports has declined by nearly half since 1958: from 10.3 to 5.8 percent. Latin American exports to the Community have done better than those of ACP countries, but substantially less well than those of both the Mediterranean countries and the Asian NICs (Table 4.5). As observed by Sandro Sideri, the tormented economic development of this region is well reflected in its halting participation in world trade.[48]

As to the causes of these trends, while the Europeans have traditionally attributed them to the anti-trade bias present in the economic strategies of Latin American countries and pointed to the export success of East Asian countries in Community markets as indicative of the lack of binding trade policy constraints put in place by the EC,[49] Latin Americans have stressed the closure of EC markets to their exports, and lately, the growing effect of EC non-tariff protectionism on their manufactures.[50] Even for those Latin Americans ready to accept the fact that, on the basis of the tenets of international specialization and open trade, their continent should concentrate on the production of foods and raw materials for export, advocating such strategies has been made difficult by the existence of the EC common agricultural policy and the associated trade protectionism. Moreover, the greater success of some Latin American countries in exporting manufactures to the United States than to Europe in the late 1980s can hardly be divorced from relative market openness. More penetrable and certain, the US market has offered Latin American exporters of manufactures far better opportunities than the EC.

When not countering Latin Americans' expressions of concern with inane answers, denying, for example, the importance of the barriers to Latin America's exports generated by the CAP,[51] or when not countering their concerns at all,[52] the Community has tended to emphasize that GSPs give Latin American industrial products a significant degree of preferential access to EC markets and that the preference system now in place can be made progressively more flexible and less restrictive.[53] Recently, the Commission, at least in its communications to the Council, has even gone "as far" as to recognize that the reform of the CAP, however gradual, could have some positive repercussions for the Latin American countries,[54] while at the same time denying the undeniable—that "over-protection by the Community of industry or even agriculture had been a significant limiting factor for Latin America's exports".[55]

The Common Agricultural Policy and its Effects on Latin America

Even though recognition of past sins does not necessarily and immediately become redemption, the Commission seems to have at least begun to confront one critical aspect of Community relations with Latin America: the obstructionist presence of the CAP. The Council, on the other hand, has shown much greater reluctance to do so, at least publicly.[56] Naturally the reform of the CAP, inevitable as a final result, will not occur simply because of the requirements of EC-Latin American relations. Even the "global bargaining needs" of the Uruguay Rounds may not be sufficient to give it a decisive jolt. The beginning of the process may have to await further progress along the road of EC integration, when the CAP will no longer constitute a critically important unifying factor. What is important, however, is that the effects of such a reform on EC-Latin American relations are explicitly factored into the decision-making process. It is in fact improbable that a relationship between the two continents can begin in the absence of substantial change in the trade relations between them, a change that necessarily implies a reform of EC protectionism in agriculture, or a substantive economic compensation for its negative effects on Latin America.

The negative effects of the CAP on many developing countries that export, or could export, temperate-zone agricultural products are well recognized. They have to do, first, with the reduction in the volume of exports to the Community caused by the existence of very restrictive barriers to entry put in place to make the support of domestic production possible. Since this is done by offering domestic producers prices higher than those prevailing in international markets, protection from import competition becomes absolutely necessary. Internal price support requires barriers to imports that insulate the domestic market. The variable levies on imports of many temperate-zone agricultural products, equal to the generally positive difference between supported internal prices and international market prices, do just that. Efficient outside exporters of the protected products—such as grains, meat and dairy products—are shut out of the EC markets and thus damaged in their trade possibilities. These are the direct, trade diversionary, effects of the CAP: more efficient outside producers are replaced by less efficient inside suppliers.

The fact that the Community has become self-sufficient in most temperate-zone agricultural products (one of the key objectives of the policy) has neither stopped the CAP process nor put stringent limits to it. Excess production and artificially low domestic consumption caused by excessively high prices inside the EC continue to generate export surpluses. The Community has helped dispose of this excess production in many ways: through food aid, direct subsidies to exports (euphemistically called "export restitutions") and easy credit. Inevitably, EC-subsidized exports displace those of other producers in third markets, thus further damaging their interests. These are the indirect, external effects of the CAP on developing country producers, such a those of Latin America.

Finally, the CAP cuts off EC producers of many agricultural commodities from the international market. This transfers the burden of adjustment to market changes to non-protected (or less protected) producers in the rest of the world, which consequently face lower and less stable market prices than those that would prevail in the absence of the CAP. Protected EC domestic producers do not have to contract production when market prices fall. In their production decisions they respond to support prices set by fiat, not to international market prices. If support prices are not adapted to changes in international prices, EC producers keep producing even in a declining international market, thus pushing prices below what they would have been in the absence of internal support. The price depressing effects of subsidized EC agricultural production and exports are also well known. As a result, other exporters, among them the Latin American ones, see revenue shrink not only because their volumes diminish as a consequence of overproduction in the Community, but also because the unit prices that they actually fetch for the sale of their products are lower than what they would be in the absence of production support inside the Community. These are the international market price depressing effects of the CAP.

By shielding a portion of total world production from the dictates of the market, the CAP also contributes to greater instability of agricultural prices.[57] By failing to cut production in a declining market, EC suppliers accentuate downward swings in international prices. Similarly, by failing to increase production in a rising market, EC producers tend to accentuate upward swing in international prices. If a substantial portion of producers do not contribute to the adjustment of production to market price changes, the dynamics of the adjustment necessarily become more complicated, and greater price instability ensues. Price instability renders producers' decisions more uncertain, and thus complicates them. It also constitutes an obstacle to efficient resource allocation if producers' expectations are less than rational and stimulates substitution in consumption, which may or may not be reversible.[58] It may also generate macroeconomic difficulties wherever exports are highly concentrated, and total export revenues are highly sensitive to price variations. For all of these reasons, price instability is thought to place additional economic costs on the export suppliers that have to face it.

There are many estimates of the external effects of the common agricultural policy. They are based on a variety of models aimed at gauging the effects of price support, EC market protection and EC policies on the disposal of the quantities produced in excess of what would have happened in the absence of these policies, on the international market prices of the affected products.[59] Results obtained vary depending on estimation methodologies, commodity coverage, assumptions made about key parameter values and about changes in the CAP policies being considered. Yet, some broad common conclusions about its external effects can be derived from the available empirical evidence.[60] The first is that the CAP exerts a sizeable downward pressure on international market prices of temperate-zone agricultural products. The orders of magnitude are 5 to 9 percent for wheat, 3 to 15 percent for maize, 1 to 3 percent for rice, 10 to 17 percent for meat, 6 to 10 percent for sugar and 12 to 25 percent for dairy products.[61] The second conclusion is that trade volumes are also considerably affected by the CAP.

Its abolition would increase them considerably, as EC net imports of temperate-zone agricultural commodities would rise substantially, especially of wheat, grains and dairy products that are the most protected.

These are also the commodities in which Latin America specializes and holds sizeable comparative advantages.[62] Finally, the variability of the international market prices of CAP affected products would be substantially reduced: by half for dairy products, by a quarter to a half in the case of wheat, and by 10 to 20 percent in the case of coarse grains, rice, meat and sugar.

All this indicates that the Latin American countries would derive considerable benefits from a reform of the CAP, in terms of higher export volumes and higher and more stable export prices. While regional estimates of these effects are not numerous, those available point to sizeable overall magnitudes.[63] To deny the existence or to ignore the indicative value of this evidence is untenable from the standpoint of facts and is economically counterintuitive. It does not help the credibility of the Community and its external projection. Nor is it justifiable, beyond a certain point and a certain time, to continue to evoke the "political realities" that would make it virtually impossible to change the CAP, except in the very long run. Such long runs never occur.

Political realities inimical to the reform of the CAP do exist and they are indeed strong. The political economy of the CAP is quite well understood.[64] But the costs of the CAP to EC consumers and EC taxpayers are also well known. Total transfers associated with agricultural policies in the Community amounted in the late 1980s to more than ECU 90,000 million a year, or nearly 2 percent of the Community's GNP. Even when the gains to producers are factored in, the net economic costs of the CAP are estimated at about 1 percent of GNP.[65] Given the size of these costs, it is plainly incredible to argue that there are not other and less expensive ways to guarantee the incomes of the less fortunate among the EC farmers. The reform of the CAP is clearly in the interests of the EC countries, not to mention beneficial to the Latin American and other efficient producers of temperate-zone agricultural products in the rest of the world.

Other EC Trade Policies and Latin America

Aside from protecting its agricultural sector, the Community has long maintained a tight watch, and often strict control, over imports of steel and textile–clothing products. In both of these industrial sectors, where EC comparative advantages were felt to be on the wane, protection against import competition has increased over time, particularly through the use of non-tariff instruments: (a) import quotas on textile and clothing products, first within the context of the Short and Long Term Arrangements on Cotton Textiles and then the Multifiber Arrangements; and (b) quotas and minimum prices on imports of steel. Less formal market arrangements have reportedly been at work in other sectors, such as synthetic fibers, at least during some periods.

The restrictive import regime for textiles began in the early 1960s and continued in the following two decades. About half of all EC imports of textiles and clothing products are currently subject to quantitative limitations or to close surveillance. Another 25 percent are subject to the so-called basket-exit mechanism, whereby any outside supplier whose exports exceed a threshold share of total EC imports would be subject to further controls. Only the remaining 25 percent of imports, which come from other industrial countries, are totally unrestricted.

The imposition of quantitative restrictions on imports into the Community has not spared Latin American exporters. In 1990, of the twenty-eight bilateral MFA-type agreements in existence for the purpose of regulating imports of textile and clothing products to the Community, eight were with Latin American countries. Of these, three provided for quantitative restraints on thirteen imports from Argentina, Peru and Brazil. The remaining five, with Uruguay, Colombia, Guatemala, Haiti and Mexico, contained no specific quantitative restrictions.

The tightening of the import regime for steel began in the mid-1970s. The EC import regime has since varied in its degree of restrictiveness depending on the conditions prevailing in domestic and international markets, but steel markets have always remained heavily regulated. Currently about 15 percent of all EC imports are managed through voluntary export restraints (VERs). Brazil is a party to an export restraint agreement with the Community, one of the six now in effect. It is also the only developing country singled out in this way by the Community. The other five VERs now in existence in the steel sector are with Eastern European countries. Brazil and Venezuela have also been the target of other EC discriminatory trade practices in the iron and steel sector. Between 1980 and 1988, eleven anti-dumping investigations were initiated by the EC against Brazilian and two against Venezuelan exports of iron and steel products.

The EC resorted to using non-tariff barriers with noticeably increased frequency against imports from specific countries in the mid-1970s. The utilization of well publicized surveillance measures, the initiation of anti-dumping or anti-subsidy investigations on imports, the negotiation of export restraints outside the textile sector, the imposition of "price undertakings" on exporters (often as the result of anti-dumping or anti-subsidy actions)[66] became widespread in the first half of the 1980s, when recession hit Europe hard,[67] but did not cease when economic conditions improved. While not directed at Latin American exports in particular this type of non-tariff protection became another negative factor in EC–Latin American trade.

In the area of anti-dumping investigations alone, twenty-four (or nearly 7 percent of the total) were initiated against imports from Latin America between 1980 and 1988. While not overwhelming in total number, they still represented about one-third of all EC anti-dumping investigations against all developing country exporters (Table 6.5). Moreover, they concentrated on four Latin American NICs, with emphasis on Brazil (in the iron and steel sector) and Mexico (in the synthetic fibers sector). While the trade restricting effects of these EC measures are difficult to estimate, they certainly contributed to uncertainty about market access and possibly to the limitation of export investments in the affected sectors. For other non-tariff measures used by the EC against Latin American exports the trade restraining effects are quite clear. For example, voluntary restraints on sheep meat, the only major type of meat imported by the EC in substantial quantities, were imposed on all suppliers, including Argentina and Uruguay.

At the same time, the Community granted tariff preferences on imports of many industrial products from non-associated developing countries, thus giving exporters in Latin America

Table 6.5 Anti-dumping Investigations Initiated by the EC

Investigations Against	No. of Investigations 1980-88 (cumulative)	Percentage of Total
Industrial countries		
US	25	7.2
Western Europe	69	19.8
Canada	6	1.7
Japan	27	7.7
Others	5	1.4
Total	132	37.8
Developing countries		
Asian NICs[a]	30	8.6
Latin American NICs[b]	24	6.9
Others	22	6.3
Total	76	21.8
Centrally planned economies		
China	21	6.0
Eastern Europe	119	34.1
Others	1	0.3
Total	141	40.4
Total investigations	349	100.0

[a] Hong Kong, Korea, Taiwan and Singapore.
[b] Argentina, Brazil, Mexico and Venezuela.
Source: Commission of the European Communities, *Seventh Annual Report of the Commission on the Community's Anti-Dumping and Anti-Subsidy Activities,* Doc. COM(90) 29 final, Brussels, 1990.

and Asia a competitive advantage over those located in other industrial areas.[68] While not general from either the country or the product point of view, the system of trade preferences enacted by the Community in 1971 represented a substantial concession to middle-income developing countries on their way towards industrialization. EC GSPs seemed to be tailor-made for many Latin American countries and capable of offering them appreciable advantages and in some ways compensation for the trade preferences, mostly affecting tropical agricultural products, previously granted by the EC to the associated countries of Africa. With its expanding potential for producing industrial goods, Latin America seemed well placed to take advantage of the EC preferences.

Granted after considerable internal debate, and after substantive modifications to the proposals submitted by the Commission,[69] the EC preferential system implied duty-free treatment, within limits, for all manufactures and semi-manufactures imported from designated beneficiary countries. The beneficiaries were the developing countries that belonged to the Group of 77.[70] The limits consisted of the amounts of imports—the so-called ceilings or tariff quotas—to which the preferential treatment applied. For sensitive products, those which competed most strongly with domestic substitutes, the ceilings were rigidly enforced. Imports in excess of the specified limits were subject to the normal duty. For semi-sensitive products application of the normal duty was kept on reserve.[71] Non-sensitive products could be imported under the preferential tariff regime in practice without limitations. The lists of products subject to ceilings were specified by the EC. The product ceilings were then subdivided into specific amounts that could be exported at preferential rates to a given EC member—the member state shares. Maximum amounts exportable at preferential rates by any beneficiary—the so-called *butoirs*—were also specified at some proportion of the ceilings. Sensitive products faced ceilings, member country shares and *butoirs*. Semi-sensitive products were subject to ceilings and *butoirs*. Non-sensitive products were subject only to *butoirs*.

Only a few processed agricultural goods were included in the EC system of preferences, and those included were given only a small tariff margin. Textiles and clothing imports were granted preferential tariff treatment only if originating from countries that had submitted to "voluntary export agreements" under the Long Term Arrangement on Cotton Textiles.[72] To benefit from these preferences, which were granted unilaterally by the Community for a period of ten years and subject to annual verification, developing exporting countries had to respect specific "rules of origin". Finally, the Community's interests remained protected by a general safeguard clause, under which the EC reserved the right to suspend tariff preferences if they were considered to cause serious disruption in the domestic market.[73]

Marginally enlarged in product and country coverage,

liberalized in the actual treatment of covered products and extended for another ten years in 1981, the Community's GSP has maintained its original selective character at both the product and country levels and has never become a general system.[74] Textiles and clothing products have been kept under MFA management. Agricultural products coverage has remained partial.[75] The selective *modus operandi* of the scheme also has remained the same. *A priori* restrictions on the amounts of imports of covered products to which preferential treatment is applicable have been kept. Therefore, the scheme has failed to give beneficiary countries ample, or even general, tariff advantages.[76] In addition, applying largely to industrial products, the principal object of tariff liberalization under GATT, the scheme has seen even its limited preferential value erode over time.[77]

For all these reasons, in particular the less than average preference granted to processed agricultural exports, the GSPs were not of great advantage to Latin American countries. The percentage of utilization of EC GSPs by Latin American countries remained virtually stagnant between 1976 and 1986, while the actual coverage of Latin American exports by the EC system of preferences declined in the 1980s, after increasing substantially in the 1970s.[78] Only Brazil, Mexico and Venezuela seem to have derived some benefits from it in terms of increased exports to the Community.[79] On the whole this scheme mattered little to most eligible countries,[80] including the middle-income beneficiaries of Latin America that had lobbied long and hard for it.

Aid to Latin America: Little and Late

Alluded to in the Commission's 1971 memorandum on development policy, justified in the "Fresco" Document three years later,[81] concretely spelled out in the 1975 Action Program,[82] financial aid to the non-associated developing countries of Latin America (and Asia) did not begin until 1976, and it was little more than a token gesture. A clear enunciation of its fundamental objectives had to wait until 1981, when the Council finally laid them down as "improvement in the living conditions of the most needy sections of the population of the countries concerned", with special attention paid "to the development of the rural environment and to improving food production".[83] Allocations of financial assistance to non-associated Latin American countries, all in the form of grants, increased from about ECU 75 million a year in 1976–80 to over ECU 260 million a year in 1981–85 (Table 6.2), and declined to little over ECU 200 million a year in 1986–89.

In 1978, Latin America, with a population of about 400 million (approximately the same as that of the ACP countries), received the equivalent of only 6 percent of the programed grant aid going to the ACP countries from the Community. The bias of EC grant aid distribution against non-associated countries becomes even greater if aid to Asia is also considered. Asia receives five times less financial aid from the Community than the ACP countries, notwithstanding a population six times as large.

Intended by the Commission for distribution according to the average income levels of the recipient countries, which was taken to be a "pertinent indicator of the needs and capacities of these countries, including any shortage of the basic infrastructure for development",[84] financial aid to Latin America has been extended over the years to eleven countries: those of the Central American Common Market (Honduras, Nicaragua, Costa Rica, El Salvador and Guatemala), those of Hispaniola (Haiti and the Dominican Republic), and Bolivia, Ecuador, Colombia and Peru in South America. Aid to Colombia and Ecuador was minuscule. Disaster relief aid was granted to Mexico once. In addition, financial aid was given to regional organizations, especially the Junta of the Andean Pact (JUNAC) and various bodies related to the Central American Common Market. Regional aid has grown in relative terms, to represent 59 percent of total aid to Latin America in 1986–89.

In actuality, geographical distribution of EC financial aid within Latin America corresponds only roughly to even the simple criteria adopted by the Commission to meet the Council's objectives. The poorer countries of Central America did receive more aid over the 1976–88 period than the richer ones in the Andean Pact or in the rest of South America. This applied to both absolute and per capita aid levels. Yet, Haiti and the Dominican Republic received only a little more than half the aid per capita that went to Central American countries, notwithstanding their much lower income per capita (Table 6.6).

Table 6.6 Direct EC Aid to Latin America

Recipient countries	1987 GNP per capita US$	Population (million)	1976-88 (cumulative) Financial Aid[a] (million ECU)	Total Aid[b] (million ECU)	Financial Aid per capita[c] (ECU)	Total Aid per capita (ECU)
Hispaniola[d]	555	13	44.1	89.9	3.4	6.9
Central America[e]	1,011	27	175.4	398.3	6.5	14.8
Andean Pact[f]	1,485	89	179.7	336.9	2.0	3.8
Rest of South America[g]	2,079	270	25.2	143.8	0.1	0.5
Total Latin America[h]	1,825	399	424.4	968.9	1.1	2.4

a   Excluding regional aid.

b   Including financial aid, food (direct and indirect) aid, humanitarian aid, economic cooperation assistance, plus miscellaneous aid.

c   Based on 1987 populations.

d   Haiti and Dominican Republic (before their membership in Lomé).

e   Costa Rica, Guatemala, Honduras, Nicaragua, Salvador.

f   Bolivia, Colombia, Ecuador, Peru and Venezuela (Andean Pact), plus Paraguay.

g   Argentina, Brazil, Chile, Mexico and Uruguay.

h   Excluding the countries associated to the EC through Lomé.

Sources: Commission of the European Communities, *Thirteen Years of Development Cooperation with the Developing Countries of Latin America and Asia*, Doc. SEC(89) 713 final, Brussels, 1989; Commission of the European Communities, *Eleventh Report from the Commission to the Council and the European Parliament on the Implementation of Financial and Technical Assistance to Latin American and Asian Developing Countries*, Doc. COM(88) 715 final, Brussels, 1989.

The picture of the geographical distribution of EC aid to Latin America does not change if, in addition to direct financial assistance, one also considers food aid and contributions to economic cooperation. The poorer Central American countries receive more than those in the Andean Pact and in the rest of South America, but the even poorer countries of Hispaniola are treated much less generously, in aid per capita terms, than those of Central America, whose income per person is almost twice as high.

The sectoral distribution of EC financial aid was kept more strictly in conformity with the Council's 1981 guidelines: 67 percent of the aid committed to Latin American countries in 1876-87 went to agriculture, 13 percent to trade and industry, 8 percent to services, and 7 percent to reconstruction schemes. Within the agricultural sector, 40 percent of EC aid was devoted to integrated rural development programs and about 30 percent to support for agrarian reform,[85] goals whose importance was specifically underscored by the Council in its annual guidelines to the Commission.

ODA flows from the Community to Latin America are not only small in absolute amounts and in most cases minuscule in relation to population, they are also quite small compared to those from other sources. They make up only about 8 percent of total ODA reaching both Central and South America. Much more important is bilateral aid from EC countries, especially in the case of South America where it is more than 40 percent of total ODA (Table 6.7).

Direct EC financial assistance to Latin America has therefore remained a limited affair not only for the region as a whole, but also for most of the poorest countries within it, on which it was originally supposed to be concentrated. While recognized as an essential instrument of the "global" cooperation experiment started in the late 1970s, financial assistance to non-associated countries was never assigned sufficient resources to become a significant factor. No amount of rhetoric about concentration on the poorest parts of this "middle income" region, or politically skillful use of it in support of regional initiatives, can hide the fact that EC direct aid remained a marginal instrument of development cooperation with Latin America. It was a kind of last resort, emergency tool usable whenever local crisis situations emerged requiring a visible—

Table 6.7 ODA Flows to Latin America (net disbursements, million US$)

	1970	1975	1980	1985
Aid to South America[a]				
EC(7) bilateral aid	76.9	172.2	295.4	283.5
EC multilateral aid	—	—	18.2	59.4
US	335.0	182.0	28.0	217.0
Japan	-15.7	41.2	87.3	136.2
Total ODA	400.7	411.4	438.4	694.7
Aid to Central America[b]				
EC(7) bilateral aid	4.4	24.6	88.3	109.9
EC multilateral aid	—	—	25.5	76.8
US	78.0	92.0	176.0	735.0
Japan	0.2	2.1	17.5	21.5
Total ODA	82.6	122.3	288.4	927.1
Aid to Latin America[c]				
EC(7) bilateral aid	92.3	223.0	511.0	490.9
EC multilateral aid	—	—	64.6	147.3
US	458.0	306.0	281.0	1,317.0
Japan	-15.3	46.6	115.6	218.3
Total ODA	494.3	616.3	996.4	2,169.6
Memorandum items:				
EC(7) bilateral as % of total aid to SA	19.2	41.8	67.3	40.8
EC multilateral as % of total aid to SA	—	—	4.2	8.6
EC(7) bilateral as % of total aid to CA	5.3	20.1	30.6	11.9
EC multilateral as % of total aid to CA	—	—	8.8	8.2

Note: Total includes ODA from all DAC countries and multilateral sources.
[a] Bolivia, Chile, Peru, Ecuador, Colombia, Brazil, Paraguay, Uruguay, Argentina, Venezuela.
[b] Nicaragua, Honduras, Costa Rica, El Salvador, Guatemala, Panama.
[c] South America, plus Central America, plus Haiti, Dominican Republic, Cuba, Mexico.
Sources: Instituto de Relaciones Europeo-Latinoamericanas (IRELA), Economic Relations Between the European Community and Latin America: A Statistical Profile, Working Paper No. 10, Madrid, Irela, 1987; G. Ashoff, La Cooperacion Para el Desarrollo Entre la Communidad Europea y América Latina: Experiencias y Perspectivas, Working Paper No. 16, Madrid, Irela, 1989; OECD, Geographical Distribution of Financial Flows to Developing Countries, Paris (various issues).

if often token—EC presence. Even in a framework of fulfillment of only basic human needs, the development of EC-Latin American cooperative relations still awaits the allocation of financial and other aid resources adequate to the task and the establishment of a regular program of cooperation between the two regions. That sensible Latin Americans can look at the EC-Mediterranean model as an improvement over the current state of affairs,[86] is a sign of both constrained expectations and paucity of the *"acquis communautaire"* in this area.

Notes to Chapter 6

[1] S. Sideri, "Europe and Latin America in the World Crisis", *Rivista di Diritto Valutario e di Economia Internazionale*, Vol. 23, No. 2, 1985, p. 359.

[2] Some observers have found little relevance in these factors, and have instead pointed to the competitive nature of the relationship between Europe and Latin America in manufactures, the most dynamic sector of trade between the two regions: L. Krause, "Latin American Economic Relations with Western Europe", in R.W. Fontaine and J.D. Theberge, eds., *Latin America's New Internationalism*, New York, Praeger, 1976, pp. 146-51. This view, however, is based on the traditional notion of specialization and trade. It does not take into account, for example, the potential for inter-industry trade that exists between the two regions.

[3] This was explicitly recognized by the EC Commission: Commission, *European Development Aid*, 1971, p. 20, where it is stated that "in the area of trade preferences the Community has always attempted to balance its responsibilities towards the associated countries with those it had against all developing countries as a whole". The Community in fact lowered its general import duties on certain tropical products, notably coffee and cocoa, thus reducing the level of preferences granted to the associates.

[4] The EC addressed Latin America with such a Memorandum soon after the signature of the Treaty of Rome, stating the goal of good and close relations with Latin America, and trying to dispel at the same time the fears of either "a fortress Europe" or "a Europe bent on Africa". See Commission of the European Communities, "Memorandum of Intention", Brussels, 1958 (mimeo.).

[5] These preoccupations were clearly reflected in the Punta del Este Document of August 1961, which stressed the urgency for all

members of the Organization of American States (OAS) to coordinate their efforts aimed at convincing the Community to end its discriminatory trade preferences in favor of associated countries: A. Lerman Alperstein, "Evolutión Histórica de las Relationes Comerciales entre América Latina y la CEE", *Commercio Exterior*, Vol. 41, No. 2, February 1991, p. 180.

6 This was the opinion voiced by J.M. Ribas, "Latin America's European Market", *Americas*, No. 14, October 1962, pp. 3–7.

7 United Nations Economic Commission for Latin America (UNECLA), *Recent Developments and Trends in Latin American Trade with the European Community*, Doc. E/CN 12/631, New York, 1962, p. 2. This is a feeling that has re-emerged in recent times in many developing countries with respect to Project 1992. The origin is the same: the apparent lack of concern by EC members for the external effects of their internal market unification. Nor has the Commission done much so far to change this outside perception. No study of the possible external effects of internal market unification, which is to be achieved in 1992, has yet been publicized. It is not even clear whether any such a comprehensive study, as opposed to internal memoranda on specific aspects of the Community's relationship with the rest of the world, was ever conducted by the Commission or on its behalf. Europeans, when it comes to integration, appear to be so convinced that what is "good for them is also good for the world", that they tend to ignore outside perceptions running in the opposite direction.

8 *Ibidem*, p. 3.

9 See, for example, D. Tussie, "Latin American Integration: From LAFTA to LAIA", *Journal of World Trade Law*, Vol. 16, No. 5, October 1982, pp. 400–9.

10 UNECLA, *Recent Developments and Trends*, p. 2; Ribas, "Latin America's European Market", p. 3; and, more recently, Mower, *European Community and Latin America*, p. 38.

11 Notable on the Latin American side was the "Memorandum of 1966", which set out the objectives to be pursued by the countries of the region in dealing with the EC and also contained their explicit request for a comprehensive interregional economic policy and a permanent joint committee of EC and Latin American representatives.

12 See, for example, E. Lerdau, "The Impact of the EEC on Latin America's Foreign Trade", *Economiá Latinoamericana*, Vol. 1, No. 1, 1963, pp. 116–17. The author concluded that "if the Community develops an outward looking approach, and fixes prices of temperate zone foods at levels low enough to be in rough line with costs

and prices in the rest of the world, the administration of the import determining mechanism will have to permit the entry of foreign supplies. But the policy tools created by the Treaty of Rome and the CAP also make it perfectly possible to exclude imported cereals as well as beef completely, should a narrowly protectionist attitude prevail."

[13] C. Furtado, *Economic Development of Latin America*, Cambridge, Cambridge University Press, 1976 (2nd edition), pp. 131-40, and C. Fartado, "Las Relaciones Commerciales Entre la Europa Occidental y América Latina", *El Trimestre Económico*, Vol. 50, No. 199, July-September 1983, p. 1322.

[14] V. Corbo, "Problems, Development Theory, and Strategies of Latin America", in G. Ranis and T.P. Schultz, eds., *The State of Development Economics*, New York, Basil Blackwell, 1988, pp. 157-62.

[15] M.S. Wionczek, "The Relations Between the European Community and Latin America in the Context of the International Economic Crisis", *Journal of Common Market Studies*, Vol. 19, No. 2, 1980, p. 163.

[16] Corbo, "Problems, Development Theory and Strategies".

[17] On the evolution of Latin American membership in GATT, see Hudec, *Developing Countries in the GATT Legal System*, pp. 23-38. Brazil and Chile had been the only two Latin American countries that joined GATT at its inception. On the role of Latin American countries in the early challenges to GATT and in the movement for its reform, see Hudec, *Ibidem*, pp. 39-67, and Tussie, *Less Developed Countries*, pp. 25-32.

[18] A. Pio, "Caratteristiche ed Evoluzione degli Investimenti Europei nel Processo di Sviluppo Latino Americano," in A. Pio, ed., *Europa-America Latina: Nouve Forme di Cooperazione*, Milan, Unicopli, 1988, p. 125. In 1978 European direct investments made up more than 40 percent of the stock of foreign investments in Argentina and Brazil and nearly 25 percent of those made in Colombia and Peru.

[19] J. Loeff, "European Community and Latin America", in *Incontro Sulla Cooperazione dell'Europa allo Sviluppo dell'America Latina*, Rome, Istituto Latino Americano, 1980, pp. 98-9. Mr Loeff was a member of the Directorate for External Relations of the Community when the paper quoted above was delivered. Three years before, the then Director General for External Relations in the EC Commission, Roy Denman, had characterized Latin America as the "middle class of the [developing] world". This quotation is reported in B. Muniz, "EEC-Latin America: A Relationship to be Defined", *Journal of Common Market Studies*, Vol. 19, No. l, 1980, p. 58. The EC Commission

itself made reference to the same spurious concept in its "Fresco" document on aid, where it observed, in a clear reference to Latin America (and also possibly to the oil exporting countries of the Middle East) that "other [countries], tomorrow's rich, are becoming the new bourgeois of the third world, with all that involves in the way of passion for success, harshness in their relations with others and will to liberate their people from the constraints which only yesterday still lay upon them". Commission, "Development Aid: Fresco of Community Action Tomorrow", 1974, p. 7.

20 This was an *ad hoc* Committee formed in 1963 to coordinate Latin American positions over issues to be discussed at the first UNCTAD Conference.

21 An agreement with Mexico was reached in 1975. This agreement, however, contained a "development clause", which the others did not have. For a Community intensely preoccupied with energy dependence, Mexico, then as a major producer of oil and a non-member of OPEC, was worth better terms than other Latin American countries. The commercial agreement with Brazil became a Cooperation Agreement in 1980.

22 Muniz, "EEC–Latin America", p. 59.

23 Council of the European Communities, "Decision of July 1974", *Bulletin of the European Communities*, 7/8, 1974, para. 1222.

24 Commission, "Development Aid: Fresco of Community Action Tomorrow", 1974, pp. 17–19, which represented the Commission's response to the invitation issued by the Council "to give its thoughts on Community Cooperation with the third world in the coming years in the context of the world economic situation".

25 Wionczek, "Relations Between the European Community and Latin America", p. 161. The establishment of SELA filled the gap left by LAFTA in providing an institutional framework for regional dialogue and cooperation with Europe.

26 The bilateral agreement reached with Mexico has already been mentioned. The interest of the Community in the financing of large mining projects capable of meeting long-term demand, and at the same time diversifying supply sources, is well illustrated by its direct interest in the development of the Carajas mining basin in Brazil during the second half of the 1970s. Eventually a loan of $600 million was made by the Economic and Steel Community in 1982 (under art. 54 of the ECSC Treaty) to help develop iron ore production in Carajas.

[27] E. Duran, *European Interests in Latin America*, London, Routledge & Kegan Paul (for the Royal Institute of International Affairs), 1985, pp. 13-14.

[28] Sistema Económico Latinoamericano, *América Latina y la Comunidad Económica Europea*, Caracas, Monte Avila Editores, 1984, pp. 173-8.

[29] The Latin American Council adopted its Decision N.150 in September 1983, expressing the political will of the member states to start again the dialogue with the Community. *Ibidem*, pp. 163-4.

[30] Established in 1969, the Andean Pact aimed at fostering economic cooperation among five Andean nations: Bolivia, Colombia, Peru, Ecuador and Venezuela. An agreement with the EC was reached in December of 1983, but ratified only in 1987.

[31] Commission of the European Communities, "Latin America: A Community Strategy", Brussels, September 1980 (mimeo.), p. 17.

[32] The countries belonging to the General Treaty on Central American Economic Integration were El Salvador, Guatemala, Honduras, Nicaragua and Costa Rica. Those belonging to the Contadora Group were Colombia, Mexico, Panama and Venezuela.

[33] W. Grabendorff, "Las Relaciones de la Comunidad Europea con América Latina: Una Politica sin Ilusiones", *Foro Internacional*, Vol. 29, No. 1, September 1988, pp. 51-3; G. Granda, V. Mate and M. Moreno, *La Cooperación entre América Latina y Europa*, Madrid, CIDEAL, 1988, p. 21.

[34] Commission of the European Communities, *Guidelines for the Strengthening of Relations Between the Community and Latin America*, Doc. COM(84) 105 final, Brussels, 6 April 1984, p. 1.

[35] *Ibidem*, pp. 12-13.

[36] G. Ashoff, "Consequences of Southward Enlargement for EC-Latin American Relations", *Intereconomics*, No. 5, September/October, 1982, pp. 225-33; A. von Gleich, M. Eheke, H.J. Petersen and P. Hrubesch, *The Political and Economic Relations Between Europe and Latin America in View of the Southern Englargement of the European Community due to the Entry of Spain and Portugal*, Hamburg, Institut fur Iberoamerika-Kunde, 1983, pp. 36-45.

[37] Ashoff, "Consequences of Southward Enlargement", pp. 226-8, and A. Tovias, "Iberian Countries, Iberoamerica and the European Community", *The World Economy*, Vol. 12, No. 1, March 1989, pp. 105-14.

[38] "Joint Declaration of Intent on the Development and Intensification of Relations with Countries of Latin America" issued by the 12 EC Members in 1985, immediately after the accession of Spain and Portugal, in Office for Official Publications, *Documents Concerning the Accessions to the European Communities*, 1987, p. 675.

[39] Commission of the European Communities, *The European Community and Latin America*, Doc. COM(86) 720 final, Brussels, 2 December 1986.

[40] Council of the European Communities, "Conclusions Adopted by the Council on Relations with Latin America", *Bulletin of the European Communities*, No. 6, 1987, para. 3.5.1.

[41] For a detailed examination of the Council's decision, see G. Ashoff, *La Cooperación Para el Desarollo Entre la Comunidad Europea y América Latina: Experiencias y Prospectivas*, Working Paper No. 16, Madrid, IRELA, 1989, pp. 89-111.

[42] These doubts had become stronger since early 1985, when the new Commission, headed by Jacques Delors, was inaugurated. Helped by the Commissioner in charge of North-South relations, Claude Cheysson, the former foreign minister of France, Delors attempted to promote an active role of the Community in the debt area. Cheysson in particular openly criticized the CAP for the limits it put on the export possibilities of Latin American debtor countries. He also started a political dialogue between the Commission and the Latin American debtor countries' Group of Cartagena on the foreign debt problem. G. Wiegand, *Western Europe and the Latin American Debt Crisis*, Working Paper No. 12, Madrid, IRELA, 1988, pp. 47-50.

[43] See, for example, the position taken in 1984 by Karl Haferkamp, EC Commissioner for External Relations, as reported in Wiegand, *Latin American Debt Crisis*, p. 48; and Commission of the European Communities, *The European Community's Relations with Latin America*, Europe Information Doc. EN 06/X/96, Brussels, December 1989, p. 5.

[44] In "Report of the EC Monetary Committee of 10 March 1986' (mimeo.), p. 13.

[45] The main exception was, of course, Peru.

[46] By its inertia in this area, the Community probably lost not only a unique opportunity to cement its relationship with Latin America, but to gain credibility as an autonomous partner in development throughout the developing world. The questions of its unwillingness or inability to play a role are still open to debate.

[47] Wionczek, "Relations Between the European Community and Latin America", p. 166; A.V. Lorca, A. Martinez and A. Fuertes, "Espana-América Latina y la Communidad Económica Europea, *Foro Internacional*, Vol. 22, No. 3, January-March 1982, p. 272; Furtado, "Relaciones Comerciales", pp. 1326-8; E. Baldinelli, "Turning Page in Relations Between Latin America and the European Communities", *CEPAL Review*, No. 30, December 1986, p. 89; I. Basombrio, "América Latina y la Comunidad Europea: Una Compleja Relación", in SELA, ed., *Relaciones Económicas Internacionales de América Latina*, Caracas, Editorial Nueva Sociedad, 1987, pp. 171-2.

[48] Sideri, *La Comunità Europea Nell'Interdipendenza Mondiale*, p. 193.

[49] J. Loeff, "European Community and Latin America", pp. 103-4; R.J. Langhammer, "EEC Policies and Latin American Export Performance: A Discussion of Causalities", *Intereconomics*, September-October, 1980, pp. 246 and 251. Indirectly, but rather clearly, this contention is also found in Commission, *Guidelines for the Strengthening of Relations Between the Community and Latin America*, 1984, p. 5.

[50] J.M. Vacchino, "América Latina y Europa Comunitaria", *Comercio Exterior*, Vol. 31, No. 2., February 1981, p. 132. See, in addition, the recent study by SELA on the effects of the EC commercial policy on Latin American trade: Sistema Económico Latinoamericano, "La Politica Comercial de la CEE y sus Efectos Sobre el Comercio de América Latina", *Comercio Exterior*, November 1985, pp. 1100-10.

[51] Loeff, "European Community and Latin America", p. 102. This EC official states: "even if there could be a slight reduction in the self supply rates [of EC agriculture], the resulting slight expansion of import capacity would spur on a number of non-Latin American countries—some of them able to produce considerably greater volumes of subsidies—to increase exports to the Community, and it seems hard to imagine that Latin America could win any appreciable share of the Community's slightly increased import capacity"

[52] This has been a near general tendency until very recently. Neither of the two official public information briefs issued by the Commission in the 1980s on relations between the EC and Latin America mentions the existence and effects of the CAP on Latin American exports: Commission of the European Communities, *The European Community and Latin America*, Europe Information Doc. No. 82/85, Brussels, November 1985; Commission, *European Community's Relations with Latin America*, 1989.

[53] Commission, *Guidelines for Strengthening of Relations Between the Community and Latin America*, 1984, p. 5; and Commission, *The European Community and Latin America*, 1985, p. 16.

[54] Commission, *Guidelines for Strengthening of Relations Between the Community and Latin America*, 1984, p. 5.

[55] *Ibidem*, p. 5.

[56] The political stickiness of the reform of the CAP is clearly reflected in the June 1987 Statement of the Council on "Relations with Latin America" in which the Council members managed to ignore it totally, no doubt for good measure. Council of the European Communities, "Relations with Latin America", Conclusion adopted on 22 June 1987, *Bulletin of the European Community*, June 1987, pp. 138-9.

[57] The international prices of most agricultural products are by themselves unstable, at least in the short run, since neither their demand nor their supply is very responsive to price changes. The price inelasticity of demand and supply generate wide price changes whenever either the market demand or supply schedules for these products shift.

[58] Substitution of man-made products, such as artificial sweeteners for sugar, is helped by wide price variations of the natural product.

[59] Partial equilibrium trade models based on the relevant supply and demand elasticities inside and outside the EC constitute the most common frame of reference. To allow for the multiplicity of CAP price support and protection mechanisms, and for the effects of price variations in other markets, multi-country and multi-commodity models are at times used. They make possible the definition of complex counterfactuals. An example of this second category of models is that of Tyers and Anderson, which was used by the World Bank to estimate the effects of agricultural protection in industrial countries for the 1986 World Development Report: R. Tyers and K. Anderson. Distortions in World Food Markets: A Quantitative Assessment, World Bank, *Development Report Background Paper*, Washington D.C., 1986 (mimeo.). Some general equilibrium frameworks have also been used to estimate the external effects of the CAP. This third class of models explicitly accounts for the relationships between commodity and factor markets, agricultural and non-agricultural sectors, policies and the macroeconomy. An example is the model used by Burniaux and Waelbroeck to estimate the effects of the CAP on developing countries: J.M. Burniaux and J. Waelbroeck, "The Impact of the CAP on Developing Countries: A General Equilibrium Analysis", in C. Stevens and J.V. van Themaat, eds., *Pressure Groups, Policies and Development: EEC and the Third World:*

A *Survey 5*, London, Hodder and Stoughton, 1985, pp. 123–40. Another example is the model of the Australian Bureau of Agricultural Economics: J. Breckling, S. Thorpe and A. Stoeckel, *Effects of EC Agricultural Policies: A General Equilibrium Approach, Initial Results*, Canberra, Bureau of Agricultural Economics and Centre for International Economics, 1987.

[60] Such evidence is summarized and compared in three recent surveys: A. Matthews, "The CAP and the Developing Countries: A Review of the Evidence", in Stevens and van Themaat, *Pressure Groups, Policies and Development* pp. 105–20; D.G. Demekas, K. Bartholdy, S. Gupta, L. Lipschitz and T. Mayer, "The Effects of the Common Agricultural Policy on the European Community: A Survey of the Literature", *Journal of Common Market Studies*, Vol. 27, No. 2, December 1988, pp. 113–45; and J. Rosenblatt, T. Mayer, K. Bartholdy, D. Demekas, S. Gupta and L. Lipschitz, *The Common Agricultural Policy of the European Community: Principles and Consequences*, Occasional Paper No. 62, Washington D.C., The International Monetary Fund, 1988.

[61] These are the ranges obtained by ignoring the lowest and highest of the available estimates.

[62] Depending on the products, the United States (in grains), Canada (in grains) and Australia (in meat) would also substantially gain from the abolition of the CAP in terms of both higher trade volumes and higher prices. Clearly, the countries that are net importers of these food products, including many low-income developing countries, would have to shoulder higher costs for their imports. The net effects on developing countries as whole, however, are positive in most commodities. Gainers could compensate the losers, and leave the group as a whole better off than with the CAP. Any such compensation, however, would not take place automatically. It would have to be negotiated and implemented.

[63] J. Zietz and A. Valdes, "The Potential to LDCs of Trade Liberalization in Beef and Sugar by Industrial Countries", *Weltwirtschaftliches Archiv*, Vol. 122, No. 1, 1986, pp. 101–8; A. Valdes, "La Agricultura en la Ronda de Uruguay: Los Interests de los Países en Desarrollo", *Comercio Exterior*, Vol. 38, No. 9, September 1988, pp. 788–810.

[64] See, for example, M. Petit, *Determinants of Agricultural Policies in the United States and the European Community*, Research Report No. 51, Washington, D.C., The International Food Policy Research Institute, 1985.

[65] OECD, *Agricultural Policies, Markets and Trade, 1990*, Paris, 1990, pp. 110–11 for the most recent estimates of total transfer costs. Others are available, for example, a survey can be found in D. Blandford,

"The Costs of Agricultural Protection and the Difference Free Trade Would Make", in F.H. Sanderson, ed., *Agricultural Protectionism in the Industrialized World*, Washington D.C., Resources for the Future, 1990, pp. 398-409. For a recent survey of estimates of the net economic costs of the CAP, see Rosenblatt et al., *Common Agricultural Policy*, p. 39.

66 "Price undertakings" are engagements assumed by exporters, often under stress, to keep export prices within limits acceptable to the Community, so as to minimize price competition with domestic producers.

67 On the causes of non-tariff protection see E. Grilli and E. Sassoon, "Contemporary Protectionism: What Have We Learned?", in E. Grilli and E. Sassoon eds., *The New Protectionist Wave*, London, Macmillan, 1990, pp. 168-77.

68 ACP exporters enjoyed duty free entry for all their manufactures under the Yaoundé and Lomé Conventions.

69 On the development of the EC GSPs, including the roles played by the various Community institutions and interest groups, see P. Tulloch, *The Politics of Preferences: EEC Policy Making and the Generalized System of Preferences*, London, Croom Helm (in association with the Overseas Development Institute), 1975, pp. 53-87; and A. Weston, V. Cable and A. Hewitt, *The EEC's Generalized System of Preferences*, London, ODI, 1980, pp. 21-55.

70 This excluded, among others, both Taiwan and China (which became eligible in 1980). In the case of textiles, clothing and footwear only independent states could be beneficiaries. This was yet another way of excluding a potentially tough competitor such as Hong Kong.

71 This product category was abolished in 1981 for all industrial products except textiles.

72 This is a particularly absurd treatment: competitive producers of these products are first subject to quantitative restrictions on their exports to the Community, then given preferential duty treatment on those limited quantities.

73 The safeguard clause was never invoked by the Community, as ceilings, which can be changed annually, offered sufficient protection of domestic interests.

74 For a description of the new scheme which entered into effect in 1982, and of its innovations see A. Weston, "Who is More Preferred? An Analysis of the Generalized System of Preferences", in Stevens, ed., *EEC and the Third World: A Survey 2*, pp. 78-82; and A. Borrmann,

C. Borrman, C. Langer and K. Menck, *The Significance of the EEC's Generalized System of Preferences*, Hamburg, Verlag Weltarchiv GMBH, 1985, pp. 23–45. Products covered, in terms of 6-digit NIMEXE items, increased from 5015 in 1973 to 6511 in 1982: *Ibidem*, p. 32. The coverage ratio of the EC GSPs, i.e. the ratio between imports covered under the scheme and MFN dutiable imports increased from .65 in the mid-1970s to .75 in the mid-1980s: UNCTAD, *Comprehensive Review of the Generalized System of Preferences, Including its Implementation, Maintenance, Improvement and Utilization*, Report No. TD/B/C.5/130, Geneva, 1990, Annex Table 1. The number of beneficiaries increased from 91 independent countries and 41 dependent territories in 1971 to 128 independent countries and 20 dependent territories in 1987: Borrman et al., *Significance of the EEC's Generalized System of Preferences*, p. 28; and Commission of the European Communities, *Generalized Preferences for the Third World*, European File No. 16/87, Brussels, October 1987, p. 5.

75 The number of agricultural products covered by GSPs increased from 145 in 1971 to 338 in 1983, accounting for 74 percent of the total.

76 The utilization ratio, i.e. the ratio between imports to which GSP tariff rates were applied and GSP eligible imports, increased only slightly, from 0.35 in 1976–78 to 0.39 in 1986–88: UNCTAD, *Comprehensive Review of the Generalized System of Preferences*, Annex Table 1. This ratio measures the extent to which beneficiaries were able to take advantage of the preferences. It reflects the limitations on access, specific country or product exclusions and the degree of information available to beneficiaries. A low utilization indicates that some or all of these factors are at work in preventing full use of the preferences. Slow growth reflects slow change in the possibilities to use the preferences.

77 The average unweighted preferential margin of the EC GSPs declined from 10 percent in 1973 to 7 percent in 1982: Borrmann et al., *Significance of the EEC's Generalized System of Preferences*, p. 33.

78 H. Julienne, "Hacia una Revitalización de la Cooperación Económica entre América Latina y la Comunidad Económica Europea", in Fundación Friedrich Ebert, ed., *Relaciones Económicas Entre América Latina y la Comunidad Económica Europea*, Madrid, Graficas Geranios, 1988, p. 69.

79 R.J. Langhammer, "Ten Years of the EEC's Generalized System of Preferences for Developing Countries: Success or Failure?", Kiel Working Paper No. 183, Institut fur Weltwirtschaft an der Universitat Kiel, Kiel, 1983 (mimeo.), pp. 19–23; D.K. Brown. "Trade and Welfare

Effects of the Generalized System of Preferences", *Economic Development and Cultural Change*, Vol. 37, No. 4, July, 1989, pp. 768–9; R.J. Langhammer and A. Sapir, *Economic Impact of Generalized Tariff Preferences*, Aldershot, Gower (for the Trade Policy Research Center), 1987, pp. 48–59.

[80] The results of the various studies of the effects of the EC's GSP are reviewed and summarized in two recent surveys: D.K. Brown, "Trade Preferences and Developing Countries: A Survey of Results", *The Journal of Development Studies*, Vol. 24, No. 3, April 1988, pp. 335–59, and C.R. MacPhee, "A Synthesis of the GSP Study Program", Doc. UNCTAD/ITP/19, Geneva, 1989 (mimeo.), pp. 3–15. The estimates of the trade and welfare effects of the EC preference schemes vary somewhat, depending on methodology (*ex-ante* or *ex-post* analysis, and within the first type of analysis depending on the types of models used—partial or general equilibrium), assumptions concerning key parameters (elasticity values, preference margin estimates, treatment of quantitative restrictions), coverage of product trade and time period covered.

[81] See Chapter 2, p.

[82] Cited in Commission, *Development Policy: 1981–1983*, 1984, p. 72.

[83] Art. 3 of "Council's Regulation No. 442/81" of 17 February 1981 on "Financial and Technical Aid to Non-Associated Developing Countries", *Official Journal of the European Communities*, No. L48, 21 February 1981, pp. 8–10.

[84] Commission, *Thirteen Years of Development Cooperation*, 1989, p. 5.

[85] Commission of the European Community, *Eleventh Report from the Commission to the Council and the European Parliament on the Implementation of Financial and Technical Assistance to Latin American and Asian Developing Countries as of 31 December 1987*, Doc. COM(88) 715 final, Brussels, 16 January 1989, pp. 13–14.

[86] SELA, *América Latina y la Comunidad Económica Europea*, pp. 144–5.

7
EC and Asia: Growing Farther Apart

Asia lies even farther at the periphery of EC development concerns than Latin America, despite the strong links with Europe developed in colonial times and preserved thereafter. The countries of Indochina had maintained cultural and political ties with France after independence. India, Pakistan, Ceylon, Malaysia and several other countries of Asia had kept strong cultural, commercial and political links with Great Britain. Indonesia had also retained in its post-independence period, an appreciable relationship with the Netherlands, as shown, for example, by the share of Dutch bilateral aid it received.[1] Notwithstanding this multiplicity of past and ongoing relations between Asian countries and individual EC members, the Community and Asia never found strong common ground for development cooperation in the post-colonial era.

Yet, there were good reasons, in addition to history, for cooperation between these two areas. Asia could have been an alternative source of the tropical agricultural products imported by Europe. Palm oil, coconut oil, and natural rubber could have been obtained from Asia instead of Africa. Asian nations could have supplied the same tropical beverages, hardwood and spices as the former African colonies of many EC members, in addition to agricultural raw materials such as cotton, jute, hard fibers and some important metals.

By and large, however, in the 1950s this region did not have the same inherent appeals for Europe as Africa or even Latin America. Asia was geographically more distant and potentially more vulnerable to Soviet-Chinese influence than Africa, and thus a less secure source of the raw materials critical to Europe. It was also a much less attractive outlet for European exports and investments than Latin America. Asia was then mostly poor. Its largest countries were poorly endowed with natural resources and faced with seemingly insurmountable population problems. All through the 1950s most Asian countries appeared condemned to slow growth and a very unpromising economic future. Even the prospects of Korea and Taiwan seemed bleak. Poor natural resource endowments, unproductive agricultural sectors and relatively large populations appeared to sentence them to permanent dependence on aid from the United States.

In addition, European colonialism in Asia, shattered by World War II, had never recovered, despite its last gasps in Indochina and Indonesia. Soon after the end of the second world conflict Asia forcefully asserted its independence from Europe and embarked on its own path to political and economic emancipation. Post-colonial institutional links with Europe rested mainly on the British Commonwealth, an organizational structure that some continental European leaders held in deep suspicion, as too inherently Anglo-Saxon.[2] The fact that the United Kingdom originally refused to join the Common Market being created among continental European nations further retarded EC relations with the newly independent nations of Asia, which were seen to be very much in the British "domain".

In the post-independence period Asia came to project two different economic images, which the EC found equally troublesome. The first reflected the immense existential (even before economic) odds that South Asia seemed to face, exemplified by racial and religious diversity, food deficiency and unchecked population growth in countries such as India, Bangladesh, Nepal and to a lesser extent Pakistan. These seemed to be huge challenges, well beyond the means available to the Community in those years to cope with them. They also clashed with the focus on Africa that development cooperation policies had taken early in the life of the Community. The second economic image which became clearer in the late 1960s, reflected the dimension of competition between Europe and South East Asian countries. Vital economic and trade interests of the Community came to be seen as threatened by several of the countries of South East Asia, which were following Japan's footsteps in producing and exporting an increasing variety of industrial commodities.

There were other obstacles to the development of cooperation between EC Europe and Asia. Distance was one. The exposure of the region to communist threat was another. The perception that the region was politically vulnerable to communism could have, in principle, stimulated EC cooperation, at least for the purpose of helping these countries develop stronger economic systems as a barrier to it. In those years, however, EC nations were only too happy to leave to the United States the task, and to the related burden, of helping Asia withstand whatever threat it faced. Political–military non-involvement in that region was considered wise. The tensions that continued to exist inside the Community between the globalist and regionalist views of EC development cooperation were yet another obstacle to a deeper EC involvement in Asia. The regionalists, who had gained the upper hand early on in the struggle to shape the geographical reach of EC development cooperation, kept a careful watch on the evolution of both the development philosophy and practice of the Community, ensuring that they would never stray too far from a pre-eminent focus on Africa. Any move towards enlarging the scope of EC development cooperation to Asia was thus carefully, if discreetly, checked.

Asia, with is daunting development challenges, was a natural pole of attraction for those in EC Europe who considered the satisfaction of basic human needs anywhere in the world as the highest goal of development cooperation. The attraction that Asia had for the globalists was only too well understood by those who favored only a regional development cooperation projection by the Community. Even when the United Kingdom finally joined the Community, creating the concrete possibility for an expansion of EC development cooperation toward some parts of Asia, the regionalists defined the boundaries of EC associationism so carefully that no Asian country could be included in the Lomé Convention.[3]

Neither the standard rationale of foreign trade and investments nor the Community's desire to contribute to the economic development of this area motivated the EC to establish relations with Asia having a well-defined, overall shape. Instead, these relations have remained fragmented and largely defined over the years by the changing perceptions of economic competition between Europe and the various components of the Asian region (Table 7.1). The Community has tended to cooperate with those Asian countries that it perceived as not posing a threat to its narrowly defined economic interests, and to keep at arm's length those count-

Table 7.1 Growth in Asia and Export Competition with EC(9)

	Real GDP Growth	Total Export Growth (volume)	Export Growth to EC(9)[a] (volume)	Manufactures'[a] Export Growth to EC(9) (volume)	Penetration[b] of EC Import Market	Penetration of EC[b] Import of Manufactures
	(percentage per annum)				*(percentage share)*	
South Asia[c]						
1961–70	3.9	3.1	-2.9	4.9	1.4	1.4
1971–80	3.5	6.3	6.3	9.8	1.0	1.8
1981–90	5.5	6.5	9.8	11.4	1.4	1.9
East Asian NICs[d]						
1961–70	9.1	12.9	9.7	12.7	1.6	3.5
1971–80	9.4	13.6	13.4	14.8	3.5	8.3
1981–90	8.7	12.5	8.7	9.7	7.0	10.8
ASEAN countries[e]						
1961–70	5.3	5.5	-2.2	21.2	1.5	0.2
1971–80	7.1	8.4	8.4	27.5	1.9	1.1
1981–90	5.0	8.3	11.5	15.0	2.5	2.1

[a] For years 1962–70; 1971–80; 1981–88.
[b] For last year of period; excludes intra-EC trade.
[c] India, Bangladesh, Pakistan, Nepal, Sri Lanka.
[d] Korea, Taiwan, Hong Kong, Singapore.
[e] Indonesia, Malaysia, Thailand, Philippines.
Sources: United Nations, COMTRADE database; World Bank, *World Tables*, Washington D.C. (various issues).

ries that were seen as economically threatening.

Along the spectrum of potential (or actual) economic competition with Europe, different groups of Asian countries were seen by the Community as occupying sharply different positions. At the low end always stood the nations of South Asia—such as India, Pakistan, Bangladesh, Nepal—by which the Community never felt threatened in any important way. These were the poorest countries of Asia to which a modicum of economic assistance could be extended on humanitarian grounds: food aid, some of which had already been granted in the 1960s to alleviate acute local shortages, and direct financial aid, focused on food production, were initiated in the second half of the 1970s, in partial and unofficial compensation for their exclusion from the benefits of Lomé.

At the opposite end of the competitive spectrum lay, from the early 1970s, the first group of NICs of East Asia—Korea, Taiwan, Hong Kong and Singapore—towards which the EC progressively assumed a defensive trade posture, and with which neither economic nor political cooperation was ever attempted. These were the countries that first threatened the EC textile industry with their exports, and then successfully competed with EC domestic producers of ships, steel and chemical products, and finally entered the EC markets for consumer semi-durable goods.

In the middle of the spectrum stood, for a long time, the countries that had coalesced into the Association of East Asian Nations (ASEAN). These countries were rich in natural resources, politically well-disposed towards the West (with the brief exception of Sukarno's Indonesia) and seemingly threatened by their communist neighbors in Indochina and China. Towards these countries, seen to some extent as politically and economically complementary to Europe, the EC assumed a position of benevolence, showing readiness in the mid-1970s to develop a policy of limited cooperation. However, as these countries developed more and more clearly the characteristics of second generation Asian NICs, becoming, for example, successful producers and exporters of textiles and electronic products, and as the perception of communist threat subsided, the Community's benevolence towards them also waned.

EC and South Asia

Towards the populous and very poor nations of South Asia the Community has maintained since the beginning a mildly sympathetic posture, if with minimal effective involvement in terms of economic assistance. Some tariff concessions for specific exports were made to South Asian countries in 1964. India, for example, was granted duty-free entry for handloom fabrics and handicrafts. The Community also suspended its duty on the import of bulk tea from India. Food aid was extended to Asia in 1968, with India and Bangladesh as the main beneficiaries. In giving GSP benefits to non-associated developing countries in 1971, the Community considered Bangladesh, Bhutan and Nepal as least developed countries, thus giving them the most favorable GSP regime. None of these countries, however, produced or exported manufactures, except for jute textiles that were subject to stringent import limitations. By and large, therefore, these were not very significant concessions, either compared with those the EC granted to other least developed countries in Africa or in relation to the acute needs of the intended beneficiaries in Asia.

Some deepening of the EC economic cooperation efforts towards South Asia occurred in the 1970s, when Commercial Cooperation Agreements were signed with several countries of the region (India in 1973, Sri Lanka in 1975, Pakistan and Bangladesh in 1976) and when the program of technical and financial aid for non-associated developing countries was launched, with India, Bangladesh, Pakistan and Sri Lanka as immediate beneficiaries.[4] The bilateral agreements were traditional in form and content. Trade was to be based on most-favored nation treatment. The norm was no preferential treatment on imports from Asian countries. There were specific sector arrangements included in some of the agreements,[5] but on the whole they simply constituted general frameworks for the expansion of trade relations on the basis of non-discrimination between the signatories, with only a minimum of specific institutional support.[6]

As in the case of Latin America, financial assistance from the Community to Asia was generally granted for rural development operations, mostly food related. In addition, some assistance for disaster relief was envisaged. EC aid was provided in the form of grants, covering both the import costs and local expenditures of the projects being financed. Co-financing with member states was also foreseen. Given the humanitarian objectives being pursued, EC financial assistance to Asia almost necessarily favored agriculture as the main sector of destination and had to be concentrated in the poorest of the Asian countries, that is, in those of South Asia.

The agreements with India and Pakistan were transformed into commercial and economic cooperation agreements during the 1980s.[7] In addition, the Community offered some financial assistance to the South Asian Association for Regional Cooperation (SAARC) established in 1985 among Bangladesh, Bhutan, India, Nepal, Pakistan, Sri Lanka and the Maldives. The commercial and economic cooperation agreements with the largest countries, however, contained little beyond good intentions about technical and scientific cooperation and the transfer of technology. In the trade area, exports of textile and clothing products remained subject to MFA restraints, while even small concessions such as the preferential treatment of Indian cane sugar exports were switched on and off depending on EC internal market circumstances.[8] Regional cooperation attempts with SAARC countries hardly went beyond minimum levels. More importantly, the Community extended STABEX coverage in 1987 to Bangladesh and Nepal, as least developed countries, and to Burma in 1988. It did not, however, grant analogous treatment to India, the largest country in South Asia, despite the fact that its per capita income was not much higher than that of the two new STABEX beneficiaries in the region.[9]

South Asian countries were not particularly damaged by EC sectoral policies (with the general exception of the MFAs), but by the same token they did not derive much help from general tariff preferences for manufactures either. With some exceptions, their capacity to generate industrial exports remained limited until the 1980s. And where such capacity existed earlier, as in jute textiles and coir products, EC import policies were quite restrictive and harmful to them. India, Bangladesh and Nepal, for example, all relied heavily on exports of jute textiles during the 1960s and 1970s. Despite the low value added and the labor intensity of most of these textiles,[10] and thus the clear competitive advantage in their production held by the processing industries of Asia, the EC continued to protect domestic jute manufacturing by quantitatively limiting imports. Moreover, effective protection of EC domestic industry, that is the protection of the value added by local manufacturing, remained even higher than the tariff equivalent of the import quotas on manufactures, because raw jute imports were kept duty free. The final result of these policies was a progressive substitution of synthetic products for jute in EC markets. Local jute manufacturing all but disappeared and so did jute consumption, as the lower-cost industries of Bangladesh and India were effectively prevented from competing with synthetic substitutes in European markets.

Aid remained the most substantive component of the cooperative policy followed by the EC, but in both absolute and relative terms it never became too important a factor. Financial assistance reached ECU 100 million a year in the mid-1980s, with India receiving more than half (Table 7.2). As a proportion of total EC financial aid to developing countries, it never exceeded 7 percent. EC members such as Germany, the Netherlands, Denmark and the United Kingdom gave more assistance than the Community through their bilateral aid programs. The orientation of the bilateral assistance of most of these EC members toward recipients' needs generated a strong focus on the large and most poor countries of South Asia, with India and Bangladesh at the top of the list. The Community, however, never shared such an orientation, even though India, in absolute terms, received the largest amounts of direct EC financial assistance. Seen against the population of India, these amounts immediately fade in importance.

With direct food aid the Community nearly doubled the value of its financial assistance to South Asia.[11] Yet, even when all food and other aid are taken into account, the one billion or so recipients in the region bring its value to only about ECU 2 per capita over the entire 1976–88 period. While measuring aid received by large countries on a per capita basis biases the result downward, since all donors tend to discriminate against large countries in aid allocations, viewed against the size and needs of the populations of the Indian sub-continent, EC assistance loses much of its aggregate significance in whatever terms one measures it.

As for the orientation of its aid to South Asia, the Community

Table 7.2 Country Distribution of EC Financial Aid to Asia (million ECU)

	1976–80 (average)	(%)	1981–85 (average)	(%)	1986–89 (average)	(%)
South Asia						
Afghanistan	0.2		—		—	
Bangladesh	6.5		16.6		17.4	
Bhutan	—		1.8		0.9	
Burma	1.2		1.6		1.0	
India	19.5		52.5		66.5	
Maldives	0.1		0.3		—	
Nepal	1.0		3.2		0.6	
Pakistan	4.9		10.5		15.3	
Sri Lanka	4.9		4.0		6.3	
Total	38.3	(73.3)	90.5	(68.1)	108.0	(69.4)
South East Asia						
Indonesia	5.6		14.3		7.8	
Philippines	1.6		3.6		11.4	
Thailand	4.3		18.4		16.4	
Vietnam	0.5		—		—	
Laos	0.8		0.2		2.9	
Total	12.8	(24.5)	36.5	(27.6)	38.5	(24.7)
China	—	—	2.4	(1.8)	6.0	(3.9)
Regional organizations	1.1	(2.2)	3.3	(2.5)	3.1	(2.0)
Total Asia	52.2	(100)	132.7	(100)	155.6	(100)

Note: Includes direct EC financial aid for standard and disaster relief projects (aid to agricultural research centers is not included).
Source: Commission of the European Communities, *Thirteenth Annual Report to the Council and Parliament on the Implementation of Financial and Technical Co-operation to Developing Countries in Asia and Latin America*, Doc. COM(90) 204, final, Brussels, 1990.

stuck to the original purpose of helping the poor, while also financing some original activities with this type of assistance. One-third of financial aid to India was devoted to small-scale irrigation schemes, one-quarter to water management, one-quarter to oilseed development and the remainder to the building of storage facilities for agricultural production.[12] All this was consistent with the objective of improving food supply and food security in India. Nearly 70 percent of the finance for these projects came from the sale of EC fertilizers (and more recently vegetable oil), the proceeds of which were used to meet local project and program costs. Much of the food sent to India was used to support Operation Flood, which was aimed at directly and immediately improving local nutrition levels by ensuring adequate supplies and distribution of milk in the areas covered by the program and by supporting the development of the dairy sector in the longer run. This operation received an overall positive assessment, in absolute and relative terms, even from the normally skeptical Court of Auditors of the European Communities.[13]

Yet, with more than two and a half times the population of sub-Saharan Africa and a substantially lower per capita income, South Asia received five times less financial aid from the Community during 1976–88. This is a rather large anomaly, which can be at least partially understood only when examined from the standpoint of EC economic interests in South Asia. As noted by Arun Banerji, among South Asian countries, even India has little to offer the Community in economic terms, both in the absolute as well as in relation to what other developing countries could offer. Lack of emphasis of EC aid on South Asia becomes, if seen in this perspective, at least somewhat less anomalous. Official rhetoric notwithstanding, EC economic interests in South Asia are marginal and likely to remain so in the future. The EC, however, continues to be an important economic partner for South Asia, and the policies it adopts, particularly in the domain of trade, are bound to affect South Asian interests.[14] This asymmetry in EC–South Asia relations is destined to persist.

Yet, the stringent limits to the Community's concerns over South Asia become a rather clear expression of an incomplete, and perhaps even faulty, view of cooperation, when seen from either the point of view of development effectiveness and basic human needs fulfillment, or that of broad political purpose. South Asia not only contains most of the world's poor, but also the world's largest functioning democracy. European concerns with human rights and democratic forms of government, as well as the basic human development thrust of EC cooperation policy, will not achieve much credibility, internally or externally, if the attention paid to the needs of the South Asian poor continues to be too limited. Ignoring, or simply underplaying, this region in development assistance is certainly short-sighted and probably also incompatible with the political ambitions of the new Europe.

EC and the East Asian NICs

After practically ignoring the East Asian NICs in the 1960s, the EC turned decisively hostile towards them in the 1970s. One of these countries, Taiwan, was totally excluded from the GSPs. Hong Kong's preferential treatment was originally limited to some specific areas.[15] Korea became an early target of non-tariff barriers to trade erected by the Community and of "graduation" initiatives. Only foreshadowed in the late 1960s, the reality of economic competition between these countries and the Community became much clearer, and was perceived by Europe as more threatening, in the second half of the 1970s, when the crisis that followed the first oil shock worsened the relative competitive position of EC industry.[16] As several EC sectors came under pressure from competition from the Asian NICs—textile-clothing, shipbuilding, steel and specific sub-sectors of the chemical and electronic industries—the response of the Community (and of its members individually) became protective.

Regulation of trade in textiles and clothing products was extended to new sectors and rules were tightened. The Long Term Arrangement on Cotton Textiles was substituted in 1974 by the first Multifiber Arrangement covering trade in articles made of all major natural and synthetic fibers. After some lax enforcement of its rules at the Community level, it was followed in 1979 by a much tighter second Arrangement. The principal objects of most of the EC attention were the Asian NICs and their expanding manufacturing sectors. Imports of footwear, and in particular rubber footwear, from Korea and Taiwan were also targeted. Shipbuilding in the Community was defended from external competition by heavy subsidies at the national level. Imports of certain types of steel products were subject to VERs and minimum prices. Korean steel, guilty of being produced most efficiently, was a target of choice until 1990. Chemical products, and later consumer electronics, became the objects of other community discriminatory trade measures.

Even EC tariffs on imports from newly industrializing countries, though following the general trend of declining over time, remained higher than those on imports coming from other developing countries. This was particularly true of tariffs on industrial goods. The NICs were highly competitive in many of those products, which were euphemistically called "sensitive" by the EC when the European industry felt particularly vulnerable to import competition.[17] When average nominal tariffs on industrial imports are broken down into finer product categories, the correlation between high tariffs and sectors where export competitiveness by NICs is high becomes clear. Nominal EC tariffs, pre- and post-Tokyo Round, have deviated substantially from the average for products such as cotton fabrics, bed linen, clothing, electronic goods, rubber footwear and cutlery, which the Asian NICs exported most successfully in the 1970s and 1980s. The deviation from the average tariff protection on imports having special importance for the Asian NICs is even stronger if effective, rather than nominal, tariffs are considered. Effective tariff rates of 20 to 40 percent became common for these products.[18]

The defensive bent of EC trade policies towards the NICs continued in the 1980s. As late as 1989, the generally benevolent Economic and Social Committee of the EC adopted an opinion on relations between the EC and the NICs of East Asia, which is quite telling of the way in which these countries are now commonly viewed in Europe and of the policy impulse that they elicit. Accused of exchange rate manipulations, unfair targeting of export markets and social dumping, the NICs of East Asia were depicted as dangerous competitors, bent on annihilating critical parts of European industry, and thus to be severely dealt with in trade relations by the Community.[19] The fact that these Asian countries were able, through market and product diversification, to sustain their export drive even in the 1980s and to continue to penetrate EC markets should not obscure the fact that Community trade policies towards them remained protectionist, and that in the absence of non-tariff barriers and other export-retarding and uncertainty-creating trade tactics used by the Community, their export growth would have been much faster.[20] In the presence of increasingly hostile trade policies by the Community, past success by Asian countries in penetrating EC markets does not ensure that the trend can continue into the future.

Aside from quantitative limits on exports of textiles and clothing to the Community negotiated within the framework of the various MFAs, East Asian NICs still have to "voluntarily" restrain exports to the EC, or to specific EC markets, of products such as footwear (Korea and Taiwan), electrical and electronic equipment (Korea), umbrellas (Taiwan), and metal flatware (Korea).[21] In addition, in the 1980–88 period alone, the four East Asian NICs were together the target of thirty anti-dumping or anti-subsidy actions by the Community, equivalent to 8 percent of the total number of procedures of this kind adopted by the EC against all countries, and to almost 40 percent of those adopted against imports from all developing countries.[22]

On the positive side, the NICs of East Asia appear to have been among the top beneficiaries of the Community's GSP. The empirical evidence on this point is less then overwhelming,[23] but the conclusion that GSPs mostly benefited the NICs is both plausible on *a priori* grounds[24] and fits the data available on the main GSP suppliers to the Community. It is also confirmed, if indirectly, by studies on the aggregate trade effects of the main industrial countries' GSPs.[25] In the absolute, however, these benefits may not have been too large, given the limited size of the overall trade creating impact of the EC preferential scheme.

EC and ASEAN Countries

While not high in the priorities of EC interests in developing countries, members of ASEAN commanded enough attention in the 1970s to become the object of an attempt by the Community to establish bloc-to-bloc cooperation with them.[26] There were essentially three reasons for this official EC interest. The first was the entry of the United Kingdom into the Community, and the consequent need to make some alternative arrangements for those developing countries that had lost Commonwealth preferences.[27] The second was the US military pullout from Indochina and the hegemony subsequently established by North Vietnam over that region. These events exposed the ASEAN countries to a much stronger external threat than in the past and spurred European nations to help them cope with it, at a time when the exercise of US power and influence over the region seemed to be severely limited by domestic dissent. The third was the economic interest—commercial and strategic—of the Community in the ASEAN region.[28] While overall EC trade with the ASEAN nations was quite small, with exports to the region accounting in 1970 for only 2 percent of the world total,[29] trade with ASEAN countries was relatively more important for EC members, such as the Netherlands and the United Kingdom. These two countries also maintained strong investment interests in the region. EC total imports from ASEAN countries were even smaller than exports in relative terms, but more than 70 percent were raw materials, some of which had strategic importance for the Community.[30]

Consistent contact between the EC and ASEAN nations began in 1972. Regular meetings of the Joint Study Group started in 1975 and periodic Ministerial Meetings began in 1978. The first EC-ASEAN Economic and Commercial Cooperation Agreement was reached in 1980. The EC had already offered in 1974 commercial cooperation agreements similar to that concluded with India, but ASEAN nations refused them, opting instead for regional relations with the Community.[31] This meant subordinating the development of EC–ASEAN relations to political–institutional progress within ASEAN. Since such progress was slow in coming, EC–ASEAN relations at the regional level did not begin to materialize until the early 1980s.

The EC–ASEAN agreement, moreover, was not particularly far-reaching in mapping trade and economic collaboration between the two regions. The two contracting parties assumed few, if any, solid reciprocal obligations concerning trade. Each pledged to take the market access needs of the other into account, to consult with the other on measures likely to affect mutual trade and to study how to remove existing trade barriers. The basic (preferential) export regime unilaterally extended by the EC in 1971 to non-associated developing countries, including those in ASEAN, was not altered in any way by the 1980 Cooperation Agreement. In the economic sphere the agreement foresaw industrial and technological cooperation among firms in the two regions. In development cooperation, it basically relied on the existing EC aid programs for non-associated developing countries.

Given these premises, it is hardly surprising that EC–ASEAN

economic cooperation has not blossomed over the past decade. If the ASEAN nations expected the EC to prove its interests in the region by enhancing market access for their exports and helping to steer European investments to ASEAN countries, these expectations were not fulfilled.[32] Only trade with the EC developed in the 1980s, but quite independently from the Cooperation Agreement. As once observed by Commissioner Cheysson, EC attitudes towards ASEAN remained largely commercial in nature.[33] Cooperative relations between these two groups of countries did undergo a modest institutional deepening over the years, but without yielding, up to now, any conspicuous economic results.[34]

There are many explanations for this outcome. One can be found in the historical development of the relationship between EC and ASEAN nations. When feeling most exposed politically and militarily, after the US withdrawal from South Vietnam, the ASEAN nations needed some compensatory support from Europe, in part to cover up the inadequacies of the political and economic cooperation that they had been able to reach with one another. By the time ties with the Community were institutionalized the needs for EC political support had largely disappeared, but the Community was facing serious economic difficulties and feeling a commercial threat from Asia, including the ASEAN countries. The lowering of the rank of the ASEAN countries in the hierarchy of EC development priorities was already quite evident in the Pisani Memorandum of 1982.[35] A closely related reason is the similarity with Japan that EC nations see in the Asian NICs, old and new. The very success of ASEAN nations' exports, fostered in part by Japanese investments, and more recently by investments originating in the first generation NICs, has tended to heighten European economic fears.

Given these circumstances, the relatively rigid posture of EC trade policy towards ASEAN countries becomes more understandable. While not yet a target of open EC trade hostility, like the first generation NICs of Asia, the ASEAN nations were granted no trade preferences beyond GSPs. In agricultural trade, moreover, they were discriminated against in products such as cocoa and palm oil by the tariff preferences granted by the Community to associated developing countries and given only limited access for exports such as rice, sugar and tapioca—products that competed with grains, sugar and feeds produced inside the Community.[36]

EC economic concessions to the Asian nations were few and far between. However, unlike the United States, the EC nations had backed the creation of the International Tin Agreement in 1959, which supported market prices of this metal by limiting export supplies, and they had continued to be a party to the agreement throughout its long history. The EC also supported in 1980, this time together with the United States, the formation of an International Rubber Agreement, aimed at stabilizing natural rubber prices through the operation of a buffer stock. The Community also continued to extend some financial assistance to ASEAN countries, in particular Thailand and Indonesia, but in small quantities and at a declining rate (Table 7.2). They too were countries marching rapidly towards "the middle class" of the developing world.

Finally, the GSPs, which had not meant much for ASEAN countries in the 1970s when their exports to the EC were mostly made up of primary commodities,[37] became more important in the 1980s, when the capacity to export manufactures in ASEAN countries increased drastically. Gains from GSPs, however, were very small for ASEAN nations between 1975 and 1980. The estimated export-enhancing impact of the EC tariff preferences was less than 1 percent when measured against total ASEAN exports, and falling. Measured against the export of products covered by the scheme, it was about 5 percent and also falling over time.[38]

The actual effects of GSPs on ASEAN countries' exports in the 1980s have not yet been gauged with precision. Available data on trade flows indicate, however, that exports of manufactures to the EC have become considerably more important for ASEAN countries and growth appears to have been fast, both in textile–clothing and electrical machinery.[39] Yet, this growth can hardly be unambiguously attributed to the effects of GSPs.[40] Utilization of GSP preferences is still only about 50 percent of the potential for the four largest members of ASEAN, and much smaller for Singapore and Brunei. Utilization rates at the end of the 1980s were still not significantly higher for manufactures than for total exports, and were considerably lower for textiles–clothing than the average for ASEAN manufactures.[41] Quantitative restrictions on textiles–clothing exports to the EC were still reducing the value of GSPs to ASEAN countries in the 1980s. In the current MFA, branded by some as relatively less restrictive than the previous ones, forty-six Community limits are in effect against exports from ASEAN countries.

The competitive element in EC–ASEAN relations seems to be increasing over time almost naturally, as these countries partake more and more of the economic and export structure of the "first generation" of Asian NICs.[42] The weakening of the political element in the EC approach towards ASEAN countries, an inescapable effect of the relaxation of political–ideological tensions in Asia and elsewhere, seems to be making the Community's posture towards them even more influenced than in the past by its increasingly competitive economic substratum.

Aid Policies Towards Asia

Directed at satisfying basic human needs in a region where poverty abounds and inequalities are still pervasive, aid could have become the clearest expression of the Community's global development concerns and created a more solid bond between the new Europe and Asia.

EC financial assistance to the whole region between 1976 and 1988 amounted to ECU 1,300 million. Total aid was more than twice as much, with food aid accounting for most of the additional development assistance supplied by the Community. This effort was not marginal in the budgetary aid framework of the Community. It was marginal, however, in relation to the needs of the more than 2.5 billion people towards which it was aimed (2 billion in India and China alone).

Devoted, like in Latin America, to the improvement of living conditions of the poorest in the recipient countries, EC aid should have been allocated by country in a roughly inverse relationship to per capita income. The Community failed to do so, not only by discriminating heavily against China, which received practically no aid, but also by devoting more aid per capita to ASEAN countries than to the South Asian countries, despite the fact that income per person was more than twice as large in the former than in the latter group. The Community also gave even less aid per person to the countries of Indochina, which had the lowest per capita income in the entire region (Table 7.3).

These distributional patterns, contradictory to the avowed

Table 7.3 Direct EC Aid to Asia

	1987		1976–88 (cumulative)			
	GNP Per Capita US$	Population (million)	Financial Aid[a] (million ECU)	Total Aid[b] (million ECU)	Financial Aid per capita[c] (ECU)	Total Aid per capita[c] (ECU)
Indochina[d]	194	113	26.6	151.1	0.24	1.33
South Asia[e]	285	1,090	939.3	2,367.0	0.86	2.17
China	300	1,069	32.7	180.2	0.03	0.17
ASEAN[f]	623	298	320.1	432.9	1.07	1.45
Total Asia	327	2,570	1,318.7	3,131.2	0.51	1.22

a Excluding regional aid.
b Including financial aid, food aid (direct and indirect), humanitarian aid, economic cooperation assistance, and miscellaneous aid (e.g. STABEX aid to least developed countries and co-financing with NGOs).
c Computed on the basis of 1987 populations.
d Cambodia, Laos, Vietnam (plus Burma).
e Bangladesh, India, Pakistan, Nepal, plus Bhutan, Afghanistan, Sri Lanka and Maldives.
f Indonesia, Malaysia, Philippines and Thailand.

Sources: Commission of the European Communities, *Thirteen Years of Development Cooperation with the Developing Countries of Latin America and Asia*, Doc. SEC(89) 713 final, Brussels, 1989; Commission of the European Communities, *Eleventh Report from the Commission to the Council and the European Parliament on the Implementation of Financial and Technical Assistance to Latin American and Asian Developing Countries*, Doc. COM(88) 715 final, Brussels, 1989.

aims of EC aid, can only be explained by the overwhelming interference of political factors in the allocations of assistance. For the same reason that China, Vietnam, Cambodia and Laos were discriminated against by the Community in aid giving, Thailand and Indonesia were heavily favored. Aid went to discourage communist influence over South East Asia after the withdrawal of US military forces from South Vietnam. Only economic assistance to the nations of the Indian sub-continent remained relatively free from political considerations and in conformity with stated objectives of poverty alleviation. The main problem here was scale. Direct EC aid was hardly sufficient to make a dent in the needs of these vast populations.

In looking at its aid to Asia, the Commission is fond of pointing out that the Community has been able to establish through it a presence in almost every part of the third world: a significant step in the universalization of EC development assistance. The Commission is also keen to stress that its aid implementation has been effective, that the range of its aid instruments has widened over time and that the destinations of EC assistance have become more numerous and diversified.[43]

EC aid presence in Asia is nonetheless paper thin, not only in China and Indochina, but also in the Indian sub-continent. The basis for drawing conclusions about implementation success is very limited.[44] The sectoral destination of financial aid to Asia is overwhelmingly in agriculture (81 percent of the total in 1976–88) and in infrastructure within the agricultural sector (36.5 percent of the total over the same period). Food aid has been as large as financial aid. STABEX support to least developed countries and cofinancing with non-governmental organizations (NGOs) have remained minuscule (respectively ECU 15 million and ECU 71 million over twelve years). What the Community calls economic cooperation—for training, scientific and technical activities, trade, industrial and energy promotion—has remained very small in total size and heavily skewed in favor of trade promotion.[45]

Nowhere, moreover, did the Commission squarely face the issue of the adequacy of the Community's aid to Asia, evaluating the scale, concentration and thrust of a deeper program aimed at meeting more of the basic development needs of Asia's poor populations. Public statements in this area have so far more resembled whispers than recognizable stands.[46]

Asia and Europe seem to be growing apart from one another. EC member countries seem at times concerned about the increasing Japanese influence over this region, yet always unwilling to combat it concretely. Economic competition between Europe and Asia is perceived as growing, partly because the second generation of NICs is seen to be following in the footsteps of the first. Improved food self-sufficiency in the Asian sub-continent is taking away some of the basic. rationale for food aid. Human rights and governance concerns about Asia are growing within the Community—witness the hard positions taken on aid to China after the suppression of student dissension and on rights abuses in some of the ASEAN countries.[47] The affected countries are responding defensively, alleging interference in their internal affairs.[48] These developments are negatively influencing not only EC trade policies towards South East Asia, but also aid policies vis-a-vis the Asian sub-continent. Even the modest links between the Community and Asia developed so far are in danger of withering away.

Notes to Chapter 7

[1] In 1960 about 25 percent of Dutch aid still went to Indonesia. Similarly, 33 percent of British aid went to Asia.

[2] See, for example, de Gaulle, *Memoirs of Hope*, p. 200.

[3] See Chapter 1, pp.

[4] On the origins of the program, see Chapter 2, pp.

[5] The Commercial Cooperation Agreement between the EC and India, for example, established a new trade regime for jute and coir textiles and for some cotton textiles as well. Tariffs on imports were eliminated, but India had to restrain its exports to the Community. For the contents of this agreement see Commission of the European Communities, *The European Community and India*, Europe Information Doc. No. 50/81, Brussels, 1981. The agreement is also discussed in K.B. Lall and H.S. Chopra, "The EEC and India", in K.B. Lall, W. Ernst and H.S. Chopra, eds., *India and the EEC*, New Delhi, Allied Publishers, 1984, pp. 1–20.

[6] The agreements typically foresaw the constitution of a Joint Committee between the EC and the signatory country, entrusted with the task of supporting the purposes of the agreement and developing closer commercial cooperation between the parties.

7 In 1981 and 1985 respectively. On the EC–India agreement see Lall and Chopra, "The EEC and India", pp. 12–16 and K.G. Ramanathan, *Indo-EEC Trade under CCA*, in Lall et al., eds., *India and the EEC*, pp. 140–8.

8 On EC trade policies towards India see, T. Bhat, "Current Trends in EEC's Commercial Policies—An Indian Overview", in Lall. et al., eds., *India and the EEC*, pp. 122–39.

9 According to the World Bank, which computes per capita income of developing countries on the basis of a uniform methodology, in 1986 per capita income of Nepal was $150, that of Bangladesh, $160, and that of Burma, $200. The per capita income of India was $290, lower than those of such African associated countries as Zambia, Sierra Leone, Sudan, Lesotho, Ghana, Mauritania, Senegal, Liberia, Nigeria, Ivory Coast, Botswana, Cameroon, Congo, Mauritius, all of which enjoyed STABEX privileges under Lomé.

10 These are sacks, industrial wrapping cloth, backing for carpets, tarpaulin and twines, for which 50–60 percent of total costs are made up by the fiber. Most of the remainder is labor cost.

11 Between 1976 and 1988 the EC committed ECU 903 million in financial and technical aid to India, Bangladesh, Pakistan and Sri Lanka. Over the same period direct food aid to these countries amounted to ECU 840 million. See Commission, *Thirteen Years of Development Cooperation*, 1989, pp. 16 and 76.

12 Commission of the European Communities, *Eleventh Report from the Commission to the Council and Parliament on the Implementation of Financial and Technical Assistance to Latin American and Asian Developing Countries*, Doc. COM(88) 715 final, Brussels, 16 January 1989, pp. 41–2.

13 Court of Auditors of the European Communities, "Special Report No. 6/87 on Food Aid Supplied to India Between 1978 and 1985 (Flood II Operation)", *Official Journal of the European Communities*, No. C31, Vol. 31, Brussels, 4 February 1988, p. 13.

14 A.K. Banerjim, "From Mutual Indifference to Cooperation: EEC's Priorities and the Evolution of Indo-EEC Economic Relations", in Lall et al., eds., *India and the EEC*, pp. 85 and 90.

15 Tulloch, *Politics of Preferences*, p. 7.

16 On the European perceptions of competition coming from East Asia in the late 1970s see Y. Berthelot and G. Tardy, *Le Défi Economique du Tiers Monde*, 2 Vols, Paris, La Documentation Française, 1978. On the origin and evolution of European attitudes towards the NICs, see also L. Turner, "Western Europe and the NICs", in L. Turner

and N. McMullen, eds., *The Newly Industrializing Countries: Trade and Adjustment*, London, George Allen & Unwin (for the Royal Institute of International Affairs), 1982, pp. 135-43. On the specific attitudes of the Community vis-a-vis outward oriented industrial development and the NICs see Kahler, "Europe and its Privileged Partners", pp. 201-14.

[17] R. Langhammer, "EC Trade Policies Towards Asian Developing Countries", *Asian Development Review*, Vol. 4, No. 2, 1986, pp. 99-100; Grilli, "Contemporary Protectionism in an Unstable World Economy", pp. 144-72.

[18] General Agreement on Tariffs and Trade (GATT), *Textiles and Clothing in the World Economy*, Geneva, 1984, p. 68, and Langhammer, "EC Trade Policies Towards Asian Developing Countries", p. 101.

[19] The ESC opinion advocated some limited cooperation between EC and NIC firms, but supported helping the domestic industry in research and development activities and the use of defensive trade measures by the EC. The report advocatd that Korea, Hong Kong and Singapore be excluded from GSPs, that they be required to apply ILO labor standards and be subject to retaliatory trade measures whenever found to be subsidizing their production or generally engaged in unfair trade practices (presumably by the EC). The ESC opinion went as far as to advocate an "improvement" of the New Community Instrument "to make it at least as effective as Article 301 of the US Trade Act" (to keep up, one can presume, the best standards of EC trade policy and not to fall victim to unfair competition from the United States in the use of restrictive trade practices): Economic and Social Committee of the European Communities, *Opinion on the Relations Between the European Community and the Newly Industrializing Countries of South East Asia*, Doc. CES 439/89, Brussels, 1989, pp. 2-9.

[20] On this point, see E. Grilli, "Responses of Developing Countries to Trade Protectionism in Industrial Countries", in C. Pearson and J. Riedel, eds., *The Direction of Trade Policy*, Cambridge, Mass., Basil Blackwell, 1990, pp. 108-25.

[21] General Agreement on Tariffs and Trade (GATT), *Trade Policy Review Mechanism: The European Community*, Doc. C/RM/S/10B, Brussels, 1991, pp. 18-23.

[22] United Nations Conference on Trade and Development (UNCTAD), *Selected Issues on Restrictions to Trade*, Doc. UNCTAD/ITP/24, Geneva, 1990, p. 55 and Table 6.5.

23 Langhammer and Sapir, *Economic Impact*, pp. 57-8; Brown, "Trade and Welfare Effects", pp. 768-9.

24 These were the beneficiary countries that had the capacity to produce efficiently and export competitively a fairly large variety of industrial goods, and thus had the strongest opportunity to take advantage of the price wedge created in their favor by EC tariff preferences.

25 R.E. Baldwin and T. Murray, "MFN Tariff Reductions and the Developing Country Trade Benefits Under the GSP", *The Economic Journal*, Vol. 87, March 1977, pp. 43-44; G. Karsenty and S. Laird, "The GSP, Policy Options and the New Round", *Weltwirtschaftliches Archiv*, Vol. 123, 1987, pp. 272-3.

26 ASEAN was set up in 1967 for the purpose of enhancing cooperation in the economic, social and cultural fields among the following countries: Indonesia, Malaysia, the Philippines, Singapore and Thailand. Brunei became a member in 1984, after receiving independence from Great Britain.

27 These were Malaysia and Singapore.

28 For an analysis of EC interests in the ASEAN countries and a history of their relations see Harris and Bridges, *European Interests in ASEAN*. An overview of ASEAN-EC trade relations can be found in N. Akrasanee, "ASEAN-EC Trade Relations", in N. Akrasanee and H.C. Rieger, eds., *ASEAN-EC Economic Relations*, Singapore, ASEAN and Institute of South East Asian Studies, 1982, pp. 10-51.

29 Statistical Office of the European Communities, *EC-ASEAN Trade: A Statistical Analysis 1970-1984*, Foreign Trade, Series D, Studies and Analyses, Luxemburg, 1987, p. 17. These shares were virtually unchanged in the mid-1980s, at respectively 3 percent and 8 percent.

30 Lumber, rubber and tin were among them. In addition the EC imported tapioca and vegetable oils from the region.

31 Commission of the European Communities, *ASEAN and the European Community*, Europe Information Doc. No. 66/83, Brussels, 1983, p. 3.

32 H. Mynt, "ASEAN-EEC Cooperation", Washington D.C., School of Advanced International Studies, 1990 (mimeo.), pp. 36-45. This paper provides a thoughtful review of the potential and limits of EC-ASEAN cooperation. An indepth review of the patterns, origins, distribution and determinants of foreign investments in ASEAN countries, can be found in C.S. Yue, "EC Investment in ASEAN", in N. Akrasanee and H.C. Rieger, eds., *ASEAN-EC Economic Relations*, Singapore, ASEAN and Institute of South East Asian Studies, 1982, pp. 256-314.

33 "The EC has tended to look at its relations with ASEAN from the purely buy and sell angle." Statement reported in C.P. Luhulima, "Political Aspects of ASEAN-EEC Cooperation", *Asian Pacific Community Quarterly*, Fall 1984, p. 33.

34 This is the conclusion of a careful student of EC-ASEAN relations: R.J. Langhammer, "EC-ASEAN Relations: Institutional Deepening but Modest Economic Impact", in C. Stevens and J.V. van Themaat, eds., *Europe and the International Division of Labour: EEC and the Third World—A Survey 6*, London, Hodder and Stoughton, 1987, pp. 133-49.

35 This point is extensively argued by Christopher Stevens, who refers to the emphasis found in the memorandum on Africa and the Mediterranean countries as priority areas in EC development cooperation policies and to the use of aid as the preferred instrument of these policies: C. Stevens, "Implications of the EC's Development Policy for ASEAN", *ASEAN Economic Bulletin*, Vol. 1, No. 1, March 1985, pp. 226-8.

36 Exports of tapioca (or cassava) from Thailand and Indonesia were subject to quantitative restraints—of the "voluntary" kind—by the EC.

37 Almost 75 percent of the total throughout the 1970s.

38 M. Davenport, *Trade Policy, Protectionism and the Third World*, London, Croom Helm, 1986, pp. 103-4.

39 In value terms, the share of manufactures in total exports to the EC increased dramatically in the 1980s: from 46 percent to 64 percent. This was due in part to more rapid volume growth and to relative price changes, in particular the decline in the relative export prices of fuels. Textiles, and less so clothing, exports enjoyed the fastest growth in the 1980s, causing ASEAN's share of EC imports of these products from developing countries to go up. They were followed by exports of electrical machinery: Commission of the European Communities, *The European Community's Relations with ASEAN*, Europe Information Doc. No. 127/X/91, Brussels, April 1991, pp. 2-4.

40 This inference is drawn by the Commission on the basis of computations covering only two years: 1988 and 1989. *Ibidem*, pp. 4-5. The Commission's document appears to be highly selective in offering information and over time comparisons of the actual export performance in manufactures.

41 *Ibidem*, p. 5.

42 "Growth in the ASEAN region during the 1980s", the Commission recently observed, "has been so dramatic as to lead the region as a whole to a new level of economic achievement. The fact is that,

broadly speaking, the ASEAN countries are no longer struggling with problems of rural development, but nearly all have graduated to the status of advanced developed countries . . . Asian regional developments inevitably have affected EC-ASEAN relations . . . The main [EC] policy change is to be found in the greater emphasis now being placed on economic cooperation." *Ibidem*, pp. 1-2. In the Commission's official terminology, economic cooperation means cooperation among near-equal parties, as opposed to aid and trade cooperation that fit relations between economically unequal parties.

43 Commission, *Thirteen Years of Development Cooperation*, pp. 71-4.

44 Only a third of the schemes financed have actually been completed. The Commission's evaluation of the development impact of its projects in mid-1989 was limited to only fourteen projects in the agricultural sector for Asia and Latin America combined. *Ibidem*, p. 63. More evaluations were said to be planned during 1990-91.

45 *Ibidem*, pp. 13-22.

46 *Ibidem*, p. 69.

47 Commission of the European Communities, *XXIIIrd General Report on the Activities of the European Communities 1989*, Brussels, 1990, point 828; and *XXIVth General Report on the Activities of the European Communities 1990*, Brussels, 1991, point 745.

48 *Washington Post*, 21 July 1991.

8

Eastern Europe: The Newest Development Challenge for the Community

Official relations between the EC and the countries of Eastern Europe were slow to evolve. Even slower and more difficult to develop were relations between the EC and the Council for Mutual Economic Assistance (CMEA), the association comprising the Soviet Union in addition to the Eastern European nations.[1] The cold war, with the consequent reduction in political and other links between the countries of Western and Eastern Europe, poisoned the environment for many years after the end of World War II. Reciprocal suspicions ran high. Partly as a consequence, Soviet attitudes towards European integration remained consistently and extremely hostile until the early 1960s.

There were other reasons for the difficulties experienced in EC–Eastern European relations. Eastern Europe was not considered an area for development cooperation with the Community. The Treaty of Rome did not even mention Eastern Europe. Relations between the EC and the Eastern European countries could develop only in the general framework of the Community's external relations. In particular, trade relationships between the EC and these countries fell squarely in the domain of the common commercial policy by virtue of art. 113 of the Treaty of Rome. After a transitional period, this article of the Treaty foresaw that trade relations with third countries would be conducted by the Community on the basis of uniform principles. The conclusion of trade agreements with third countries was explicitly recognized to fall in the domain of the common commercial policy. The Commission was given direct responsibility for making recommendations to the Council about the negotiation of such agreements and for conducting them after receiving the necessary authorization. From the standpoint of the EC, much of the relationship with Eastern Europe until the late 1980s did in fact revolve, in a formal sense, around the twin questions of the implementation of the CCP and the role of the Commission in it. Political relations with the East, however, were not affected by the Treaty of Rome and were left exclusively to the individual EC members.

The fact that relations between the Community and Eastern Europe improved enormously and rapidly in the late 1980s and that a drastic change occurred in their basis, which, as far as the Community was concerned, moved in some important respects from external trade policy to development cooperation, has tended to overshadow the past. Once the political climate changed and Eastern Europe became free to choose its political and economic course, and once the economic, social and environmental challenges facing many of the region's countries became clear, the natural response of the European Community to the plight of Eastern Europe was one of economic cooperation, along the lines of its previous response to developing countries' demands. The Community quickly adapted and extended its "cooperation-through-association" model to Eastern Europe, as it had done with the countries of Southern Europe and the Mediterranean basin. It used the model in a more nuanced fashion than in the past and included political conditionality in it, thus abandoning its avowed political neutrality, but it once again fell back on a time-tested framework for relations with a neighboring region that had suddenly assumed a high priority.

After a brief first phase of trade-cum-cooperation agreements that lasted until 1990, association was offered to Eastern Europe. This happened so quickly and seemed so effortless that EC relations with Eastern Europe may appear to have long been based on a substratum of economic and political cooperation. This is, however, only recent history.

Many of the same changes have occurred in EC relations with the former Soviet Union. Association with the Community of the countries resulting from the breakup of the Soviet state is not being considered as of now. However, in April 1990 the Soviet Union and the EC signed an agreement on trade and economic cooperation, and the EC, as well as its individual members, have extended various forms of economic assistance first to the Soviet state and subsequently to its former components (especially Russia). These actions represent such a swift and radical break with the past—after decades of indecision, resistance to change and extreme caution even in adjusting actual behaviors to changed realities—that models and interpretations cannot keep up with the breakneck speed at which events are taking place and decisions are being made. For these very reasons, framing current EC relations with Eastern and Central European countries in an historical perspective is more necessary than ever.

Soviet Policy Towards the EC

Relations between Eastern and Western Europe became an early victim of the cold war soon after the end of World War II. In fact much of the cold war had roots and key manifestations in Europe specifically in the forcible submission of Eastern Europe to Soviet political and military control. Within the cold war framework relations between the two halves of Europe could only be difficult, even in the economic domain. The Soviet Union maintained strong opposition to any cooperative effort among Western European nations, and especially to any effort at economic integration among them. Having condemned the Marshall Plan as an attempt to rehabilitate and eventually rearm Germany, which eventually occurred in the framework of the North Atlantic Treaty Organization, the Soviet state opposed the creation of the Coal and Steel Community in 1951 and, six years later, the establishment of the European Community. This position it took the Soviet Union nearly two decades to change in substance, and another to modify also in form.

Soviet opposition to European economic cooperation was both political and ideological. The roots of political opposition are to be found in the "German problem" and more generally in a deeply felt need to prevent Western Europe from coalescing too strongly against a Soviet state weakened by a very costly war and by reduced ideological commitment of the masses, itself a consequence of the war. The roots of ideological opposition are easily traceable to Leninist thinking about capitalism, its last stage (imperialism), its inherent contradictions and the inevitability of its collapse. Seen through the lens of ideology, the EC was an inherently ephemeral construction doomed to failure. There was therefore no need for the Soviet state to deal with it as if it were a reality. Both these strands of thought are evident in the "17 Theses on the Common Market", delivered by the Moscow Institute of World Economy in January 1957, just before the Spaak Committee finished its report on European integration.[2] From these political and ideological premises followed the policy of non-recognition of the EC, a stance that the Soviet Union observed with punctilious care for many years and that it attempted to impose on its more reluctant Eastern European allies. Even if bypassed in practice in later years, first by the Eastern European nations and then by the Soviet Union itself, the policy of non-recognition of the EC formally lasted until 1988.

A modest reappraisal of the EC, however, occurred during Nikita Khruschchev's time and continued until the early 1970s. The "32 Theses on the Common Market", prepared in 1962 with the help of Western European Communist parties, in particular the Italian and French, and the nearly simultaneous speech by the supreme leader of the Soviet Union on "The Vital Questions on the Development of the World System", began the tortuous process of legitimization of relations with the EC. These were small, but important, official first steps. Others would follow, as it became clear that, though possibly an ephemeral entity, the EC was still there and its collapse could not be dated precisely. It had, therefore, to be dealt with, at least for the time being, as an economic and political reality. Later on, the rapid progress that the Community seemed to be making, particularly when compared with that of CMEA, certainly must not have escaped even the least realistic Soviet leaders.

Economic reform attempts in Eastern European countries, all implying some devolution of planning responsibilities from the central authorities to the productive enterprises and the substitution of indirect for direct methods of economic management, focused Soviet attention on the CMEA, its purposes and potential. In fact the notion of economic integration among member countries began to surface officially after 1968, very much at the initiative of the Soviet Union. Three years later a "Complex Program of Socialist Economic Integration" was adopted by the CMEA. In March 1972, Leonid

Brezhnev felt secure enough about the balance of interests achieved with the Eastern European allies to indicate in his speech to the 15th Congress of the Soviet Trade Unions that "the Soviet Union was far from ignoring the situation actually existing in Western Europe, including the existence of such economic groupings of capitalist countries as the European Common Market". In the view of the Soviet leader, CMEA integration was providing the right basis for an EC-CMEA dialogue. In December of the same year the president of the Soviet Union publicly answered the implicit question of business relations between the CMEA and the EC: such relations were now "probably" possible.[3]

Several factors, aside from the apparent fortification of the CMEA, were playing a role in the Soviet reappraisal of the EC. Mutual integration notwithstanding, most of the Eastern European states remained in favor of normalization of relations with the Community. Trade with the West and western credits had become too important for many of them to be left to casual or even informal relations. Politically, Eastern European preferences for better and more explicit relations with the EC could not be safely ignored by the Soviet Union in the aftermath of the invasion of Czechoslovakia. Nor could the threat of West Germany be used any longer in the early 1970s to keep the Eastern European countries in line. The signing of the German-Soviet pact in May 1972 had put an effective end to this option. Finally, the Soviet Union's economic weakness was beginning to become clear to its leaders. If much needed western capital and technology—the wherewithal for the modernization of the Soviet productive system—were to be obtained, Western Europe had to be considered not only a critically important source in itself, but also a necessary partner to avoid too strong a dependency on the United States. Dealing with Western Europe meant, necessarily, dealing with the EC as well.[4]

EC Policy Towards Eastern Europe and the CMEA

EC policies towards Eastern Europe and the CMEA, essentially defensive until the mid-1970s, were very protective of the stability of the Community up to 1964. The trade dealings of member states with selected Eastern European countries were seen in Brussels as a threat to the implementation of the common commercial policy at the end of the transition period foreseen by the Treaty of Rome. Dependence on supplies from Eastern Europe was considered dangerous for the Community, and thus to be minimized. Imports from Eastern Europe were viewed more often than not as disruptive to the internal market. The non-market economies of Eastern Europe could not be relied on, as could the other trade partners of the Community, when it came to trade behavior. They appeared not to be bound by standard price considerations or by enterprise profit and loss relations when engaging in international trade. Trading for them was a state affair, guided by the laws of politics and political interest.

In retrospect this EC posture appears to have been too cautious and apparently dictated by false, or at least exaggerated, economic preoccupations. Yet, the Community was young then and still wobbly. The Soviet Union was plainly hostile to it, to the point of lobbying openly against its creation in 1957–58 and refusing to recognize its legal status after that. Moreover, the difficulties on the road to the development of a common market in Europe seemed numerous: first the creation of a customs union among the EC member states and the centralization of commercial policy, then the setting up of a common agricultural policy and then the extension of common policies to other sectors of the economies of the member states. The EC Commission, in particular, was not taking any chances when it came to relations with Eastern Europe. "Better safe than sorry" seemed to be a key characteristic of its *modus operandi* in those years.

Moreover, in the early years of the EC, trade with both the Soviet Union and Eastern Europe was of little importance to the member states. World War II and its aftermath had combined to reduce to near insignificance what had been an extensive network of trade relations between the two halves of the continent.[5] There were therefore few reasons to worry about what was no longer significant. Only in the 1960s did trade relations between EC members and Eastern European countries develop sufficiently to become a factor again. In the late 1950s, EC(6) trade with Eastern Europe, including the Soviet Union, represented 2.7 percent of total exports and 2.9 percent of total imports (including intra-trade). In the early 1970s, the share of EC(6) imports from Eastern Europe had grown to 3.3 percent, while exports to Eastern Europe represented 3.4 percent of the total. If intra-EC trade is excluded, the share of the Community's exports to Eastern Europe can be seen to have grown even more: from 4 to nearly 7 percent between 1958 and 1971, and similarly for the share of imports (Table 8.1).[6] It was in many ways the development of East–West trade relations that forced the EC to deal with Eastern Europe. These relations developed naturally between EC and CMEA members and could not be ignored by the Community. The Commission tried instead to

Table 8.1 EC Trade with Eastern Europe

	1958	1971	1981	1989
	(million ECU)			
Exports to:				
USSR	208	1,118	8,257	12,610
Other Eastern Europe	415	2,292	9,846	13,268
Total Eastern Europe	623	3,410	18,103	25,878
	percentage			
As a share of total EC exports	2.7	3.4	3.2	2.5
As a share of EC exports (excluding intra-trade)	3.9	6.7	6.8	6.3
	(million ECU)			
Imports from:				
USSR	274	1,084	14,180	15,079
Other Eastern Europe	403	2,097	9,091	13,813
Total Eastern Europe	677	3,181	23,271	28,892
	percentage			
As a share of total EC imports	2.9	3.3	3.8	2.7
As a share of total EC imports (excluding intra-trade)	4.2	6.5	7.3	6.5

Note: EC(6) in 1958 and 1971; EC(12) in 1981 and 1989.
Sources: D. Hiester, "The European Community and the East Bloc", in J. Lodge, ed., Institutions and Policies of the European Community, New York, St. Martin's Press, 1983; EUROSTAT, Foreign Trade Monthly Statistics, 1958-1974 (special number), Brussels, 1975; and External Trade Statistical Yearbook: Recapitulation 1958-1989, Brussels, 1990.

manage them as tightly as possible, for without careful management of these relations the passage to a common trade policy could have become imperiled.

The attempt by the Commission to take control of the management of East-West trade relations began with the advocacy of only short-term trade agreements between the EC member states and the Eastern European countries. In 1961 the EC Council limited the duration of these agreements to one year, unless they included a clause that automatically amended them to conform with the EC common trade policy when it came into effect.[7] Similarly, when it became evident that Community members were competing among themselves on the conditions of credit extendable to Eastern European countries, creating a situation that could possibly complicate the adoption of a common commercial policy, the Commission pushed for consultations among them on these matters. The Council accepted the Commission's position in 1962.[8] EC policies concerning trade in steel and agricultural products with Eastern Europe were also kept tight in those years. The Commission was exercising strict surveillance on imports, while *de facto* attempting to enforce restraints on EC-CMEA trade relations.

The Commission also pushed hard in the same years to get the Council to accelerate the definition and enactment of a common policy concerning trade with state-trading countries, arguing that internal as well as external reasons made it imperative that this be done quickly. According to this view, the internal market was being jeopardized and important opportunities connected to GATT negotiations were being lost by member countries pursuing individual relations with Eastern Europe. However, confronted with the strong reluctance of several of the member states to arrive at an early unification of national policies towards Eastern Europe, the Commission relented in its efforts to restrain the more open attitudes of some of them. After the failure of the major effort launched in 1962-64 (a series of communications to the Council on the subject, on which the executive organ of the Community in practice refused to act), the Commission adopted a less interventionist posture, trying instead to simply oversee trade and credit relations with the centrally planned economies of Eastern Europe.

In the following years several EC members began to liberalize their commerce with state-trading countries. The end of the transition period foreseen in the Rome Treaty came and went without a CCP in place, even vis-a-vis Eastern European countries, with which EC members were stubbornly trying to preserve the right to conclude bilateral agreements, at least when "exceptional" circumstances could be shown to prevail.[9] As the deadline for the implementation of a common commercial policy was pushed forward by the Council, first to the end of 1973 and subsequently to the end of 1974, the Commission was forced to follow, instead of lead, its member states in the implementation of this critical policy step. Regulation of relations with Eastern Europe did not become an avenue for a faster pace towards a common external trade policy as the Commission had earlier envisaged. The adoption of a clear general policy concerning agreements between member states and third countries had to wait until 1974, following yet another proposal by the Commission in the previous year.[10]

If finding a consensus on bilateral relations between members and state-trade countries was a lengthy affair, the definition of a common EC policy towards Eastern Europe, and a formal position vis-a-vis the CMEA, turned out to be a difficult and tortuous process even in the 1970s, notwithstanding the revision in the position of the Soviet Union towards the Community, the conclusion of the Soviet–German Treaty and the relaxation of political and military tensions in Europe that ensued.[11] On the one hand, the Community wanted to pursue economic cooperation with the countries of Eastern Europe. Aside from economic advantage, the Community was seeking to enlarge, in any way possible, the maneuvering margins of the Eastern European countries, especially Romania, Hungary and Poland, which were the most independent-minded of the group. On the other hand, the Community did not wish to legitimate the CMEA by using it as a generalized vehicle for its relations with Eastern Europe, which was exactly the opposite of what the Soviet Union dearly wished.

Reconciling these different objectives proved to be difficult. The task was complicated moreover by the strong desire of the Commission to gain control, as soon as possible, over those specific aspects of the commercial policy towards Eastern Europe that had until then been in the domain of the member countries, particularly, import quotas and MFN trade status. In pursuing its different goals the Commission proposed a two-pronged approach: a "specimen cooperation agreement" to be used by the EC in dealing directly with individual Eastern European countries, thus totally bypassing the CMEA, and a common commercial policy towards Eastern Europe that would represent the minimum common denominator of those of member countries, but be applied immediately. The outline agreement foresaw long-term, non-preferential trade arrangements between the EC and the individual Eastern European countries that wished to enter into direct relations with the Community, instead of arrangements between individual Eastern European countries and single EC members, as had been the case before. The proposed agreements were to be based on the principle of reciprocal advantages and commitments. The Community envisaged granting MFN status to the signatories and taking into account their specific trading structures. Trade in agricultural products and textiles, however, was as usual excluded from the ambit of application of these agreements, and safeguard mechanisms were also specifically to be built into them. The Commission was still taking no chances where trade with state-trading Eastern European countries was concerned.

Inside the Community things went smoothly. The Council accepted in substance the Commission's position during 1974, and an "invitation to negotiate" was sent to the Soviet Union and to the Eastern European countries. In the meantime, the Community would apply an autonomous policy aimed at maintaining the status quo in trade.[12] Making the Soviet Union accept the position that relations with the EC were to be based on bilateral agreements with individual countries in which the CMEA would have no substantive role proved to be more difficult than anticipated. The Soviet Union agreed in substance to the EC position only in 1988, when official relations between the two institutions were finally established. Meanwhile the often absurd ballet of EC–CMEA contacts went into full swing.[13]

The Commission, in pursuing *de facto* the old policy of not affording the Soviet Union any direct or indirect chance for increasing its control over the Eastern European countries, stuck to the formally correct position that the CMEA had no "constitutional right" to represent the members in negotiating trade and cooperation agreements with the EC. The Commission in effect hoped that by stalling on this point it would entice some of the Eastern European countries to break rank with the Soviet Union, and to enter into direct negotiations with the Community at the expiration of the previously negotiated bilateral agreements. Romania had already done so in 1972, when it had requested and obtained GSP treatment from the Community. It did so again in 1976 by negotiating an agreement on exports of textiles with the Community and by signing with it, in 1980, a full trade and cooperation agreement. Sectoral trade policies, however, proved to be the Trojan horse the Community desired. A proposal made by the Council in 1977, that all countries exporting steel to the Community negotiate agreements over prices in order to prevent disruption of Community markets, was accepted first by Czechoslovakia in 1978. Several other Eastern European countries followed suit by signing trade agreements with the EC over textiles and steel. Even the Soviet Union and East Germany, the two hardliners in CMEA, could not avoid entering (together with Poland) into direct negotiations with the EC in 1977 over fishing rights in the North Sea.[14]

The farthest that the Community was willing to go in its direct relations with the CMEA as a whole was to propose that a framework agreement be negotiated between the two organizations, provided that CMEA members be allowed to conclude bilateral trade and cooperation agreements with the Community. This offer was first made in one of the EC–CMEA meetings in 1976. Negotiations over the draft agreement began in 1978, but led nowhere. The EC was being successful in breaking, piece-by-piece, the common front between the Soviet Union and its Eastern European allies, and was therefore not prone to compromise, while the Soviet Union, though stagnating economically, was not yet weak enough to accept what was in practice an EC diktat. An additional problem was the inclusion of Berlin in any contractual agreement between the EC and CMEA, which the Soviet Union opposed.[15]

Eventually the Community won the point. Conditions in Eastern Europe were evolving in its favor.[16] The financial situation of several Eastern European countries worsened drastically in the early 1980s as external debt burdens, in part a consequence of the easy credit policies followed by the EC members in the 1970s against the Commission's wishes, became crippling. The Polish and Romanian debt crises of 1981 and 1982 epitomized this trend. Worsening financial conditions brought to a head many of the structural problems that beset the productive structures of these countries, attempts to reform them notwithstanding.[17]

Politically, the rise to power of Mikhail Gorbachev in the Soviet Union and the policies that he implemented in close succession led to a drastic improvement in East-West relations and to increased Soviet interest in a better relationship with Western Europe—itself in part a consequence of the worsening of internal economic conditions. These policies also set in motion a process of change in Eastern Europe that culminated in the unification of Germany, and in the realization of first political independence and subsequently democracy in much of Eastern Europe.

In June 1988 the "Joint Declaration on the Establishment of Official Relations between the European Community and the Council for Mutual Economic Assistance"[18] formally sanctioned the victory of the EC position. Conspicuously absent from the declaration was any attribution of representation functions to the CMEA. Not only did the Soviet Union have to renounce its long-held demand that the CMEA be the vehicle for EC-Eastern Europe cooperation, but it also had to assure the Community that the establishment of official relations between the EC and the CMEA would not adversely affect the development of EC bilateral relations with individual CMEA countries. This assurance was given implicitly in the declaration itself, which not once, but twice, circumscribed cooperation between the two parties to areas falling within their respective competence, and explicitly in a letter to the Community delivered two years before.[19] The agreements on trade and economic cooperation concluded by the Community with Hungary just three months after the Declaration and with Poland a year or so later sealed this issue. Establishment of formal relations between the EC and the CMEA did indeed sanction the freedom of Eastern European countries to pursue their autonomous economic relations with EC Europe.

EC Response to Political and Economic Liberalization in Eastern Europe

Drastic political and economic change in Eastern Europe occurred at a propitious time for the Community. By the time liberalization started in Eastern Europe, the Community was well on its way towards the creation of a unified internal market and the shaping of a definite path to monetary unification. The EC construction had not only regained political momentum in the late 1980s, but also enjoyed renewed economic credibility. EC Europe was growing; it was exuding confidence and it was willing to take bolder steps than at any time since the early 1970s.

West Germany was given strong cooperation by its EC partners during its reunification with East Germany. This delicate process was handled smoothly with regard to its implications for the Community. East Germany was integrated into the Community as soon as reunification occurred in October 1990, without any overt fuss over costs and burden sharing.[20] Residual Soviet and Eastern European fears were thus allayed and the transition process, instead of generating complications, resulted in the creation of an even earlier and more extensive political entente between Eastern and Western Europe.[21] The existence of the Community, its political cohesion and forward economic projection contributed decisively to the speed and relative ease of the East–West settlement in Central Europe.

The EC response to the changes occurring in Eastern Europe in the late 1980s took three specific dimensions. There was an aid response addressed to the most urgent needs of the Central European countries that were affected by profound, and at times seemingly explosive, economic crises. There was complementary action in the field of trade, aimed at improving the access to the EC market of all the Eastern European countries' exports. Finally, there was the early development of institutional frameworks within which economic and political relations between Western and Eastern European countries could take place. In many ways it was the speed and breadth of the institutional answer that most distinctly characterized the overall EC response to the challenge coming from Eastern Europe in the late 1980s. The basic content of such a response was in fact traditional in nature, being akin to much of the Community's previous development cooperation efforts. But the quickness of the response was unparalleled in Community history.

The Aid Response

The EC's immediate reply to the urgent economic needs of some of the Eastern European countries was to supply assistance— in the form of both food and financial aid—on a case-by-case basis. The member countries were mobilized, and so were the major Western allies. At the Paris Summit of July 1989, at the request of the European participants, a program of economic assistance to Poland and Hungary was adopted: Operation PHARE (Poland–Hungary: Assistance for the Restructuring of the Economy). The initiative, to which twenty-four countries adhered, is still ongoing.[22] The Community was not only an autonomous party to it, but was also given the task of coordinating its activities.[23] The "aid packages" of the single participants that PHARE coordinated became in time more varied in form and comprehensive in nature than originally envisaged. Food deliveries, new credit, investment guarantees, and technical assistance grants were accompanied by official debt relief measures, bridge-loans and even a stabilization fund for Poland.[24] Assistance also was extended from the short to the medium term and woven into the programs of such international organizations as the International Monetary Fund and the World Bank.[25]

Within PHARE the Community granted emergency food aid to Poland beginning in 1989, to Romania in 1990, and to Bulgaria, Albania and Romania in 1991. In addition, EC financial assistance for economic restructuring in Poland, Hungary, Czechoslovakia, Bulgaria and Yugoslavia was allocated in both the 1990 and 1991 budgets. Total EC direct economic assistance reached ECU 500 million in 1990 and it is expected to reach ECU 785 million in 1991 (Table 8.2). The Council also approved in early 1990 a structural adjustment loan to Hungary of ECU 870 million over five years, which was proposed by the Commission as an exceptional gesture towards a country facing tough medium-term economic conversion problems.[26] The first tranche of the loan, conditional on the conclusion of an agreement between

Table 8.2 EC Aid Commitments to Eastern Europe (million ECU)

	1990	1991[a]
Humanitarian Aid		
Hungary and Poland	42	—
Romania	15	16
Albania	—	5
Bulgaria	—	10
Economic Restructuring Aid		
Poland	181	197
Hungary	90	114
German Dem. Rep.[b]	34	—
Czechoslovakia	30	99
Bulgaria	25	75
Yugoslavia	35	6
Romania	—	103
Multidisciplinary Aid[c]	13	7
Regional Programs	35	88
Total Aid	500	775

[a] Estimated on the basis of preliminary information.
[b] Eligible until reunification.
[c] For program studies, infrastructure and other uses.
Source: Commission of the European Communities, *EC-Eastern Europe Relations*, (DGX Background Brief), Brussels, 1991; Data Supplied by the European Commission.

Hungary and the IMF and on the pursuit of economic reform, was released in early 1990; the second in early 1991.[27] Outside PHARE the Community also worked on setting up a program of assistance for the Soviet Union. In December 1990, at its Rome meeting the EC Council decided to extend ECU 250 million of food aid and ECU 400 million of technical assistance to the Soviet Union, in addition to the extension of credit guarantees for ECU 500 million. The delivery of both the food aid and the technical assistance funds was postponed as a result of events in the Baltic republics during January 1991 when the Soviet Union used force to try to subdue independence movements. Food aid was resumed by decision of the Council in March 1991. The relaunching of full EC–USSR cooperation was decided in May of the same year at the second meeting of the Joint Committee, previously established to ensure the operation of the economic and commercial cooperation agreement between the EC and the USSR.[28] It did not last very long, however, as the Soviet state broke up in late 1991 to reconstitute, in part, as a Commonwealth of Independent States (CIS). But EC aid to the constituent republics, especially Russia, resumed almost immediately. EC food aid featured prominently in the attempt made by Western donors to support price liberalization in that country at the beginning of 1992.

Aside from direct economic assistance, the European Investment Bank was empowered in February 1990 to make project loans to Poland and Hungary for a total amount of ECU 1,000 million over three years. A year later Czechoslovakia, Bulgaria and Romania were also declared eligible for EIB loans,[29] and an increase of the loanable funds to ECU 2,000 million was proposed by the Commission.[30]

The Trade Policy Response

Economic assistance to Eastern Europe was from the very beginning accompanied by measures aimed at strengthening commercial ties between the two halves of Europe. Their purpose was in part to restore pre-World War II conditions, in part to re-anchor the Eastern European economies to the West, and in part to try to ensure that internal stabilization and reform in these economies would have a better chance. Improving market access for Poland and Hungary was one of the prime objectives of Operation PHARE as early as 1989. Trade and aid had always gone together in EC cooperation policies. The Community almost naturally used these twin instruments in dealing with the Eastern European situation. Depending on the state of trade relations with the various Eastern European countries, this meant granting MFN status to some of them (Hungary, Bulgaria and Romania),[31] granting GSP treatment to most of them (first to Poland and Hungary, then to Bulgaria and Czechoslovakia),[32] and liberalizing trade with all of them (including the former Soviet Union).

Phased elimination of the specific quantitative restrictions on imports from Eastern European countries was foreseen in the various trade and cooperation agreements that came into being after 1988. But in the context of Operation PHARE the Community decided on early elimination of these significant trade restrictions. Those in force with Poland and Hungary were abolished as of the beginning of 1990. Quotas on imports from Bulgaria, Czechoslovakia and Romania were abolished from October of the same year.[33] Non-specific quantitative restrictions on imports from Hungary and Poland were suspended for the year 1990.[34] Recognizing that in moving towards freer trade with Eastern Europe the Community had to go first and to move faster, if it really wanted to contribute to the economic recovery of that area, the Commission pushed the Council to take action in the field of trade policies as early and consistently as possible.[35]

Yet, the coherence in EC trade policies towards Eastern Europe that the Commission was able to ensure from the Council was far from complete. Quantitative restrictions on imports of steel, textiles and agricultural products remained in place.[36] Some limited relief was granted to Eastern European countries by extending them GSP treatment for textile products and by increasing the steel import quotas in force by 15 per cent,[37] but EC sectoral trade policies, including agriculture, were too hard to crack, even in the case of Eastern Europe. They remained in force and effectively limited Eastern European exports to the Community in some of the areas where expansion of exports was most feasible.[38]

The Institutional Response

The EC response to the changes occurring in the political and economic conditions of Eastern Europe showed a strong institutional dimension from the very beginning. This was so even when the speed of economic and political change in this region was less than clearly appreciated. The bilateral trade and cooperation agreements negotiated with the major Eastern European countries immediately after the Joint Declaration of 1988 were known instruments, which had been usefully employed before in developing relations with Southern Europe, the Mediterranean, Asia and Latin America. Aside from being time-tested tools, by historical practice these agreements had well served the Community in the first stage of its relations with third countries. The choice was therefore indicative of both the general preference for known institutional frames of reference in dealing with Eastern European countries and of the expectations held in Brussels, at least until 1989, about the speed at which the situation in Eastern Europe was evolving. The view was then that the Community's relations with Eastern Europe would be developed in an orderly and systematic fashion, beginning with the widening of trade links and the setting up of the basic premises for economic cooperation.

When the pace and direction of events in Eastern Europe became clearer, the decisions to extend these "first generation" agreements from Hungary (September 1988), Czechoslovakia (December 1988), and Poland (September 1989) to the Soviet Union (December 1989), Bulgaria (May 1990) and Romania (October 1990) were based on a less traditional rationale. According to the Commission, the quick conclusion of these agreements would help Eastern European countries significantly in the transition period, by signifying to the outside world the willingness of their governments to anchor their economies to Western Europe.[39] By then, the Commission thought that the external demonstration effects, and perhaps even the mere symbolism, of these agreements would be as important as their specific content for the Eastern European countries that were entering into them. Even when the pace of events seemed to overtake the negotiations—as in the case of the first trade agreement with Czechoslovakia, which had to be renegotiated in May 1990, or the Trade and Cooperation Agreement with East Germany concluded just four months before reunification— the new rationale given by the Commission seemed to apply, at least for the short term.

The bilateral agreements on trade and economic cooperation negotiated by the Community between 1988 and 1990 (Table 8.3) varied very little in specific objectives and contents.[40] Their stated purpose was to develop and diversify trade between the contracting parties. In the area of trade they were aimed at establishing basic governing principles (non-discrimination and reciprocity in trade relations), at the reciprocal concession or reaffirmation of MFN status, plus the gradual elimination of all EC specific quantitative restrictions on imports from the Eastern European parties.[41] The liberalization of trade that these agreements foresaw was to apply to all products except textiles, steel and agricultural imports, which were covered by sectoral arrangements. The Community, moreover, maintained ample

Table 8.3 Agreements Between the EC and Eastern European Countries

GSP and Sectoral Agreements Under the MFAs and the ECSC Treaty	Trade and Cooperation Agreements Under Art. 113 of the Treaty of Rome	Association Agreements Under Art. 238 of the Treaty of Rome
GSP: Romania (1972) Textiles Trade: Romania (1976 and 1977) Textiles Trade: Poland (1978) Textiles Trade: Hungary (1978) Steel Import Quotas: Czechoslovakia, Hungary, Poland, USSR (1978)		
	Hungary (1988) Czechoslovakia (1988) Poland (1989) USSR (1989) Bulgaria (1990) Czechoslovakia (1990) Romania (1990)	
		Hungary (1991) Poland (1991) Czechoslovakia (1991)

Note: Years in parentheses refer to dates of signature of the various agreements.
Sources: P. Marsh, "EC Foreign Economic Policy and the Political Management of East-West Economic Relations", *Millenium—Journal of International Studies*, Vol. 9, No. 1, Spring 1980; *Official Journal of the European Communities* (various issues).

safeguard rights, although consultations with the signatory countries were foreseen if safeguard actions ever became necessary.

The agreements generally contemplated cooperation in industry, mining, agriculture and agro-business, transport, telecommunications, tourism, science, and the environment. In some cases (Poland and Bulgaria) health and vocational training were also indicated as sectors for cooperation. In other cases (Bulgaria and Czechoslovakia) the energy (including nuclear energy), and the banking, insurance and financial service sectors were added to the list. In the case of the Soviet Union, the European Atomic Energy Community (EURATOM) became a contracting party of the agreement, to emphasize the importance attached to cooperation in the field of nuclear energy, including safety standards. The main instruments of cooperation were to be exchanges of information, investment promotion and protection schemes, business contacts, technical assistance from the Community, and in some cases joint research and development activities. All the agreements foresaw the establishment of a joint committee to ensure their proper functioning.

The EC institutional response included, in addition to the establishment of the aid coordinating process under Operation PHARE,[42] the creation of the European Bank for Reconstruction and Development (EBRD), a multilateral development bank exclusively devoted to the satisfaction of Eastern European investment needs.[43] Neither institution represented a new departure in the use of instruments of assistance. Aid coordinating groups had long existed under the stewardship of multinational bodies such as the World Bank and the Organization for Economic Cooperation and Development (OECD). Regional development banks existed for Africa, Asia and Latin America. A European Investment Bank was operating in the EC and associated developing countries, and its activities could have been permanently extended to Eastern Europe. The special significance of the new institutions set up for Eastern Europe was that they reflected the material support specifically coming from both Europe and the rest of the Western world. For the Western countries, including the EC members, the greatest value of these institutions was in the political message of support that they embodied and delivered.

Operation PHARE, aside from being assigned to the Commission for coordination, was from the beginning anchored to the establishment of "the rule of law, the respect of human rights, the establishment of multi-party systems, the holding of free and fair elections and economic liberalization with a view to introducing market economies" in the associated countries of Eastern Europe. These were all political themes, either *strictu* or *latu sensu*. EC Europe was in the forefront of the specification and pursuit of these objectives.[44] EBRD was also unique in a number of respects: it was to foster market orientation in the economies of the borrowing countries and multi-party democracy (a rather novel objective for a development bank). It moreover included the Soviet Union among its members and its economic mandate was overwhelmingly in the direction of helping the private sector to take root in the borrowing countries.

Associationism Extended: From "Trade and Cooperation" to the "European" Agreements

The second phase of the EC institutional response to changes in Eastern Europe began while the first was still under way. As early as December 1989, the EC Council, meeting in Strasbourg, expressed the consciousness of the Community (and its member states) of "the common responsibility which devolved on them in this decisive phase in the history of Europe", their readiness "to develop with the USSR and the other countries of Central and Eastern Europe . . . closer and more substantial relations based upon an intensification of political dialogue and increased cooperation in all areas". As for the ways of doing so, the Council stated that the Community would "continue its review of appropriate forms of association with those countries [which were then] on the road to economic and political reform".[45] Aside from being timely, this declaration of intent stressed the political conditionality being built into the second phase of EC cooperation with Eastern Europe. Closer cooperation was now openly and strongly predicated on the pace of Eastern Europe's progress in both political and economic reforms.

The desirability of the Community proceeding towards "a form of association [with the Eastern European countries] once the first generation of agreements is complete" was expressed by External Relations Commissioner Andriessen to the European Parliament while it was debating the Community's relations with Central and Eastern European countries in January 1990.[46] Practically at the same time, the Commission, in a Communication to the Council, was arguing that "the Community should play an important role in reinforcing the process of political reform and economic liberalization which is under way" in Eastern Europe, and that "the development of bilateral relations with these countries should take place within the framework of an *overall* Community Policy". The Commission continued, "association agreements with these countries should have common elements covering trade, cooperation and financial support, *modulated according to the needs and the capacities of each country as well as its progress towards open political and economic systems*" (emphasis added).[47]

These concepts were further developed by the Commission in response to a request from the Council, meeting informally in Dublin in January 1990. In a communication forwarded to both the Council and the Parliament at the end of February the Commission argued that the Eastern European countries (now called "partners") were "looking beyond normalization, and toward a type of relationship reflecting geographic proximity, shared political, economic and cultural values, and increased interdependence". Developing the foreign policy rationale for its position, the Commission went on to advocate that the Community respond positively to the interest shown by these countries and offer them association agreements "both as a sign of solidarity to democratic forces in neighboring countries and because of the Community's own interests". As for the benefits of these agreements to the potential signatories, the Commission stated that "early approval of the goal of association will contribute to political stability . . . and strengthen the confidence on the part of economic operators".[48]

The foreign policy motivation now openly guiding the Commission in making its recommendations to the Council in this area is further shown by the argument it simultaneously made that the Soviet Union be considered as a "special case" and not be offered association. With respect to this country, according to the Commission, the Community should seek "to obtain the highest level of reciprocal benefits from the new trade and cooperation agreement . . . and treat constructively any request of assistance".[49] Nothing more was needed or contemplated for the time being.

For the other Eastern European countries, association agreements should be of value in themselves, the Commission argued, and should not be construed as being simply a step towards accession to the Community. Association and accession should be kept separate from one another. The conservative position taken by the Commission on accession by the Eastern European countries was surprising. By not attempting to support even the relatively safe objective of eventual accession, to occur at the end of an unspecified or a specified transition period (as in the case of Greece and Turkey), the Commission appeared to trade off possible longer-term gains in favor of pushing association immediately, with all its practical implications such as the supply of aid in a certain, medium-term framework (instead of a yearly basis) and expanded trade privileges for the associates. It also appeared to try to avoid taking a definitive position on a matter on which divisions abounded both inside itself and the Council.

As far as content, the views of the Commission were that association agreements should include trade (with the goal of free trade), economic and commercial cooperation (embodying new forms and instruments), technical and financial assistance (according to the need and absorption capacity of each partner), and cultural cooperation and information exchange. In addition the agreements should specifically embody processes for political dialogue.[50] In the area of trade, association would mean, in practice, faster progress towards free trade, that is, rapid completion of the process started with the trade and cooperation agreements. With respect to financial assistance, the meaning of the Commission's recommendation was also clear. Like all previous association agreements negotiated by the Community, those with Eastern Europe would have a financial protocol attached to them, detailing the amount and time frame of the Community's direct aid.

The meaning attached to "economic cooperation" with Eastern European countries was less precise. Nor was the reference to "new forms and instruments of cooperation" ever made clear. The experience with previous agreements with other associated countries, like those of the Mediterranean, is also quite negative in this particular area. Economic cooperation is a nice sounding objective, but a difficult one to achieve in practice beyond a few areas that are in the public sector domain. The contours of political dialogue, let alone its contents, were also left vague. Reference was made by the Commission to an "institutionalized framework for regular exchange of views on bilateral and wider international issues", but nothing more specific was said about it.[51]

The Commission's vision of "an association framework",

though reconfirmed and juridically framed with increased precision in a subsequent Communication to the Council,[52] was not fleshed out until August 1990, when a general outline of the association agreements was presented to the Council. On that occasion the Commission framed the objectives of the association agreements in clearer terms. First, they "should create a climate of confidence and stability favoring political and economic reform and *allowing the development of close political relations which reflect shared values*" (emphasis added). Second, they "should strengthen the foundations of the new European architecture . . . and enable partners in Central and Eastern Europe to participate in the wider process of European integration".[53]

The "European Agreements" in the Commission's views were to help consolidate a new political climate in Europe and to lay the foundations for an integrated continent. Even though the specific forms of the integration plan were not spelled out in the Community's document, the political goals pursued could not have been made more transparent, and could not have contrasted more strongly with those set out in most other association agreements. The Commission was also careful to list the more conventional economic objectives being pursued— from creating a better climate in the partner countries for private sector economic agents, to assisting the governments of these countries in managing the transition from command to market economy and the necessary restructuring—but the primacy of the political goals being pursued could not have been more strongly emphasized.[54] Associationism was in such a way being extended to the outer limits of its potential in the political sphere.

Consistent with the strategy being proposed by the Commission to the Council were the suggestions that exploratory conversations begin with Czechoslovakia, Hungary and Poland "in light of the conditions [prevailing in these countries] and the request received by their governments". These were the countries that historically had had the strongest western orientation and that had been more fully integrated with Western Europe before World War II. They were the most eager to "rejoin" Europe and were proceeding more rapidly towards democratic government in the aftermath of the collapse of their previous Communist regimes. For these reasons they were the natural "first comers" and the preferred candidates for association with the Community. Bulgaria and Romania were clearly behind them in political evolution and had, in the past, traditionally gravitated more strongly towards Russia. They could wait. And so could the Soviet Union "which raised specific questions in the context of internal reform, relations with the Community and integration into the international economic system".[55]

It took, however, until December 1990 for the Council to adopt directives enabling formal negotiations between the Community and the governments of Czechoslovakia, Hungary and Poland. There were certainly questions about the content of the agreements that needed to be sorted out at the Council level. But the key unanswered question was about the ultimate outlet of association. A debate over the question of membership in the Community for the associable countries at the end of a transition period went on inside the Council and the Commission. The alternative to membership was the French idea of a European Confederation, associating all states of the continent in a common and permanent organization of trade, peace and security. This was an idea also favored by the Commission's president, Jacques Delors, who had often spoken of his preference for a Europe organized in concentric circles, at the core of which would stand the Community, constituting a kind of federation inside the wider confederation of all the European nations.[56] For the partner countries of Eastern Europe, the question was where they would find their place, in the inner circle or in the outer one. The August 1990 Communication by the Commission foreshadowed the second of these alternatives.[57]

Both Germany and the United Kingdom favored association of the Eastern European countries with a view to integration, a position expressed by both Mrs Thatcher and Mr Kohl, who saw the interests of both Eastern and Western Europe better served by association leading to eventual membership than by association without a precise final anchor.[58] Inside the Community, as late as April 1991, Commissioner Leon Brittan was openly taking a position apparently at odds with that of the Commission's president, by stating that he "regarded membership in the European Community as a legitimate goal for these countries, and one which we support and welcome".[59] While the meaning of the "we" used by Mr Brittan is not clear, the public dissent of a commissioner from the views of his president revealed that profound divisions on this issue still existed inside the Commission. At practically the same time, President Mitterand of France, rejecting the pleas of the democratic governments of Hungary, Poland and Czechoslovakia, was reiterating that the Eastern European countries should abandon the goal of joining the Community and consider instead building closer ties with the West through a European-wide confederation that would serve as "an intermediate phase lasting tens of years".[60]

While the apparent lack of success of the exploratory talks between the Commission and the governments of Hungary, Poland and Czechoslovakia about association in the second half of 1991 seemed due to the rigidity of the Community's position (reflecting the strong uneasiness of some member countries such as France and Italy) on dismantling protection in the trade of steel, textiles and farm products, the negative bearing of the unsolved membership problem on the ongoing negotiations cannot be discounted.[61] The Commission publicly stuck to the position that "the discussions confirmed that the three countries hoped gradually to integrate with the Community, the ultimate aim being accession, . . . [while] the Community made it clear that it could not at this stage give any promises about eventual accession".[62] But disagreement over the issue must have loomed large because President Mitterand was induced to speak again in favor of his position as late as June 1991.

Both sides, however, were foreseeing eventual membership in the Community for Hungary, Poland and Czechoslovakia when association agreements between these countries and the EC were finally signed in December 1991.[63] Reached after almost a year of hard negotiations, the agreements had an economic content spanning trade in goods and services, aid and competition policies, and protection of investors' and workers' rights. They also had an explicit political content and foresaw political coordination at a high ministerial level. As for their economic structure, at the end of a transition period, which is different for each country and shorter for the Community than for any of the three associates, the association agreements contemplated that trade in goods would be free in both directions. Free entry and national treatment in services would also follow. Partial exceptions to the timetable set for the creation of a free trade area between the EC and each of these three countries were agreed upon for such "sensitive" products as textiles, steel and food. Bit except for the latter, all impediments to their imports into the Community are to disappear. For agricultural products covered by the CAP, Czechoslovakia, Hungary and Poland will only obtain preferential access to EC markets.[64]

Notes to Chapter 8

[1] The CMEA, also known as COMECON, predated the EC. It was set up in 1949 by the USSR, Bulgaria, Czechoslovakia, Hungary, Poland, Romania and Albania (which withdrew in 1961). East Germany became a member in 1950. Outer Mongolia was admitted in 1962. China, North Korea and North Vietnam were associated with the Council as observers between 1956–57 and 1960. Yugoslavia was an observer between 1956 and 1958. After their independence Angola and Mozambique also became observers. CMEA mostly regulated trade and payments relations among the member countries. Details can be found in M. Kaser, *Comecon*, London, Oxford University Press, 1967; S. Ausch, *Theory and Practice of CMEA Cooperation*, Budapest, Akademiai Kiado, 1972; J. Wilczynski, *The Economics of Socialism*, London, Allen and Unwin, 1970.

[2] On the Soviet Union's position towards the EC see C. Ranson, *The European Community and Eastern Europe*, Totowa, N.J., Rowman and Littlefield, 1973, pp. 22–35; I.G. John, "The Soviet Response to Western European Integration", in I.G. John, ed., *EEC Policy Towards Eastern Europe*, Hants, Saxon House, 1975, pp. 41–54; J. Pinder, "Soviet Views of Western European Integration", in G.N. Yannopoulos and A. Shlaim, eds., *The EEC and Eastern Europe*, Cambridge, Cambridge University Press, 1978, pp. 107–26.

[3] John, "Soviet Response", pp. 46–9.

[4] On the factors determining Soviet re-thinking vis-a-vis the Community see John, "Soviet Response", pp. 49–54; and P. Marsh, "The Development of Relations between the EEC and CMEA", in Yannopoulos and Shlaim, eds., *The EEC and Eastern Europe*.

[5] In 1938, for example, exports to Eastern Europe accounted for over 15 percent of the total exports of Western Europe: League of Nations, *The Network of World Trade*, Geneva, 1942, Annex III, pp. 168 and 171.

6 In addition, see J. Pinder and P. Pinder, *The European Community's Policy Towards Eastern Europe*, London, Chatham House-PEP, 1975, Table 1, p. 8.

7 This was the meaning of the so-called "EC clause" adopted by the Council the year before, which was to be inserted in all the future bilateral agreements reached by the EC members with Eastern European countries. With the same 1961 decision the Council also limited the maximum duration of these bilateral trade agreements to the transition period of the Treaty (which was to end in 1969), and established a prior consultation procedure among the members whenever such an agreement was being considered: *Official Journal of the European Communities*, No. 71, November 4, 1961, pp. 1273-4.

8 Ranson, *European Community and Eastern Europe*, pp. 38-40.

9 In 1969 the Commission had presented another proposal to unify the procedures for negotiating bilateral agreements with state-trading countries. EC member countries resisted it in practice by trying to limit the common approach to only those situations where "special circumstances" did not exist. They wanted also to remain the judges of that *Ibidem*, pp. 45-7.

10 *Official Journal of the European Communities*, No. C.106, December 6, 1973, pp. 22-3.

11 This relaxation of tensions in Europe found its most visible manifestation in the Helsinky Conference on European Security of 1974, attended by both Western and Eastern European countries.

12 The decision was made by the Council on March 27, 1975: Commission of the European Communities, *The European Community and the Countries of Eastern Europe*, Europe Information Doc. No. 12/78, Brussels, 1978, p. 4.

13 For an account of the early movements, see Marsh, "Relations Between the EEC and CMEA", pp. 53-5.

14 Commission, *European Community and the Countries of Eastern Europe*, 1978, pp. 3-4; P. Marsh, "The European Community and East-West Economic Relations", *Journal. of Common Market Studies*, Vol. 23, No. 1, September 1984, pp. 2-3.

15 R. Hrbek, "The EC and the Changes in Eastern Europe", *Intereconomics*, May/June 1990, p. 133.

16 The conviction that time was on the Community's side emerges clearly even in the normally balanced resolutions on Eastern Europe passed by the European Parliament in those years. In October 1982, for example, commenting on relations between the European

Community, the East European state-trading countries and the CMEA, the European Parliament characterized as "unacceptable" the fact that trade between the Community and individual CMEA countries was not still generally regulated by trade agreements despite the offer of negotiations made by the Community in 1974. It called on other CMEA countries, in addition to Romania, to conclude such agreements: *Official Journal of the European Communities*, No. C 292, pp. 16–17. Similarly, a 1985 report of the European Parliament, which was extremely favorable to the establishment of a wide-ranging dialogue between the Community and Eastern Europe, cast the EC role in the following terms: "[the EC should] seek to establish increasingly extensive bilateral relations with all Eastern European countries" that shared the same vision, and went as far as to characterize the CMEA as an "international talking shop and civil service". European Parliament, *Report on Relations Between the European Community and the Countries of Central and Eastern Europe*, Working Document A2-111/85, 1985. The Rapporteur was Mr V. Bettiza. Academic opinions over the EC stance were considerably more varied and, on the whole, less sympathetic to the Community's position. Some academic observers, struck by the reluctance of EC members to move towards collective action in the field of trade policies, fretted that the Commission would end its "long march" towards a common commercial policy towards Eastern Europe with little to show: J. Pinder, "A Community Policy Towards Eastern Europe", *The World Today*, Vol. 30, No. 3, March 1974, pp. 119-23. Others saw the EC position on the CMEA as illogical and potentially sterile, demanding recognition on its own terms, but unwilling to offer the same to the CMEA for fears of adding greater legitimacy to the Soviet Union: D. Hiester, "The European Community and the East Bloc", in J. Lodge, ed., *Institutions and Policies of the European Community*, New York, St. Martin's Press, 1983, pp. 194-5. Others recognized that the Community's position was rooted in its legitimate interest that CMEA states remain as disunited as possible, but noted that such a position was at the same time scarcely consistent with EC traditions: Marsh, "Relations Between the EEC and the CMEA", p. 68.

[17] These attempts were particularly marked in Poland and Hungary, which also became members of the International Monetary Fund and the World Bank and attempted with some determination to cope in an orthodox way with internal economic reform (particularly enterprise reform) and external debt.

[18] *Official Journal of the European Communities*, No. L. 157, 24 June 1988, pp. 35-6.

19 An exchange of letters to this effect between the Foreign Ministries of the European members of the CMEA and the Community occurred between January and May 1986.

20 The European Council at its Dublin meeting on 28 April 1990 had already welcomed without reservation the process of German unification occurring "under a European roof" and had stated that integration in the Community would occur as soon as unification became legally binding. No revision of the Treaties was considered necessary for this purpose: Final Communique, in *Bulletin of the European Communities*, No. 4/90, 1990, p. 8. This position found strong support in the European Parliament, which expressed it in a Resolution on the Unification of Germany passed on 17 May 1989.

21 This was no doubt helped by the signing of the agreement between Germany and Poland over their common frontiers.

22 Hence the Group of 24, or G-24, denomination. Members of PHARE are all the EC countries, the EFTA countries, Australia, Canada, Japan, New Zealand, Turkey and the United States.

23 Commission, *XXIIIrd General Report—1989*, Para. 786. Operation PHARE provided a common umbrella for the participants' assistance in the areas of emergency food aid, access to Western markets for the Eastern European countries' exports, the promotion of investments and joint ventures, the environment, and management and vocational training. Its geographical reach was eventually extended to Bulgaria, Czechoslovakia and Yugoslavia in July 1990. The German Democratic Republic was also included, but just until reunification in October of the same year.

24 The stabilization fund—a line of credit up to $1,000 million, designed to assist Poland reach currency convertibility at the end of 1989, was financed for more than half of the total by EC member states.

25 United Nations Economic Commission for Europe (UNECE), *Economic Survey of Europe in 1989-90*, New York, 1990, Chapter 4, pp. 4.33-4.35.

26 Commission of the European Communities, *Operation Phare*, Information Memo 3/90, Brussels, 11 January 1989; Commission of the European Communities, *EC-Eastern Europe Relations*, Brussels, DGX Background Brief, 12 March 1991; UNECE, *Economic Survey*, pp. 38-9.

27 The tranches amounted to ECU 350 million and ECU 260 million respectively.

28 *Financial Times*, 14 January and 22 January 1991; *Washington Post*, 20 February 1991; *Financial Times*, 24 May 1991; and Commission of

the European Communities, *EC-Eastern Europe Relations*, DGX Background Brief, 8 July 1991.

[29] Yugoslavia was already eligible.

[30] Commission of the European Communities, *Communication from the Commission to the Council on the Extension to the Other Central and Eastern European Countries of the Facilities for the European Investment Bank to Finance Projects in Poland and Hungary*, Doc. COM(90) 384 final, Brussels, 14 September 1990.

[31] As members of GATT, Poland, Yugoslavia and Czechoslovakia already traded with the Community on an MFN basis.

[32] Romania and Yugoslavia already enjoyed GSP preferences from the Community.

[33] Commission, *Operation Phare*, 1989; *Communication from the Commission to the Council on the Implications of Recent Changes in Central and Eastern Europe for the Community's Relations with the Countries Concerned*, Doc. SEC(90) 111 final, Brussels, 23 January 1990, p. 5; Commission, *EC-Eastern Europe Relations*, 1991, pp. 2–7; *Financial Times*, 18 October 1990.

[34] Regulation EEC No. 3691/89

[35] For a clear enunciation of the Community strategy in the field of trade policies, see Commission of the European Communities, *Communication from the Commission on the Development of the Community's Relations with Countries of Central and Eastern Europe*, Doc. SEC(90) 717 final, Brussels, 18 April 1990, p. 4.

[36] GATT, *Trade Policy Review*, Annex, pp. 16–23. Voluntary export restrictions on steel products are currently in force with Bulgaria, Czechoslovakia, Hungary, Poland and Romania. Within the MFA framework, agreements limiting the export to the Community of textile products are in force with Czechoslovakia, Hungary, Poland, Romania and the Soviet Union. Self-restraint agreements covering agricultural product exports are in force with most of the Eastern European members of the CMEA.

[37] Commission of the European Communities, *Press Release* No. 1556, Bruxelles, 20 January 1990; Commission, *EC-Eastern Europe Relations*, 1990, p. 12.

[38] According to press reports, in negotiations about association with Poland, Hungary and Czechoslovakia, the EC was offering a ten-year plan towards free trade, with asymmetric concessions by the Community in the first five years, in all sectors except agriculture, steel and textiles, *Financial Times*, 26 March 1991. See also *Financial Times*, 19 April 1991.

[39] According to Prof. Hrbek, in early 1990 the Commission was characterizing the trade and cooperation agreements already concluded, or being concluded at that time, as the "first step" towards normalization of relations with the countries of Eastern Europe. With the exception of the Soviet Union, these countries would have considered the intensification of relations with the EC as a means for re-establishing their European bonds after the artificial separation of the previous several decades. The author quotes two draft documents prepared by the Commission for the Special Summit held in Dublin in April 1990: Hrbek, "EC and the Changes in Central and Eastern Europe", p. 135.

[40] The text of the agreement with Hungary is in the *Official Journal of the European Communities*, No. L327, Brussels, 11 December 1988, pp. 1–34; the agreement with Poland is in the *Official Journal of the European Communities*, No. L339, Brussels, 22 November 1989, pp. 1–52; the second agreement with Czechoslovakia and the agreement with Bulgaria are both in the *Official Journal of the European Communities*, No. L291, Brussels, 23 October 1990, pp. 29–46 and 9–28 respectively; the agreement with the Soviet Union can be found in the *Official Journal of the European Communities*, No. L68, Brussels, 15 March 1990, pp. 1–20. The latest EC cooperation agreement, with Romania, is published in the *Official Journal of the European Communities*, No. L79, 4 March 1991, pp. 12–26.

[41] Imports of sensitive products could remain subject to restrictions at the end of the transition period. As previously mentioned, the four-to-five-year timetable for the phasing out of these restrictions was short-circuited in the framework of Operation PHARE. By 1990 all these restrictions were abolished, except those against the Soviet Union that were, since the beginning, supposed to be eliminated only in part.

[42] Aside from being an aid coordination mechanism, PHARE represented a way of ensuring an acceptable sharing among Western allies of the burden of assistance to Eastern Europe. The burden-sharing aspect of PHARE was particularly important for the Western European countries, which wanted to ensure adequate contributions from both the United States and Japan.

[43] EBRD was formally established in May 1990 under the leadership of Jacques Attali and became operational in early 1991. Membership includes the twelve EC countries, the European Community, the European Investment Bank with a total of 51 percent of the shares, The United States with 10 percent, other European countries—Austria, Cyprus, Finland, Lichtenstein, Malta, Norway, Sweden, Switzerland, Turkey—with 10.72 percent, non-European members—

Australia, Canada, Egypt, Israel, Japan, South Korea, Mexico, Morocco, New Zealand—with 14.82 percent, and the borrowing members—Bulgaria, Czechoslovakia, Hungary, Poland, Romania, the former USSR and Yugoslavia—with the remainder, 11.90 percent of the total. See Commission of the European Communities, *The European Bank for Reconstruction and Development*, ICC Background Brief, Brussels, 12 December 1990. Albania also became a member in mid-1991.

44 Commission of the European Communities, *Communication to the Council and the Parliament on the Development of the Community's Relations with the Countries of Central and Eastern Europe*, Doc. SEC(90) 196 final, Brussels, 1 February 1990, p. 3. The same political themes had been underlined in the Declaration of Ministers of the Group of 24 for Economic Assistance to Poland and Hungary at their first meeting at the end of 1989. See *Europe Information*, Brussels, IP(89)953, 13 December 1989.

45 Europe Information, "Declaration on Central and Eastern Europe by the European Council", Strasbourg, 9 December 1989 (mimeo.).

46 Europe Information, *Debate on the Community's Relations with the Countries of Central and Eastern Europe: Introduction by M. Andriessen*, Strasbourg, 17 January 1990.

47 Commission, *Implications of Recent Changes in Central and Eastern Europe for the Community's Relations with the Countries Concerned*, 1990, pp. 1 and 5.

48 *Ibidem*, p. 6.

49 Commission, *Development of the Community's Relations with the Countries of Central and Eastern Europe*, 1990, p. 5.

50 *Ibidem*, p. 7.

51 *Ibidem*, p. 10.

52 The "European Agreements" were to be based on art. 238 of the Treaty of Rome. *Ibidem*, p. 3.

53 Commission of the European Communities, *Communication from the Commission to the Council and the Parliament on Association Agreements with the Countries of Eastern and Central Europe: A General Outline*, Doc. COM(90) 398 final, Brussels, 27 August 1989, pp. 7-17.

54 *Ibidem*, pp. 2-3.

55 *Ibidem*, p. 3.

56 See Agence Europe Note No. 1552, Bruxelles, 1 June 1990.

57 Commission, *Association Agreements with the Countries of Eastern and Central Europe*, 1990, p. 2.

58 *Financial Times*, 6 August 1990 and *Washington Post*, 13 June 1991. Mrs Thatcher had publicly argued in Aspen, Col., that membership be offered to EC countries "clearly, openly and generously" once democracy had taken root and their economies were capable of sustaining it. Meanwhile, association agreements could be used as an "intermediate step". Mr Kohl had, instead, argued in favor of early EC membership for Poland, Hungary and Czechoslovakia in fear that, outside a strong and supportive framework, their fragile economies could collapse and a new wave of social and political instability, threatening Western interests, could ensue.

59 Mr Brittan made this statement in a speech to the Bradford Chamber of Commerce on the subject of "Eastern and Central Europe: The Task Ahead", *Europe Information*, Doc. No. IP(91)328, Brussels, 19 April 1991.

60 *Washington Post*, 13 June 1991.

61 On the specific disagreements between the Community and the three Eastern European associables over trade policies see *Financial Times*, 26 March 1991.

62 *Europe Information*, Doc. No. IP(90)859, Brussels, 23 October 1990.

63 *Financial Times*, 23-24 November 1991 and 17 December 1991.

64 The texts of the Association Agreements are not yet available. Their content, however, was discussed in general newspaper reports and in interviews granted by officials of the negotiating parties.

9

EC Development Policies: Retrospect and Prospects

EC development policies are important because they effectively determine the conditions under which developing countries can access the largest common market in the world as well as the ways in which the EC allocates a sizeable portion of its aid resources among them. Community policies are also important because they influence the aid and cooperation strategies of the member states and the positions that they take within the international organizations that operate in the field of development. Collectively, EC countries already represent the biggest source of economic assistance to developing countries. They are also the largest group of shareholders in the World Bank and the International Monetary Fund. EC development policies, moreover, are destined to become even more important in the future. The trade policy component of these policies will soon concern a single market, and the conditions of access to it, which in certain areas (textiles, agricultural products, steel, clothing, footwear, electronics) are of vital importance to many developing countries. Community policies regarding aid, moreover, are also likely to become even more important than in the past in setting best practices for member countries to follow and possibly in determining the flows of assistance to developing countries, as individual country policies and common aid policies become more integrated within the Community.

At their origin, the development policies of the Community were a direct and nearly inevitable product of the colonial experience of the member countries. In 1958, existing political and economic realities had dictated that the colonial (and in some cases former colonial) possessions of the Community member states be associated to the Community. This was done unilaterally with the Treaty of Rome, almost as a by-product of the establishment of the European Common Market. Association to the Community of the "countries and territories" still under the jurisdiction of the member states came nonetheless to shape in a lasting fashion the development cooperation posture of both the Community and of its members. For the Community it effectively set the upper bound, in content and form, of the policies of cooperation with the rest of the developing countries. For the members it established a set of common priorities that came inexorably to influence their own development cooperation policies and practices.

Goals of EC Development Cooperation

EC development policies began as and remained regional in scope. The geographical preference originally built into them by history, and consolidated by necessity and political expedience, was never fundamentally altered. Over the years the preferred domain of EC development policies continued to be Africa. A true globalization of these policies never occurred, despite the continued existence of a "globalist" pole among the member countries and despite the adaptations of the original regional stance to changing political realities inside and outside the Community, particularly during the 1970s when the need to enlarge and diversify the geographical reach of EC development cooperation was felt more strongly. Another important enlargement of the sphere of application of EC development policies is currently under way toward Eastern Europe.

History played a critical role in molding the development posture of the EC and its members. The weight of the economic and other ties that were established during colonial times inevitably shaped the path of relations between Europe and Africa. Partly for this reason, France, which had the strongest colonial past and the widest African interests among the original EC member countries, maintained an undisputed leadership in Community policies towards developing countries. This helped to give EC development policies continuity with the past and, for many years, a seemingly coherent foundation. But at the same time it also helped to keep the focus of these policies firmly on Africa, at the expense of relations with other developing areas, especially Latin America, and now possibly even Eastern Europe.

The notion of a natural partnership between Europe and Africa, which the Community could develop outside the original colonial framework and make a cornerstone of associationism toward Africa, was unmistakably French. France's influence, exerted from Paris and Brussels, contributed decisively to the acceptability and continued prominence of this notion at the EC level. Meshed with the more modern concept of interdependence, it became in the 1970s the standard justification for continued privileged relations with Africa. The basic notion of EurAfrica, however, if accurately descriptive of the key production and trade links between the two regions— one rich in land and other natural resources and specialized in the production of primary commodities, the other well endowed with capital and skilled labor and specialized in the production of manufactures—rested on shaky economic grounds. Its logic was much less solid than it appeared to be at first glance.

To begin with, relative factor endowments *per se* constitute a less than decisive determinant of production decisions and trade flows across countries and regions. The development of the natural endowment and the evolution of technology, as determinants of specialization and trade, are critically important, particularly if one of the parties is relatively undeveloped. Economic policies also play a key role in shaping the growth of undeveloped economies. In addition, apart from being based on static foundations and being neutral with respect to technological progress and economic policies, the notion of EurAfrica was inimical to the aspirations of most developing countries in Africa and elsewhere. They generally rejected the specialization model it implied and advocated instead development strategies and policies aimed at radically altering the traditional division of labor that lay at the basis of EurAfrica. In pursuit of industrialization, they sought a new and different paradigm of international division of labor. The Community never dealt explicitly with the degree of acceptance of the EurAfrica concept (and later of interdependence) by the very African countries that were supposed to be partners in it. The Community simply chose to proclaim its importance, ignoring in substance the issue of acceptability, and continued to preach complementarity of economic interests and interdependence between the two areas in a "raw materials-for-manufactures" exchange mode. At the same time the Community made concessions to Africa, in trade and other fields, that were at least nominally directed at changing the very basis of the production and trade relations on which its policy of cooperation was supposed to rest.

Yet, if Europe was in many ways fundamentally bound to Africa by history and existing economic interests, the links with the European metropoles could not be disregarded by the former African colonies even after they became politically independent. Colonial production and trade patterns, difficult to change, tied them, at least for some time, to the EC and other European markets. Raw materials flowed from Africa to Europe and manufactures and capital in the opposite direction. Europe was critical to Africa both as a market for primary commodities and as a source of investments for the development of these commodities. For the Africans, the beginning of their post-independence economic relationship with Europe was predetermined by history, but the end was open. Starting from the colonial inheritance, they wanted to restructure the economic relationship with Europe by enlarging the productive capacity of their economies and developing in the process an endogenous industrial base. Industrialization was for them a synonym of development. If the Community, deep down, thought otherwise, it certainly did not let it be known to its African associates. EC trade preferences and aid were for the associates the means to achieve industrialization, not to maintain or deepen the traditional model of specialization imposed on them in colonial times.

Africa's immediate economic importance for Europe at large was quite limited. As a market for Europe's manufactures it had only relatively small value. European investment flows to Africa were closely connected with plantation agriculture and mining and were not large in absolute terms. The Community, however, attributed to Africa strategic importance as a secure source for raw materials (especially metals) that seemed to exceed its direct economic value as an outlet for exports and capital investments. The paradox of this situation was that, in order to maintain its strategic value to Europe, Africa had to remain specialized in the production and export of raw materials (the opposite of what it wanted) while the Community, to maintain credibility for itself was obliged to underwrite, at least in words, the very changes in the economic structure of African countries that would have reduced their value to the Community as suppliers of raw materials. How to construct on these premises a new relationship, reflective of the developmental desires and objectives of the African partners and of the economic interests of the Community, was never squarely faced by either party. No amount of rhetoric over forms and principles embodied in the association conventions negotiated between them—especially Lomé—was sufficient to hide this basic inconsistency between the declared objectives and actual interests underlying development cooperation between the EC and Africa.

Economic interdependence between these two regions did not mean in any case economic equality between them. Africa needed Europe much more than Europe needed Africa. The Africans always knew this, and never forgot it—except perhaps during the exhilarating years of "commodity power" in the mid-1970s. The Community could pretend otherwise, and even at times believe the opposite, but the underlying asymmetry in the economic relationship with Africa was never changed, either by events or by behaviors motivated by the desire to reduce it. The two regions were unevenly dependent on one another, yet existing reciprocal linkages were important enough that neither side could afford to disregard them. There was therefore a basis for an economic relationship between the EC and Africa, a common terrain that both parties felt worth preserving. But it was never as wide or as solid as the Community's rhetoric chose to depict it for many years (in practice until the Pisani Memorandum of 1982) and the associated countries had to accept it at face value.

Security of supply of raw materials was indeed one of the primary interests pursued by EC countries in developing cooperative relations with the newly independent nations of Africa. The OPEC experience and the commodity shortages of the early 1970s heightened the feeling in Europe of dependency on the imports of raw materials and thus the importance of Africa as a secure source, and supplied strong economic and political credibility to the policies of cooperation with Africa that had been pursued until then at the EC level. If the stability of supply of raw materials had appeared in 1957 as a sufficiently large common interest for all EC members, best pursuable by common policies, experience in the 1970s seemed only to confirm the wisdom of such a "strategic" choice. France, which had shepherded this choice, took most of the intellectual and political credit for it.

However, this seemingly plausible basis for cooperating with Africa led in time to a rather acritical acceptance at the Community level and in most member countries of the security of supply argument. An excessive emphasis on the interdependence of economic interests between Europe and Africa led to the conclusion that in many ways the economic destinies of Europe and Africa were inextricably tied to one another. This misplaced and fundamentally implausible emphasis continued even after the importance of African raw materials to Europe had clearly begun to wane, indicating the existence of laggard thinking or at least a marked reluctance at the Community level to dispose of a justification that had long served to vindicate the wisdom of the original EurAfrican choice.

Other factors played a role in the establishment and continuation of this relationship. Bipolarism and competition between the superpowers in the 1950s heightened the importance of Europe maintaining the political allegiance (or simply the friendship) of newly independent states in Africa and elsewhere. Europe, in a way, had to "hold on" to at least one traditional area of influence, if it wanted to maintain some power and influence in the post-World War II international order. This was the political interest of Europe in Africa, which again dovetailed with French foreign policy goals, at least after General de Gaulle came to power in France. All this was not totally artificial. As the political and military role of Western Europe had become regional in substance after World War II, the Community's focus on Africa did fit well into that regional mold.

Regionalism in EC development policies did not go unchallenged either inside or outside the Community, but it remained, despite some adjustment, the hallmark of these policies for years to come. Inside the Community, Germany and the Netherlands were the least Africa-focused members, and the most globalist when it came to development cooperation policies. Italy maintained a distinct interest in Latin America. Outside the Community, both the United States and the USSR vied for the political sympathies of the newly independent African nations in the aftermath of decolonization. In some sense the two tendencies may have offset each other. As long as the Africa-oriented members could point to outside challenges to the residual European influence in Africa, its defense by the Community would be instinctively, if superficially, more credible an objective of common policy.

The Community held its political and economic ground in Africa mostly by extending trade and aid privileges to the colonies or former colonies of France, Belgium and Italy, and subsequently to those of the United Kingdom, while mandating from them in return very modest trade concessions at first and subsequently nothing at all. The substance of this "cooperative" relationship based on unilateral concessions from the Community never changed. The associative framework designed to govern it also remained substantially intact even after the associates became independent and grew in number. Only its forms were adapted to prevailing circumstances. Instead of unilateral association, conventions of association between the former colonies and the Community were formally negotiated and signed. The Yaoundé Convention of 1963 started this trend. After the United Kingdom's accession to the Community, and the contemporaneous entry of the former British colonies in Africa into association with it, the Lomé Conventions became the general structure for EC policies. Yet, despite the passage from *association octryée* to *association négociée*, the Community continued to maintain control of the economic terms of the association policies towards Africa, for it held the purse strings.

EC development cooperation was extended in time to other regions. First to Southern Europe and the Mediterranean area, in which the members of the Community maintained a clear, if never too precisely defined, security interest, which was promptly rediscovered after the first oil crisis. The association model was also applied to the parts of this area, which were eventually included in the Community's second expansion, an event that took nearly three decades to mature and that occurred on the basis of a less than pristine application of principles—witness the continued exclusion of Turkey and the island states of the Northern Mediterranean from the Community. Second, cooperation was offered to parts of Asia and Latin America, but in a much reduced form and to a more economical extent, as no specific challenge to the Community emanated from these areas for many years. Cooperation entailed in all these cases, with the exception of the Maghreb and Mashreq, only modest aid flows and no significant trade concessions. Finally, Eastern Europe became the object of intense interest at the Community level towards the end of the 1980s, when socialism collapsed in the area. Community cooperation with Eastern Europe also began in a low-key fashion, with standard trade and cooperation agreements, but it moved rapidly in the direction of association when the accelerating pace of change in Eastern Europe began to be more clearly appreciated in the West.

This limping regionalism practiced by the Community has been differently interpreted, but it seems to have been much more the result of chance, than of design. As aptly observed a few years ago by Miles Kahler, "the grand design" in the policies of development cooperation of the European Communities "often ill fitting, was imposed later".[1]

Instruments of EC Development Policy

From the beginning EC development policy employed two main instruments—trade preferences and direct aid—graduated according to the interests that the Community had in the countries with which it wanted to cooperate economically or politically. The graduated use of the two instruments, as well as the choice of the institutional devices utilized to frame economic cooperation with different groups of countries, looked for a while like it belonged to a preordained scheme. Marginal countries seemed to be offered only non-preferential trade arrangements, while countries more important to the Community generally received some trade preferences and aid in the context of trade and cooperation arrangements, with the most important among them receiving wide-spread preferences and multi-year aid programs in the framework of full-fledged association agreements. Yet, apart from the top preference always reserved for associated African countries, who got what, when and why among the other developing countries never had a clear and consistent rationale. The sequencing of the EC relations with different groups of developing countries, and often their development cooperation content, appear to have been haphazard, reactive and more dictated by events, and sometimes fashions, than by plans, principles or even a broad strategy. The only recognizable constant in the maze of changing regional ties developed by the Community was the preservation of the relative primacy of the associated African (and subsequently Caribbean and Pacific) countries among those receiving concessions.

The development cooperation instruments used by the Community were far from new, either in kind or in the use made of them. Bilateral aid to the colonies already existed when Community aid was established. French assistance, in particular, was already quite substantial in the 1950s. The addition of multilateral (i.e. direct EC) aid to that coming from the member countries was a modest innovation introduced by the Rome Treaty. Another innovation was the multi-year framework within which EC direct financial assistance was offered. This gave greater certainty to the recipients and favored a more planned use of the resources made available to them by the Community. Additionality of Community aid, a politically powerful, if economically misleading, notion was also forcefully proclaimed. It found a tangible expression in the rule that the European Development Fund would be financed out of the national budgets of the members. This apparently had another advantage: it kept aid to associated countries clear of the compensation "games" that were inevitably expected to arise among the members in the context of the Community budget. Similarly, free access to the markets of the respective metropoles already existed for each of the colonial territories. Extending it to the entire Community for all of them was a necessity dictated by the establishment of a common market that included France, Belgium and Italy.

Community aid to developing countries was also declared to be policy-neutral in the name of non-interference in the development strategies and economic policy choices of the recipients. In substance, however, this was a rather opportunistic position that the Community took largely to please the ruling elites in the recipient countries and to expedite the administration of aid. The concept of aid neutrality sold well in the political market of international development cooperation during the 1960s and 1970s. This seemed enough for the Community, apparently more interested in accrediting in that market the "new" development model (associationism in particular) that it was ostensibly pursuing than in testing its effectiveness even locally.

Trade preferences for developing countries were hardly a new concept. Great Britain had maintained its preferences for Commonwealth countries, many of them undeveloped, and had successfully defended their legitimacy in the negotiations leading to the establishment of GATT. Before signing the Treaty of Rome, EC member states had generally kept the imports from their colonies or former colonies free of duties, thus granting them preferential treatment. Itself born in one of GATT's grey areas, the Community never felt too sensitive to the charge of diffusing discriminatory trade arrangements which may have been legally dubious within GATT. Attachment to results, rather than principles, was from the beginning a hallmark of Community action in the field of trade policies. The Commission and the Council strove for what they considered to be necessary and politically acceptable to the major trading partners of the Community. When under pressure (mostly from the United States) for their preferential trade policies towards developing countries, they resorted alternatively to legal and political justifications, invoking GATT loopholes (such as art. XXIV on customs unions and free-trade areas), general principles (such as their UN Charter-derived duty to foster the economic and social development of the associated countries and territories), or simply the "facts of life"—among them the existence of strong economic and cultural links with many African countries. More often than not, the Community also pictured itself as the politically most acceptable avenue for maintaining western influence in the developing world. As such, Community behavior was presented as deserving greater than normal tolerance from its western partners.

There were other reasons for this choice of instruments by the Community. Preferential trade policies, aside from being consistent with the basic Common Market philosophy of economic cooperation among the six member countries, were also in line with the economic development orthodoxy of the time. To support their industrialization efforts, through scale economies, positive externalities and learning by doing, developing countries needed privileged access to industrial countries' markets. For without industrialization there could be no real development. This strategy was highly valued by developing countries which espoused and emphasized it in international fora such as UNCTAD, until it was recognized as sound by industrial countries and accepted in the framework of GATT. External aid was the natural complement to trade. It represented a net injection of foreign savings into the economies of the recipients. It made possible both higher investment rates in countries where saving was scarce and, in the final analysis, higher growth of output. Aid could, moreover, be easily targeted to the needs of the recipients, as perceived at a particular time, and switched to others when it became expedient to do so. When received in the form of grants, the prevailing rule for EC assistance to African and other poor countries elsewhere in the developing world, aid represented an injection of free resources, particularly welcome by countries whose capacity to borrow and service external debt was also minimal.

In time, trade concessions were extended to non-associates as well. In 1971, for example, the EC entered its Generalized System of Preferences, applicable to the exports of industrial products from nearly all developing countries. As long as they made some difference, trade agreements involving preferential access to the Community markets for products other than those covered by the GSPs were signed with Maghreb and Mashreq countries. This occurred in 1976–77. Other countries in Southern Europe and the Mediterranean basin were granted trade privileges at different times: Greece in 1961, Turkey in 1963, Spain, Israel and Malta in 1970, and Cyprus and Portugal in 1972. Asian and Latin American developing countries were, on the contrary, never extended trade preferences in excess of those included in the GSPs. Lying at the outer reach of EC development concerns, these countries were always granted lower trade (and aid) concessions than both the associates and (generally) the countries of the Mediterranean basin. East Asia, in particular, came over time to be perceived more as a threat to Europe, in industry and trade, than as a subject of economic cooperation, and the Community's response to this type of challenge soon became a protective one. Eastern Europe is now being granted associated status, involving trade concessions and large amounts of aid—a treatment indicative of the high priority attached by the Community to this neighboring area.

Community aid, once depicted as a model of political neutrality and non-interference in the internal choices of the recipient countries, is now becoming distinctively more political in its objectives. Actual distribution of aid is also being made more conditional than in the past on policy actions by recipients. Politicization of aid is a recent, but already established, trend. It began with assistance to Central America, designed to favor a peaceful settlement of the conflicts plaguing that area, and it is now the most pervasive characteristic of the aid to Eastern Europe, which has been granted with the express purpose of sustaining political change and democratic forms of governments in that region.[2] Economic policy conditionality of EC aid is, on the contrary, just beginning. It first appeared, in a formal sense, in Lomé IV, connected to the portion of Community aid that was designated to sustain structural adjustment in ACP countries. It reappeared even more explicitly and forcefully in the bilateral loan made by the Community to Hungary in 1990 and in the assistance extended to Eastern European countries by the Group of 24, which the Community coordinated.

The orientation of Community aid, though influential in shaping the distribution of bilateral aid flows, which also became more and more concentrated on the associated countries with the passage of time, never overrode the preferences of the single member states. The Community was given specific competence in the area of trade and trade policies by the Treaty of Rome. Nothing of the sort, however, was envisaged in the field of aid. Member countries volunteered very little in this area, striving instead to maintain autonomy in their national aid policies and control of the destination of their bilateral aid resources. Coordination of member countries' aid policies, though often recognized as desirable, was never entrusted to any significant degree to the EC Commission. EC members also exercised the equivalent of strict control over the Community's aid purse strings by never accepting the budgetization of financial assistance to the associated countries, and thus continuing to contribute to the European Development Fund from their national budgets.

The ever present dichotomy between Community and

member countries' aid policies and practices seems to have contributed to the relative inefficacy of their overall aid efforts, even in Africa where most of the EC resources were directed. The success of external assistance, however, does not only depend on the particular forms of "aid giving". It also, and in large part, depends on the economic context within which it is utilized, and thus on the policies of the recipient countries. By purposefully shying away until very recently (in practice until Lomé IV), from any influence on the policy environment, in even the most preferred aid recipients, and from relating the supply of economic assistance to the quality of the recipients' economic policies, the Community made it more difficult to evaluate the effectiveness and developmental value of its direct resource transfers. It also tended to validate the notion, strong among many of the recipients, that EC direct aid was a form of political compensation for the associated countries whose use of the aid should not be evaluated only through the standard criteria of economic efficiency and development effectiveness.

If the results obtained through aid are difficult to ascertain, the effects of EC trade preferences on recipients are not at issue. Tariff privileges did not by themselves prevent the recipients, especially those of Africa, from losing market shares in the EC, nor did they bring about (at least so far) any widespread diversification of the exports of the beneficiary countries to the Community. In EC markets associated countries' exports were outperformed by those of the non-associated, less preferred countries. If it is true that EC preferences gradually lost their worth for the beneficiaries because of the progressive liberalization of tariffs under GATT, and because they were restrictively administered by the Community, it is also generally true that trade preferences are not by themselves a sufficient condition for the export success of those that receive them. Here again, production and export policies pursued by the preference receiving countries at the national level are of paramount importance. There is strong evidence that most of the beneficiaries of EC trade preferences failed to put in place the domestic policies that would have maximized the value of privileged market access to the Community. Yet, by not becoming concerned with production and trade policies in associated countries, and especially with the economic incentives afforded to the production of exportable goods, the

Community in effect renounced the possibility of· helping beneficiaries maximize the advantage of the trade privileges that it granted.

Nor were the preferences granted to all developing countries on industrial product exports to the Community generally more effective than those extended to the associates. A few countries took advantage of them, but for most others the export enhancing effects of the preferences were negligible. The countries that benefited most were probably the NICs of East Asia and a few of the Mediterranean and Latin American countries—in general, the countries that were following the most coherent and determined export-oriented policies and providing the necessary incentives to the production of tradable goods. For the most part these were also the countries that the Community did not especially wish to help, since they were the least poor and least undeveloped of the group. They were also the most competitive with the Community, in domestic as well as third country markets.

New Forms and Directions of EC Development Cooperation

The regional emphasis of EC development policies, embedded in the Treaty of Rome, continued with the Yaoundé conventions and extended to its maximum by the Lomé agreements, has in many ways become both an anachronism and a straightjacket for EC Europe. What suited the interests and economic means of the Community's original six member states—and conformed to the limited foreign policy space of Europe after World War II—can hardly be expected to continue to fit equally well the needs of what has become the largest economic bloc in the world or its plans to become a cohesive economic union. This realization was slow to surface among EC members, despite a tradition of globalism among some of them, as long as they felt constrained by the existing political–strategic balance between East and West. In the multipolar world that now seems to be rapidly emerging, these constraints are being lifted, and old frames of reference are being re-evaluated. The process of reassessment of EC cooperation policies is in substance already under way.

Several factors and tendencies are shaping the pace of adjustment in EC development policies. One has to do with the realization that Africa, far from remaining the natural economic complement of Europe, is of little direct economic value and has become a quasi-permanent burden for it. This is a valuation not yet openly expressed at the official level, but one whose existence and implicit acceptance at the policy-making level in EC Europe is already quite evident. The purely economic weight of Africa has been shrinking in relative terms, instead of increasing. Its contribution, actual or potential, to the economic security of Europe now appears to have been overestimated and perhaps also willingly overstated.

Perhaps more importantly, it is becoming increasingly clear that neither the specialization model implicit in the European notion of EurAfrica, nor the variant of this paradigm closer to the African point of view, succeeded in pointing this continent in any clear direction, in fostering its growth or in furthering its structural change. Africa appears at best to be "stuck" economically. At worst it appears to be inexorably declining. Preferential trade with the EC and the receipt of aid have neither helped deepen the traditional specialization of Africa in the production and export of raw materials, as relative factor endowments would have predicted, nor have they contributed in any visible way to efficient import substitution or to the creation of a modern industrial structure. Africa simply failed to advance in either direction.

Such failure is not simply attributable to the lack of potency of its privileged economic nexus with the Community. The restrictiveness of EC trade policies in some areas, such as textiles, may have hurt the diversification prospects of some African countries. The stingy support extended by the Community to industrial development in associated countries may also have been a restraining factor. Aid flows that were not maintained in real terms, let alone fully adjusted for the increase in population in the ACP countries, did not provide much of a cushion. It was the domestic policies that failed in Africa in a very fundamental sense; however, the special relationship with Europe did not prevent in any significant way Africa from failing in whatever strategy it attempted to pursue.

Extending preferential relations to Africa, moreover, does not appear to have advanced any of the key strategic interests of

Europe. Trade with Africa has declined in relative terms. The contribution that Africa can make to security of raw materials supplies has dwindled. Security of supply itself lost much of its original relevance for the Community as technological progress lessened dependence on them and the global political–strategic balance was altered by endogenous failures in the socialist bloc. EC private investment flows have found different geographical outlets even in the area of natural resource development. Only public support for Africa in the form of financial aid and official credit has increased, but with less than encouraging results. Africa's development failures and its reduced strategic importance to Europe are eroding, in most EC capitals as well as in Brussels, the credibility of much of the previous economic justification for a special cooperative relationship with Africa. Of all the EC member countries, only France appears to be still committed to a pro-African policy, if more in a West-Central African than Pan-African sense. But finding a credible rationale even for France's cooperation policy with Africa is becoming progressively more difficult.[3]

Some of the lessons of past experience are slowly sinking in. The failure of aid to spark growth in Africa, for example, has led to some changes in EC aid practices. Part of the aid to the ACPs foreseen in Lomé IV has been earmarked for structural adjustment and will be extended only if specified macro and sector conditions are met by the governments of the recipient countries, that is if some of the conditions for efficient and effective utilization of aid are created and maintained. At the same time, the context within which EC development cooperation is taking place has also changed so rapidly and profoundly in recent years that simple adaptation to these changes has already significantly altered the direction of EC cooperation policies. As a result, strict or even predominant regionalism with emphasis on Africa, soft and unconditional Community aid as a complement to bilateral flows, and acceptance of recipient countries' priorities and preferences appear to be losing much of the justification they once had, and are quickly becoming notions of the past.

Notwithstanding continuous supply of aid (through both regular and special channels) and public debt cancellations, the attention of Europe is already moving away from Africa. Careful observers of EC–African relations have noted that the very renegotiation of the Lomé Convention in 1985 and the supply by the EC of an unchanged amount of real aid to the associated countries of Africa, the Caribbean and the Pacific were remarkable results, given the context in which they occurred. These judgments apply *a fortiori*, and maybe even more strongly, to the contents of the recently negotiated Lomé IV, despite the clear increase in the conditionallity associated with EC aid.

If Africa remains, at the beginning of the 1990s, a priority in EC development cooperation, it is more for historical and humanitarian reasons, and perhaps because of the inertia built into long-followed practices, than for the protection of European economic interests considered to be vital. This conclusion finds support, for example, in the shifts in the determinants of the geographical distribution of aid to associated countries that have occurred in the 1980s. In this period bilateral aid was allocated much more on the basis of recipient needs, and less on the basis of donor interests, than in the previous decade. It is also supported by the generous contributions of EC countries to special multilateral initiatives in favor of Africa, such as the Special Facility for Africa set up under World Bank auspices in 1985, the Special Program of Assistance for low-income, debt-distressed sub-Saharan African countries created in late 1987 and also coordinated by the World Bank, and the Structural Adjustment Facility set up by the IMF in 1986. These contributions were obviously motivated by the needs of the intended beneficiaries and not by European economic interest in Africa.

Another tendency that is becoming more evident in EC development cooperation is the search for wider complementarities with developing areas than those offered by Africa. While South East Asia, with its successful NICs, projects an image, as well as a reality, of competition with the EC, Latin America offers much more promising avenues for mutual cooperation with the Community, and so does Eastern Europe. Full exploitation of the existing potential for specialization and trade with these two areas is still to be achieved. To do so would require changes in the CAP and the progressive dismantling of restrictive import regimes in sectors such as steel and textiles. But the realization that substantive net benefits for both parties could be derived from it is gaining ground.

Many of the changes in existing EC trade and sectoral policies necessary to develop economic relations with Eastern Europe and Latin America in the short to medium term are in any case inevitable. The costs of the CAP to the Community, for example, are unbearable in economic terms, and they far exceed the most often talked about budgetary consequences of the EC agricultural policy. The Community can hardly afford such costs to protect a sector whose comparative advantages are dwindling and whose strategic importance is waning. Resources have to move out of, instead of be kept in, the agricultural sectors of most of the member countries.

Managed trade in textiles and clothing is costing EC consumers enormous amounts and shielding a sector whose characteristics do not appear to justify the assistance it has received for so many years. It is a mature sector, in which income elasticity of demand is not very high, but in which technical progress is swift, entry is easy and competition is potentially keen. Several portions of the industry are highly capital intensive (particularly in textiles) and capable of withstanding foreign competition from whatever source. Specialization is an asset and is being fully exploited in many segments of this EC industry. Clothing, in particular, has large components of design, merchandising and marketing—areas in which EC manufacturers have considerable competitive advantages. The industry, therefore, would certainly not disappear if the tariff and non-tariff protection afforded to it in the framework of the MFAs were to be abolished.

The EC textile and clothing industry has had ample time to restructure. The MFAs, after all, were started in the early 1970s as temporary managing devices, but have lasted until now. The industry has in fact already restructured to a considerable extent. Certain lines of production have shrunk. Capacity has moved south, both within Europe and from Europe to the developing world. Aside from physical migration, portions of the industry have been reorganized along more flexible and competitive production modes. Technological innovation has spread from the spinning and weaving sectors, to knitting, cutting, sewing and various other phases of clothing production. To try to save those portions of the industry, whose long-term prospects are poor under any reasonable set of economic circumstances, by using generalized protection is plainly too wasteful, aside from being economically futile.

The need for protection of the steel sector has also run its course in the EC. A good and competitive steel sector is essential to both the consumer durables and investment goods industries. The EC steel industry was reorganized in the 1980s and much excess capacity existing then has been shed. A competitive market in steel, with a local industry operating in it in conditions of parity with the rest of the world, is of critical importance to the industry of Europe. Without a competitive steel sector, several key EC industries—such as motor vehicles—will not be able to operate successfully in an open European market.

Several Latin American and Eastern European countries would benefit handsomely from the liberalization of the EC agricultural policy, especially in the form of larger and more remunerative exports of cereals, meats and dairy products. They would also benefit, if less than Asian countries, from a more liberal import regime in textiles and clothing, as well as from the possibility of competing freely in Europe and in third markets with EC steel. The Community as a whole would also benefit from such policy changes.

In the medium term, both Latin America and Eastern Europe have a double attraction for EC Europe. They represent large and growing markets, which are moreover being rendered ever more accessible by extensive liberalization of import regimes. Latin America, and to a large extent also Eastern Europe, represent complementary economic areas for EC countries— areas with which trade can be expanded along both "traditional" inter-industry and "new" intra-industry lines. Latin America, for example, can easily and almost immediately exploit its existing comparative advantages in agriculture and resource-based industries such as steel, other basic metals, paper, leather and wood products, while importing manufactures from Europe at the middle and high end of the technological spectrum. In the medium term it can also exploit the potential for successful intra-industry specialization and trade with Europe in many lines of production—from mechanical products, to electronics, to consumer semi-durables. Some of the same considerations apply to Eastern Europe. Many countries in both these regions have good technological bases, skilled and abundant labor forces and an economic environment which is becoming more and more hospitable to industrial cooperation with the developed countries.

Eastern Europe, in addition, has the advantage of location and it is becoming a strong center of attention for EC industry and finance. The economic reconstruction of Eastern Europe, a political and economic imperative for Western Europe, will also require a massive and prolonged official involvement of the EC countries.[4] Aside from assisting Eastern Europe financially and extending to it immediate trade concessions, the Community is already moving towards the definition of an association policy. This trend will inevitably lead to the integration of much of Eastern Europe with the EC. If there is competition between Eastern Europe and Latin America, and *a priori* there seems to be some, particularly in industry, association could give Eastern Europe a significant edge in EC markets.

Strongly collaborative relations with much of the former Soviet Union will also be inevitable for many of the same reasons. The interests of peace and stability in Europe will in time be seen by most as being best served by a growing and modernizing set of countries where the Soviet Union once was. To foster such a process, massive technical and financial help will have to be extended by Europe to these countries. Some of it, particularly in the immediate period, may even have to be at concessional terms. In the longer term, under the right conditions, private investment capital can be expected to flow in abundance from Europe and elsewhere in the industrial world to the main constituent elements of the former Soviet Union. Trade between the EC and many of the components of today's Commonwealth of Independent States will also have to be liberalized in the short term, but not necessarily in a symmetrical fashion at the beginning of the process.

What Future for EC Development Cooperation?

The key question at this juncture is not whether EC development policy is taking a wider geographical and political dimension (it already is) and some new forms (they are already quite apparent), but whether there is a rational design behind it, as opposed to a set of *ad hoc*, piecemeal responses to unfolding events. No clear design, old or new, seems to lie yet at the basis of EC development cooperation in the 1990s. The experience of the two previous decades is being repeated. EC development cooperation is still driven by exogenous changes, it is saddled by a burdensome past and it is not helped by any improvement in its institutional framework. That some lessons of experience and reactions to exogenous challenges have pushed it, in the past few years, towards greater diversification of objectives and some changes in forms was on the whole a rather casual, if fortunate, outcome.

Another important question is whether a change of direction in EC development policies, away from limping regionalism, is sustainable. Sustainability depends on an agreed strategic design, shared goals and sound operational principles, as well as on the availability of adequate instruments to pursue them. Some agreement on new directions has obviously developed in recent times—witness the swift changes in policies towards Eastern Europe and some revival of interest in cooperating with the Mediterranean and, to a lesser extent, the Latin American countries. Goals, however, have so far mostly been defined only in the short term. Long-term sustainability of even current policy trends is in no way assured—witness the disagreements among members on the eventual participation of Eastern Europe to the Community, and the north–south divide still evident in the definition of new relations with the Maghreb and Mashreq. The lack of fully shared long-term objectives is also indicated, among other things, by the process for allocating aid resources, which has been and still is haphazard at best, and has not yielded either clear or credible choices. The balance between national and Community action in development cooperation has remained precarious even when changes of direction have occurred, as in the cases of Eastern Europe and the Gulf crisis. The Community has been given some extensions of its mandate in cases of acute need, but without assured continuity and without a new definition of its role in it. Policy *ad hocism* may well be a nearly normal tendency for the Community, but it is neither necessary nor productive in the area of development cooperation.

Equally evident is that of the two principal instruments of EC development policies—trade and aid—the first has lost much of its relevance, except in specific situations, either sectoral such as the CAP and the MFA, or geographical such as Eastern Europe and Latin America. Relaxation of existing trade barriers can help specific groups of developing countries. Latin America, for example, would gain considerably from a reform of EC agricultural policies. Both Eastern Europe and Latin America (as well as the Community) would gain from a reduction or elimination of import restrictions on steel and to a lesser extent on clothing. EC sectoral and development policies cannot be kept forever separated. This is a lesson that the Community should recognize and incorporate in its actual behavior. A reduction in much of the informal protectionism practiced by the Community with increasing frequency in the 1970s and 1980s would also help developing countries, if largely the NICs of Asia, Brazil, Mexico, Poland and perhaps Hungary and Czechoslovakia. In any case most of the trade preferences still in existence have little general consequence for the intended beneficiaries. A drastic simplification of these preference policies would have in itself some of the benefits that are carried by reductions in informal barriers to trade.

Direct economic aid and the facilitation of investment flows to priority countries and regions remain important instruments of development cooperation for EC Europe. If aid flows towards Africa are to be maintained for the foreseeable future, in the context of Lomé and other multilateral initiatives to which the EC should continue to adhere, meeting new demands for EC economic assistance in priority areas will inevitably require that more resources are devoted to aid by the Community. The problem of the sufficiency of Community aid, especially in view of the stated objectives pursued in Eastern Europe, has already been forcefully put to the attention of its EC partners by Italy. Despite the hiatus that followed the proposal made by the Italian Foreign minister Gianni De Michelis for increased Community assistance to developing countries, EC Europe can hardly put off for long the question of the amount of resources to be devoted to development assistance since it has to rely increasingly on aid as the main instrument of its development cooperation. Avoiding this question will mean in the years to come having to make even sharper choices among otherwise irreconcilable aims and having to reduce more rapidly than is desirable the scope of European development cooperation with Africa.

The effectiveness of the use of aid will also have to be

increased. Existing practices are badly in need of change. These include more general and effective coordination between bilateral and multilateral aid (and thus the definition of the Commission's mandate in this field), the targeting of financial assistance more towards the support of policy reform than towards project financing (and thus the establishment of a policy advisory capacity at the Commission level), and increasing budgetization of aid (and thus a greater oversight role of the European Parliament on what has been so far a largely executive process). Other departures from past practices will undoubtedly occur. For without a more precise definition of the shared goals and priorities of EC development cooperation, and of the changes needed in development cooperation practices, neither a simple increase in the flows of EC development aid nor a modification in trade and sectoral policies, however important, will be sufficiently effective in supporting a broader EC development projection or politically sustainable in the long term inside the Community.

Private investments to priority areas should be strongly encouraged. What needs to be kept in mind in this area, however, is that private capital flows are driven by their own profit-maximization logic. They can only marginally be influenced from the outside. While private investors never shy away from seeking comfort from public authorities, resources devoted to these purposes are hardly ever well spent. What are vastly more effective, as they act directly and positively on the expectations of investors, are changes in the regulatory framework and domestic economic policies in the host countries. These inside changes should be supported by all available means, including technical assistance and policy-based financial support. In the end, domestic policies and actual economic performance act as the most potent magnets (or repellents) of private capital flows.

Cooperation in other areas, including industrial cooperation and transfer of technology, needs to be carefully defined. The Community has in the past acted too "politically" in these areas, promising what it did not want to give or could not deliver. Disconnected from direct investments, transfers of technology involve direct arrangements between firms, because firms, not governments, possess much of the know-how that is needed in developing countries. The Community can help in the development of standards and rules to facilitate intra-firm cooperation, but faces stringent limits in most other areas of direct intervention. It should, therefore, promise what is feasible and deliver what it promises. This means that cooperation agreements with developing countries must carefully clarify objectives and instruments of industrial and technological cooperation and leave as little as possible to interpretation.

Development cooperation will continue to pose a considerable challenge to the Community in the years to come. Like most other public activities it does not and will not become easier simply with the passage of time. The learning curve in these activities is never very steep and continuous. Development cooperation is no exception, as the underlying realities of economic and social development also have a tendency to keep changing. Intellectual and political fashions also change, sometimes rapidly, making continuity of action even more difficult. Economic development is a complex task, about which outsiders have generally a lot to say, but little to contribute. All of this will continue to make Community cooperation with developing countries as difficult in the future as it has been in the past, but in no respect a less necessary or noble task for the "new Europe".

Notes to Chapter 9

1 Kahler, "Europe and its Privileged Partners", p. 1.

2 The so-called "Euro–Arab dialogue" that started in the mid-1970s also had a rather evident political connotation. It was always considered as a political dialogue by the Arab side, which sought to change through it EC members' positions on the Arab–Israeli conflict. The EC, however, never utilized aid or trade concessions in dealing with the mostly oil-rich Arab states. In this instance there was, therefore, no actual utilization of developmental instruments for the achievement of political objectives.

3 An updated case for the traditional preference for Africa in French development cooperation is made in F. Magnard and N. Tenzer, *La Crise Africaine: Quelle Politique de Coopération pour la France*, Paris, Presses Universitaires de France, 1988, pp. 165–95. To do so, however, the authors must resort to such notions as: (a) French economic influence in the service of the free world, and (b) stability of Africa as vital for France. The first of these notions relied heavily on the

stated need to contrast Soviet and Libyan influence in Africa. The second on the existence of a "world vocation" of France to which Africa would lend credibility and "precious" support in the United Nations. Neither was particularly convincing at the end of the 1980s.

[4] R. Portes, *The European Community and Eastern Europe After 1992*, CEPR Occasional Paper No. 3, London, Center for Economic Policy Research, 1990.

Bibliography

Books, Book Chapters, Reports and Articles

Adams, G.M., "Community Foreign Policy and Political Integration: Lessons of the African Association", in S.J. Warnecke, ed., *The European Community in the 1970s*, New York, Praeger, 1972.

Agarwal, J.P., M. Dippl and R.L. Langhammer, *EC Trade Policies Towards Associated Developing Countries: Barriers to Success*, Tubingen, Mohr, 1985.

Aggarwal, V.K., *Liberal Protectionism*, Berkeley, University of California Press, 1985.

Akrasanee, N., "ASEAN-EC Trade Relations", in N. Akrasanee and H.C. Rieger, eds., *ASEAN-EC Economic Relations*, Singapore, ASEAN and Institute of South East Asian Studies, 1982.

Andreis, M., *L'Africa e la Communità Economica Europea*, Torino, Einaudi, 1967.

Angarita, C., and P. Coffey, eds., *Europe and the Andean Countries*, London, Pinter Publishers, 1988.

Ashoff, G., "Consequences of Southward Enlargement for EC-Latin American Relations", *Intereconomics*, No. 5, September–October, 1982.

Ashoff, G., *La Cooperación Para el Desarrollo Entre la Comunidad Europea y América Latina: Experiencias y Perspectivas*, Working Paper No. 16, Madrid, IRELA, 1989.

Ausch, S., *Theory and Practice on CMEA Cooperation*, Budapest, Akademiai Kiado, 1972.

Austin, D., "The Transfer of Power: Why and How", in W.H. Morris-Jones and G. Fischer, eds., *Decolonization and After: The British and French Experience*, London, Frank Cass, 1980.

Balassa, B., *Incentive Policies and Agricultural Performance in Sub-Saharan Africa*, PPR Working Paper No. 77, Washington D.C., The World Bank, 1988.

Baldinelli, E., "Turning Page in Relations Between Latin America and the European Communities", *CEPAL Review*, No. 30, December 1986.

Baldwin, R.E., and T. Murray, "MFN Tariff Reductions and the Developing Country Trade Benefits Under the GSP", *The Economic Journal*, Vol. 87, March 1977.

Balogh, T., "Africa and the Common Market", *Journal of Common Market Studies*, Vol. 1, No. 1, 1962.

Banerji, A.K., "From Mutual Indifference to Cooperation: EEC's Priorities and the Evolution of the Indo-EEC Economic Relations", in K.B. Lall, W. Ernst and H.S. Chopra, eds., *India and the EEC*, New Delhi, Allied Publishers, 1984.

Baron, F., and G. Vernier, *Le Fond Européen de Développement*, Paris, Presses Universitaires de France, 1981.

Basombrio, I., "América Latina y la Communidad Europea: Una Compleja Relación", in SELA, ed., *Relaciones Económicas Internacionales de América Latina*, Caracas, Editorial Neuva Sociedad, 1987.

Beenstock, M., "Political Econometry of Official Development Assistance", *World Development*, Vol. 8, No. 1, 1980.

Berg, E., "Intra African Trade and Economic Integration", Vol. 1, Alexandria, Va, E. Berg Associates, 1985 (mimeo.).

Berthelot, Y., and G. Tardy, *Le Défi Economique du Tiers Monde*, 2 Vols, Paris, La Documentation Française, 1978.

Betts, F.R., *Assimilation and Association in French Colonial Theory: 1890-1914*, New York, Columbia University Press, 1961.

Bhat, T., "Current Trends in EEC's Commercial Policies—An Indian Overview", in K.B. Lall, W. Ernst and H.S. Chopra, eds., *India and the EEC*, New Delhi, Allied Publishers, 1984.

Billerbeck, K., *Europeanization of Development Aid: Integration Through Coordination of National Aid Policies of EC Member States*, Berlin, German Development Institute, 1972.

Blanford, D., "The Costs of Agricultural Protection and the Difference Free Trade Would Make", in F.H. Sanderson, ed., *Agricultural Protectionism in the Industrialized World*, Washington D.C., Resources for the Future, 1990.

Bornstein, M., Z. Gitelman and W. Zimmerman, *East-West Relations and the Future of Eastern Europe*, London, Allen and Unwin, 1981.

Borrmann, A., C. Borrmann, C. Langer and K.W. Menck, *The Significance of the EEC's Generalized System of Preferences*, Hamburg, Verlag Weltarchiv GMBH, 1985.

Bourrinet, J., *La Coopération Economique Euroafricaine*, Paris, Presses Universitaires de France, 1976.

Bouvier, P., *L'Europe et la Coopération au Développement: La Convention de Lomé*, Brussels, Editions de L'Université de Bruxelles, 1980.

Breckling, J., S. Thorpe and A. Stoeckel, *Effects of EC Agricultural Policies: A General Equilibrium Approach, Initial Results*, Canberra, Bureau of Agricultural Economics and Centre for International Economics, 1987.

Bridge, J.M., "The EEC and Turkey: An Analysis of the Association Agreement and its Impact on Turkish Economic Development", in A. Shlaim and G.N. Yannopoulos, eds., *The EEC and the Mediterranean Countries*, Cambridge, Cambridge University Press, 1976.

Broder Krohn, H., "La Communauté Elargie et les Pays en Voi de Développement", in H. Brugmans et al., eds., *La Politique Economique Extérieure de la Communauté Européenne Elargie*, Bruges, De Tempel, 1973.

Brown, D.K., "Trade Preferences and Developing Countries: A Survey of Results", *The Journal of Development Studies*, Vol. 24, No. 3, April 1988.

Brown, D.K. "Trade and Welfare Effects of the Generalized System of Preferences", *Economic Development and Cultural Change*, Vol. 37, No. 4, July 1989.

Burniaux, J.M., and J. Waelbroeck, "The Impact of the CAP on Developing Countries: A General Equilibrium Analysis", in C. Stevens and J.V. van Themaat, eds., *Pressure Groups, Policies and Development: EEC and the Third World—A Survey 5*, London, Hodder and Stoughton, 1985.

Cheysson, C., "Security and Development: A View from Europe", Lecture Delivered to a World Bank Managers' Retreat, Annapolis, Md., April 1981 (mimeo.).

Cline, W.R., *The Future of World Trade in Textiles and Apparel*, Washington D.C., Institute for International Economics, 1987.

Corbo, V., "Problems, Development Theory and Strategies of Latin America", in G. Ranis and T.P. Schultz, eds., *The State of Development Economics*, New York, Basil Blackwell, 1988.

Cosgrove Twitchett, C., "Patterns of ACP/EC Trade", in F. Long, ed., *The Political Economy of EC Relations with African, Caribbean and Pacific States*, Oxford, Pergamon Press, 1980.

Cosgrove, Twitchett, C., *Europe and Africa: From Association to Partnership*, Westmead, Saxon House, 1978.

Cosgrove, Twitchett, C., *A Framework for Development: The EC and the ACP*, London, George Allen and Unwin, 1981.

Cousté, B.P., L'Association des Pays d'Outre-Mer à la Communauté Economique Européene, Paris, Libraries Techniques, 1959.

Cova, C., *La Politique Arabe de la Communauté*, Brussels, Bureau d'Informations Européennes, 1983.

Cuddy, J., *International Price Indexation*, Lexington, Mass., Lexington Books, 1976.

Curzon, G., and V. Curzon, "Neo-Colonialism and the European Community", in *The Yearbook of World Affairs*, London, Stevens and Son (for the Institute of World Affairs), 1971.

D'Agostino, A., "Bisogni Essenziali ed Aiuti allo Sviluppo", Doctoral Dissertation, Milan, Bocconi University, 1989.

Davenport, M., *Trade Policy, Protectionism and the Third World*, London, Croom Helm, 1986.

Daveri, F., and E. Grilli, "Modelli di Distribuzione Geografica degli Aiuti Pubblici allo Sviluppo", ISPI Working Paper, Milan, 1991 (mimeo.).

De Gasperi, A., *Discorsi Parlamentari*, Vol. I, Rome, Ufficio Pubblicazioni della Camera dei Deputati, 1985.

De Gaulle, C., *Memoirs of Hope: Renewal and Endeavor*, New York, Simon and Schuster, 1971.

de Limbourg, I., "Aide au Développement de la CE en Chiffres", *Objectif Europe*, Vol. 4, No. 2, 1979.

Delorme, N., *L'Association des Etats Africains et Malgache à la Communauté Economique Européenne*, Paris, Librairie Pichon et Durand-Auzias, 1972.

Demekas, D.G., K. Bartholdy, S. Gupta, L. Lipschitz and T. Mayer, "The Effects of the Common Agricultural Policy of the European Community: A Survey of the Literature", *Journal of Common Market Studies*, Vol. 27, No. 2, December 1988.

Deschamps, H., *Les Méthodes et les Doctrines Coloniales de la France*, Paris, Librairie Armand Colin, 1953.

Dodoo, C., and R. Kuster, "The Road to Lomé", in A.M. Alting von Geusau, ed., *The Lomé Convention and a New International Economic Order*, Leyden, A.W. Sijthoff, 1977.

Dolan, M., "The Changing Face of EEC Policies Towards the Developing Countries: Reflection of Economic Crisis and the Changing International Division of Labour", *Journal of European Integration*, Vol. 7, Nos. 2-3, 1984.

Donges, J., "The Economic Integration of Spain with the EEC: Problems and Prospects", in A. Shlaim and G.N. Yannopoulos, eds., *The EEC and the Mediterranean Countries*, Cambridge, Cambridge University Press, 1976.

Duran, E., *European Interests in Latin America*, London, Routledge & Kegan Paul (for the Royal Institute of International Affairs), 1985.

Eden, A., *Facing the Dictators*, Boston, Houghton Mifflin Co., 1962.

Faber, G., *The European Community and Development Cooperation*, Assen, Van Gorcum, 1982.

Faber, G., "The Economics of Stabex", *The Journal of World Trade Law*, Vol. 18, No. 1, January-February, 1984.

Featherstone, K., *Socialist Parties and European Integration: A Comparative History*, Manchester, MUP, 1988.

Featherstone, K., "The Mediterranean Challenge: Cohesion and External Preferences", in J. Lodge, ed., *The European Community and the Challenge of the Future*, New York, St. Martin's Press, 1989.

Fejto, F., *The French Communist Party and the Crisis of International Communism*, Cambridge, The MIT Press, 1967.

Frey-Wouters, E., *The European Community and the Third World*, New York, Praeger, 1980.

Frisch, D., *The Lomé Convention: Practical Aspects, Past Experience and Future Prospects*, Europe Information Doc. X/57/1985, Brussels, European Communities, March 1985.

Furtado, C., *Economic Development of Latin America*, 2nd edition, Cambridge, Cambridge University Press, 1976.

Furtado, C., "Las Relaciones Comerciales Entre la Europa Occidental y la América Latina", *El Trimestre Económico*, Vol. 50, No. 199, July-September, 1983.

Galtung, J., *The European Community: A Superpower in the Making*, London, Allen and Unwin, 1973.

Gorell Barnes, W., *Europe and the Developing World*, London, Chatham House-PEP Paper, 1967.

Goto, J., "The Multifiber Arrangement and its Effects on Developing Countries", *The World Bank Research Observer*, Vol. 4, No. 2, July 1990.

Grabendorff, W., "Las Relaciones de la Comunidad Europea con América Latina: Una Politica sin Ilusiones", *Foro Internacional*, Vol. 29, No. 1, September 1988.

Granda, G., V. Mate and M. Moreno, *La Cooperación entre América Latina y Europa*, Madrid, CIDEAL, 1988.

Green, R.H., "The Child of Lomé: Messiah, Monster or Mouse?", in F. Long, ed., *The Political Economy of EEC Relations with African, Caribbean and Pacific States*, Oxford, Pergamon Press, 1980.

Grilli, E., "Responses of Developing Countries to Trade Protectionism in Industrial Countries", in C. Pearson and J. Riedel, eds., *The Direction of Trade Policy*, Cambridge, Mass., Basil Blackwell, 1990.

Grilli, E., "Contemporary Protectionism in an Unstable World Economy", in G. Sutija and G. Fels, eds., *Protectionism and International Banking*, London, Macmillan, 1991.

Grilli, E., and M. Riess, "EC Aid to Associated Developing Countries: Distribution and Determinants", in Weltwirtschaftliches Archiv, Vol. 128, No. 2, 1992.

Grilli, E., and E. Sassoon, eds., *The New Protectionist Wave*, London, Macmillan, 1990.

Grilli, E., and E. Sassoon, "Contemporary Protectionism: What Have We Learned?", in E. Grilli and E. Sassoon, eds., *The New Protectionist Wave*, London, Macmillan, 1990.

Gruhn, I.V. "The Lomé Convention: Inching Towards Interdependence", *International Organization*, Vol. 30, No. 2, Spring 1976.

Hager, W., "The Mediterranean: A European Mare Nostrum?", *Orbis*, Spring 1974.

Hamilton, C., ed., *Developing Countries and the Multifiber Arrangements*, Washington D.C., World Bank, 1990.

Harmand, J., *Domination et Colonisation*, Paris, E. Flammarion, 1919.

Harris, S., and B. Bridges, *European Interests in ASEAN*, London, Routledge and Kegan Paul (for the Royal Institute of International Affairs), 1983.

Henig, S., "Mediterranean Policy in the Context of the External Relations of the European Community", in A. Shlaim and G.N. Yannopoulos, eds., *The EC and the Mediterranean Countries*, Cambridge, Cambridge University Press, 1976.

Hewitt, A., "The European Development Fund as a Development Agent: Some Results of EDF Aid to Cameroon", *ODI Review*, No. 2, 1979.

Hewitt, A., "The Lomé Conventions: Myth and Substance of the Partnership of Equals", in M. Cornell, ed., *Europe and Africa: Issues in Post-Colonial Relations*, London, ODI, 1981.

Hewitt, A., "The Lomé Conventions: Entering a Second Decade", *Journal of Common Market Studies*, Vol. 22, No. 2, 1984.

Hewitt, A., "Malawi and the EEC: The First Seven Years", in C. Stevens, ed., *EEC and the Third World: A Survey 4—Renegotiating Lomé*, New York, Holmes & Meier Publishers, 1984.

Hewitt, A., "Stabex and Commodity Export Compensation Schemes: Prospects for Globalization", *World Development*, Vol. 15, No. 5, 1987.

Hewitt, A., "ACP and the Developing World", in J. Lodge, ed., *The European Community and the Challenge of the Future*, New York, St. Martin's Press, 1989.

Hiester, D., "The European Community and the East Bloc", in J. Lodge, ed., *Institutions and Policies of the European Community*, New York, St. Martin's Press, 1983.

Hitiris, T., *Trade Effects of Economic Association with the Common Market: The Case of Greece*, New York, Praeger, 1972.

Holmes, P., "Spain and the EEC", in D. Bell, ed., *Democratic Politics in Spain*, London, Francis Pinter, 1983.

Hrbek, R., "The EC and the Changes in Eastern Europe", *Intereconomics*, May/June 1990.

Hudec, R.E., *Developing Countries in the GATT Legal System*, London, Gower (for the Trade Policy Research Center), 1987.

Isaken, J., "Western European Reaction to Four NIEO Issues", in E. Lazlo and J. Kurtzman, eds., *Western Europe and the New International Economic Order*, New York, Pergamon Press, 1980.

Jackson, C., and P. Price, "Who Controls Community Aid", in C. Cosgrove and J. Jamar, eds., *The European Community's Development Policy: The Strategies Ahead*, Bruges, De Tempel, 1986.

Jensen, F.B., and I. Walter, *The Common Market: Economic Integration in Europe*, Philadelphia, J.B. Lippincott Co., 1965.

Jepma, C., "'An Application of the Constant Market Share Technique on Trade Between the African and Malagasy States and the

European Community: 1958-1978", *Journal of Common Market Studies*, Vol. 20, No. 2, 1981.

John, I.G., "The Soviet Response to Western European Integration", in I.G. John, ed., *EEC Policy Towards Eastern Europe*, Hants, Saxon House, 1975.

Julienne, H., "Hacia una Revitalización de la Cooperación Económica Entre América Latina y la Comunidad Económica Europea", in Fundación Friedrich Ebert, ed., *Relaciones Económicas Entre América Latina y la Comunidad Económica Europea*, Madrid, Gráficas Geranios, 1988.

Kahler, M., "Europe and its Privileged Partners in Africa and the Middle East", *Journal of Common Market Studies*, Vol. 21, Nos. 1-2, September-December 1982.

Kalamotousakis, G.J., "Greece's Association with the European Community: An Evaluation of the First Ten Years", in A. Shlaim and G.N. Yannopoulos, eds., *The EEC and the Mediterranean Countries*, Cambridge, Cambridge University Press, 1976.

Karsenty, G., and S. Laird, "The GSP, Policy Options and the New Round", *Weltwirtschaftliches Archiv*, Vol. 123, 1987.

Kaser, M., *Comecon*, London, Oxford University Press, 1967.

Keesing, D., and M. Wolf, *Textile Quotas Against Developing Countries*, London, Trade Policy Research Center, 1980.

Kibola, H., "Stabex and Lomé III", *The Journal of World Trade Law*, Vol. 18, No. 1, January-February, 1984.

Killick, T., "Whither Lomé? A Review of the Lomé III Negotiations", *Third World Quarterly*, Vol. 7, No. 3, July 1985.

Killick, T., "The Development Effectiveness of Aid to Africa", PRE Working Paper No. 646, Washington D.C., The World Bank, 1991 (mimeo.).

Kitzinger, U.W., *The Politics and Economics of European Integration*, New York, Praeger, 1963.

Krause, L., "Latin American Economic Relations with Western Europe", in R.W. Fontaine and J.D. Theberge, eds., *Latin America's New Internationalism*, New York, Praeger, 1976.

Lall, K.B., and H.S. Chopra, "The EEC and India", in K.B. Lall, W. Ernst, and H.S. Chopra, eds., *India and the EEC*, New Delhi, Allied Publishers, 1984.

Langhammer, R.J., "EEC Trade Policies and Latin American Export Performance: A Discussion of Causalities", *Intereconomics*, September-October 1980.

Langhammer, R.J., "Ten Years of the EEC's Generalized System of Preferences for Developing Countries: Success or Failure?", Kiel Working Paper No. 183, Kiel Institut fur Weltwirtschaft an der Universitat Kiel, 1983 (mimeo.).

Langhammer, R.J., "EC Trade Policies Towards Asian Developing
    Countries", *Asian Development Review*, Vol. 4, No. 2, 1986.
Langhammer, R.J., "EC-ASEAN Relations: Institutional Deepening but
    Modest Economic Impact", in C. Stevens and J.V. van Themaat,
    eds., *Europe and the International Division of Labour: EEC and the
    Third World—A Survey 6*, London, Hodder and Stoughton, 1987.
Langhammer, R.J., and A. Sapir, *Economic Impact of Generalized Tariff
    Preferences*, Aldershot, Gower (for the Trade Policy Research
    Center), 1987.
Langhammer, R.J., and U. Hiemenz, *Regional Integration Among
    Developing Countries: Opportunities, Obstacles and Options*, Tubingen,
    J.C.B. Mohr, 1990.
Lawrence, R., "Primary Products, Preferences and Economic Welfare:
    The EC and Africa", in P. Kennen and R. Lawrence, eds., *The
    Open Economy*, New York, Columbia University Press, 1968.
Lele, U., and J. Rahul, Synthesis: Aid to African Agriculture, in U. Lele,
    ed., "Aid to African Agriculture: Lessons from Two Decades of
    Donor Experiences", Washington D.C., The World Bank, 1989
    (discussion draft).
Lemaignen, R., *L'Europe au Berceau: Souvenirs d'un Technocrate*, Paris,
    Plon, 1964.
Lerdau, E., "The Impact of the EEC on Latin America's Foreign Trade",
    Economía Latinoamericana, Vol. 1, No. 1, 1963.
Lerman Alperstein, A., "Evolución Histórica de las Relaciones
    Comerciales Entre América Latina y la CEE", *Comercio Exterior*,
    Vol. 41, No. 2, February 1991.
Lister, M., *The European Community and the Developing World*, Aldershot,
    Avebury, 1988.
Loeff, J., "La Communauté Elargie et l'Espace Méditerranéen", in
    H. Brugmans et al., eds., *La Politique Economique Extérieure de la
    Communauté Européene Elargie*, Bruges, De Tempel, 1973.
Loeff, J., "European Community and Latin America", in *Incontro Sulla
    Cooperazione dell'Europa allo Sviluppo dell'America Latina*, Rome,
    Istituto Latino Americano, 1980.
Lorca, A.V., A. Martinez and A. Fuertes, "España-America Latina y la
    Comunidad Económica Europea", *Foro Internacional*, Vol. 22,
    No. 3, January-March 1982.
Luhulima, C.P., "Political Aspects of ASEAN-EEC Cooperation", *Asian
    Pacific Community Quarterly*, Fall 1984.
MacPhee, C.R., "A Synthesis of the GSP Study Program", Doc.
    UNCTAD/ITP/19, Geneva, 1989 (mimeo.).
Magdoff, H., *Imperialism*, New York, Monthly Review Press, 1978.
Magnard, F., and N. Tenzer, *La Crise Africaine: Quelle Politique de
    Coopération pour la France*, Paris, Presses Universitaires de France,
    1988.

Maizels, A., and M. Nissanke, "Motivations for Aid to Developing Countries", *World Development*, Vol. 12, No. 9, 1984.

Manning, P., *Francophone Sub-Saharan Africa 1880-1895*, Cambridge, Cambridge University Press, 1988.

Marsh, P., "The Development of Relations Between the EEC and CMEA", in G.N. Yannopoulos and A. Shlaim, eds., *The EEC and Eastern Europe*, Cambridge, Cambridge University Press, 1978.

Marsh, P., "EC Foreign Economic Policy and the Political Management of East-West Economic Relations", *Millenium—Journal of International Studies*, Vol. 9, No. 1, Spring 1980.

Marsh, P., "The European Community and East-West Economic Relations", *Journal of Common Market Studies*, Vol. 23, No. 1, September 1984.

Martin, G., "Africa and the Ideology of Eur-Africa: Neo Colonialism or Pan-Africanism", *Journal of Modern African Studies*, Vol. 2, No. 2, June 1982.

Matthews, J.D., *Association System of the European Community*, New York, Praeger, 1977.

Matthews, J.D., "The CAP and Developing Countries: A Review of the Evidence", in C. Stevens and J.V. van Themaat, eds., *EEC and the Third World: A Survey 5*, London, Hodder and Stoughton, 1985.

McQueen, M., "Some Measures of the Economic Effects of Common Market Trade Preferences for the Mediterranean Countries", in A. Shlaim and G.N. Yannopoulos, eds., *The EEC and the Mediterranean Countries*, Cambridge, Cambridge University Press, 1976.

McQueen, M., "Lomé and the Protective Effects of Rules of Origin", *Journal of World Trade Law*, Vol. 16, No. 2, March-April 1982.

McQueen, M., and R. Read, "Prospects of ACP Exports to the Enlarged Community", in C. Stevens and J.V. van Themaat, eds., *Europe and the International Division of Labour*, London, Hodder and Stoughton, 1986.

McQueen, M., and C. Stevens, "Trade Preferences and Lomé IV: Non-Traditional ACP Exports to the EC", *Development Policy Review*, Vol. 7, 1989.

Medina Ortega, M.M., "Les Relations entre l'Espagne et la Communauté Depuis 1945", in Institut d'Etudes Européennes, ed., *L'Espagne et les Communautés Européennes*, Brussels, Editions de l'Université de Bruxelles, 1979.

Minet, G., "Spanish and European Diplomacy at a Crossroads", in G. Minet, J. Siotis and P. Tsakaloyannis, eds., *Spain, Greece and Community Politics*, Sussex European Paper No. 11, University of Sussex, 1981.

Mishalani, P., A. Robert, C. Stevens and A. Weston, "The Pyramid of Privilege", in C. Stevens, ed., *EEC and the Third World: A Survey 1*, New York, Holmes & Meier Publishers, 1981.

Morrice, J., *The EC's Development Policy: From Lomé to the North-South Dialogue*, Brussels, Agence Européenne d'Information, 1984.

Mortimer, E., *France and the Africans: 1944-1960*, London, Faber and Faber, 1969.

Moss, J., *The Lomé Conventions and Their Implications for the United States*, Boulder, Col., Westview Press, 1982.

Moss, J., and J. Ravenhill, "Trade Developments During the First Lomé Convention", *World Development*, Vol. 10, No. 10, October 1982.

Moss, J., and Ravenhill, J., "The Evolution of Trade under the Lomé Conventions: The First Ten Years", in C. Stevens and J.V. van Themaat, eds., *Europe and the International Division of Labour*, London, Hodder and Stoughton, 1987.

Mower, A.G., Jr., *The European Community and Latin America: A Case Study in Global Role Expansion*, Westport, Conn., Greenwood Press, 1982.

Muniz, B., "EEC-Latin America: A Relationship to be Defined", *Journal of Common Market Studies*, Vol. 19, No. 1, 1980.

Musto, S.A., "Southward Enlargement and Developing Countries: A Shift in the Community's Policy of Preferences?", in C. Stevens and J.V. van Themaat, eds., *Europe and the International Division of Labour*, London, Hodder and Stoughton, 1987.

Mynt, H., "ASEAN-EC Cooperation", Washington D.C., School of Advanced International Studies, 1990 (mimeo.).

Ntumba, L.L., "L'Aide Financière et Technique de la CEE aux Paus en Voi de Développement d'Asie et d'Amérique Latine", *Revue du Marché Commun*, No. 328, June 1989.

Okigbo, P.N.C., *Africa and the Common Market*, London, Longmans, 1967.

Olu Sanu, E., "The Lomé Convention and the New International Economic Order", Lecture Series No. 18, Lagos, Nigerian Institute of International Affairs, 1982.

Ouattara, A., "Trade Effects of the Association of African Countries with the European Economic Community", *IFM Staff Papers*, Vol. 20, No. 2, 1973.

Parfitt, T.W., "EEC Aid in Practice: Sierra Leone", in C. Stevens, ed., *EEC and the Third World: A Survey 4—Renegotiating Lomé*, New York, Holmes & Meier Publishers, 1984.

Pearson, L.B., *Partners in Development*, New York, Praeger, 1969.

Petit, M., *Determinants of Agricultural Policies in the United States and the European Community*, Research Report No. 51, Washington D.C., The International Food Policy Research Institute, 1985.

Pinder, J., "A Community Policy Towards Eastern Europe", *The World Today*, Vol. 30, No. 3, March 1974.

Pinder, J., "Soviet Views of Western European Integration", in G.N. Yannopoulos and A. Shlaim, eds., *The EEC and Eastern Europe*, Cambridge, Cambridge University Press, 1978.

Pinder, J., and P. Pinder, *The European Community's Policy Towards Eastern Europe*, London, Chatham House-PEP, 1975.

Pio, A., "Caratteristiche ed Evoluzione degli Investimenti Europei nel Processo di Sviluppo Latino Americano", in A. Pio, ed., *Europa-America Latina: Nouve Forme di Cooperazione*, Milan, Unicopli, 1988.

Pisani, E., *La Main et l'Outil*, Paris, Robert Laffont, 1984.

Pomfret, R., "Trade Effects of the European Community Preferences to Mediterranean Countries", *World Development*, Vol. 10, No. 10, 1982.

Pomfret, R., *Mediterranean Policy of the European Community*, London, Macmillan (for the Trade Policy Research Center), 1986.

Pomfret, R., and B. Toren, *Israel and the European Common Market: An Appraisal of the 1975 Free Trade Agreement*, Tubingen, Mohr, 1980.

Portes, R., *The European Community and Eastern Europe After 1992*, CEPR Occasional Paper No. 3, London, Center for Economic Policy Research, 1990.

Prebish, R., *The Economic Development of Latin America and its Principal Problems*, New York, United Nations, 1950.

Rajana, C., "The Lomé Convention: An Evaluation of EC Economic Assistance to the ACP States", *Canadian Journal of Development Economics*, Vol. 2, No. 2, 1981.

Ramanathan, K.G., "Indo-EEC Trade Under CCA", in K.B. Lall, W. Ernst and H.S. Chopra, eds., *India and the EEC*, New Delhi, Allied Publishers, 1984.

Ranson, C., *The European Community and Eastern Europe*, Totowa, N.J., Rowman and Littlefield, 1973.

Rathbone, R., "The Legacy of Empire", in M. Cornell, ed., *Europe and Africa: Issues in Post-Colonial Relations*, London, ODI, 1981.

Ravenhill, J., *Collective Clientelism: The Lomé Conventions and North-South Relations*, New York, Colombia University Press, 1985.

Ravenhill, J., "Europe and Africa: An Essential Continuity", in R. Boardman, T.M. Shaw and P. Soldatos, eds., *Europe, Africa and Lomé III*, Lanham, Md., University Press of America, 1985.

Ribas, J.M., "Latin America's European Market", *Americas*, No. 14, October 1962.

Rivkin, A., *Africa and the West*, New York, Praeger, 1962.

Rivkin, A., *Africa and the European Common Market: A Perspective* (revised 2nd edition), Monograph Series in World Affairs No. 4, Denver, University of Denver, 1966.

Robinson, K., *The Dilemma of Trusteeship: Aspects of British Colonial Policy Between the Wars*, London, Oxford University Press, 1965.

Robson, P., *Integration, Development and Equity: Economic Integration in West Africa*, London, Allen & Unwin, 1983.

Rosenblatt, J., T. Mayer, K. Bartholdy, D. Demekas, S. Gupta and L. Lipschitz, *The Common Agricultural Policy of the European*

Community: Principles and Consequences, Occasional Paper No. 62, Washington D.C., The International Monetary Fund, 1988.

Roy, M.P., "La Convention de Lomé: Amorce d'une Nouvel Ordre Economique International", Notes et Etudes Documentaires, Vol. 30, Nos. 4313-4315, 1976.

Roy, M.P., La CEE et le Tiers Monde: Hors Convention de Lomé, Paris, La Documentation Française, 1984.

Roy, M., La CEE et le Tiers Monde: Les Conventions de Lomé, Paris, La Documentation Française, 1985.

Secchi, C., "Una Valutazione Critica della Politica Comunitaria nei Confronti dei Paesi in Via di Sviluppo", in F. Pocar, ed., Le Politiche delle Comunità Europee, Milan, Unicopli, 1986.

Secchi, C., "Protection, Internal Market Completion, and Foreign Trade Policy in the European Community", in E. Grilli and E. Sassoon, eds., The New Protectionist Wave, London, Macmillan, 1990.

Shlaim, A. and G.N. Yannopoulos, eds., The EEC and the Mediterranean Countries, Cambridge, Cambridge University Press, 1976.

Sideri, S., "Europe and Latin America in the World Crisis", Rivista di Diritto Valutario e di Economia Internazionale, Vol. 23, No. 2, 1985.

Sideri, S., La Comunità Europea nell'Interdipendenza Mondiale, Milan, Unicopli, 1990.

Srinivasan, T.N., "Food Aid: A Cause of Development Failure or an Instrument for Success?", The World Bank Economic Review, Vol. 3, No. 1, January 1989.

Stevens, C., Food Aid and the Developing World: Four African Case Studies, London, Croom Helm, 1979.

Stevens, C., "The European Community and Africa, the Caribbean and the Pacific", in J. Lodge, ed., Institutions and Policies of the European Community, New York, St. Martin's Press, 1983.

Stevens, C., "Implications of the EC's Development Policy for ASEAN", ASEAN Economic Bulletin, Vol. 1, No. 3, March 1985.

Stevens, C., "The Impact of EC Preferential Trade Policies", World Development Report Background Paper, Washington D.C., The World Bank, 1986 (mimeo.).

Stevens C., "Obstructions to the Development of Trade Between the ACP and the EC", Paper Presented to the NIEO-Lomé Symposium, Amsterdam, 1988 (mimeo.).

Stevens, C., and J.V. van Themaat, eds., Europe and the International Division of Labour, London, Hodder and Stoughton, 1986.

Stevens, C., and A. Weston, "Trade Diversification: Has Lomé Helped?", in C. Stevens, ed., EC and the Third World: A Survey 4— Renegotiating Lomé, New York, Holmes and Meier, 1984.

Tovias, A., Tariff Preferences in Mediterranean Diplomacy, New York, St. Martin's Press (for the Trade Policy Research Center), 1977.

Tovias, A., "Iberian Countries, Iberoamerica and the European Community", *The World Economy*, Vol. 12, No. 1, March 1989.

Tsoulakis, L., *The European Community and its Mediterranean Enlargement*, London, Allen and Unwin, 1981.

Tulloch, P., *The Politics of Preferences: EEC Policy Making and the Generalized System of Preferences*, London, Croom Helm (in association with the Overseas Development Institute), 1975.

Turner, L., "Western Europe and the NICs", in L. Turner and N. McMullen, eds., *The Newly Industrializing Countries: Trade and Adjustment*, London, George Allen & Unwin (for the Royal Institute of International Affairs), 1982.

Turner, L., and N. McMullen, eds., *The Newly Industrializing Countries: Trade and Adjustment*, London, George Allen & Unwin (for the Royal Institute of International Affairs), 1982.

Tussie, D., "Latin American Integration: From LAFTA to LAIA", *Journal of World Trade Law*, Vol. 16, No. 5, October 1982.

Tussie, D., *The Less Developed Countries and the World Trading System*, New York, St. Martin's Press, 1987.

Tyers, R., and K. Anderson, "Distortions in World Food Markets: A Quantitative Assessment", *World Development Report Background Paper*, Washington D.C., The World Bank, 1986 (mimeo.).

Vacchino, J.M., "America Latina y Europe Comunitaria", *Comercio Exterior*, Vol. 31, No. 2, February 1981.

Valdes, A., "La Agricultura en la Ronda de Uruguay: Los Intereses de los Países en Desarrollo", *Comercio Exterior*, Vol. 38, No. 9, September 1988.

van den Noort, P., "The Political Realities of European Agricultural Protection", in P. Coffey and M.S. Wionczeck, eds., *The European Community and Mexico*, Dordrecht, Martinus Nijhoff Publishers, 1987.

van Wijnberger, S., "Aid, Export Promotion and the Real Exchange Rate: An African Dilemma", Economics and Research Staff Discussion Paper No. 199, Washington D.C., The World Bank, 1986 (mimeo.).

Verney, S., "Greece and the European Community", in K. Featherstone and D.K. Katsoudas, eds., *Political Change in Greece Before and After the Colonels*, London, Croom Helm, 1987.

Viesti, G., ed., *Tra Cooperazione e Competizione: Le Relazioni Economiche tra la CEE ed i PVS*, Bologna, Il Mulino, 1991.

Vignes, D., *L'Association des Etats Africains et Malgache à la CEE*, Paris, Librairie Armand Colin, 1970.

von Gleich, A., M. Ehrke, H.J. Petersen and P. Hrubesch, *The Political and Economic Relations Between Europe and Latin America in View of the Southern Enlargement of the European Community due to the Entry of Spain and Portugal*, Hamburg, Institut fur Iberoamerika-Kunde, 1983.

Wall, D., "The European Community's Lomé Convention: Stabex and the Third World's Aspirations", London, Trade Policy Research Center, 1976 (mimeo.).

Wartman, H.R., *Essays on the European Common Market*, Information Bulletin No. 57, Bloomington, Ind., Indiana University Graduate School of Business, 1966.

Weston, A., "Who is More Preferred? An Analysis of the Generalized System of Preferences", in C. Stevens, ed., *Hunger in the World: EEC and the Third World—A Survey 2*, New York, Holmes & Meier Publishers, 1982.

Weston, A., V. Cable and A. Hewitt, *The EEC's Generalized System of Preferences*, London, ODI, 1980.

Wiegand, G., *Western Europe and The Latin American Debt Crisis*, Working Paper No. 12, Madrid, IRELA, 1988.

Wilczynski, J., *The Economics of Socialism*, London, Allen and Unwin, 1970.

Wionczek, M.S., "The Relations Between the European Community and Latin America in the Context of the International Economic Crisis", *Journal of Common Market Studies*, Vol. 19, No. 2, December 1980.

Yannopoulos, G.N., "Patterns of Response to EC Tariff Preferences: An Empirical Investigation of Selected Non-ACP Associates", *Journal of Common Market Studies*, Vol. 25, No. 1, 1986.

Young, C., "Decolonization in Africa", in H. Gann and P. Duignan, eds., *Colonialism in Africa: The History and Politics of Colonialism*, Vol. 2, Cambridge, Cambridge University Press, 1970.

Young, C., "Association with the EC: Economic Aspects of the Trade Relationship", *Journal of Common Market Studies*, Vol. 11, No. 2, 1972.

Yue, C.S., "EC Investment in ASEAN", in N. Akrasanee and H.C. Rieger, eds., *ASEAN-EC Economic Relations*, Singapore, ASEAN and Institute of South East Asian Studies, 1982.

Zartman, I.W., *The Politics of Trade Negotiations Between Africa and the European Economic Community*, Princeton, Princeton University Press, 1971.

Zartman, I.W., "Europe and Africa: Decolonization or Dependency", *Foreign Affairs*, Vol. 54, No. 1, January 1976.

Zartman, I.W., "Lomé III: Relic of the 1970s or Model for the 1990s", in C. Cosgrove and J. Jamar, eds., *The European Community's Development Policy: The Strategies Ahead*, Bruges, De Tempel, 1986.

Ziet, J., and A. Valdes, "The Potential to LDCs of Trade Liberalization in Beef and Sugar by Industrial Countries", *Weltwirtschaftliches Archiv*, Vol. 122, No. 1, 1986.

EC Documents and Publications

Commission of the European Communities, "Memorandum of Intention", Brussels, 1958 (mimeo.).

Commission of the European Communities, *Opinion on the Application for Membership Received from the United Kingdom, Ireland, Denmark and Norway for Submission to the Council Under Art. 237 of the EC Treaty*, Doc. COM(67) 758, Brussels, 29 September 1967.

Commission des Communautés Européennes, *Evolution du Régime Douanier, Fiscal et Contingentaire des Principaux Produits Tropicaux Importés dans les Etats Membres de la Communauté Economique Européenne de 1958 à 1968*, Brussels, 1968.

Commission des Communautés Européennes, *Le Rôle de l'Aide Publique des Pays de la CEE dans l'Aide Mondiale aux Pays en Voi de Développement (1962-1966)*, Doc. 7055/VIII/B/68-F, Brussels, June 1968.

Commission des Communautés Européennes, *Les Echanges Commerciaux entre la CEE et les Etats Africains Associés*, Série Aide au Développement, No. 2, Brussels, 1969.

Commission of the European Communities, *Economic Union and Enlargement: The European Commission's Revised Opinion on the Application for Membership from the United Kingdom, Ireland, Denmark and Norway*, Brussels, October 1969.

Commission of the European Communities, "Commission Memorandum on a Community Development Cooperation Policy", Supplement 5/71 to the *Bulletin of the European Communities*, 1971.

Commission of the European Communities, *European Development Aid: How the European Community is Helping the Developing Countries*, Brussels, 1971.

Commission of the European Communities, "Memorandum from the Commission on a Community Policy on Development Cooperation: Program for Initial Actions", Supplement 2/72 to the *Bulletin of the European Communities*, 1972.

Commission of the European Communities, *Memorandum on a Community Policy on Development Cooperation: Appendices*, Brussels, 1972.

Commission of the European Communities, "Memorandum to the Council on the Future Relations Between the Community, the Present AAMS States and the Countries in Africa, the Caribbean, the Indian and Pacific Oceans Referred to in Protocol No. 22 to the Act of Accession", Supplement 1/73 to the *Bulletin of the European Communities*, 1973.

Commission of the European Communities, "Development Aid: Fresco of Community Action Tomorrow", Supplement 8/74 to the *Bulletin of the European Communities*, 1974.

Commission of the European Communities, *European Development Fund*, Brussels, 1976.

Commission of the European Communities, "The Development Cooperation Policies of the European Community from 1971 to 1976", Brussels, April 1977 (mimeo.).

Commission of the European Communities, *Europe and the Third World: A Study in Interdependence*, Collection Dossiers, Development Series No. 2, Brussels, February 1978.

Commission of the European Communities, *The European Community and the Countries of Eastern Europe*, Europe Information Doc. No. 12/78, Brussels, 1978.

Commission of the European Communities, *The Lomé Convention and the Evolution of EEC-ACP Cooperation*, Information Note No. P-74, Brussels, July 1978.

Commission of the European Communities, "Latin America: A Community Strategy", Brussels, September 1980 (mimeo.).

Commission of the European Communities, *The European Community and India*, Europe Information Doc. No. 50/81, Brussels, 1981.

Commission of the European Communities, *European Development Fund Procedures*, Development Series No. 4, Brussels, 1981.

Commission of the European Communities, *Commission Communication to the Council on a Mediterranean Policy for the Enlarged Community*, Doc. COM(82) 353 final, Brussels, 24 June 1982.

Commission of the European Communities, *Cooperation Agreements Between the EEC and the Maghreb Countries*, Europe Information Doc. DE 36, Brussels, 1982.

Commission of the European Communities, "Memorandum on the Community's Development Policy", Supplement 5/82 to the *Bulletin of the European Communities*, 1982.

Commission of the European Communities, "Problems of Enlargement: Taking Stock and Proposals", Supplement 8/82 to the *Bulletin of the European Communities*, 1982.

Commission of the European Communities, *ASEAN and the European Community*, Europe Information Doc. No. 66/83, Brussels, 1983.

Commission of the European Communities, *Commission Communication to the Council on Better Coordination of Development Cooperation Policies and Operations within the Community*, Doc. COM(84) 174 final, Brussels, 26 March 1984.

Commission of the European Communities, *Commission Report to the Council on the Exploratory Talks with the Mediterranean Countries and the Applicant Countries and the Commission Proposals Concerning the Implementation of a Mediterranean Policy for the Enlarged Community*, Doc. COM(84) 107 final, Brussels, 11 May 1984.

Commission of the European Communities, *Commodities and Stabex*, Europe Information Doc. No. DE 49, Brussels, September 1984.

Commission of the European Communities, *The European Community's Development Policy: 1981-83*, Brussels, 1984.

Commission of the European Communities, *Europe-South Dialogue*, Brussels, 1984.

Commission of the European Communities, *Guidelines for the Strengthening of Relations Between the Community and Latin America*, Doc. COM(84) 105 final, Brussels, 6 April 1984.

Commission of the European Communities, *The Community and the Mediterranean Countries: Guidelines for Economic Cooperation*, Doc. COM(85) 517 final, Brussels, 26 September 1985.

Commission of the European Communities, *The European Community and Latin America*, Europe Information Doc. No. 82/85, Brussels, November 1985.

Commission of the European Communities, *The European Community and Latin America*, Doc. COM(86) 720 final, Brussels, 2 December 1986.

Commission of the European Communities, *Ten Years of Lomé*, Europe Information Doc. DE 55, Brussels, 1986.

Commission of the European Communities, *Generalized Preferences for the Third World*, European File No. 16/87, Brussels, October, 1987.

Commission of the European Communities, *The Europe-South Dialogue*, Brussels, 1988.

Commission of the European Communities, *Official Development Assistance from the European Community and its Member States*, Europe Information Doc. DE 57, Brussels, 1988.

Commission of the European Communities, *Eleventh Report from the Commission to the Council and the European Parliament on the Implementation of Financial and Technical Assistance to Latin American and Asian Developing Countries as of 31 December 1987*, Doc. COM(88) 715 final, Brussels, 16 January 1989.

Commission of the European Communities, *The European Community's Relations with Latin America*, Europe Information Doc. EN 06/X/96, Brussels, December 1989.

Commission of the European Communities, *Fourth Lomé Convention*, Information Memo No. P-76, Brussels, 1989.

Commission of the European Communities, *Operation Phare*, Information Memo 3/90, Brussels, 11 January 1989.

Commission of the European Communities, *Redirecting the Community's Mediterranean Policy—Communication to the Council*, Doc. SEC(89) 1961, Brussels, 23 November 1989.

Commission of the European Communities, *Thirteen Years of Development Cooperation with the Developing Countries of Latin America and Asia: Data and Results*, Doc. SEC(89) 713 final, Brussels, 10 May 1989.

Commission of the European Communities, *Communication from the Commission on the Development of Community's Relations with the*

Countries of Central and Eastern Europe, Doc. SEC(90) 717 final, Brussels, 18 April 1990.

Commission of the European Communities, *Communication from the Commission to the Council and the Parliament on Association Agreements with the Countries of Eastern and Central Europe: A General Outline*, Doc. COM(90) 398 final, Brussels, 27 August 1990.

Commission of the European Communities, *Communication from the Commission to the Council on the Extension to the Other Central and Eastern European Countries of the Facilities for the European Investment Bank to Finance Projects in Poland and Hungary*, Doc. COM(90) 384 final, Brussels, 14 September 1990.

Commission of the European Communities, *Communication from the Commission to the Council on the Implications of Recent Changes in Central and Eastern Europe for the Community's Relations with Countries Concerned*, Doc. SEC(90) 111 final, Brussels, 23 January 1990.

Commission of the European Communities, *Communication to the Council and the Parliament on the Development of the Community's Relations with the Countries of Central and Eastern Europe*, Doc. SEC(90) 196 final, Brussels, 1 February 1990.

Commission of the European Communities, *The European Bank for Reconstruction and Development*, ICC Background Brief, Brussels, 12 December 1990.

Commission of the European Communities, *Redirecting the Community's Mediterranean Policy: Proposals for the Period 1992–96— Communication to the Council*, Doc. SEC(90) 812 final, Brussels, 1 June 1990.

Commission of the European Communities, *Seventh Annual Report of the Commission on the Community's Anti-Dumping and Anti-Subsidy Activities*, Doc. No. COM(90) 29 final, Brussels, 13 June 1990.

Commission of the European Communities, *Thirteenth Annual Report to the Council and Parliament on the Implementation of Financial and Technical Co-operation to Developing Countries in Asia and Latin America*, Doc. No. COM(90) 204 final, Brussels, 22 June 1990.

Commission of the European Communities, *XXIIIrd General Report on the Activities of the European Communities 1989*, Brussels, 1990.

Commission of the European Communities, *EC-Eastern Europe Relations*, DGX Background Briefs, Brussels, 12 March 1991 and 8 July 1991.

Commission of the European Communities, *The European Community's Relations with ASEAN*, Europe Information Doc. No. 127/X/91, Brussels, April 1991.

Commission of the European Communities, *XXIVth General Report on the Activities of the European Communities, 1990*, Brussels, 1991.

Cooperation Agreement Between the EC and Algeria, *Official Journal of the European Communities*, No. L263/1, 27 September 1978.

Cooperation Agreement Between the EC and Jordan, *Official Journal of the European Communities*, No. L268/1, 27 September 1978.

Cooperation Agreement Between the EC and Syria, *Official Journal of the European Communities*, No. L269/1, 27 September 1978.

Cooperation Agreement Between the EC and Tunisia, *Official Journal of the European Communities*, No. L265/4, 27 September 1978.

Cooperation Agreement Between the EC and Hungary, *Official Journal of the European Communities*, No. L327, 11 December 1988.

Cooperation Agreement Between the EC and Poland, *Official Journal of the European Communities*, No. L339, 22 November 1989.

Cooperation Agreement Between the EC and the Soviet Union, *Official Journal of the European Communities*, No. L68, 15 March 1990.

Cooperation Agreement Between the EC and Bulgaria, *Official Journal of the European Communities*, No. L291, 23 October 1990.

Cooperation Agreement Between the EC and Czechoslovakia, *Official Journal of the European Communities*, No. L291, 23 October 1990.

Cooperation Agreement Between the EC and Romania, *Official Journal of the European Communities*, No. L79, 4 March 1991.

Council of the European Communities, "Final Declaration of the Conference of the Heads of States and Governments of the European Community", Paris, 19–21 October 1972.

Council of the European Communities, *Copenhagen Declaration*, reprinted in *Bulletin of the European Communities*, 12/73, Annex I, 1973.

Council of the European Communities, "Decision of July 1974", *Bulletin of the European Communities*, No. 7/8, 1974.

Council of the European Communities, "Council's Regulation No. 442/81 on Financial and Technical Aid to Non-Associated Developing Countries", *Official Journal of the European Communities*, No. L48, 21 February 1981.

Council of the European Communities, "Conclusions Adopted by the Council on Relations with Latin America", *Bulletin of the European Communities*, No. 6, 1987.

Council of the European Communities, "Relations with Latin America", Conclusions adopted on 22 June 1987, in *Bulletin of the European Communities*, June 1987.

Council of the European Communities, *Compilation of Texts, Vol. IV— Cooperation*, Brussels, 1988.

Council of the European Communities, *Compilation of Texts Adopted by the Council 1981–88*, Brussels, 1989.

Council of the European Communities, *Compilation of Texts, Vol. V— Cooperation*, Brussels, 1989.

Council of the European Communities, "Resolution of 16 May 1989 on Coordination in Support of Structural

Adjustment in ACP States", *Bulletin of the European Communities*, No. 5, 1989.

Council of the European Communities, *Press Release on the 1464th Council Meeting*, No. 10871/90, Brussels, 18–19 December 1990.

Court of Auditors of the European Communities, "Annual Report Concerning the Financial Year 1980, Part II, The European Development Funds", *Official Journal of the European Communities*, No. C344, Vol. 24, 31 December 1981.

Court of Auditors of the European Communities, "Annual Report Concerning the Financial Year 1981, Part II, The European Development Funds" *Official Journal of the European Communities*, No. C344, Vol. 25, 31 December 1982.

Court of Auditors of the European Communities, "Special Report on the Coordination of Community Aid to Third Countries", *Official Journal of the European Communities*, No. C224, Vol. 27, 25 August 1984.

Court of Auditors of the European Communities, "Special Report No. 6/87 on Food Aid Supplied to India Between 1978 and 1985 (Flood II Operation)", *Official Journal of the European Communities*, No. C31, Vol. 31, 4 February 1988.

Economic and Social Committee of the European Communities, *Opinion of the Economic and Social Committee on the Mediterranean Policy of the European Community*, Doc. CES(89) 835, Brussels, 12 July 1989.

Economic and Social Committee of the European Communities, *Opinion on the Relations Between the European Community and the Newly Industrializing Countries of South East Asia*, Doc. CES 439/89, Brussels, 1989.

Economic and Social Committee of the European Communities, *Report on the Mediterranean Policy of the European Community*, Doc. CES(89) 386 final, Brussels, 26 June 1989.

Economic and Social Committee of the European Communities, *Additional Opinion of the Economic and Social Committee on the Mediterranean Policy of the European Community*, Doc. CES(90) 512, Brussels, 26 April 1990.

European Parliament, *Report on Relations Between the European Community and the Countries of Central and Eastern Europe*, Working Document No. A2-111/85, Brussels, 1985.

Office for Official Publications of the European Communities, *Treaties Establishing the European Communities*, Luxemburg, 1987.

Office for Official Publications of the European Communities, *Documents Concerning the Accessions to the European Communities*, Vol. II, Luxemburg, 1988.

Parlement Européen, *Rapport sur la Politique Commerciale de la Communauté dans le Bassin Méditerranéen*, Document de Séance No. 246, February 1971.

Statistical Office of the European Communities, *Analysis of Trade Between the European Community and the ACP States*, Luxemburg, 1979.

Statistical Office of the European Communities, *EC-ASEAN Trade: A Statistical Analysis 1970-1984*, Foreign Trade, Series D, Studies and Analyses, Luxemburg, 1987.

Other Documents and Publications

ACP Group, *Memorandum on ACP Guidelines for the Negotiations for a Fourth ACP/EC Convention*, Brussels, 1989.

Africa, Caribbean and Pacific ACP—European Community, "Dossier Lomé", *The Courier*, Special Issue, No. 31, May 1975.

Agence Europe, *La Politique Globale de la CEE dans le Bassin Méditerranéen d'Après les Suggestions de la Commission Européenne*, Doc. No. 708, Brussels, 30 November 1972.

Development Committee, *Aid for Development: The Key Issues*, Washington D.C., The World Bank, 1986.

European Cooperation and Solidarity, EC Commission and Council of Europe, *Europeans and Development Aid in 1987*, Brussels, 1988.

General Agreement on Tariffs and Trade (GATT), *Trends in International Trade, A Report by a Panel of Experts*, Geneva, 1958.

General Agreement on Tariffs and Trade (GATT), *The Tokyo Round of Multilateral Trade Negotiations*, Geneva, 1980.

General Agreement on Tariffs and Trade (GATT), *Textiles and Clothing in the World Economy*, Geneva, 1984.

General Agreement on Tariffs and Trade (GATT), *Trade Policy Review Mechanism: The European Community*, Doc. C/RM/S/10B, Geneva, 1991.

House of Lords Select Committee on the European Communities, *Development Aid Policy*, London, HMSO, 1981.

Institut d'Etudes Européennes, *L'Espagne et les Communautés Européennes*, Brussels, Editions de l'Université de Bruxelles, 1979.

Instituto de Relaciones Europeo-Latinoamericanas (IRELA), *Economic Relations Between the European Community and Latin America: A Statistical Profile*, Working Paper No. 10, Madrid, 1987.

Italian Ministry of Foreign Affairs, "Iniziativa dei Paesi CEE verso i paesi dell'Est Europeo, del Mediterraneo e dei Paesi in via di Sviluppo", Note presented to the EC Council of Ministers of 16 July 1990 (mimeo.).

League of Nations, *The Network of World Trade*, Geneva, 1942.

Organization for American States (OAS), "The Effects of the European
    Community on the Latin American Economies", Washington
    D.C., 1963 (mimeo.).
Organization for Economic Cooperation and Development (OECD),
    Twenty-five Years of Development Cooperation: A Review, Paris, 1985.
Organization for Economic Cooperation and Development (OECD),
    Development Cooperation in the 1990s, Paris, 1989.
Organization for Economic Cooperation and Development (OECD),
    Agricultural Policies, Markets and Trade 1990, Paris, 1990.
Overseas Development Administration, *DAC, Arab and Multilateral Aid:
    Geographical Distribution: 1982–88*, London, 1990.
Sistema Económico Latinamericano (SELA), *América Latina y la
    Comunidad Económica Europea*, Caracas, Monte Avila Editores,
    1984.
Sistema Económico Latinamericano (SELA), "La Política Comercial de
    la CEE y sus Efectos Sobre el Comercio de América Latina",
    Comercio Exterior, November 1985.
United Nations, *International Economic Assistance to Less Developed
    Countries*, Doc. E/3395/Rev. 1, New York, 1961.
United Nations, *Proceedings of the United Nations Conference on Trade and
    Development*, Vol. 1, New York, 1964.
United Nations, *Proceedings of the United Nations Conference on Trade and
    Development—Second Session*, Vol. 1, New York, 1968.
United Nations Conference on Trade and Development—United
    Nations Development Program (UNCTAD-UNDP), "Market
    Access Conditions for Agricultural Raw Materials, Tropical and
    Natural Resource-Based Products of Sub-Saharan Africa",
    Geneva, 1987 (mimeo.).
United Nations Conference on Trade and Development (UNCTAD),
    *Comprehensive Review of the Generalized System of Preferences,
    Including its Implementation, Maintenance, Improvement and
    Utilization*, Report No. TD/B/C.5/130, Geneva, 1990.
United Nations Conference on Trade and Development (UNCTAD),
    Selected Issues on Restrictions to Trade, Doc. UNCTAD/ITP/24,
    Geneva, 1990.
United Nations Economic Commission for Africa (UNECA), *African
    Alternative Framework to Structural Adjustment Programmes for Socio-
    Economic Recovery and Transformation*, Doc. E/ECA/CM. 15/6, Rev.
    3, Addis Ababa, 1989.
United Nations Economic Commission for Europe (UNECE), *Economic
    Survey of Europe in 1989–90*, New York, 1990.
United Nations Economic Commission for Latin America (UNECLA),
    *Recent Developments and Trends in Latin American Trade with the
    European Community*, Doc. E/CN 12/631, New York, 1962.

World Bank, *Accelerated Development in Sub-Saharan Africa: An Agenda for Action*, Washington D.C., 1981.

World Bank, *Towards Sustained Development in Sub-Saharan Africa: A Joint Program of Action*, Washington D.C., 1984.

World Bank, *Population Data Files*, BESD Data Bank, Washington D.C.

Index

Rivkin, A., *18-19*
Romania
    aid to, *309*
    and cooperation with the EC,
        306, 313
    see also Poland-Hungary
        Assistance for the
        Reconstruction of the
        Economy (PHARE)
Rossi Report, *186*
Roy, M., *185*
rules of origin of the EC, *167-8*
rural development
    and aid to associated
        countries, *116*
    and Lomé Conventions, *117*
Russia, *298, 311*

Senegal
    aid to, *121-3*
    access to Yaoundé, *119*
    independence of, *15*
    and Lomé, *27*
Senghor, L., *18, 45n*
Sideri, S., *245*
Sierra Leone, *124-5*
Sistema Economico Latino
    Americano (SELA), *237-8*
Spain
    access to the EC, *198*
    and cooperation with the EC,
        181
social Christian parties and
    colonialism, *3*
socialist parties and colonialism,
    3
Somalia
    access to Yaoundé, *19*
    end of Italian mandate, *7*
South Asian Association for
    Regional Cooperation
    (SAARC), *277*
Soviet Union (and former
    Soviet Union after
    December 1991)

aid to, *310, 311*
    agreement with the EC, *306,
        311, 313, 315*
    EC trade policy towards, *311*
    importance to the EC, *349*
    perception of the EC, *298*
    policy towards the EC,
        299-300, 301
Sri Lanka
    commercial cooperation
        agreement with the EC, *276*
    EC aid to, *279*
STABEX, *27-30, 37, 113, 115, 277*
Sudan
    access to Yaoundé, *19*
    independence of, *14*
Sugar Protocol, *see* Lomé
    Conventions
"Surprix" system, *see* France
Syria, *188*
SYSMIN, *37, 113*

Taiwan, *281, 283*
Thatcher, M., *320*
Togo, *19, 27*
Touré, S.
    and French Community, *2*
    and Pan-Africanism, *18*
    and Yaoundé, *18*
Tovias, A., *190-1*
trade
    EC-AAMS trade relations,
        140-1, 158-61
    EC-ACP trade relations,
        161-4
    EC-Mediterranean trade
        relations, *180*
    see also trade policies of the
        Community
trade policies of the
    Community
    constraints to trade
        augmenting effects of EC
        preferences towards
        African associates, *164-74*